Thinking about
Criminal Justice in Canada

Karla O'Regan
St. Thomas University

Susan Reid
St. Thomas University

2013 • EMOND MONTGOMERY PUBLICATIONS • TORONTO, CANADA

Emond Montgomery Publications Limited
60 Shaftesbury Avenue
Toronto ON M4T 1A3
http://www.emp.ca/highered

Printed in Canada on recycled paper.

We acknowledge the financial support of the Government of Canada through the Canada Book Fund for our publishing activities.

Acquisitions and development editor: Mike Thompson
Marketing manager: Christine Davidson
Director, sales and marketing, higher education: Kevin Smulan
Supervising editor: Jim Lyons
Copy editor: Deanna Dority
Proofreader: Jamie Bush
Production editor: David Handelsman
Text designer and typesetter: Tara Wells
Indexer: Paula Pike
Cover designers: Stephen Cribbin & Simon Evers
Cover image: Eldar Curovic

Library and Archives Canada Cataloguing in Publication

O'Regan, Karla
    Thinking about criminal justice in Canada / Karla O'Regan, Susan Reid.

Includes index.
ISBN 978-1-55239-517-2

    1. Criminal justice, Administration of—Canada—Textbooks.
I. Reid, Susan   II. Title.

HV9960.C2O738 2012   364.971   C2012-903131-3

Contents

Foreword

A Note to Instructors

In our classrooms, over coffee, during office hours, and, hopefully, through this text and the conversations students will have about it, we see many opportunities to consider—and reconsider—the criminal justice issues that confront all of us on a daily basis. We are teaching to transform, to alter the ways in which our students view the world and act within it. We often present this approach to students by way of a "cocktail party" metaphor, in which part of their role as learners is that of teachers: to live the experience of having new knowledge by imparting that knowledge to others as an advocate, both inside and outside the classroom. A "cocktail party" lends itself well to this transformative knowledge because it is in these informal conversations where the new knowledge one has gained is acted upon, and a new view of the world is offered to another individual. This runs contrary to the views held by many about the processes of teaching and learning, in which instructors fill the minds of unsuspecting students with information. Students often believe they are surrounded by experts whose command of knowledge enables them to definitively answer their questions. When confronted with real-world applications, however, students are likely to utilize the learning strategies and logic they have already developed, as opposed to engaging with new ideas or skills. In order to put this new knowledge to work, students need to explore, test, compare, and defend multiple points of view on an issue.

This is why criminal justice is so well situated within the liberal arts. The development of critical thinking skills is a lifelong endeavour, requiring not only that we question our basic assumptions about the world around us, but also that we assist others in doing the same. When students begin to question the vision of society they have inherited, they move beyond the role of passive observers and into that of independent thinkers. Through the development of alternative insights, we can each hope to challenge our more comfortable assumptions, and as teachers, we can know we have done our job of providing fertile ground for the cultivation of critical thought and innovative action.

This philosophy of teaching and learning forms the backbone of this book. We teach criminology and criminal justice at a small liberal arts university, and believe that the study of these disciplines is well suited to the art of learning as freedom. While it is not common for criminal justice practitioners to be trained in traditional liberal arts disciplines, we work within a multidisciplinary department that builds on the integration of these different fields. Further, the day-to-day work of criminal justice professionals can often involve making decisions, which, if they become too routinized, can lead them to forget about the situations and circumstances that led a suspect, inmate, or parolee to become enmeshed in the criminal justice system in the first place.

In our view, the infliction of pain on another—whether couched in terms of punishment, deterrence, or retribution—must be done with a clear vision of the outcome that is expected. When referring to capital punishment, for example, we need to consider why a society would kill someone in order to demonstrate why killing people is wrong. In order to fully appreciate the impact of sanctions on another individual, we believe it is important to consider issues from a variety of perspectives, and this is how we have approached this book.

Our goal from the outset has been to create a "teachable text." Working against the dominant model of providing students with "information" that they read independently before attending lectures and are later assessed on, we envisioned this text as a kind of in-class workbook. We will encourage our students to mark up the pages, and to complete the enclosed exercises both in class and in the book. We imagine stopping our own lectures to tease out the themes touched upon in the various critical thinking questions, to open up class discussion using the *What Do You Think?* sections, and to coordinate small group projects or presentations around the topical case studies. Highlighted boxes throughout the text will encourage our students to "take a sidebar" and probe some of the more tangential or analytical questions the material raises, before returning to the main "course of action."

Similarly, Chapter 16 is not meant to be a "catch-all" for topics that couldn't be slotted into previous chapters, nor do we envision that it should be read sequentially as a stand-alone chapter. Instead, we hope instructors will find ways of using it that best fit within their own pedagogical approach. Students can be referred there for extended reading on particular issues, or they can use it as fodder for "special topics" seminars (throughout the text, margin "bubbles" direct readers to related sections in Chapter 16). The two of us plan to use the chapter in very different ways: one of us will use it as a "go-to" list for year-end poster presentations, the other as a resource for an in-class essay-writing workshop. In any case, *how* you use the final chapter and the other teaching tools in the text is entirely up to you. We simply hope that they are, in fact, used—ideally, in collaboration with your students.

Acknowledgments

We have wanted to write a book together for some time and the opportunity to do so with a text that will be used by our own students has been a true privilege. We want to thank them for the inspiration they brought to us at each stage of this writing process.

This project would not have taken off without the enthusiasm and vision of Mike Thompson and the support of the rest of the team at Emond Montgomery Publications, who have improved this text at every stage of its development: Jim Lyons, Deanna Dority, Tara Wells, Katy Littlejohn, David Handelsman, and Jamie Bush.

We and EMP wish to thank the following people for reviewing the project at various stages and offering their feedback and suggestions: Jane Barker (Nipissing University), Leo de Jourdan (Canadore College), Walter de Keseredy (UOIT), Alison Dunwoody (University of Alberta), Ronald Hinch (UOIT), Jessie Horner (Kwantlen Polytechnic University), Anne-Marie Singh (Ryerson University), and Jeanine Webber (Humber College).

Finally, we acknowledge the patience, enthusiasm, and insights offered by our contributing authors, as well as the consistent support of our families and friends, particularly our colleagues at St. Thomas University. We feel incredibly fortunate to make a living doing what we love and in an environment as committed to undergraduate teaching as ours.

Karla O'Regan and Susan Reid
Fredericton, New Brunswick

Website

Please visit the accompanying website for this text, emp.ca/cj, for a full glossary of criminal justice terms and other resources.

About the Authors

Jane Barker is an associate professor and chair of the School of Criminology and Criminal Justice at Nipissing University.

Leo de Jourdan is a former police officer and is currently the coordinator of the Police Foundations Program at Canadore College.

Julian Hermida is an associate professor in the Department of Law and Politics at Algoma University.

Ronald Hinch is a professor in the Faculty of Social Science and Humanities at the University of Ontario Institute of Technology.

Graham Hudson is an assistant professor in the Department of Criminal Justice and Criminology at Ryerson University.

Christine Hudy designs police training and is the lead educational methodologist at RCMP's Depot Division in Regina.

Kouri Keenan is a consultant and PhD student at Simon Fraser University.

Karla O'Regan is an associate professor in the Department of Criminology and Criminal Justice at St. Thomas University, Fredericton.

Susan Reid is a professor in the Department of Criminology and Criminal Justice at St. Thomas University, Fredericton, and director of the Centre for Research on Youth at Risk.

Stephen Schneider is an associate professor in the Department of Sociology and Criminology at Saint Mary's University.

Graham Stewart was the executive director of The John Howard Society of Canada until his retirement in 2007.

D. Scharie Tavcer is an associate professor in the Department of Justice Studies at Mount Royal University.

Jeanine Webber is the program coordinator and a professor of criminal justice in the School of Social and Community Services, Humber Institute of Technology and Advanced Learning.

Canada's Criminal Justice System: An Overview

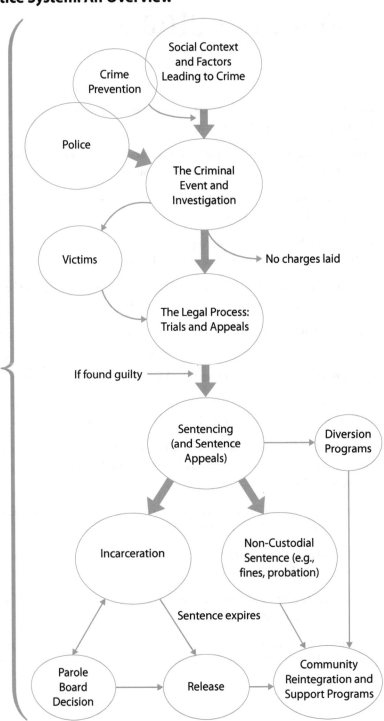

PART ONE
Introduction

You Be the Judge

Karla O'Regan

The presiding judge, Honourable
Chief Justice Barry Stuart
Source: Barry Stuart.

Sometimes, when we hear about a case involving a violent crime, we rush to a hasty conclusion about whether the judge's sentence was fair; we don't consider important principles such as justice, mercy, vengeance, shame, human rights, and public safety, and what these mean. The goal of this book is to help you think more searchingly, critically, and by the time you reach the end, we hope, a bit differently about these and other core principles of Canada's criminal justice system. Chapter 1, which begins after this case study, provides a framework for discussing the theories, institutions, and issues around criminal justice in Canada today. This case study provides you with an opportunity to test your own preconceptions about the criminal justice system. Read the following description of a real criminal offence committed in Canada, including information about the victim and the offender.* What sentence would you give? What would be your reasons? At the end of the book, you'll have an opportunity to revisit this case to see whether your opinion or your reasons for having it have changed.

The Offence

A young man (whom we'll call J) broke into the victim's home shortly after midnight, wearing a ski mask and carrying a knife. He woke the victim from a deep sleep and used duct tape to bind her hands and feet and to cover her eyes and mouth. He left only her nose exposed, so she could breathe. For more than two hours, J physically and sexually assaulted the victim. He forced her to inhale a number of harsh, offensive substances, including chili pepper, and he cut the waist-length hair she had worn for more than 20 years. At one point, J violently ripped off the duct tape covering his victim's eyes, removing some of her skin and eyebrows. Throughout the assaults, the

---

* Note to readers: This case, as well as some others described in this book, involves a very violent offence. Many of the facts are disturbing and should be discussed with sensitivity and respect.

victim was in constant fear of death. Even after the assault had ended, she lay paralyzed with terror until she heard no more noise in the house, struggled free, and fled out into the street. Numerous bruises and cuts covered her body. Her lungs suffered burns from the toxic inhalations, and she subsequently became asthmatic. The emotional, social, and psychological damage she suffered was severe and immeasurable.

The Victim

The victim chose not to address the court in person during sentencing. Instead, she submitted a victim impact statement to relay her experience of the crime and of the pain and suffering it caused her. Excerpts of that statement are included below:

> I am unnaturally afraid, terrified even, under what before the attack were normal, positive situations. I am afraid to be in my own home alone, especially at night-time and that makes it, at times, impossible for me to sleep. I have disturbing dreams. I don't sleep deeply. I am hyper vigilant a lot of the time. I find myself peeping outside of the windows regularly to see if anyone is lurking around, to see if there are footprints on the patio. I keep all of my doors and windows closed and locked. I am terrified to leave my own home on foot, alone, in broad daylight—it is not even an option for me. I am a prisoner in my own home. Things that used to be freedom, like going for walks, or gardening in my yard, or taking the garbage out … when I'm alone, I just can't do them.
>
> This incident has curtailed my freedom of movement. I won't walk to the end of my driveway. I can only leave my home in a cab or if a friend is with me. My mailbox is right outside my front door. I couldn't check my mail after the assault. I do now, but I have to peep through the window first to see if anyone is around before I can open the door.
>
> When the house makes a noise, I hit the ceiling. In other words, I have very exaggerated startle responses. I am frequently in a state of high anxiety and have frequent panic attacks. Also, my ability to deal with normal day-to-day stresses has been lessened. Being in normal social situations makes me extremely tense at times, like going to a social function. I no longer feel comfortable in public situations, in any situation where I don't know everyone. Trusting people is an issue for me. I don't trust people and society as I used to. I still freak out getting into a cab with a male driver if I don't know him. …
>
> Towards the end, not long before he [J] finally left, I was certain he intended to kill me before he left. I begged him not to, telling him my daughter needed me. I no longer feel safe in my own community. Subsequent attacks on other women in the community were triggers for me and severely hampered my efforts to normalize my life. I feel a great fear and distrust towards most men. I feel I have lost much of my joy of life and find I need

to work very hard to regain it. This is something that consumes most of my time on a daily basis.

See also mini chapter 16.3
Victims' Rights

When somebody commits a crime, he has not just broken the law: he's broken a person along with it.

At the sentencing hearing, the court took note of how the offender's actions had harmed the wider community by fostering fear, as well as anger, resentment, confusion, and grief, among many of its members.

The Offender

J is a member of a First Nation in Canada's Yukon Territory. At the time of his birth, his mother was severely addicted to drugs and alcohol, which strongly suggests that J was born with fetal alcohol spectrum disorder (FASD) (Spencer, 2011). When he was only seven months old, his mother took him to live with his maternal grandparents. Subsequently, a number of visits by Social and Family Services revealed that he was suffering from severe neglect and abuse. On one visit, before J was even two years of age, social workers found him alone in a bedroom with a board across the door, dirty and hungry. A year later, he was found lying in the middle of the road; a bus driver, after narrowly avoiding running over him, took him to child-protection services. He was returned to his home, but within a year was taken to hospital with injuries believed to be caused by physical abuse. Before he was four, his aunt (herself only nine years old) died after falling off the back of a truck in the yard, while an uncle died of exposure after becoming drunk and unconscious out of doors. Over the course of the next few years, Social and Family Services was called numerous times, and the personnel there documented evidence of physical and sexual abuse suffered by J at the hands of his uncles. Social Services reports indicate that whenever J was deemed "too difficult" or his grandmother became financially unstable, he would be dropped off at Social Services for months at a time (although his guardian would not allow J to be adopted when the opportunity arose).

J eventually moved through several foster homes. By the time he was seven years old, the schools he attended began to report a number of problems with J, including severe temper tantrums, **truancy**, stealing, indecent acts of vandalism (including smearing feces on walls), inappropriate sexual activities, and cruelty and violence to animals and other children. When J was only 8 years old, a teacher observed the following: "He has been through a great deal of stress and unhappiness. Time is crucial in getting him the professional help he

Truancy is a term used by courts, schools, and social service organizations to refer to students who voluntarily choose to skip or not attend school. It refers only to compulsory schooling—that is, where the law requires students to attend. In Canada, school is compulsory for everyone up to the age of 16, except in Ontario, New Brunswick, and Manitoba, where all youths are required to attend school until the age of 18.

desperately needs. This is a little boy who deserves something good to come into his life."

J's grandmother died when he was eight, and he was returned to state custody. This necessitated a psychiatric examination. During this assessment, J was shown a picture of a little boy and asked to tell a story about it. He responded as follows:

> He is crying. He wishes his mom could come back. He misses her. He is going to be stealing, no one is ready to feed him, no one is ready to get his socks on, no one combs his hair, no one gets him cleaned up for school, he goes to school dirty. Someone is ready to steal him a killer and he kills him and gets his meat, cuts him open and cooks his meat. If he does that Lord will punish him. Nobody loves this little boy. He cries and cries.

J continued to move from foster home to foster home, demonstrating chronic anti-social behaviour, including acts of sexual aggression, until he was sixteen and returned to the home of his grandfather—the same home he had earlier been removed from amid reports of neglect and abuse. No follow-up treatment or visits were provided. J left school in grade 10 and, before he was 17, incurred 20 criminal convictions and spent time in jail.

At the time of the offence described above, J was 21 years old. He was unemployed and not attending school. He had no significant marketable skills, no work history, and the equivalent of a grade 10 education. He supported himself through social assistance and through stealing, and he had a significant alcohol and drug addiction. His home was a hotel room. He had never received the treatments recommended for the particular forms of harm he had suffered—neglect, abandonment, and sexual and physical abuse. His anger, inappropriate sexual behaviour, and substance abuse were not dealt with in counselling or in treatment programs. None of the recommendations made by numerous professionals over the course of J's life were implemented, which led the judge in the case to determine that J had been a "ticking time bomb" in the community.

What Do You Think?

1. What sentence would you give J in this case? Why?
2. What factors would you take into account when deciding on this sentence?
3. What principles guide your decision?
4. What do you hope your sentence will accomplish?

REFERENCES

Spencer, B. (2011). A different kind of justice. *The National*, *20*(5), 18–28.

Studying Criminal Justice

Introduction

Cases like the one that opened this book reveal the complexity of the criminal justice system and the challenges inherent in its study. No doubt there were many disagreements among your colleagues about the appropriate sentence for J and the reasons for it. Working through these debates is a key component of the criminal justice profession and the many different agencies, institutions, and stakeholders it involves. These differences of opinion are also why studying criminal justice can be such an interesting endeavour. There is always more than one side to a story. Crime is, after all, an aspect of social life. Some theorists, such as the French sociologist Émile Durkheim, argue that crime is a necessary part of human societies and their development. It exists in all civilizations regardless of political leadership, financial circumstances, geography, religious belief, cultural history, demographic composition, language, or levels of industrialization—although each of these factors can influence how much crime there is and how it is dealt with.

Criminology and Criminal Justice: Liberal Arts Endeavours

Understanding how much crime there is, on the one hand, and determining how to address it, on the other hand, marks the distinction between criminology and criminal justice. Criminology is interested in how and why crime happens, while criminal justice is concerned with what to do about criminal activity once it has occurred. Those are, of course, simplistic definitions of both fields and it is important to keep in mind that criminology and criminal justice rely on the work and expertise of each other. Criminology, for example, wants to know more about "the criminal mind" and what factors motivate an offender to commit illegal acts. Research in this area often relies on psychology, biology, sociology, and the studies that emerge from criminal justice experts about existing offenders and their treatment programs. Similarly, criminal justice scholars are sometimes interested in how to rehabilitate an offender while in prison or how to help her reintegrate into her community after being released. This challenge is made easier with the help of criminological studies that aim to learn more about what motivates people to commit crimes in the first place and how an offender's community can play a role in the prevention, commission, and control of crime. The purpose of the criminal justice system is to prevent and control crime in a way that both maintains and promotes justice. Criminology uses a scientific method to explain the interactions of law-making, law-breaking, and the reactions of society to these processes. The study of criminal justice is characterized by the need to understand how the system works, how the criminal law affects that system, and how the system should be administered. This has sometimes led to criminal justice studies being housed in political science or sociology departments, given the discipline's interest in studying social control and the various ways it is exercised in defining and reacting to criminal behaviour.

ideology
A system of beliefs or assumptions about the correct or proper order of things, particularly with respect to morality and political arrangements; a value system that shapes a person's position on specific issues.

Williams and Robinson (2004, p. 379) suggest that liberal arts education "has at its centre four practices that distinguish it from other kinds of learning: critical thinking, continuing examination of life, encounters with difference, and the free exchange of ideas." They go on to suggest that most criminal justice texts ignore issues crucial to the very foundation of all criminal justice processes, such as power, **ideology**, politics, and the manipulation of the law through lobbying by special interest groups. We would argue that the liberal arts encourage a more critical approach to the study of the criminal justice system and its agencies, where it is essential to debunk the dominant myths of crime and criminal justice. This text encourages the use of ideology as a framework for understanding both the intended and unintended consequences of a crime policy or program; it thus engages in a more critical analysis of the systems of criminal justice, placing the discipline firmly within the tradition of the liberal arts. The utility of ideology as a means of understanding the criminal justice system will be further explored throughout this chapter.

Criminal Justice: Areas of Study and Key Players

Given its interest in *responding to* crime, the field of criminal justice can be understood as the study of the many institutions and agents that are involved in the investigation of criminal activity, the enforcement of the criminal law, and the correctional arm of the state. These agencies can be broadly understood to fall within one of three general areas of criminal justice work— namely, policing, courts, and corrections. This book is organized around these three subfields of specialization. The first of these is the work of the various policing services in Canada and their affiliated agencies, including municipal, provincial, and federal levels of policing, community-based strategies, and specialized forces such as the First Nations police service, surveillance and investigative teams, and the forensic science services used by police throughout the country.

A second area of criminal justice work centres on the criminal law and its procedures. This field of study involves the work of many court-based personnel, including lawyers, judges, and their research teams (comprising paralegals, legal secretaries, and law clerks). It is also an area interested in the work of court services personnel, including bailiffs, registrars, jury attendants, and court reporters, as well as criminal justice professionals who provide services and support to victims and witnesses, such as victim services organizations and social workers.

The third subfield of criminal justice is also one of its largest areas of research: corrections. It focuses on the procedures and institutions of imprisonment in terms of the assessment, treatment, rehabilitation, and reintegration of offenders. Correctional officers, security personnel, and prison administration workers (such as the warden or superintendent of the institution) are key players in this criminal justice field. The work of post-incarceration personnel, such as parole officers, drug and alcohol abuse counsellors, and mental health workers, is also of interest to criminal justice scholars of corrections. Community-based work among criminal justice professionals that doesn't take place in jail, court, or prison is also a part of the corrections area and includes halfway house counsellors, attendance

centre program personnel, educational consultants, youth workers, probation officers, group home workers, and diversion or alternative measures
coordinators.

It is also important to mention the programs that are operated within the
community which aim to prevent crime through both voluntary groups
(e.g., crime prevention associations, Neighbourhood Watch groups) and
other non-governmental organizations (e.g., John Howard Society, Elizabeth
Fry Society). These programs and agencies provide assistance to the more
formal state-run institutions with the help of a broad base of community
volunteers.

This is far from an exhaustive list, but it should give you some indication
of the wide variety of work that is conducted within the criminal justice
system and the exciting opportunities such diversity creates for those who,
like you, have chosen criminal justice as a field of study.

How Do We Come to Know What We Know About Crime and Criminal Justice?

The appeal of criminology and criminal justice courses may lie in the fascina-
tion that people have with the subject matter, but is perhaps further enhanced
by the many popular TV dramas that explore issues of crime and justice,
such as *Law and Order*, *Criminal Minds*, and *CSI*. Many of us are subject to
a daily barrage of images about crime and disorder through news media,
television, and Internet sources. Crime constitutes a constant and significant
portion of the total news portrayed on radio and television, and in the print
media. Both the news and entertainment industries are notorious for con-
sistently taking the least common crime or criminal justice event and making
it appear to be the most common crime or justice image. Such practices can
make anyone seem like an instant authority on crime, but all too often such
ideological beliefs impede our ability to look for alternative solutions to the
crime phenomenon. Consumers of a steady diet of crime and criminal
justice images from the media have been subjected to a vocabulary of force,
where police are portrayed as crime fighters in the "war" on crime. This
prepares a student entering a course in criminal justice to hold beliefs that
crime must be "fought" rather than prevented, reduced, or solved. Students
who do not learn about how the law is made or who do not appreciate that
it is by definition partial, incomplete, and biased in favour of some interests
over others will not understand the present realities of criminal justice
practice and its challenges. One of the purposes of this text is to dispel the
myths surrounding crime and criminal justice and enable you to more critically evaluate criminal justice policies in light of competing views about the

nature of crime, the methods of intervention, and the possible intended and unintended outcomes of these various methods.

Thinking Critically About the Issues

In asking you to think critically about the issues in this text, we want you to embark on a process of reasonably deciding what to do and/or believe while considering what sources, images, ideas, and arguments helped you reach these positions. We want you not only to be able to assess your own and others' arguments, but also to be able to construct good arguments where the issues are controversial. Criminal justice scholars should always be striving to create counterarguments and examples supported by empirical evidence while remaining sensitive to their own biases and values. We are asking for a commitment to open-mindedness and fairness, empathy for others' positions, openness to self-criticism, and an appreciation of the value of looking at criminal events from multiple points of view. This may mean a change in some of the beliefs you already have about crime and how it should be addressed, and this kind of shift is not always easy to undertake. Yet, as Mark Twain once suggested, "Education consists mainly of what we have unlearned," and when it comes to society's reactions to and treatments of criminal activity, you might say there is a great deal of "unlearning" to do.

Sherman (1981, p. 17), in his work on preparing criminal justice professionals, suggested that "the business of criminal justice is forcing people to do what they do not want to do, on the basis of threat of pain, physical harm, or in those countries which still have capital punishment, death." Few commentators on the criminal justice system and even fewer students of criminal justice think about the social and ethical responsibilities of this task before becoming involved with the system themselves; when they do encounter the system, Sherman suggests the result is a "substantial reality shock" (p. 18). We all have a responsibility to act thoughtfully in our support for public policies within the realm of crime prevention and control when we pick our government leaders through the democratic process. In order to prepare you for the tasks you will face in the future, whether as a practitioner in the criminal justice system or as a Canadian citizen, it is important that you clearly understand the implications of any given criminal justice practice from several viewpoints. As we have noted, the police, the courts, and the state's correctional arm are the principal areas of focus in criminal justice studies. This is not only a reflection of how our current system *responds* to crime, but also how it *defines* crime. It is important to keep in mind how the choices of lawmakers and government officials can influence what behaviours are targeted and by whom. Thus, the very existence of police, courtrooms, and correctional institutions informs us about how the criminal justice system is organized as well as its underlying assumptions. Remember, however, that these are not the only ways of responding to crime. Many alternative approaches to policing or to determining punishments for offenders are explored in criminal justice studies each year (some of which are examined in Chapter 16 of this book).

Implementing criminal justice policy in policing, criminal law, or corrections requires an understanding that focusing on one form of crime control will affect the quality of life not only of the targeted segment of the population, but of the population as a whole. If any one method is used exclusively, it will have limited returns, and we must be mindful of the need to consider alternative processes. Through a systematic practice of recognizing our own beliefs and being open to the insights of others, we have an opportunity to explore the beliefs that might marginalize others and to consider all sides of an often conflicting array of alternatives. This book is not only about the *how* of criminal justice, but more importantly about the *why* of the law, police, courts, and corrections.

How Much Crime Is There? Debunking the Myths

Crime and society's response to it are frequent features in news media reports, leaving many issues of policing, the court system, and the correctional system open to public scrutiny. How often have you overheard conversations about a high-profile criminal case or a piece of government legislation designed to "get tough on crime"? Often, public opinion focuses on the failure of the system to keep citizens safe and the injustice of an offender getting off on a "technicality," but few of these attitudes consider the complexity of the system. This is an understandable oversight given the breadth of issues involved in any case or criminal event. Equally, the complexity surrounding counting crime and reporting on **crime rates** to the general public is another area that requires considerable awareness of the processes involved (see the sidebar on page 14).

Despite politicians' frequent claims to the contrary, the national crime rate has been falling steadily for the past 20 years and is now at its lowest level since 1973 (Statistics Canada, 2011). In 2010 alone, the crime rate declined 5 percent from 2009. The homicide rate fell to 1.62 for every 100,000 members of the population—its lowest level since 1966, representing less than 1 percent of all violent incidents (Mahoney, 2011). This tells us that not only are there fewer crimes occurring in Canada than ever before, but also that the crime that is committed is less violent.

There is also a misperception that homicides and other violent crimes are more prevalent in large cities. The most recent statistics reveal in fact

FIGURE 1.1   The Police-Reported Crime Rate, 1962–2010

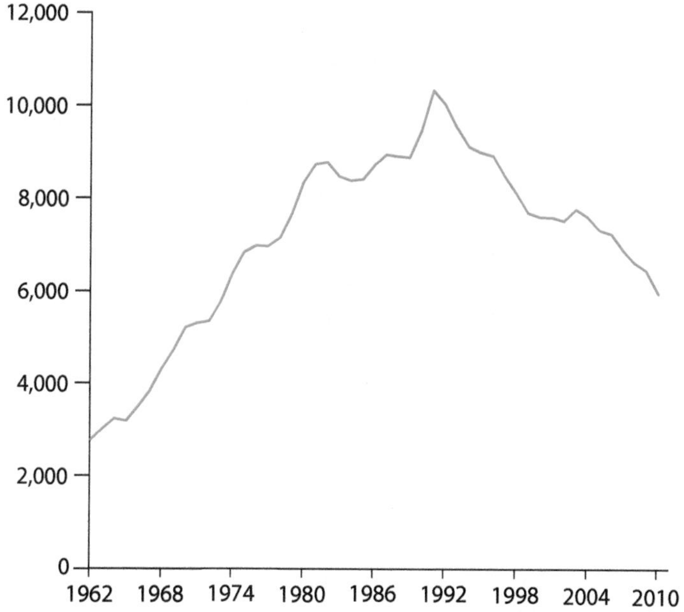

The police-reported crime rate, which measures the overall volume of crime, has been falling for decades. The Crime Severity Index, which measures the severity of crime, has also been declining.

Source: Statistics Canada (2011). Rate is calculated per 100,000 population.

that the incidence of homicide was below the national average in Canada's three largest cities: Toronto, Montreal, and Vancouver. Indeed, among the country's census metropolitan areas, Thunder Bay reported the highest homicide rate for the second year in a row, followed by Saskatoon and Regina (Mahoney, 2011). Does this mean that it is more dangerous to live in Thunder Bay? Not necessarily. What is needed is an understanding of how a change in the rate per 100,000 population is calculated and how the increase of even one homicide in a region can dramatically increase the rate. It is important to remember that while murder is a very serious event, it is not commonplace.

The crime rate, which measures the overall volume of police-reported crime, counts all offences equally, so that one incident of bicycle theft is counted the same as one incident of murder. As such, the crime rate tends to be driven by high-volume, less-serious offences, such as minor thefts and mischief rather than the more violent offences people often imagine when

---

SIDEBAR

Crime Rate

The "crime rate" is a measure of how much crime is known about for any given region or population. It is calculated by adding up all of the criminal incidents that have been reported to the police and dividing by the population (i.e., rate per every 100,000 persons). In Canada, this data is taken from the Uniform Crime Reporting (UCR) Survey, which collects information filed by police departments across the country about the number of crimes reported, the number of criminal charges that were laid, how these were addressed (e.g., were they "cleared" or solved by police?), as well as the age and gender of the offenders. Because it does not include information about any crimes that were not reported, the crime rate is only one indicator of how much crime really occurs.

---

they hear the word "crime." In order to have a better understanding of the more serious crimes in Canada, the Crime Severity Index (CSI) was introduced in 2006. In addition to the volume of crime reported to the police, the CSI also gives a weight to each offence based on the average sentences handed down by the courts. The more serious the average sentence, the higher the weight for the offence on the CSI. As a result, in the calculation of the sum of the weighted offences (divided by the population), the more serious offences such as murder will have a greater impact on changes in the index from year to year (Wallace, Turner, Babyak, & Matarazzo, 2009). In 2010, the CSI reached its lowest point since 1998, which was the first year for which index data were available (Statistics Canada, 2011). The compatibility between the crime rate and the CSI data for the year 2010 suggests that crime is going down.

There are a number of other sources for crime rate data in Canada. Human Resources and Skills Development Canada has constructed a series of statistical measures, referred to as Indicators of Well-Being in Canada (see Figure 1.2). The website provides data from different sources and "presents a comprehensive, up-to-date picture of the well-being of Canadians and Canadian society" (Human Resources and Skills Development Canada, 2012).

Unreported Crime: The Dark Figure

The crime rate as an indicator of well-being in Canada falls under the category of "security," and provides, in addition to police-reported and self-reported crimes (from victim surveys like the General Social Survey), an overview

FIGURE 1.2   Areas of Well-Being in Canada

Source: Human Resources and Skills Development Canada (2012).

of how Canadians feel about their sense of personal safety and their level of satisfaction with the police. Self-report studies are particularly useful given their ability to provide data on crimes that are not reported to police and are thus omitted from national measurements of the crime rate. We never really know how much crime is out there because not all of it is reported. Criminologists and law enforcement personnel refer to this unknowable statistic as the "dark figure of crime."

The General Social Survey (GSS), which began in 1985 and runs every five years, is one of the largest sources of data about unreported crime. It polls a sample of the Canadian population (sample size (n) = 25,000) aged

---

SIDEBAR

Dark Figure of Crime

The "dark figure of crime" is a term used in criminology and criminal justice studies to refer to the vast amount of criminal activity that is not reported to police. The term reminds us that the total amount of crime in any given society is impossible to know. How much crime goes unreported is thought to vary depending on the offence. For example, sexual assault is believed to have the lowest reporting rate of any criminal offence, estimated to be less than 6 percent. This means that of every 100 sexual assaults that occur, only 6 of them are ever reported to the criminal justice system, leaving the remaining 94 incidents "in the dark."

15 years and older living in the ten provinces and asks a series of questions aimed at learning more about (1) changes in the living conditions and well-being of Canadians over time by gathering data on social trends; and (2) current or emerging issues in Canadian society. Theme areas include:

- health
- time use
- victimization
- education, work, retirement
- family
- social support and aging
- social engagement.

In 2009, the survey estimated that 7.4 million Canadians were a victim of a criminal incident in the preceding 12 months. This self-reported rate was essentially unchanged from 2004. According to the data from the GSS, one-third (31 percent) of incidents were reported to the police in 2009, down slightly from 2004 (34 percent) (Smith, 2011). About 36 percent consisted of household incidents (namely, break-ins, thefts of motor vehicles or parts, vandalism, or theft of household property), while 34 percent consisted of theft of personal property. Violent incidents accounted for 30 percent.

"The prison for unreported crime" (Prime Minister Stephen Harper and Cabinet Minister Stockwell Day)

Source: Artizans. Reprinted by permission.

Stockwell Day, who was a federal Cabinet minister at the time, claimed in 2010 that 88 percent of sexual assaults go unreported to the police. But this number actually came from the GSS, which asked the question: "During the past 12 months has anyone ever touched you against your will in any sexual way (unwanted touching, grabbing, kissing, or fondling)?" When the respondents to the GSS were asked why they did not report this behaviour to the police, they told StatsCan interviewers it was because "the incident was not important enough." This reveals one of the drawbacks to self-report studies. Despite their ability to provide some insight into the dark figure of crime, they depend on the individual respondents' honesty and understanding of the questions posed—including particular definitions of crime. Would the general public, for example, in reading the statistic Day referred to, be aware that there are three levels of sexual assault,[1] or would they believe the statistic to be referring only to what used to be called rape? How each person might read and understand the GSS question about unwanted sexual touching has an effect on how the rate of sexual assault (and its unreported levels) is understood by criminal justice researchers and professionals and can also alter how crime-control policies are developed.

Crime Rates Versus Fear of Crime

Some critics have pointed out that commentary about the falling crime rates is couched in elitism and that the criminologists and scholars who are criticizing the government for promoting a tough-on-crime agenda are divorced from the reality of crime in their lives. Ian Lee (2011), writing for the Macdonald-Laurier Institute, an Ottawa social policy think tank, has suggested that

> [a]ffluent, older privileged people in … any community with average incomes three or four or five times the Canadian income average, have little existential experience with crime. … [T]his suggests that governments need to adopt outreach programs to inform those privileged Canadians, who perhaps do not understand the lived reality of many Canadians, of the data and the relationship between the data, the concerns and fears of many Canadians and the public policy initiatives undertaken to address those real concerns of ordinary Canadians. (pp. 17–18)

When we look at the StatsCan data that Lee (2011) makes reference to, we find that the majority of Canadians (93 percent) felt satisfied with their personal safety and that this has been a continuing trend (1999, 91 percent; 2004, 94 percent). Similarly, when respondents were asked about specific situations (e.g., walking alone in their neighbourhood at night), 90 percent reported feeling safe and about 83 percent said they were not at all worried when they were home alone at night. About 58 percent of those who used public transportation reported that they were also not concerned for their safety when waiting for or using these services after dark (Statistics Canada, 2010).

Why, then, amid declining crime rates and an increased sense of safety among Canadians, are get-tough approaches still so prevalent? Criminologist Julian Roberts (2001) has suggested that the reporting practices of the mass media have a significant influence on public attitudes and beliefs about crime. News reports tend to focus on violent offences (despite their rarity) while paying less attention to declining crime rates in general, leading more Canadians to believe that violent crime is on the rise. This might explain why, despite the statistics that suggest Canadians are generally feeling safer, there continues to be wide support for the federal government's tough-on-crime policies. A 2009 public opinion poll revealed that more than 76 percent of Canadians supported tougher legislation to deal with gang-related crime and tougher sentencing provisions to send marijuana growers to jail (Angus Reid Strategies, 2009a). Another poll conducted that same year showed overwhelming public support for the federal government's proposed changes to mandatory minimum sentencing, including 72 percent of Canadians being in favour of eliminating the existing **faint hope clause** and 91 percent supporting a mandatory two-year jail term for anyone caught selling drugs at or near a school (Angus-Reid Strategies, 2009b).

SIDEBAR

Faint Hope Clause

Canada's faint hope clause is found in s. 745.6 of the *Criminal Code*. It gives persons convicted of the country's most serious offences (i.e., murder or high treason), who have been sentenced to life imprisonment without the eligibility for parole, the opportunity to apply for parole after they have served 15 years of their sentence. It is not permitted in cases where the offender has committed more than one murder. It is called the "faint hope" clause because of how few applications made under this provision have been successful: about 10 percent since its inception in 1976 (Jenish, 1997). Following amendments to the *Criminal Code* in March 2011, the faint hope clause was effectively removed. It is no longer available for anyone whose offence was committed after December 2, 2011.

In this area of counting crime and determining how best to respond to it, it is clear that an individual's political and ideological perceptions influence the questions that are asked and the way that the data is interpreted. This is also true when you consider the ways that we think about who should "count" as a criminal.

Who Are the "Criminals"?

By definition, a criminal is anyone who has been convicted of a crime. Contrary to public opinion, of the many individuals who come in contact with Canada's criminal justice system, the smallest group comprises persons convicted and sentenced to a term in prison. After a person commits a crime, the crime must be reported and investigated before an arrest (if any) can be made. The arrest, as you will learn throughout the course of this book, represents only the beginning of a criminal prosecution. Many decisions by police, lawyers, probation officers, judges, and juries will affect whether a conviction for the crime will occur or, after conviction, what type of sentence will be imposed. There is far more crime than the number of sentences served would suggest. This is because, as cases move through the criminal justice system, various factors affect whether they will continue to the next stage. Many cases are dropped long before they reach the sentencing phase, let alone a sentence of incarceration. This funnelling process is known in criminal justice circles as **attrition** and is estimated in recent Statistics Canada data to be about 5 percent in Canada, meaning that if 100 crimes occurred over the year (which would be very low!), only 5 of these would result in a sentence of imprisonment.

attrition
The filtering process that criminal cases undergo as they move through the criminal justice system.

Figure 1.3 illustrates this process for the year 2010. Although almost 2.4 million crimes were committed in Canada, only 9 percent (262,616) resulted in a conviction and approximately 31 percent of those convicted were sentenced to provincial prisons, while only 2 percent (5,434) were sentenced to federal penitentiaries (Public Safety Canada, 2011, p. 13).

The crime funnel serves as a good example of what the study of criminal justice is like. We often begin with broad-based concerns or topics, but must narrow them in order to reach a fuller understanding and effect any change. This is particularly the case when what some criminologists refer to as the "social context" of crime is considered. This perspective views the social conditions in which crime takes place (e.g., the existence of inequality or discrimination) as central to understanding how crime is treated by the criminal justice system, including how crime and criminals are defined.

SIDEBAR

The Crime Funnel

The crime funnel, also known as attrition, refers to the reduction of cases as they make their way through the various parts of the criminal justice system. This leaves a small percentage of the total number of cases investigated by police resulting in conviction, and even fewer that end in a custodial sentence. There are several key points within this funnelling process where attrition is greatest. These include:

1. The victim's decision to report the crime to police.
2. The police investigation and decision process with respect to whether the allegation is credible or supported by sufficient evidence (i.e., "founded").
3. Discussions between police and Crown prosecutors and their joint discretion to lay a charge.
4. The criminal prosecution of an accused, including any pretrial and trial procedures that can affect whether a case goes forward.
5. The judge or jury's decision in reaching a guilty verdict or the entering of a plea from the accused.
6. The determination of an appropriate sentence.

The number of cases decreases at each of these attrition points.

Could You Identify the Criminals in Canada Today?

In 2008, the *Toronto Star* ran a five-day series on crime to help educate the general public on matters related to crime in Canada. An article by Rankin and Powell (2008), "The Criminals Among Us," starts as follows:

> On any given day in Canada, on any busy city bus, on any main street, take a look around. There are criminals among us—about ten percent of adults. Picture the 50 people on the bus, and ask yourself, which five are criminals?
>
> Many Canadians identify the wrong people.

John Hagan (2010) asks this very question in his book *Who Are the Criminals?*, arguing that the answer is largely determined by the highly political context of criminal justice policies, where elected leaders "advocate and

FIGURE 1.3   The Crime Funnel

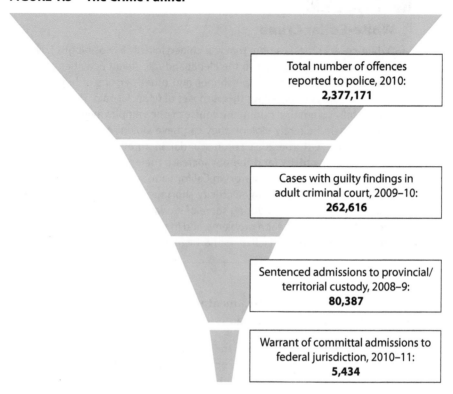

Total number of offences
reported to police, 2010:
2,377,171

Cases with guilty findings in
adult criminal court, 2009–10:
262,616

Sentenced admissions to provincial/
territorial custody, 2008–9:
80,387

Warrant of committal admissions to
federal jurisdiction, 2010–11:
5,434

Source: Public Safety Canada (2011, p. 13).

implement definitions of crime and causal arguments to suit ideological preferences, placate fears, and serve electoral needs" (Hagan, p. 3). This is one component of the argument made by Jeffrey Reiman in the classic book *The Rich Get Richer and the Poor Get Prison* (1979), in which he noted how laws protect the interests of the world's wealthy by defining crime in ways that target society's poor while avoiding the criminalization of corporate, or "white-collar," activities. Hagan's historical analysis of US crime policy drew attention to this differential targeting of criminal activity, noting a lax approach to what he refers to as "suite crime" (i.e., **white-collar crime**) and a harsh approach to street crime (e.g., common assault, break and enters). This illustrates that, in addition to how crime is defined, the ways in which crime is addressed within the criminal justice system are also subject to multiple forms of bias and discrimination, where some social statuses and

---

SIDEBAR

White-Collar Crime

"White-collar crime" is a term that was coined initially by sociologist Edwin Sutherland in 1939 to refer to the illegal and fraudulent activities of corporate executives, business personnel, and other persons of high social status that are committed for the purposes of financial gain. These crimes are typically committed during the course of one's employment, and while not considered directly violent, they can have violent consequences, as was the case with the 2001 Enron scandal. In an effort to increase the demand for electricity (and thereby increase their profits), Enron traders instructed power plant operators in California to shut down for extended periods of time, creating an electricity shortage. The resulting blackouts experienced in California during some of its warmest months led to mass droughts and severe health problems, and in some instances death among the young and elderly (Eichenwald & Richtel, 2002).

---

races experience privileged treatment at the expense of others. For example, Reiman (1979, p. 112) observed:

> *For the same criminal behavior,* the poor are more likely to be arrested; if arrested, they are more likely to be charged; if charged, more likely to be convicted; if convicted, more likely to be sentenced to prison; and if sentenced, more likely to be given longer prison terms than members of the middle and upper classes.

Crime Funnel or Crime Net?

Critiques like Reiman's suggest the possibility of a different perspective on the crime funnel. You will recall that the crime funnel suggests that only some criminal behaviour comes to the attention of the police and the courts, and that a great deal of cases are dealt with outside of the formal criminal justice system. There is therefore a certain amount of "editing out of crimes" as they proceed through the funnel.

Another way of discussing the phenomenon is what has been referred to as the "crime net." Brannigan (1984) suggested that the crime-net model brings out features of the criminal justice system that are not considered in the crime-funnel approach. The police act as "fishers" seeking criminals, but when taking out their crime "nets" must decide where to go and what fish to catch. This approach suggests that not all people who commit offences are selected for prosecution. Picture the wide but finely meshed nets used by shrimping boats. The nets are widely cast, picking up many fish and sea life of all sizes; yet, many of these nets include an "escape hatch" for larger fish, directing the smaller fish toward the back of the net through a grid that large fish cannot enter. This analogy of a fishing net illustrates how "big fish" may be able to get away from the net that is put out by the police because of the way it is designed, whom it is aiming to catch, and who falls outside their interest.

This social structural approach draws attention to the overrepresentation of some members of society within our prisons, while rich and powerful members committing equally heinous offences "swim away." It also helps illustrate how the act of defining some activities but not others as "crimes" results in different types of "criminals." The regulation of employment safety standards or the determination of the maximum number of hours in a working day, for example, hardly seems related to criminal justice; however, the exploitation of workers and their impoverished socio-economic conditions have resulted in far more deaths than all of the world's serial killers put together. The Union Carbide disaster in Bhopal, India in 1984 is a sad but effective example. Considered the world's worst industrial catastrophe, the plant's unsafe working conditions resulted in a gas leak that killed an estimated 25,000 people, severely injuring and deforming more than 550,000 others. No time in prison has been served by anyone following this incident (Sarangi, 2012).

This example demonstrates how definitions of crime, perceptions about who is a criminal, and opinions about how to address criminal activity depend on an individual's ideological perspective. In this way, attrition in the criminal justice system might be viewed as a "loss" or a "gain," just as crime rates can be understood to be "high" or "low" depending on what activities are considered criminal. Thinking through your own ideological perspective (as well as that of others) is an important tool for critical criminal justice analyses. This is also true when you are considering how best to intervene in the lives of those who come in conflict with the law. Given the difficulty of understanding how much crime there is in society and who should "count" as a criminal, it is equally likely that it will be difficult to agree upon the best way to deal with those individuals once they formally enter the criminal justice system. There has been an ongoing debate about whether it is better to treat the underlying individual and social factors that lead to crime or to make offenders pay for their crimes through punishment, denunciation, and retribution.

Observers continue to debate whether it is better to treat underlying social factors, or to make offenders pay for their crimes.

What Do You Think?

Think back to your decision about the appropriate sentence for the offender, J, in the opening case study. Which side of the crime-control debate would your punishment best represent? Were you most motivated by an interest in treating the "social context" of J's crime? Or, were you concerned primarily with the principles of denunciation or retribution?

What Works? The Debate About Crime Control Versus Rehabilitation

See also mini chapter 16.1
"Nothing Works" Revisited

Over the years, the pendulum in Canada has swung from left to right in terms of criminal justice policy for those who come into conflict with the law. At the height of the rehabilitative era, when the focus was on individualized treatment, the federal government focused its budget on assessment, treatment, and rehabilitation. Some critics of this approach argued that rehabilitation did not reduce **recidivism**; this position was reinforced by the release of a widely read article, "What Works: Questions and Answers About Prison Reform" by Robert Martinson (1974), which in essence argued that "nothing works." Martinson (1979) himself later clarified this position, stating that it was not the specific treatment programs designed for rehabilitating offenders that had the greatest predictive effect on recidivism, but rather the *conditions* under which these programs were delivered (p. 254). A similar conclusion had been reached by proponents of an effective treatment and intervention program for offenders known as "what works" (Gendreau, Little, & Goggin, 1996). This literature argued that the empirical evidence demonstrates that placing low-risk, low-need offenders in intensive "rehabilitation" programs can do more harm than good. Such intensive treatments should be reserved for those offenders who pose serious threats to the larger society. This led some advocates to propose a system of radical non-intervention based on the notion of **net widening**. In this approach, the critics put forth that doing nothing at all is sometimes superior than using the machinery of the criminal justice system. As this argument goes, the more intervention and labelling of offenders who are low risk to reoffend, the more likely it is that the net will be widened. This would

recidivism

Relapsing into criminal behaviour after treatment and/or sentencing within the criminal justice system. Most simply, it can be thought of as "reoffending."

SIDEBAR

Net Widening

"Net widening" is a term used to describe the effects of providing alternatives to incarceration that deal with offenders outside of the court system in order to reduce the numbers going to court and ultimately entering correctional systems. Such measures as diversion have cast the net wider: the total number of offenders under the control of the state has increased, while the population of those who were to benefit from this initiative has not been reduced.

mean that rather than having fewer offenders within the system, the criminal justice processing and their subsequent labelling would lead to more offenders coming into the system.

These debates highlight the complex challenges involved in determining not simply what crime is, but how best to respond to it. Part of the work of criminal justice scholars is to devise models for approaching these topics in a critical, fair, and thoughtful way. This issue will be revisited after a look at some theoretical models that are useful in considering criminal justice policy and its underlying ideologies.

The Ideology of Criminal Justice: Theoretical Models

Earlier in this chapter we defined the term "ideology" and spoke about the importance of understanding the values that drive the development and explanation of criminal justice. Political belief systems serve as the basic foundation for both law and its reform. Given that law is the basis for our criminal justice system, criminal justice operations cannot be understood without examining the role that ideology plays in shaping our systems of justice and the various competing views about their effectiveness. Williams and Robinson (2004, p. 385) have suggested that public policy is influenced by ideology and by stereotypes of criminals as much as, if not more than, by an understanding of the underlying causes of crime and the immediate situations that bring it about. In order to move beyond these stereotypes and debunk these myths, it is important to have some way of bringing together a framework to understand the various competing belief systems.

Herbert Packer (1964) developed a systematic way to conceptualize the influence of ideology on criminal justice systems. He referred to criminal justice as a paradox, characterized by a gulf between how police, courts, and corrections ought to behave and how they actually behave. In order to make explicit the value choices underlying the details of the criminal justice process, Packer suggested two main models of criminal justice procedure that fall loosely on a left-to-right ideological continuum and that have commonly been referred to as the "punishment–treatment dichotomy."

Crime control, at the far right of the continuum, is largely concerned with assuring the public that crime will not be tolerated and that, once it has been discovered, it will be severely punished.

The *welfare model*, toward the left side of the spectrum, stresses the importance of looking after the needs of the offender in order to ensure that the individual's problems are treated so that more crime will not occur in the future.

> **Deterrence** is a philosophical approach to crime that focuses on what forms of punishment are necessary to prevent crime from happening. It has two forms: specific and general. Specific deterrence seeks to punish the individual offender just enough so as to stop her from committing any future crimes. The assumption is that the offender will have learned the consequences of crime and will choose not to suffer them again. General deterrence seeks to punish offenders severely enough that the general population will choose not to commit crime. This approach aims to make an example of the offender so as to teach everyone the "costs" of crime.

rehabilitation
The treatment of offenders in order to prevent future criminal activity; a planned intervention that targets some aspect about the offender that is thought to cause the offender's criminality (e.g., attitude, cognitive processes, social relationships, and employment).

The crime-control model is based on the philosophy of **deterrence**, while the welfare model is primarily based on the tenets of **rehabilitation** and a medical model of treatment.

In addition to these two theoretical models, there have been other considerations that have been adopted and codified over the years. A variation on the crime-control model has emerged that adds a measure of accountability for human fallibility. Known as the *justice model*, it still focuses on the protection of society through deterrence principles, but it also suggests that there may be human errors in the discovery and subsequent finding of guilt for those accused of criminal conduct. As such, the justice model focuses on making sure that punishments are severe enough to deter crime but also that they are applied equally and fairly to everyone. This approach therefore focuses on the crime and not the individual who commits it, arguing that the criminal justice system should not apply differential treatment in any circumstances.

Similarly, with respect to the medical/treatment model of intervention, a great deal of work in the criminological literature has pointed to the strong positive correlation (link) between poverty and crime. This has led a number of critics to point out the need to consider the impact of external sociodemographic factors, known as the **root causes of crime**. The *community change model* picks up these root causes to suggest that the lack of access to resources and the disadvantages experienced by some members of society form the basis for the underlying factors leading to the commission of crime. From this perspective, all members of the community have a responsibility for the ongoing prevention and rehabilitation of individuals who come in conflict with the law (Reid & Reitsma-Street, 1984).

root causes of crime
Social factors in our societies, cultures (family values), economy, and systems that are more likely to lead an individual to commit crime. Examples include peer influence, poverty, unemployment, poor neighbourhoods, and poor literacy.

Based on some of the tenets of a community change model is the approach commonly referred to as "restorative justice." Restorative justice is a way of viewing the criminal justice system that puts the emphasis on healing those relationships that have been broken by conflict and crime. Viewed through this lens, crime is understood as a violation of people and their relationships, and a disruption of the peace of the community as opposed to being simply an offence against the state or an injury suffered solely by the victim. Restorative justice encourages the participation of victims, offenders, and the community in finding solutions that will achieve reconciliation and restore harmony. This approach also recognizes that sometimes the use of measures outside the criminal justice system (e.g., victim–offender mediation, circle sentencing) is the best response to the crime. Further, the restorative justice approach focuses on the importance of engaging the community in a meaningful dialogue regarding the most suitable means of repairing the harm and working toward a mutually beneficial solution for the victim and offender that will ensure that the offender understands how his or her behaviour has affected others (Reid & Zuker, 2005). You can read more about restorative justice and the use of sentencing circles in Chapter 16.

Each of these perspectives considers society from the viewpoint of either the **individualist** or the **collectivist**. Extreme individualists would argue that the state has absolutely no claims on the individual and there should be no rules, government, or constraints on individual actions (Reid, 1994). In contrast, extreme collectivists argue that society always takes precedence over individuals, and believe that the state has the right to demand conformity with the rules for the public good.[2] Regardless of the perspective, the causation of crime is the result of either **determinism** or free will, depending on the criminal justice model applied.

These two polar extremes are further differentiated by their emphasis on either extreme elitism, which suggests that there should be rulers and they should have complete power over individuals within society, or extreme egalitarianism, which says that all people should be absolutely equal in condition, not just opportunity. If these polar extremes can be envisioned as falling on a left–right continuum, at both ends there are collectivistic positions. On the far left is the position that society ought to be seen as more egalitarian, while on the far right is the position that society should be more hierarchically ordered.

individualist
A person who subscribes to the individualistic perspective, which focuses on the protection of individual autonomy against obligations that may be imposed by social institutions such as the state.

collectivist
A person who subscribes to the collectivistic perspective, which stresses the importance of group goals over individual goals and focuses on the community or broader society.

determinism
Philosophical idea that all human actions are a result of previous acts. Free will, in contrast, suggests that individuals can choose their actions and are not completely influenced by pre-existing events.

FIGURE 1.4   Theoretical Criminal Justice Models

Collectivist	Individualist	Individualist	Collectivist
Community change	**Welfare**	**Justice**	**Crime control**
Determinism	Determinism	Free will	Free will
Restorative justice			

Source: Reid (1994).

TABLE 1.1 A Comparison of Theoretical Models

	Restorative justice	Community change	Welfare	Justice	Crime control
Main tenet	When a crime is committed, it has an impact not only on the victim and the offender, but on the wider community as well.	Society is responsible for the promotion of the welfare of its citizens and must work to prevent crime and delinquency.	The treatment needs of the individual offender and his or her family must be attended to.	Interference with an individual's freedom is limited and procedures for criminal justice matters are based on consent by all parties as much as possible.	It is the responsibility of the state and the courts to maintain order in society.
Crime causation (free will vs. determinism)	All citizens have a role to play in the prevention of crime and repair of the harm done when a crime is committed.	Behaviour is seen as being determined by life consequences (e.g., poverty, lack of opportunity, social structure).	Behaviour is seen as being determined by social/psychological forces.	Freely determined: an individual chooses to commit offences.	Freely determined: an individual chooses to commit offences.
Individual or collective response	Collective: families, victims, and the community are involved to the greatest extent possible in rehabilitation, community safety initiatives, and holding offenders accountable.	Focus is on collective society rather than on the individual offender as being responsible for criminal conduct.	Individual: focus is on criminal conduct as being part of other social events affecting the individual, who needs rehabilitation and/or treatment (family dysfunction, alcohol/substance abuse, victim of family violence).	Individual: focus is on the repression of crime, but with a recognition that there is a high probability of error in informal fact finding (i.e., legal safeguards are needed to protect individual liberty and rights).	Collective: repression of criminal conduct through punishment, denunciation, and individual and general deterrence.

TABLE 1.1   Concluded

	Restorative justice	Community change	Welfare	Justice	Crime control
Criminal justice response	The individual is required to face the personal harm that his or her offending behaviour has done to the victim and the wider community; restitution, victim–offender mediation, and community service form part of the restoration of the victim, the offender, and the community.	Focus is on changing social processes that lead persons to engage in criminal conduct and to improve the quality of life for all citizens.	Focus is on evaluation of the whole individual and his or her life circumstances; the person is brought to court to be aided and assisted.	Focus is on formal adversarial system of justice; key is the protection of rights for the public and accused, legal safeguards, due process rights (e.g., right to a lawyer, right to appeal, and right to legal representation at all stages of proceedings).	Focus is on a screening process that diverts the innocent out of the courts (i.e., only the guilty go to court); no need for legal safeguards.

Source: Reid and Zuker (2005).

For individualistic ideologies on the right end of the continuum, the assumption is that government is necessary, but that its activities should be restricted to ensure that individuals have ample opportunities to exercise their initiative and talent. Individualistic ideologies on the left recognize the virtues of a free-enterprise system, but temper this by adding that some goods and services should be provided within the public realm. These individualist ideological positions fall just right or just left of the collectivistic positions. The recent rise of the American political movement the Tea Party (whose name is a reference to the American Revolution in the 18th century) is a good example of a libertarian (i.e., individualistic) perspective. A comparison of the approach of each of these models is found in Table 1.1 on pages 28–29.

What Do You Think?

How do you think the case study that opened this book might fit within these theoretical models? Was J's behaviour made worse by the system or was his "criminal mind" simply beyond aid? Here, in the consideration of an actual case, the ways in which criminal justice theory meets criminal justice practice can be seen. Viewing J's criminal career as a consequence of his personality and his choices is a position that falls on the individualistic side of criminal justice policy, whereas considering the system's role in perpetuating criminal attitudes and activities suggests a more collectivist approach. Where do your views fall?

We will be asking you to think about these ideological underpinnings throughout the remainder of this book. By including an analysis of the historical development of the structures and processes of the criminal justice system and an examination of the nature of the behaviour of criminals and the legislators and professionals who manage the system, we believe that you will be equipped with the tools to reconsider any of your deeply held assumptions and beliefs, and to be open to new ideas and evidence.

Conclusion

Although each of the contributors to this text has areas of expertise within their respective criminal justice fields, it is important to remain inquisitive about what you read, keeping in mind the many different sides to each story. Throughout the text there will be a number of places where you will be asked to stop and "take a sidebar" in order to think critically about specific events, theories, or approaches to crime and punishment. Each section opens with a case study, profiling a particular criminal event or case in Canadian history. Some of these may be familiar to you. Perhaps you will read them and immediately form an opinion about the people and events described. Try to take note of these initial thoughts and trace any changes or developments in these first impressions that may occur as you read the chapters that follow the case studies. Ideally, we would like you to leave this textbook thinking differently from when you first picked it up. The next time you hear a news story about an arrest or investigation, or about the government's latest "war" on crime or drugs, we hope you will be able to engage in the debate in a more informed fashion, with the perspectives you encountered in this text helping you to form your own criminal justice mind.

Crime is always featured prominently in the news media, and is often very sensational. The old saying "If it bleeds, it leads" still very much applies to journalism today, and demonstrates the priorities of most news organizations. The media play a central role in shaping the public's attitudes toward crime, but critical thinkers know they must look beyond sensational headlines and examine the evidence in order to properly understand the issues.

▶ IN-CLASS EXERCISE
Criminology and Criminal Justice

How well do you understand the differences between criminology and criminal justice? In small groups, discuss these two related disciplines and, using the table below, fill in a few of the key areas of concern or major types of activity found in each field. When you have finished, compare your answers with those of a neighbouring group. Did you miss any? Do you disagree with anything your colleagues wrote in? What types of research interests or activities fit less neatly than others into the table? Why?

Criminology	Criminal Justice

DISCUSSION QUESTIONS

1. Take a moment to revisit your decision with respect to the case study that opened this book. Which of the seven models of criminal justice discussed in this chapter best represents the goals you had when sentencing J? Does the sentence you chose reflect more than one of the models? In which ways? Are there any models that clearly do not fit either your sentence or that case? Why or why not?

2. Think about the issue of attrition of cases through the criminal justice system. Outline whether you think the crime funnel or the crime net (or some other analogy) best defines why some people end up in jail while others do not, and why some even go undetected. Compare your answers with others' answers. Further study might include looking at criminal cases in the next few years and considering the impact that the *Safe Streets and Communities Act* (2012) has had on their attrition. (More about this Act will be provided in the case study that begins Part Four.)

3. Look again at the Areas of Well-Being in Canada diagram (Figure 1.2) and think about the areas where the "root causes of crime" might have an impact on an individual's likelihood of being involved in crime. While it has been pointed out that the "security" indicators

may increase or decrease crime in Canadian society, there may be other indicators that affect whether the crime rate increases or decreases. What kinds of policies and laws would be needed to counteract some of these other negative outcomes, which may in turn prevent and control crime?

NOTES

1. The three levels of sexual assault are:

   Sexual assault level 1 (*Criminal Code* s. 271(1)): Any form of touching of a sexual nature that is performed without the consent of the complainant. The severity of the offence is determined by the part of the body touched, the nature of the contact, the situation in which it occurred, and any words or gestures that accompanied the act. This can range from an unwanted kiss to forced penetration.

   Sexual assault level 2 (s. 272(1)): Occurs when a person is sexually assaulted by someone who (a) uses a weapon or threatens to use a weapon (imitation or real); (b) threatens to cause harm to a third person (friend, family member, or children); (c) causes bodily harm to a third party; or (d) commits the assault with any other person (multiple assailants).

   Sexual assault level 3 (aggravated sexual assault; s. 273(1)): Occurs when a person brutally beats, wounds, maims, disfigures, or endangers the life of someone during an assault.

2. Although communism is often associated with extreme collectivism, communist states historically have only collectivized the work activities of their citizens, rather than prioritized group rights over individual ones in all cases. The community known as "Freetown Christiana" in Copenhagen, Denmark is perhaps a better example of extreme collectivism, given its self-governing nature and its abolition of private property.

REFERENCES

Angus Reid Strategies. (2009a, March 5). Canadians clearly support ideas to deal with gang violence. Vancouver. Retrieved from http://www.angus-reid.com/wp-content/uploads/archived-pdf/2009.03.05_Gangs.pdf

Angus Reid Strategies. (2009b, June 26). Canadians endorse federal anti-crime proposals. Vancouver. Retrieved from http://www.angus-reid.com/wp-content/uploads/archived-pdf/2009.06.26_CrimeBill.pdf

Brannigan, A. (1984). *Crimes, courts and corrections: An introduction to crime and social control in Canada*. Toronto: Holt Rinehart and Winston.

Criminal Code, RSC 1985, c. C-46, as amended.

Eichenwald, K., & Richtel, M. (2002, October 12). Enron trader pleads guilty to conspiracy. *New York Times*, p. C-1. Retrieved from http://www.nytimes.com/2002/10/18/business/18ENRO.html?pagewanted=all

Gendreau, P., Little, T., & Goggin, C. (1996). A meta-analysis of the predictors of adult offender recidivism: What works! *Criminology, 34*, 575–607.

Hagan, J. (2010). *Who are the criminals? The politics of crime policy from the age of Roosevelt to the age of Reagan.* Princeton, NJ: Princeton University Press.

Human Resources and Skills Development Canada. (2012). *Indicators of well-being in Canada.* Retrieved from http://www4.hrsdc.gc.ca/h.4m.2@-eng.jsp

Jenish, D'A. (1997). Faint hope: Backgrounder. *Canadian Encyclopedia (Online)* (Maclean's Magazine). Retrieved from http://www.thecanadianencyclopedia.com/articles/macleans/faint-hope-background

Lee, I. (2011). *Myths & urban legends concerning crime in Canada.* Commentary. Ottawa: Macdonald-Laurier Institute. Retrieved from http://www.macdonaldlaurier.ca/files/pdf/Ian_Lee_March_2011.pdf

Mahoney, T.H. (2011, October). Homicide in Canada 2010. *Juristat*, Catalogue No. 85-002-X. Ottawa: Statistics Canada.

Martinson, R. (1974). What works? Questions and answers about prison reform. *The Public Interest* (Spring), 22–54.

Martinson, R. (1979). New findings, new views: A note of caution regarding sentencing reform. *Hofstra Law Review*, 7, 243–258.

Packer, H. (1964). Two models of the criminal process. *University of Pennsylvania Law Review, 113*(1), 1–68.

Public Safety Canada. (2011). *Corrections and conditional release statistical overview, annual report 2011.* Ottawa: Public Safety Canada. Retrieved from http://www.publicsafety.gc.ca/res/cor/rep/_fl/2011-ccrso-eng.pdf

Rankin, J., & Powell, B. (2008, July 21). The criminals among us. *The Toronto Star.* Retrieved from http://www.thestar.com/specialsections/article/460764--the-criminals-among-us

Reid, S.A., & Reitsma-Street, M. (1984). Assumptions and implications of new Canadian legislation for young offenders. *Canadian Criminology Forum, 7*(1), 1–19.

Reid, S. (1994). *Ideology, critical thinking and current criminological issues: Using debates as a pedagogical tool in undergraduate education* (PhD dissertation). University of Toronto.

Reid, S.A., & Zuker, M.A. (2005). Conceptual frameworks for understanding youth justice in Canada: From the Juvenile Delinquents Act to the Youth Criminal Justice Act. In Kathryn Campbell (Ed.), *Understanding youth justice in Canada.* Toronto: Pearson.

Reiman, J.H. (1979). *The rich get richer and the poor get prison: Ideology, class and criminal justice.* Boston: Allyn and Bacon.

Roberts, J. (2001). *Fear of crime and attitudes to criminal justice: A review of recent trends, 2001-02.* Ottawa: Ministry of the Solicitor General.

Sarangi, S. (2012). Compensation to Bhopal gas victims: Will justice ever be done? *Indian Journal of Medical Ethics, 9*(2), 118–120.

Sherman, L.W. (1981). *The study of ethics in criminology and criminal justice curricula.* Chicago: University of Illinois.

Smith, W.R. (2011). Crime and justice. *Canada year book.* Ottawa: Statistics Canada.

Statistics Canada. (2010, September 28). General social survey, victimization. *The Daily*. Retrieved from: http://www.statcan.gc.ca/daily-quotidien/100928/dq100928a-eng.htm

Statistics Canada. (2011, July 21). Police-reported crime statistics. *The Daily*. Retrieved from http://www.statcan.gc.ca/daily-quotidien/110721/dq110721b-eng.htm

Wallace, M., Turner, J., Babyak, C., & Matarazzo, A. (2009). Measuring crime in Canada: Introducing the crime severity index and improvements to the uniform crime reporting survey. Ottawa: Statistics Canada. Retrieved from http://www.statcan.gc.ca/pub/85-004-x/85-004-x2009001-eng.htm

Williams, E.J., & Robinson, M.B. (2004). Ideology and criminal justice: Suggestions for a pedagogical model. *Journal of Criminal Justice Education*, *15*(2), 373–392.

PART TWO
Policing Practices

Canada's G20 Summit in Focus

Karla O'Regan

Source: Lucas Oleniuk/Toronto Star.

It was the largest mass arrest in Canadian history. When Toronto hosted the G20 Summit in June 2010, images of violent clashes between police and protesters spread quickly across social media and news reporting sites, as participants and onlookers attempted to make sense of the weekend's events. Over the course of two days, police made more than 1,100 arrests and moved over 900 people to makeshift detention centres in the city. Although the protest was positioned as a peaceful one, the violence that erupted in Toronto's downtown core left many people harmed, including 97 police officers who suffered injuries while carrying out their duties (Blair, 2011). Lawsuits against Toronto police for illegal arrests and Charter violations have continued to make headlines, including a $4 million suit launched in April 2012. A number of officers were subject to disciplinary action for their actions during the G20. What went wrong?

The G20, a group of finance ministers, bank governors, and heads of state from 20 of the world's major economies, has met several times since its inception in 1999 (at which point it comprised only eight countries, known as the G8). In each case, widespread social protest, heightened police action, and violent encounters between police and protesters have been commonplace, often leading to serious injuries and deaths. This was the case, for example, with the 2009 G20 Summit held in London, England, where a man died after a police officer hit him with a baton and pushed him to the ground. The officer, PC Simon Harwood, was charged with manslaughter, although a jury found him not guilty in July 2012. The deceased's family has indicated plans to pursue the matter in civil court.

Protest History

Often, G20 Summit violence is compared with the events at the World Trade Organization's 1999 meeting in Seattle, where more than 50,000 protesters marched through the streets, managing to gain access to the Summit's media room on its last day. This "Battle in Seattle" (iconized in a major motion picture in 2007) represented the largest demonstration against free trade in North American history.

In view of this history, policing authorities began planning security strategies for Toronto's G20 two years in advance. However, the location for the Summit was changed in December 2009, leaving police only six months to prepare. Toronto Police Chief Bill Blair, in his report on the Summit events, cites this short planning period as one of the major difficulties faced by police forces during the Summit (Blair, 2011).

A number of precautionary measures were put in place in the weeks leading up to the G20 meetings in Toronto. Early in June 2010, a concrete and chain-link fence measuring almost 3.5 kilometres long and three metres high was built around the area of Toronto's downtown where the political meetings were set to take place. An area of the city far removed from the Summit site was designated as the official "protest spot." Many downtown businesses closed up shop for the weekend, encouraging employees to work from home. In addition, the federal government allocated Toronto's G20 almost $1 billion for "security costs"; it employed over 20,000 officers from 26 different police services, as well as private security firms. In Chapter 2, Leo De Jourdan identifies these private security firms as one of the leading challenges facing the future of policing in Canada.

Many "pre-emptive" arrests were also conducted in the days leading up to and during the Summit. These included a raid of the graduate students' building at the University of Toronto, where out-of-town protesters were thought to have been housed (OIPRD, 2012; Popplewell & Lu, 2010). Seventy people were arrested while sleeping in the university gymnasium, although many of them were later released without being charged (Standing Committee, 2011). Before the end of the weekend, the number of arrests totalled over 1,000, and the temporary facilities established to hold these detainees were stretched beyond capacity. Prisoner accounts from these centres revealed severe overcrowding and serious rights violations, including inappropriate strip-searching procedures and little to no opportunities for the detainees to consult legal counsel, obtain medication, or access adequate toilet facilities. One 17-year-old woman reported being forced to urinate in front of male officers during her detention (Kennedy & Dempsey, 2010). Others recounted being beaten and dragged by officers who had removed or covered their badge numbers. This police violence resulted in broken limbs, open wounds, and other injuries that were left untreated until the detainees' release.

What limits should there be on police action in a democratic, rights-based society? Should pre-emptive arrests be permissible? If so, under what circumstances? How should police prepare for mass social protest? What tactics and strategies should police use to protect the democratic right to peaceful protest while ensuring the safety of those involved and of the community at large? Some criminal justice scholars have argued for a more community-based policing model of "negotiated management," a model that will promote increased cooperation between police and protesters in an effort to avoid violence (Vitale, 2005).

An estimated 20,000 protesters marched peacefully through Toronto's downtown to voice opposition to what they saw as the irresponsible actions of the G20 countries, including their role in global arms production, world poverty, and violations of labour and employment law, as well as their failures with respect to health care and democratic rights. However, not all participants protested peacefully. During one of the scheduled marches, a small group of protesters broke away from the main march to engage in "Black Bloc" tactics, setting fire to a police car and severely vandalizing a number of commercial properties in Toronto's downtown core. The police responded with force. Donning riot gear, officers fired tear gas and rubber bullets into the crowd and employed a "kettling" tactic, using shields and batons to force protesters into a small, concentrated mass. Many citizens not participating in the protest were caught in the kettle while travelling between home and Toronto's downtown and were detained for more than four hours despite pouring rain and dropping temperatures. Police also practised "snatch and grab" techniques, moving in on groups of protesters at random and concentrated intervals to make arrests, often with the use of significant force.

Chapter 3 takes a closer look at the different strategies employed by police in both their daily activities and in more specialized operations such as those employed during the G20. It discusses the challenges faced by officers in

---

The Black Bloc

First seen during social protest movements in Germany in the 1980s, Black Bloc tactics involve members dressing in black clothing and covering their faces with ski masks or handkerchiefs. They conceal both their identities and their personal individuality, in an attempt to emphasize group solidarity. They use occasions of mass social (and peaceful) protest as cover for criminal acts of violence and anarchy, often disguising makeshift weapons (e.g., poles and sharpened sticks) as protest signs. Their similar appearances and their tactic of infiltrating crowds of peaceful protesters often make them difficult for police to identify and arrest.

connection with conventions of police culture and "personality." One aspect of policing's unique culture that is discussed in Chapter 3 is what is sometimes referred to as the "blue line" or "blue wall." This term refers to the solidarity often witnessed among police force members, which discourages officers from "ratting out" fellow officers or from stepping forward to report instances of misconduct. Despite video and photographic footage of the weekend's events as well as eyewitness testimony, Toronto Police Services neither admitted to any wrongdoing nor assisted in identifying any offending officers. In the weeks following the G20 meetings, Ontario's Special Investigations Unit pursued complaints lodged against individual officers for use of excessive force, but these investigations were halted due to "lack of evidence."

Some of these investigations have been reopened, but to date only two officers have had formal charges laid against them. An additional nine officers were denied promotion because they removed their badges during the G20 conflict. Chapter 4 examines closely the legal powers police have to uphold the law and to protect citizens, as well as the limits on these powers. Many of the arrests that took place over the G20 weekend in Toronto were authorized under a new Ontario law enacted in the days leading up to the Summit. This law permitted police to arrest anyone near the G20 security zone who refused to identify themselves or consent to a police search. Despite the significant power this new law granted police, no notification of its enactment was released to the public (Paperny & Howlett, 2010). Further, when discussing the details of the new law with the media, Toronto Police Chief Bill Blair gave incorrect information, suggesting police could make arrests if anyone stepped within five metres of the security fence. When asked at a news conference if this information was true, Blair responded, "No, but I wanted to keep the criminals out" (OIPRD, 2012).

In the days after the G20 ended, the Office of the Independent Police Review Director (OIPRD) began to receive complaints about police conduct during the Summit. The OIPRD is an independent, arm's-length agency operated out of Ontario's Ministry of the Attorney General. It is staffed entirely with civilians whose responsibilities include receiving, investigating, and processing complaints against police action. In total, it received more than 350 complaints stemming from the G20 protests. Its final report found a number of serious incidents of police misconduct and rights violations, and it ordered disciplinary charges against more than 100 officers. Chapter 4 explores the following topics in greater depth: the role of the *Charter of Rights and Freedoms* in defining the justifiable use of excessive (if not lethal) force; and the laws that exist to regulate police when their actions can be said to "cross the line."

After reading news reports and watching videos of Toronto's G20 Summit protests, it can be tempting to take a simplified view of the resulting violence between activists and police and to assign all of the blame to one side or the other. We must keep in mind, however, that not all protesters were Black Bloc, and not every police officer violated citizens' rights. Many protesters walked peacefully through the city, exercising constitutional rights of assembly and free speech. Many officers acted professionally in a high-stress situation, obeying orders and struggling with poor communication strategies and incident planning. As criminal justice scholars, we need to resist simplified analyses and think critically about the issues such events raise. Toronto's G20 protests and their aftermath provide an opportunity for us to engage in serious analysis about a number of policing issues and their challenges.

What Do You Think?

1. In what ways should governments be accountable when violent clashes between private individuals and state forces occur?
2. What kind of a response to mass protest should be expected of Canada's police forces?
3. Do events like Toronto's G20 Summit suggest that Canada is moving closer to a police state?
4. How compatible was police action during the G20 Summit with Canada's *Charter of Rights and Freedoms*?

These and many other issues are explored in the following chapters, each of which challenges you to think critically about policing—its history, its operations, its legal powers, and its challenges.

REFERENCES

Ericson, R., & Doyle, A. (1999). Globalization and the policing of protest: The case of APEC 1997. *British Journal of Sociology*, 50(4), 589–608.

Hajnal, P.I. (2010). The Muskoka G8 and Toronto G20 Summits, accountability, and civil society. *International Organisations Research Journal*, 4(31), 31–42. Retrieved from http://iorj.hse.ru/en/2010--5/27488522.html

Hodgkinson, T. (2011). Is the whole world still watching? Explaining police violence during the Toronto G8/G20 meetings. (Master's thesis). Queen's University, Kingston, ON.

Hussey, I., & LeClerc, P. (2011). "The big smoke" screen: Toronto's G20 protests, police brutality, and the unaccountability of public officials. *Socialist Studies*, *7*(1/2), 282–302.

Kennedy, B., & Dempsey, A. (2010, June 29). Crowd condemns G20 policing, arrests: Female protestors strip-searched by male officers, detainee says. *Toronto Star*, p. GT.2.

Office of the Independent Police Review Director. (2012). *Policing the right to protest: G20 systemic review report*. Retrieved from https://www.oiprd.on.ca/CMS/getattachment/Publications/Reports/G20_Report_Eng.pdf.aspx

Paperny, A.M., & Howlett, K. (2010, September 22). Province to probe "secret law," G20 police powers. *Globe and Mail*. Retrieved from http://www.theglobeandmail.com/news/toronto/province-to-probe-secret-law-g20-police-powers/article1369573/

Popplewell, B., & Lu, V. (2010, June 27). Student union faces questions about hosting protestors. *Toronto Star*. Retrieved from http://www.thestar.com/news/gta/torontog20summit/article/829313--about-50-arrested-in-u-of-t-g20-raids?bn=1

Rosie, M., & Gorringe, H. (2009). What a difference a death makes: Protest, policing, and the press at the G20. *Sociological Research Online*, *14*(5). Retrieved from http://www.socresonline.org.uk/14/5/4.html

Standing Committee on Public Safety and National Security. (2011). *Issues surrounding security at the G8 and G20 summits: Report of the Standing Committee on Public Safety and National Security* by K. Sorenson. Retrieved from http://publications.gc.ca/collections/collection_2011/parl/XC76-403-1-1-04-eng.pdf

Vitale, A.S. (2005). From negotiated management to command and control: How the New York Police Department polices protests. *Policing & Society*, *15*(3), 283–304.

Behind the Blue Line: History and Organization

LEARNING OBJECTIVES

After reading this chapter, students will be able to:

- Identify historic events that shaped the early policing structure.
- Understand the origin of modern-day policing and the relevance of Sir Robert Peel's nine principles in today's police environment.
- Compare past and current practices and consider future challenges facing the policing community.
- Understand the role of the police in balancing enforcement with crime prevention.
- Contrast the various levels of police services.
- Understand the structure and mandate of the various levels of police services in Canada.

CHAPTER OUTLINE

Author's Introduction: A Career in Criminal Justice

When I was in my late teens and searching for a direction in life, my father encouraged me to consider policing as a career option. He suggested that this would be an adventurous and exciting profession that would suit my personality and active lifestyle. He then handed me a recruitment ad that he had cut from the local newspaper. My interest was sparked. Now that the calendar has advanced 30-some years, I am glad that I heeded my father's advice. But I regret that when I began my career I didn't delve more deeply into the reality of the policing profession, because I was quite ignorant of its various aspects, and had only stereotypical impressions shaped by years of exposure to television cop shows. I really had no appreciation for the profession from a historic perspective, nor did I have any real understanding of the reality of police activity in the day-to-day work environment.

The entrance and recruitment standards in today's policing organizations are very high and the battery of testing is very rigorous. Once hired, officers can expect to be held to a much greater level of scrutiny and public accountability than officers of past generations. For these reasons, those thinking of pursuing a career in law enforcement should enter the profession with their eyes wide open, and with a complete understanding of both what they can expect from the career and what the career will, undoubtedly, expect of them.

A Brief History of Policing

While it is difficult to point to one era in Canada's history as the defining moment in the creation of organized policing, certain events contributed significantly to the evolution of this profession. In the European context, there was no recognizable system of law enforcement prior to the ninth century. Essentially, rulers and emperors defended their power and sovereignty, and those who did not accept or comply with decrees met with the wrath of armies loyal to those authorities. Otherwise, citizens were left to their own resources in protecting their possessions and defending themselves from acts of aggression.

The Tithing System

Not until the ninth century did policing emerge as we know it. King Alfred the Great, who ruled over Anglo-Saxon England, decreed that he would provide security for his subjects in exchange for their absolute loyalty and obedience. To make good on his promise, Alfred ordered the landowners, or "thanes," to provide this protection to the common citizens, or "freemen." In this, the earliest form of Neighbourhood Watch, the freemen organized themselves into groups of ten families, called "tithings," to be on the lookout for any disobedience. Anyone within these groups who witnessed a crime would alert the other members by "raising the hue and cry"—a rudimentary alarm system that might involve, for example, ringing a bell. Those who heard this alert were expected to help capture the suspect, in posse fashion, in what today might be considered a kind of citizen's arrest. The tithing would then turn over the suspect to the thane, who would determine the appropriate punishment or, depending on the severity of the wrongdoing, bring the lawbreaker to the king to be dealt with.

As the system evolved, the leader of each tithing (the "tithingman") would meet periodically with the nine others. This group became known as a "hundred," so called because of the number of families it represented. From the hundred emerged a leader who took on the additional responsibilities of organizing courts, hearing civil disputes, and settling disagreements between neighbours. Representing a larger geographic area known as a "shire" and being elected to an official capacity as a "reeve," this person was referred to as the "shire-reeve." In time, these two words were combined, resulting in the more familiar term "sheriff." Within this early system of justice were the seeds of community policing, whereby citizens were actively involved in maintaining local order.

The Frankpledge System (1066)

Another historic benchmark came two centuries later following the Norman conquest of England. In 1066, post-invasion, William the Conqueror adopted the framework of the Anglo-Saxon tithing system, but renamed it "Frankpledge," a system that required citizens to pledge to uphold the law and take responsibility for the conduct of all members within the group. William reduced the responsibilities of the shire-reeve to dealing strictly with law enforcement. Judges were appointed and courts became more formalized. A "court tourn" developed from the former body of hundred to hear cases regarding less serious crimes, petty offences, and civil disputes.

For more serious crimes, 12 people were selected from the tithings to investigate offences as well as to hear and decide on cases. The structure and role of this group suggest that this is perhaps the origin of the modern-day jury system.

In some communities, courts were established to handle matters more local in scope and interest without having to involve the court tourn. This "court leet" was headed by a "comes stabuli," a term that had been previously assigned to an officer who looked after a horse stable. This evolved into **constable**, which in today's policing world is associated with the lowest rank within a policing unit. The court tourn and court leet were the forerunners of separate lower and superior courts.

The Statute of Winchester (1285)

In 1285, the *Statute of Winchester* created a code outlining police practices and introduced the concept of rural policing using the parish system to identify areas of police **jurisdiction**. Justices of the peace were also introduced, taking over the role of the shire-reeves. In urban areas, the concept of round-the-clock vigilance, referred to as "watch and ward"—watch being nighttime and ward being daytime—was created as well.

These policing practices continued for several centuries with little positive change. During this time, however, the job of law enforcement became less attractive, and finding competent people to fill this role became increasingly difficult. Corruption ensued and constables began to abuse their powers,

constable
The lowest rank of office held by a sworn police officer; a position ordinarily assigned to front-line uniformed officers in the initial stages of a police career.

jurisdiction
The authority given to a police service to carry out law enforcement responsibilities within a defined geographic area (i.e., provincial vs. federal).

take bribes, and charge and assist with the prosecutions of innocent people based on evidence that was in many cases flimsy or out-and-out fabricated. Constables routinely schemed with justices of the peace and judges to sway the outcome of judicial proceedings. Then, with the Industrial Revolution came rapid growth in urban areas of England, resulting in a spike in crimes such as thievery, prostitution, drunkenness, gambling, and violence. A more effective policing structure was clearly needed and citizens began demanding reform to deal with the judicial corruption and increasing crime.

Sir Robert Peel's Vision (1829)

In response to this cry for reform, the English government of the day considered a number of proposed changes, including adopting the French gendarme system, though that proposal was rejected because it too closely resembled a military force. Finally, in 1829, the *Metropolitan Police Act* was introduced and passed, creating the first major British police organization for the City of London.

Many democracies and English-speaking countries around the world have since adopted this model, first introduced by a British parliamentarian who would later become that country's prime minister. Sir Robert Peel, the model's architect and long considered the father of modern-day policing—

bobbies
A slang term for British police officers, which, along with "peelers," is derived from Sir Robert (Bobbie) Peel's name.

two slang terms for police officers, **bobbies** and "peelers," are both derived from his name—established nine guiding principles that would set out priorities for the newly formed London Police Force (now called the Metropolitan Police Service). These principles spelled out not only what those police officers should do, but also how they should go about doing it.

Many might be surprised to learn that law enforcement was not Peel's number one principle. His primary focus instead was on the prevention of crime and disorder. With the benefit of more than 150 years of hindsight, it seems that Peel had it right, as modern-day police agencies continue to adopt policies and put in place resources that reflect his top priority.

Although arguably the most important aspect of the profession, crime prevention is the least appealing to most people seeking careers as police officers. Candidates are likely to be more interested in the prospects of danger and intrigue, and the excitement associated with such a career. And while preventing crime and disorder is a lofty and noble goal, it is both naive and unrealistic to expect that crime can be eradicated. Weakness, poor judgment, greed, emotion, and frailty are all part of the human condition that ensures continuing criminal behaviour. Some criminologists observe

Sir Robert Peel

SIDEBAR

Sir Robert Peel's Nine Principles of Policing

1. The basic mission for which the police exist is to prevent crime and disorder.

2. The ability of the police to perform their duties is dependent upon the public approval of police actions.

3. Police must secure the willing cooperation of the public in voluntary observation of the law to be able to secure and maintain the respect of the public.

4. The degree of cooperation of the public that can be secured diminishes proportionately to the necessity of the use of physical force.

5. Police seek and preserve public favour not by catering to public opinion, but by constantly demonstrating absolute impartial service to the law.

6. Police use physical force to the extent necessary to secure observance of the law or to restore order only when the exercise of persuasion, advice, and warning is found to be insufficient.

7. Police, at all times, should maintain a relationship with the public that gives reality to the historic tradition that the police are the public and the public are the police; the police being only members of the public who are paid to give full-time attention to duties which are incumbent upon every citizen in the interests of community welfare and existence.

8. Police should always direct their action strictly toward their functions, and never appear to usurp the powers of the judiciary.

9. The test of police efficiency is the absence of crime and disorder, not the visible evidence of police action in dealing with it.

What Do You Think?

Which of these nine principles still guide policing today? What are some examples of where these principles are most prominent in Canadian policing today?

---

that the only sure way to eliminate crime is to eliminate laws. But no society would want to risk the chaos that would almost certainly follow. Moreover, the public insists not only that we have laws, but also that we have the ability and resources to enforce those laws. This was clearly demonstrated in October 1969, when police in Montreal withdrew their services over contract issues. For 16 hours the city was left without this essential service. Within a few hours, thugs and anarchists took to the streets looting, vandalizing, and rioting. Dozens were injured and millions of dollars in property damage ensued. Such incidents may lead to the conclusion that the mere presence of a policing authority deters criminal behaviour.

Policing Today

Hollywood's portrayal of the policing profession has no doubt influenced the perceived thrill associated with the job. But this same portrayal contributes to the public's misconception about police activities. While chasing and arresting "bad guys" is a very important and exciting part of law enforcement, it is nonetheless only a small part of what occupies an officer's time. The skills required for a policing career go well beyond the function of law enforcement. Just as necessary are superior social, or "people," skills, as well as literacy and effective communication. Other important personal attributes include common sense, maturity, compassion, sensitivity, discretion, civic pride, a basic understanding of human behaviour, and of course a strong set of moral and ethical values.

"Every society gets the kind of criminal it deserves. What is equally true is that every community gets the kind of law enforcement it insists on."

—Robert Kennedy

When allocating resources, police administrators constantly struggle to find the right balance between the competing interests of crime prevention and law enforcement, or, in the jargon of police administration, between "proactive" and "reactive" policing.

Civilian Oversight

Police officers are responsible for the way in which they treat members of the public, including both suspects and victims. The senior administration of a police service, which includes police chiefs and commissioners who set policy and provide leadership within the organization, are also accountable to the community through a governing body known as a police services board (see Figure 2.1 on page 61). This board consists of members who are either elected officials (members of a municipal council) or those who have been appointed to represent the interests of citizens regarding matters of public safety and fiscal responsibility. They meet regularly to review and approve the operational, administrative, and fiscal policies of the service.

The success of a police agency is usually measured in two general areas:

- the local crime rate; and
- the ability of the organization to successfully investigate and prosecute crime.

By compiling and examining local crime statistics, administrators can evaluate how effective they are from year to year. Police chiefs are quick to take credit for a reduction in crime within their jurisdiction. But those same police chiefs will use an increase in the rate of crime to make a case for an increase in fiscal and human resources.

Chiefs are also proud of statistics that show a high rate of clearance (the successful resolution of investigations, normally through charges) for criminal investigations. However, it is safe to say that in general, police administrators would prefer to have less crime to solve than a high rate of clearance in a crime-ridden community.

There are two basic questions that police services board members will ask of administrators seeking budget increases:

1. Will a sustained or increased public investment ensure the prevention or reduction of crime?
2. Would the public support such an investment?

The first question points to Peel's ninth principle: "The test of police efficiency is the absence of crime and disorder, not the visible evidence of police action in dealing with it." A senior police administrator will not likely ask for less money because of a marked reduction in criminal activity. Rather, those administrators at budget time will likely attribute the reduced level of crime to an increase in resources, and argue that any reduction in resources, in turn, could result in a return to a higher rate of crime, putting citizens at increased risk.

The second question reflects Peel's second principle: "The ability of the police to perform their duties is dependent upon the public approval of police actions." While a community would almost certainly feel more secure with twice the number of police officers on the streets, it is highly unlikely that the community would approve of the tax increase that would be needed to support such a move.

Community Policing

Another of Peel's principles, the seventh, suggests that police are citizens first, and though they have additional authority, they should not lose sight of their place in the community they are serving, or as Peel put it: "The police are the public and the public are the police."

Police have strayed from this concept over the past 170 years. Many would blame this on the introduction of the motor vehicle; as offenders became more mobile, so too did the police in order to keep up. Isolation from the very citizens the police were serving became an unintended consequence of their spending more time in their cruisers, and less time maintaining those relationships with the communities Peel was referring to. In recent times, police organizations have made a concerted effort to return to the days when officers were perceived by the public as fellow citizens who happen to be police officers, genuinely interested in making the community a better, safer place to live, work, and play. Officers are now encouraged to get out of their cruisers and interact with the public in a friendly, non-intimidating manner, building mutual trust in the community and gaining the respect and support of the citizens they serve.

Today's police officers are also encouraged to take part in non-policing activities. A demonstrated interest in the community promotes not only individual respect, but also a respect for the organization the officer represents.

Police agencies commonly reach out to the public at town hall meetings or citizen forum groups. Police authorities now routinely involve the community in helping to establish goals, plans, and priorities. The community, in turn, appreciates the opportunity to express their views and opinions. Their input has been fairly consistent, identifying issues such as the need for increased police presence and a higher level of visibility, thus contributing to the perception of a more secure environment.

What Do You Think?

What types of activities have you observed police engaged in that fall under the category of community policing?

The film *Through a Blue Lens*, produced by the National Film Board, depicts Vancouver police officers interacting with drug addicts in Vancouver's East Hastings area. In what way are such interactions similar to or different from your conception of community-based policing? (You can view a trailer for the film at http://oddsquad.com/store/through-a-blue -lens/.)

The Reality of Policing

A "typical" day in the life of today's uniformed officer could involve activities such as resolving conflict, providing counselling, administering first aid, educating the public, performing various acts of social work, comforting victims, and offering advice on matters that in many cases have little, if anything, to do with the law or any manner of law enforcement. Some might suggest this is a far cry from what Sir Robert Peel had in mind, but it might be argued that his principles are more relevant today than ever, and that officers who accept this as a part of their duties have adjusted to a return to his guiding principles.

The traditional front-line work of officers is done by the uniformed patrol units that respond to calls for service and emergencies. This is often where rookies learn the profession and cut their teeth. Many officers also find it a very exciting time as they encounter something new from shift to shift or even hour to hour. A traffic stop can suddenly turn into a violent confrontation, a lunch break can be interrupted by a call to respond to a robbery in progress, or a call to an accident scene can require the risk of injury to remove a victim from a flaming vehicle. Officers involved in such activities are often called on to make split-second decisions that could have a lasting impact on people's lives, including their own. Their actions could also be subject to scrutiny for months or even years by not only their superiors, but also by a civilian oversight agency, a judge, or members of a jury. It is truly amazing that an event lasting less than a minute can result in hundreds of hours of investigation and/or judicial or quasi-judicial review. Is it any wonder then that police services take such great care in selecting suitable candidates who can withstand the pressures of such responsibilities and public expectations?

"Every kind of peaceful cooperation among men is primarily based on mutual trust and only secondarily on institutions such as courts of justice and police."

—*Albert Einstein*

While a relatively small percentage of the working day of a front-line officer is spent looking into crime-related activities, a greater portion of that time is spent on non-crime matters such as bylaw enforcement (e.g., barking dog complaints, parking complaints, noise complaints), providing advice and assistance to the public, and conducting foot or motor patrols in response to the public demands for higher visibility.

With experience, officers in mid-size police services can move to other specialized areas, such as criminal investigation, traffic, courts, or youth office. In even larger services, they can move to homicide, fraud, organized crime, or morality units. These front-line police officers are required to attend additional courses designed to prepare them for their area of specialization.

What Do You Think?

Think back to the case study of police involvement in the G20 Summit. What "split-second decisions" were made that were later investigated?

Toronto Police Chief Bill Blair, in his report reviewing the G20 Summit, stated, "Crowd behaviour is influenced in part by the type and manner of police deployment. Premature displays of real or implied force can lead to negative crowd reactions that may escalate a situation. The initial contact by public order officers with protest groups, in the absence of clear indications to the contrary, should be low key and measured" (2011, p. 58). How do you think this kind of perspective might influence front-line police training?

Canadian Police Jurisdictions and Resources

The number of active police officers in Canada has never been higher. This is the result of both an increase in population and a need to ensure adequate police resources for all regions of the country. There are close to 70,000

sworn members serving in various police services throughout Canada. In addition to these personnel, civilian members are employed in most police services. These employees are in supportive roles such as dispatchers, administrative assistants, forensic analysts, and computer programmers.

Statistics show that there are approximately 203 police officers per 100,000 citizens, leaving the country well behind the national averages in Australia by 8 percent, England by 11 percent, and, perhaps most surprisingly, behind the United States by 17 percent (see sidebar). The agency that compiled these statistics points out that this variance may be deceiving owing to the differences in the ways that officers are categorized in other countries (Statistics Canada, 2010).

In Canada, police get their jurisdictional mandate from the level of government they are serving. Because the Royal Canadian Mounted Police (RCMP) is an agency of the federal government through the Ministry of Public Safety Canada, its members are spread to all corners of the country, even though their basic police powers are no greater than those of any other sworn police officer in any other police service. Both provincial and municipal policing services, meanwhile, act under the authority of legislation that was created within the province (e.g., *Police Services Act* of Ontario); thus, their police powers do not extend beyond the borders of the province in which they serve. So, police officers employed by the cities of Ottawa, Hamilton, or North Bay, or any other Ontario municipality, have the same authority throughout the province that a member of the Ontario Provincial Police has; both operate under the authority granted to them through provincial legislation. Although jurisdictional boundaries and mandates are clearly defined, there is a considerable sharing of resources, information, and criminal intelligence in the interest of effective policing practices. This hasn't always been the case, however, as there have been a number of occasions when police services refused to share information or cooperate with neighbouring services.

Sadly, this has caused undue delay in the identification, capture, and prosecutions of violent offenders like Paul Bernardo, who was responsible for the vicious attacks on a number of female victims and for the kidnappings and murders of Kristen French and Leslie Mahaffy. Who knows how many victims could have been spared horrifying experiences if only a high level of interservice collaboration had been in place? Steps have since been taken to prevent this from happening again, including the introduction of an integrated and coordinated system of major case management across police services (Campbell, 1996).

SIDEBAR

Sworn Officers per 100,000 Citizens

Canada	203
Australia	222
England	229
United States	244

Source: Statistics Canada (2010).

The Royal Canadian Mounted Police

In the early stages of Canada's development, the government saw the need for a federal police force, and in 1873 created the RCMP, originally called the North-West Mounted Police (NWMP). Within a year of the agency's birth, it turned its attention to the west. In that region, Hudson's Bay Company owned a large area of land that was eventually sold to the Dominion. The growth in population and fur trade activity in this region was accompanied by increased tension and conflict among and within the fur traders, the Métis, and the native communities. In an effort to maintain the peace, law, and order, the NWMP established a post at Fort Dufferin in Manitoba in 1874. In the summer of that year, 275 officers and other men, along with horses, oxen, and supplies on large carts, embarked on a western patrol. Over the next several months, in what has become known as "the March West," these officers made their way to Alberta and quickly established friendly relations with, and gained the trust of, the chiefs and citizens in First Nations' communities. Within months, the contingent successfully stemmed the whisky trade, enforcing laws on prohibition.

SIDEBAR

An Overview of the Royal Canadian Mounted Police

The RCMP was originally named the North-West Mounted Police, based on the area of the country it served and the use of horses in its policing function. In 1904, the force became the Royal North-West Mounted Police, signifying Canada's links with the monarchy and the British Commonwealth.

In 1920, after absorbing the Dominion Police (responsible for the security of Parliament and related federal buildings), the force was renamed the Royal Canadian Mounted Police.

The RCMP retains the word "mounted" in its title to reflect its history as a mounted unit and because the force continues to use horses in its world-renowned musical ride.

The RCMP's resources include five patrol vessels used for protecting Canada's coastal areas. The vessels are named after former RCMP commissioners Inkster, Nadon, Higgitt, Lindsay, and Simmonds. The Air Services Branch maintains a fleet of more than 40 aircraft.

Source: Royal Canadian Mounted Police Marine Services Branch; Royal Canadian Mounted Police, Air Services Branch.

The RCMP has grown along with Canada's population and now has a presence in all 10 provinces and three territories. While not without its challenges in recent times, the agency continues to have the respect of Canadian citizens and members of the international policing community who appreciate the agency's proud history, traditions, and effectiveness in law enforcement.

Approximately 28,000 people are employed by the RCMP. Of those, about 20,000 are sworn members, with the remaining being civilian members.

The RCMP enforces federal laws dealing with drugs, immigration, custom and excise, and inland shipping, among others. It also provides security services to the prime minister and visiting heads of state. At one time, the service also gathered intelligence concerning matters of national security. This task was taken over in 1984 by the Canadian Security and Intelligence Service (CSIS), a civilian agency, as a result of growing public concern that intelligence gathering should not be the function of the national police service (McDonald Commission Report, 1981). For the sake of comparison, the RCMP is to the FBI as CSIS is to the CIA. The first two are both investigative and law enforcement bodies, while the last two are responsible for intelligence gathering, threat assessment, and matters of national security.

The RCMP is a Canadian icon. Tourists to Parliament Hill in Ottawa love to have their photos taken with a Mountie in the red serge dress uniform, now reserved for ceremonial occasions and to promote the traditional image of the RCMP at official functions. The vast majority of the sworn members wear the working uniform: blue trousers with a wide yellow stripe down the sides, a uniform shirt with shoulder flashes bearing the identifying acronym of the agency in both official languages (RCMP/GRC), and the types of equipment typically worn by front-line police officers (i.e., gun belt, sidearm, handcuffs, protective vest).

With the exceptions of Ontario and Quebec, all provinces, and many cities and communities, contract the RCMP to provide policing services. The country is divided into divisions for administrative purposes, with each division assigned a letter. For the most part, divisions fall along provincial boundaries. However, there are some notable exceptions, such as British Columbia, with two divisions, and Ontario, with three. All RCMP officers complete their required training at "Depot" Division, the training academy located in Regina, Saskatchewan. Here the cadets complete six months of intense activities that include a mix of academic and physical courses, as well as drill (marching), defensive driving, and firearms training. The cadets are also expected to perform additional duties and follow a stringent set of rules designed to instill both self- and troop discipline. This serves to unify the troop in functioning effectively as a unit.

Although the cadets request their preferred postings and the RCMP tries to accommodate them, the decision is largely based on the staffing requirements of the various regions of the country. The need for front-line officers is much greater in the provinces and areas that contract their services. Typical assignments of officers in "contract" postings include patrol, investigations, and enforcement of the *Criminal Code* and provincial statutes such as *Highway Traffic Acts* and *Liquor Licence Acts*. In other words, the majority of RCMP officers perform the same function as police officers in Calgary, Winnipeg, Halifax, and smaller municipal and regional police services.

The RCMP also has an investigative service in each of the divisions. These units consist of veteran officers who are ready to respond to major crime investigations in either a lead or a supportive role. In many remote regions of the country, there are simply not sufficient local resources available to dedicate to investigation without compromising the day-to-day policing needs of the area. In other cases, many of these investigators have special skills, training, or experience necessary to properly investigate a more complex type of crime.

Another function of the RCMP is to enforce federal statutes in marine areas. These include the *Canada Shipping Act*, *Small Vessel Regulations*, and *Migratory Birds Convention Act*. To assist with this enforcement, the RCMP maintains a fleet of some 377 watercraft, which includes five larger coastal patrol vessels.

The other smaller craft are used in inland areas and are distributed throughout the country. It has recently become common practice for the RCMP to work with local, regional, and provincial policing authorities in patrolling inland bodies of water for the purpose of enforcing both federal and provincial law. For example, not having the proper safety equipment on board is a violation of federal law that the RCMP would typically address, while a violation of the liquor laws on a vessel would be a matter for the Ontario Provincial Police, because this would contravene the *Liquor Licence Act*, a provincial statute.

The nature of its work also demands that the RCMP maintain an Air Services branch for the following purposes: to provide air support and assistance to operational personnel through northern and regional patrols; to transport officers, prisoners, and supplies; and to help with aerial searches.

The RCMP national headquarters is located in Ottawa, where a number of sworn and civilian members work in an administrative capacity, dealing with matters such as policy, research, and budgeting. They also work with the minister and federal ministry responsible for the agency. Ottawa is also the location of the Canadian Police College, which provides advanced training courses to members of this and other police services. This city is also home to the Canadian Police Information Centre (CPIC), which is the central repository for information pertaining to charged and wanted persons, and for all criminal records. The RCMP is responsible for ensuring that the information is accessible to police services throughout the country. Both the police college and the information centre are administered by the RCMP.

paramilitary
Having features in common with a military organization, particularly in training and the organizational structure or chain of command.

chain of command
The hierarchical structure within a military-like organization. In a typical police service, the lower ranks are the non-commissioned officers, from constables to sergeants and staff sergeants; at the higher level are the commissioned ranks, from inspectors to chiefs or commissioners.

The RCMP is often described as a **paramilitary** organization. Much like the military, it has a **chain of command** with a ranking structure that sees increased responsibilities attached to the higher ranks.

Upon graduating from the Depot, a new constable is assigned a field training, or coach, officer. The front-line patrol officers who respond to calls and investigate day-to-day citizen complaints and reports are constables. After several years of experience and satisfactory work performance, a constable reaches "first class" status. Usually, local commanders are corporals, sergeants, or staff sergeants, depending on the size of the detachment. These commanders provide direction and supervision for the front-line officers and assist with more serious investigations. Beyond the level of staff sergeant are the ranks of the commissioned officers, from inspectors and superintendents, to assistant and deputy commissioners, to the lone commissioner. These levels are reserved for officers who provide senior leadership within the organization; while these members retain their basic police authorities, their internal powers are increased as their roles become more supervisory and administrative. These officers rise through the ranks and are identified in the early stages of their careers as having leadership potential.

At the head of the RCMP is the commissioner, whom some might compare to the "chief of police" of a much larger organization than a typical city police service. The commissioner is the face of the agency and is accountable to the public through elected government officials and, in particular, to the minister of justice. The commissioner is responsible for keeping the minister of justice informed on matters of public interest, and especially on matters that have drawn significant public attention through the media—for example, the incident involving Robert Dziekański, who died after being subjected to multiple tasers by RCMP officers at the Vancouver airport in October 2007 (see the mini case study on page 113). More recently, another potentially scandalous issue surfaced when a number of female members went public with allegations of sexual harassment in their work environment. The commissioner must ensure that all these types of potentially embarrassing and sometimes criminal matters are dealt with transparently and appropriately to maintain public confidence in the service. The commissioner also provides advice on matters of policy in addition to the duties that are consistent with the chief executive officer of any large organization.

William Elliot was the first civilian commissioner in RCMP history. Although his appointment in 2007 was controversial and met with general disapproval among the rank and file, the thinking at the time of this appointment was that operational skills are not nearly as important as skills related to public administration, budgeting, fiscal and corporate management, and a level of political savvy. Many, if not most, of the members might have suggested otherwise, claiming that their leader should be someone who can relate to the experiences of the front-line officers and mid-level supervisors. Elliot resigned in November 2011, and the organization returned to the tradition of promoting from within, with the appointment of Commissioner Bob Paulson.

Ontario and Quebec are the only two provinces that have established their own provincial police services, although Newfoundland and Labrador is served by the Royal Newfoundland Constabulary (RNC). The RNC is located in only a few urban areas, where it works closely with the provincially contracted RCMP.

Ontario Provincial Police

Ontario's *Police Services Act* sets out the requirement for adequate and effective policing service throughout the province. This presents no small challenge, considering that the province is geographically larger than many European countries. Moreover, the vast majority of the land mass is rural, and in many cases sparsely populated and remote. So in those areas too small to support an organized service, the Ontario Provincial Police (OPP) is tasked with providing the appropriate level of police resources. This organization also provides policing services to a number of municipalities that have opted to contract with it, rather than create their own police services— a decision usually based on which option will meet the adequacy standard and be the most cost-effective in addressing local needs.

The OPP was officially established in 1909, largely in response to the dramatic increase in criminal activity that accompanied the increase in mining activity in northern Ontario. The organization has grown in both numbers and scope, in keeping with the provincial growth in population and development. The service now has approximately 6,100 sworn officers and 2,700 civilian employees. These members are spread throughout the province in five regions. The OPP headquarters are located in Orillia, as are many of its senior administrative offices and training facilities.

The OPP has a ranking structure and chain of command similar to that of the RCMP. A recruit's career begins at the organization's training facility in Orillia. After completing both this and the training requirements at the Ontario Police College in Aylmer, the newly sworn constable is assigned a

commissioned

A high authoritative status conferred on OPP officers, usually in recognition of their leadership and management abilities.

training officer. With time and experience, officers may achieve the ranks of sergeant and staff sergeant, and possibly **commissioned** ranks. The organizational head of the agency is the commissioner (currently Chris Lewis). The commissioner is accountable to the public through the Ontario Ministry of Community Safety and Correctional Services. As with the RCMP, the commissioner informs the minister and advises on matters of policy.

Quebec Provincial Police

The Quebec Provincial Police (QPP), known also as Sûreté du Québec (SQ), is similar in nature to the OPP. Its headquarters are located in Montreal and the provincial training academy is in Nicolet. The director general is Richard Deschesnes, who oversees the police service in much the same way as the commissioners of the OPP or RCMP do their respective organizations. The agency provides policing services for the province of Quebec, as well as for many of the small communities that have contracted its services. Its responsibilities include enforcing Quebec's traffic code on all provincial highways, providing an investigative unit to take the lead or assist with major investigations, providing security for Quebec's National Assembly in Quebec City, and generally carrying out the traditional role of law enforcement and crime prevention. The QPP has approximately 5,000 sworn members. This service requires its recruits to have attended Collège d'enseignement général et professionnel (CEGEP) and get additional recruit training during the initial stages of their employment. Upon completing training, members can be posted to any location within the province.

First Nations Police Services

The studies, work, and research of various groups, including the 1990 Task Force on the Indian Policing Policy, have identified the need to address the issue of the overrepresentation of native offenders in the Canadian criminal justice system. Consequently, many First Nations communities throughout the country have taken over control of much of the policing function, ensuring the delivery of services in a manner that is both culturally sensitive and respectful of the traditions and practices of First Nations citizens. Federal and provincial governments have worked with band councils and other stakeholders in the native communities in creating 168 policing service agreements covering 408 First Nations and Inuit communities that serve well over 300,000 citizens. There are currently close to 1,300 officers working in these communities across the country.

The entrance and recruitment standards for First Nations policing are similar to those of other police services, but, understandably, the target group for recruitment purposes is First Nations citizens.

Municipal Police Services

Throughout Canada, there are many municipalities and regions that have their own police service independent of the RCMP or provincial police agencies. The largest of these is Toronto Police Service. Most of Canada's larger cities, including Halifax, Montreal, Winnipeg, Regina, Edmonton, and Vancouver, administer their own policing services. In some areas, communities and municipalities have joined together to form regional police services. Peel Regional Police is the largest such service in Canada in the western part of the GTA. Every province has its own standard for policing. These standards are set out in provincial legislation such as the Ontario *Police Services Act*. This type of legislation sets out the qualifications needed to become a police officer and the prescribed training that must be completed before carrying out the function of a fully sworn police officer.

FIGURE 2.1   Structure of a Municipal Police Force

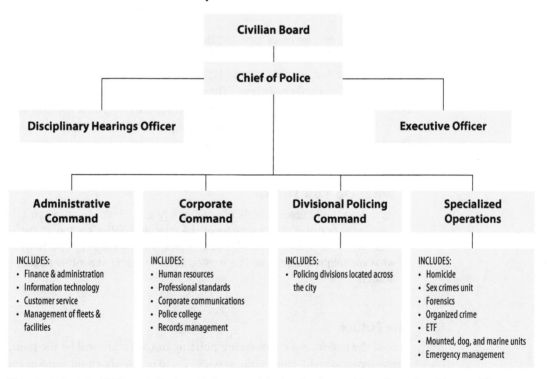

This chart depicts a fairly typical structure for a municipal police force, although smaller cities would have fewer branches, units, and resources than larger centres.

Source: Adapted from Toronto Police Services Board (2012, February 16). Retrieved from http://www.torontopolice.on.ca/orgchart.pdf.

SIDEBAR

Ten Largest Municipal Police Services in Canada

(These are forces not under contract to the RCMP. The numbers refer to sworn personnel.)

Toronto	5,588
Montreal	4,589
Peel Regional	1,895
Calgary	1,872
Edmonton	1,568
York Regional	1,433
Ottawa	1,372
Winnipeg	1,361
Vancouver	1,327
Durham Regional	894

Source: Statistics Canada (2010).

A number of provinces have academies where recruits complete their mandatory training. Although the minimum educational standard in most police jurisdictions remains grade 12, some additional education is usually expected of potential candidates. There are several post-secondary institutions throughout the country that offer programs in police studies and criminal justice, but police services still require their recruits to complete the training at their respective academies.

What Do You Think?

How does the academic study of criminology and criminal justice assist a potential police recruit before he or she attends a police academy? Are there any ideas studied in criminal justice programs that are different from what you might expect would be studied at the Depot or at another police academy?

The Future

One of the major challenges facing policing in the future will be the rising costs associated with this public service. There is already an increase in the number of private security services performing a police function that represent the interests of private property owners or, in some cases, provide security services under contract. These private security officers are typically

Sikh officers of the Vancouver Police Department. Many forces across the country have made efforts to bolster the number of visible minorities in their ranks, with mixed results.

Source: Philip M. Tong. Reprinted by permission.

seen in malls, parks, government buildings, hospitals, colleges, and universities, as well as other venues that require a recognizable presence of a uniformed authority.

The changing nature of crime—particularly in computer technology, fraud, and child pornography—will also be a significant concern as police services struggle to keep pace with the increasing activity in these areas.

Another likely challenge for police services will be in the active recruitment of members from visible minority groups to ensure that the service is representative of the demographics and diversity of the community it serves. Many citizens need to identify with male or female officers who share a common ethnic, religious, or cultural background and at the same time model and encourage respect for Canadian values and law. These officers are also instrumental in reaching out to younger members of the various visible minority groups, who also need strong role models whom they can identify with and even draw inspiration from.

Conclusion

Policing remains an attractive profession. Those entering this career will find it challenging, exciting, rewarding, occasionally dangerous, sometimes frustrating, and seldom boring. And while an officer can enjoy a comfortable lifestyle, thanks to the level of financial compensation, this can come at great personal and family sacrifice with the prospects of shift work, stress, the element of danger, and the high incidence of professional burnout.

But the benefits of such a career far outweigh the negatives, especially if a proper balance in daily family, work, and social routines is maintained. And those who engage in a policing career will likely forge close and lifelong relationships with fellow officers.

What would Sir Robert Peel think of his legacy? Would he still be able to recognize his principles woven into the policies and operations of the modern, highly technological, fast-paced policing organization? Would he still see his principles as relevant in the context of the 21st-century police profession? Certainly policing would not be what it is today without the benefit of his wisdom, vision, sense of decency, and also respect for members of the policing profession and, more importantly, the citizens those officers have sworn to serve and protect.

▶ IN-CLASS EXERCISE

You live in a town with a population of 10,000. In recent years there has been an alarming increase in all aspects of crime, including drug and property offences and violent incidents. The competence of the local municipal police service, which consists of 12 constables, two sergeants, and the chief of police, has been called into question because of its seeming inability to address this spike in crime. Two of the constables are under suspension for job-related disciplinary reasons, and a third has been reassigned to desk duties pending the outcome of a criminal investigation into allegations of excessive force during an arrest. Morale within the police service is at an all-time low. The town council has raised concerns about the policing budget because of ballooning overtime costs, which are the result of officers taking a large number of sick days, and the need to ensure that there are always enough officers on duty.

As a taxpayer and local business owner, you have been asked to lead a group of concerned citizens in working with the town council and the police services board to determine what the community should do to improve this situation. As you assess what steps should be taken, consider the following questions:

1. Is the current complement of officers sufficient, and is the number of officers consistent with the ratio of officers to population in other jurisdictions?

2. In getting back to basic policing practices and concepts, which of Peel's principles require more attention, and why?
3. What options are available to the town council with regard to contracting out police services to the provincial authority? Weigh the pros and cons of the options.
4. If the current police service is to have any hope of restoring public confidence, what needs to be done
   a. immediately
   b. in the short term (the next three weeks)
   c. in the mid-term (three weeks to six months)
   d. in the long term (beyond six months)?

DISCUSSION QUESTIONS

1. In the past, police services in Canada required their recruits to be single, male, over five feet eight inches tall, and physically strong. These requirements closed the door to many who had significant attributes in other important aspects relevant to the profession. Why were these qualifications considered to be discriminatory? What recruitment practices are now in place to ensure that police services reflect the demographics of the community in which it serves?
2. Sir Robert Peel covered a number of areas in his nine principles. In the context of today's policing environment, are there any other principles you would add?
3. During the background stage of a police application, inquiries will be made with respect to the character of the candidate. What exactly does this mean? What sorts of behaviours reflect positively or negatively on a candidate's character?
4. Police agencies always have as a goal receiving continued public support and approval. What challenges do you see in the early stages of this century that pose a threat to achieving this goal?

SUGGESTED FURTHER READINGS

Sheehan, D., Oosten, R. (2006). *Behind the Badge: History of the RCMP "Depot" Division.* Regina: Centax Books.

Police Sector Council. http://www.policecouncil.ca/pages/policing.html

REFERENCES

Blair, W. (2011). G20 Summit Toronto, ON, June 2010: Toronto Police Service after-action review. Retrieved from http://www.torontopolice.on.ca/publications/files/reports/g20_after_action_review.pdf

Campbell, A., Ontario Ministry of the Solicitor General and Correctional Services, & Ministry of the Solicitor General. (1996). *Bernardo investigation review: Report of Mr. Justice Archie Campbell*. Toronto: Solicitor General.

McDonald, D.C. (1979–1981). *Commission of inquiry concerning certain activities of the Royal Canadian Mounted Police*. Ottawa: Supply and Services Canada.

Ontario Provincial Police (OPP). http://www.opp.ca/

Police Services Act, RSO 1990, c. P.15.

Royal Canadian Mounted Police (RCMP). http://www.rcmp-grc.gc.ca/

Statistics Canada. (2010). Canadian Centre for Justice, Statistics Canada. *Police resources in Canada, 2010*. Catalogue No. 85-225-X. Ottawa: Author. Retrieved from http://www.statcan.gc.ca/pub/85-225-x/2010000/part-partie1-eng.htm

Sûreté du Québec (SQ). http://www.sq.gouv.qc.ca/

Task Force on Indian Policing Policy. (1990). *Indian Policing Policy Review*. Ottawa: Indian and Northern Affairs.

Policing Strategies and Operations

▶ IN-CLASS EXERCISE

You Are the Police Officer: Part 1

An elderly couple, Mr. and Mrs. Kovac, come into the Royal Canadian Mounted Police (RCMP) detachment one quiet Saturday morning. They approach the clerk at the front counter and ask to speak with a police officer in private. The clerk calls you out, and you take them into an office. The Kovacs appear very nervous and upset. After some hesitation, Mrs. Kovac states, "I just can't believe she would do this! Why would she do this to me? I have always treated her like family. How could she steal so much money in my name?" Mr. Kovac adds, "Don't worry, dear, the police will figure it out."

The first part of this exercise illustrates how a police investigation typically begins. You start by identifying your clients. The victim and her husband, Mrs. and Mr. Kovac, and a female suspect are clients. You also have an initial indication of what the problem may be based on the information gathered thus far. The female suspect seems to have stolen money by assuming Mrs. Kovac's identity.

As you continue to read through this chapter, write down the steps you would take in this investigation, and be prepared to discuss them in class.

Policing Strategies

Introduction

reactive policing

A policing strategy whereby police officers respond to calls for service either while an offence is in progress or after it has been committed.

Traditionally, police have adopted **reactive policing** strategies, meaning they respond to offences that are in progress or have already been committed (i.e., after the fact). When not responding to calls, police officers randomly patrol their areas with the intention of discouraging crime from occurring or of being close by should they need to quickly react to a request for service. The advantage of reactive strategies is that the community initiates, and thus tacitly approves, the work of the police by asking for their assistance. The drawback is that such strategies—and patrol in particular—are not efficient. Police presence alone is ineffective in deterring crime, and the chances of encountering an offence while it is happening, or even a suspect, during a random patrol are exceedingly slim. As well, reactive strategies result in enforcement-oriented responses that do not address the underlying causes of crime and therefore do not offer long-term solutions. A different approach to policing is needed to compensate for these shortcomings.

proactive policing

A policing strategy whereby police officers identify and respond to emerging problems, with the goal of preventing crime from occurring.

Proactive policing strategies developed in response to the need for another way to do police work. Rather than waiting to be sent to calls, police strive to prevent criminal activity in the first place. Random patrol is replaced by directed patrol, which concentrates on particular problem areas identified through specialized operations such as crime mapping and analysis (discussed later in this chapter). Proactive strategies have several benefits. Police actively engage the community in identifying and resolving crime, improving the relationship between those who enforce the law and the public as a result. More importantly, response options other than enforcement, such as service and protection, address the underlying causes of crime, leading to long-term solutions. The disadvantage is that police work is not always initiated by the community, but by the police themselves. This can be perceived by the public as a top-down approach.

Although the primary strategies used by police today are proactive, the reality is that both forms of strategies are deployed at the same time and in complementary ways, as the following mini case study illustrates.

MINI CASE STUDY

Dealing with Vandalism

A small, remote community in northern Manitoba had been experiencing an ongoing problem with vandalism. Every weekend, windows at various businesses and the school were smashed, and the walls of the buildings were spray-painted with graffiti. Police officers from the local RCMP detachment focused their patrols around the businesses and school, and identified a group of 13- to 15-year-olds as being responsible for most of the offences. They arrested and charged some of these young persons with mischief, and diverted others to extrajudicial measures (i.e., alternatives to court proceedings, such as a warning, caution, or referral to a community-based program). Although these efforts resolved the problem in the short-term, the vandalism inevitably reoccurred. The corporal in charge of the detachment called a meeting with the mayor, town council, school principal, and other community members to discuss the problem and generate possible solutions. During the meeting, several participants noted that this particular age group did not have many options for activities on the weekends. As a result, the teenagers gathered in groups and wandered around the community, bored and looking for something to do. Those at the meeting agreed to organize a series of sporting and social events at the school on the weekends. Several police officers also volunteered to assist at the events. This solution proved to be very successful. By engaging the teenagers in positive activities on the weekends, the number of mischief offences in the community dropped dramatically. As well, the relationship between the police officers and the teenagers was significantly better because they were interacting with each other more often on an informal, non-official level.

What Do You Think?

1. What reactive and proactive strategies did the police employ in this situation?
2. Why were the reactive strategies ineffective in resolving the incidence of mischief?
3. Why were the proactive strategies more effective?

This example highlights a critical point about reactive and proactive policing strategies. Ultimately, preventing offences must complement responding to offences.

The proactive strategies commonly employed in Canada today are problem-oriented policing, community policing, and intelligence-led policing.

Problem-Oriented Policing

problem-oriented policing

A proactive policing strategy whereby police focus on the problems that form the basis of crime.

Problem-oriented policing focuses on the problems underlying crime rather than on offences or calls for service. A problem typically encompasses a collection of incidents that have certain elements in common, such as the type of offence, location, time, and *modus operandi* (i.e., method used by the suspect to commit the crime). Police start by thoroughly analyzing the incidents and precisely defining the problem. A clear definition is needed to ensure the response addresses the true source of the problem, which is usually social in

---

MINI CASE STUDY

Solving the Problem

A low-income residential area in one of Ontario's larger cities was experiencing a high number of break and enters. The local municipal police agency analyzed the incidents by looking at:

- the scope of the problem
- targeted houses
- victims
- offenders
- type and value of stolen property
- locations and times of the offences
- current responses.

This analysis revealed that the crimes had several characteristics in common. The break and enters happened between 6 a.m. and 6 p.m. on weekdays when the residents were away. The offenders gained entry by forcing or breaking doors or windows, and mostly stole cash, jewellery, gaming systems, video games, and laptop computers. Geographic mapping established that a high proportion of the incidents occurred near schools. The police agency determined that much of the problem was related to youth who were chronically absent from school, and involved with gangs and drugs. The police explored numerous possible responses, and in consultation with the community, selected and implemented those responses that received the most support and had the highest likelihood of success. These included focusing on repeat offenders, controlling the stolen-property market, working with the school to reduce student absenteeism, providing advice to residents and victims in particular on how to prevent break-ins, and improving certain environmental design elements in the neighbourhood (e.g., better lighting, cutting back overgrown trees and shrubs near houses). Six months later, a follow-up research study found the number of break and enters was steadily declining.

What Do You Think?

How were the elements of problem-oriented policing applied in this situation?

nature. Next, police generate all possible responses and consider each one so as not to exclude any that are potentially useful. The responses may include enforcement, but are more often preventive, such as intervention, proactive problem solving, and education. Since this strategy is primarily police-driven, the community is engaged in the process when police feel the public has a role in resolving the problem. After implementing the selected response, police assess the success of their solution and share the findings so that their agency and others can learn what does and does not work. The strength of problem-oriented policing is its ability to directly solve problems rather than just react to the symptoms, which are the offences (Weisburd, Telep, Hinkle, & Eck, 2010; Mazerolle, Soole, & Rombouts, 2006; Braga, McDevitt, & Pierce, 2006). See Chapter 15 for more on problem-oriented policing.

community policing
A proactive policing strategy whereby police work in partnership with the community to identify and analyze policing problems, determine policing priorities, and implement responses.

Community Policing

In **community policing**, the community and police work together. Police actively engage the community at all levels of dealing with crime, using formal, organized methods of communication, such as consultative groups,

MINI CASE STUDY

Community-Based Solutions

Each year, police officers from the RCMP detachment responsible for a small southern Saskatchewan town and its surrounding rural area meet with their key stakeholders to discuss the issues that are of concern to them and their community. This input feeds into the detachment's annual performance plan, which details policing priorities for the year and the initiatives that will address these priorities. During last year's meeting, the stakeholders brought forward their concerns about the incidence of impaired driving. Community members felt the low number of offenders being charged with this offence did not reflect the actual number of individuals who were driving while intoxicated. In addition, impaired drivers had recently been involved in two separate serious collisions that resulted in the death of one passenger and significant injuries to all the other people in the vehicles. The sergeant in charge of the detachment agreed that impaired driving should be one of their policing priorities. Various initiatives were discussed during the meeting, and the following were agreed upon by all those present: eight road checks and traffic stops would be conducted throughout the year; a Report Impaired Drivers (RID) program would be permanently implemented; an Operation Red Nose program would be held for ten evenings throughout November and December; and each police officer would be given the goal of charging five impaired drivers per year. By involving the community in this process, the detachment was assured that their efforts would closely match the needs of the community they serve.

What Do You Think?

How were the elements of community policing applied in this situation?

advisory boards, and town meetings. Jointly, they identify and analyze policing problems, determine policing priorities, and implement responses. Enforcement is balanced with problem solving and preventive measures, which concentrate on the root causes of crime. Police not only aspire to keep offences from occurring, but also become involved in higher-order social objectives, such as creating safe environments and improving the quality of life. They see themselves as being in service to their client—that is, the community—and thus are more visible, accessible, and responsive to the public. This decentralized, collaborative, client-centred approach results in positive relations between citizens and police. Community policing is also effective in reducing the rates of crime while ensuring police provide accountable, professional service (Rosenbaum & Lurigio, 1994; Liou & Savage, 1996; Connell, Miggans, & McGloin, 2008).

CAPRA: A Community Policing Problem-Solving Model

To help them deal with incidents, police have long relied on problem-solving models, most notably SARA (Scanning–Analysis–Response–Assessment), which has been used by numerous North American agencies since the late 1980s. In the mid-1990s, the RCMP developed a community policing problem-solving model called CAPRA. It took conventional models like SARA one step further by incorporating all the critical elements of modern policing, including those from both community and problem-oriented approaches. CAPRA combines the traditional skills of acquiring and analyzing information (Acquire and Analyze) and responding professionally to a public safety issue (Response) with the new requirements of client service (Client), public accountability (Partners), and continuous learning (Assessment). Each component of the model asks police to answer key questions

---

SIDEBAR

The SARA Model

The SARA model was developed by Eck and Spelman (1987) to operationalize problem-oriented policing. Police begin by "Scanning" to determine whether or not a problem really exists. Next, in "Analysis," they learn everything possible about the problem by examining what is happening, when, where, and how. They then apply a customized "Response" to the problem. Last, in "Assessment," police evaluate the effectiveness of their response by looking at the process they followed and seeing if the problem was solved or reduced.

FIGURE 3.1   CAPRA Model

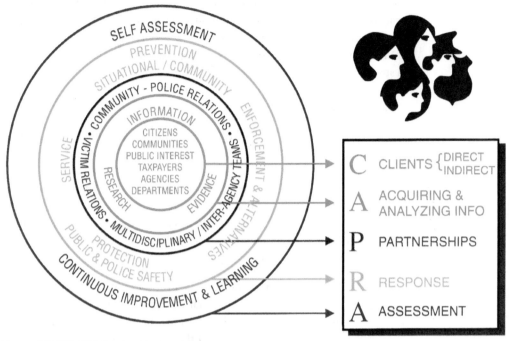

Source: © RCMP-GRC. Reprinted by permission.

to ensure the process is fully addressed. The circular design reinforces the need to continuously define, seek additional information, adapt, redefine, respond, assess, adapt responses, and reassess. Also, the circular representation focuses on the need to keep clients and partners in mind at all times. CAPRA is more than just a problem-solving model in that it provides an operational framework from which to provide policing services.

Clients

Who are my direct clients in this situation?
What are their needs, demands, and expectations?
Who are my indirect clients in this situation?
What are their needs, demands, and expectations?

Clients are the people the police interact with when delivering their services as well as those who receive these services. They are at the centre of the model because all policing is done in response to the clients' needs, demands, and expectations. As well, problems are defined in light of the clients' needs.

This requires police to understand their clients' perspectives and respond to the needs of all those they interact with. Even suspects and prisoners are considered to be clients, since the police have a professional obligation to treat them with respect for human dignity and, when suitable, to protect their well-being. Clients are involved, as appropriate, in generating and selecting response options, developing action plans to implement the selected options, and assessing the service provided.

There are two types of clients.

1. Direct clients: Those whom police interact with at various points in their service delivery or investigations (e.g., complainants, victims, witnesses, suspects, prisoners).
2. Indirect clients: Those not directly involved in an incident or its investigation, but who have an interest in its outcome either because of the way it was handled or because of the association of the incident to similar incidents (e.g., the public, other government agencies or departments, interest groups).

The "Client" component is not found in any other policing model. CAPRA is unique because it teaches police that public interest is best understood and served by learning about and working with direct clients, appreciating their needs and interests, and those of their community.

What Do You Think?

Think back to the first part of the Kovac case described in the in-class exercise. Who are your direct and indirect clients? What are the needs, demands, and expectations of each?

Acquire and Analyze

What do I already know that will help me to deal with this situation?
What do I need to know that will help me to deal with this situation?

Acquiring and analyzing information is essential to continuously assessing risk during an incident, gathering critical evidence, solving a crime, apprehending a suspect, and presenting a thorough case to ensure the fair outcome of a situation, whether through the judicial system or alternative means. When engaged in preventive problem solving, the more information police have and the better the analysis in consideration of the clients' perspectives, the more likely the police are to define the problem appropriately, based upon the clients' needs, and to arrive at a mutually agreed upon response or solution to the problem. Information is acquired from various sources, such as clients and partners, and through research. Research can be as simple as conducting computer checks on a suspect or as complex as crime mapping and geographic profiling.

What Do You Think?

Based on the first part of the Kovac case, what kind of information would you acquire and analyze to deal with the situation?

Partnerships

Who can help me to deal with this situation?

Partners are anyone within the organization (e.g., Police Dog Services, Forensic Identification Section), other government departments or agencies (e.g., Emergency Medical Services, Child and Family Services), or the community (e.g., church pastor, scientist), who can assist police in providing better-quality and more timely service.

Establishing and maintaining partnerships on an ongoing basis provides several benefits:

1. Develops the trust needed to know partners are available as required.
2. Ensures police are aware of all existing potential partners so that the best information or assistance is available to clients as soon as possible.
3. Builds contingency plans so that when assistance is required, it is immediately available.
4. Makes sure clients receive assistance and follow-up through volunteers when police have to attend to other priorities.

What Do You Think?

As you read the second part of the Kovac case exercise (page 78), identify any partners who may be able to help you deal with the situation.

Response

What is my primary responsibility?
What is the public interest, and how is it best served in this situation and in this set of circumstances?
Which client(s) should get priority at various stages of an incident?

Four types of responses are available to police.

1. Service: Assisting the public and referring them to appropriate partners.
2. Protection (public and police safety): Protecting the public, victims, and those affected by their victimization in partnership with community agencies and experts.
3. Enforcement and alternatives: Laying charges and proceeding through the judicial system so that offenders are held accountable is, at times, in the public's best interest. At other times, non-enforcement or measures such as restorative justice are appropriate.
4. Prevention (situational/community): Preventing incidents (offences or problems) from occurring or escalating through intervention, proactive problem solving, and education.

Police must determine what their primary responsibility is in terms of how the public interest is best served in a particular situation, keeping in mind two things: that elements from more than one of these responses may need to be implemented in order to address all the needs and interests of the client; and that the ideal response can change over the course of an investigation or incident.

What Do You Think?

In the second part of the Kovac case exercise (page 78), determine your most appropriate response to the problem.

Assessment

How could my partners and I have handled that better?
What should we do differently next time?
Did we consult victims and other community members who were affected by the problem?
Did we examine any trends?
Are there any lessons learned that could be shared?

Police must assess their performance in order to continuously improve the quality of their service. They must also monitor incidents and detect patterns in partnership with their clients to solve problems and prevent similar situations from occurring.

What Do You Think?

As you read the upcoming third part of the Kovac case exercise (page 89), evaluate the processes followed for dealing with the situation and the effectiveness of the response.

Intelligence-Led Policing

Intelligence-led policing is an emerging strategy that developed in response to the 9/11 terrorist attacks on New York City (McGarrell, Freilich, & Chermak, 2007; Ratcliffe & Guidetti, 2008; Carter & Carter, 2009). This approach relies on **intelligence**, created through the collection and analysis of information, to guide police work. It is typically applied to large-scale national or regional policing problems, such as terrorism and organized crime, and has also recently been used for smaller local problems, such as a string of bank robberies. Information about the problem is gathered from diverse sources, including records of calls for services and offences, interviews with offenders, surveillance, and informants. **Crime analysts** then objectively analyze the information using various research methodologies. The results help police not only to identify patterns and linkages (i.e., the who, when, and where of crime) to assist in solving investigations or predicting and preventing future crime, but also to understand the relationship between the crime and the community (i.e., the complex social and environmental issues that underlie many crime and safety problems) so that they can assist in mobilizing community resources toward an effective response. Intelligence is shared with other police and law enforcement agencies, allowing strategic and tactical decisions to be made cooperatively. In this police-driven approach, the community is an important source of information, but it does not influence policing priorities. Intelligence-led policing has shown early promise in reducing crime rates and providing a new evidence-based model (McGarrell et al., 2007; Heaton, 2009; Kirby, Quinn, & Keay, 2010).

intelligence-led policing
A proactive policing strategy whereby police make strategic and tactical decisions based on intelligence.

intelligence
Information about suspects, their associates, and criminal activity that is gathered and analyzed in order to prevent or resolve crime.

crime analysts
Those who collect, organize, and analyze data from police documents, and other law enforcement and non-law enforcement sources. They produce maps, graphs and reports that assist in identifying suspects, crime patterns and trends, as well as the allocation of police resources.

MINI CASE STUDY

Sharing Data and Information

Organized crime groups pose a threat to the economic integrity and national security of Canada. They are involved in a wide range of illegal activities that touch almost every facet of society, such as the production and distribution of illicit drugs, mass-marketing fraud, weapons trafficking, and human smuggling. Their influence extends from those in charge of the groups all the way down to the street-level offender. Many of the offences that are committed have some type of connection to organized crime. As such, the RCMP in British Columbia collected and analyzed a significant pool of data related to organized crime that was obtained from various sources, including records management systems, specialized databases, and informants. The research led to a comprehensive threat assessment for the province that outlined, in detail, all the major criminal organizations in British Columbia. In addition to sharing this information with other provincial policing agencies, the RCMP compiled joint threat assessments with American law enforcement. From the list, police agencies were able to make informed decisions about which organizations should be targeted jointly in order to make the most impact on their criminal activity.

What Do You Think?

How were the elements of intelligence-led policing applied in this situation?

► IN-CLASS EXERCISE

You Are the Police Officer: Part 2

non-custodial interview
A police interview that occurs when a person is not in police custody (i.e., not arrested) and attends the interview voluntarily. The person is provided the police caution (i.e., right to silence) and is told that he or she is free to leave at any time during the interview.

statement
A written, audiotaped, or videotaped account, taken by a police officer from a witness or suspect, that may be used as evidence in court.

You interview and obtain statements from Mr. and Mrs. Kovac. When the couple went to the bank to increase their line of credit, Mrs. Kovac discovered she has a credit card with a high outstanding balance in her name. She did not apply for the credit card. Mr. and Mrs. Kovac believe their daughter-in-law, Susan Medlow, may be responsible, as she is addicted to drugs and has talked about owing someone a significant sum of money. The next day, you call Susan in for a **non-custodial interview** and obtain a **statement** from her. She admits to having a drug addiction and being in debt to her dealer, but denies opening a credit card in her mother-in-law's name. Based on the information you have at this time, you do not have the power to arrest Susan (see Chapter 4 for more information on arrest). You obtain copies of the signed credit card application and the past month's statement from the bank, and a sample of Mrs. Kovac's signature. The signature on the credit card application does not resemble Mrs. Kovac's signature. You then locate and seize security video footage from a business that shows Susan using the credit card in question on a date and time shown on the statement. You now have the power to arrest Susan and charge her with credit card fraud (s. 342(1)(c) of the *Criminal Code*), identity theft (s. 402.2(1)), and identity fraud (s 403(1)(a)).

The second part of this exercise shows how you, as a police officer, would investigate this case. You acquire and analyze information about the incident, and engage the bank as a partner who can assist you in dealing with the situation. As the investigation progresses, you define the problem more clearly. Susan clearly assumed Mrs. Kovac's identity, forged her mother-in-law's signature on an application to obtain a credit card, and ran up a large amount of unpaid debt on that credit card. You determine that enforcement is the response that best meets the public interest.

Keeping in mind what you have read about policing strategies, write down what you think your next investigative steps should be and be prepared to discuss them in class.

Policing Operations

Introduction

Police operations are the specific techniques used by officers to carry out the strategies of their agency. These techniques have evolved over time in reaction to changes in society and the nature of policing. Key operations, such as patrol and investigation, have always been a part of modern policing, while others have emerged in response to current realities in law enforcement, criminal activity, and advances in technology.

Key Operations

Patrol

Patrol is the foundation of policing operations. Police officers make their rounds through a designated area either on foot or by other modes of transportation, such as car, bicycle, horse, or boat. **Targeted patrol** is used to place officers in locations where offences are occurring or likely to occur, while **preventive patrol** is used to deter crime through police presence. Patrol also situates officers so that they can respond rapidly to calls and raises the public's perception of safety.

targeted patrol
A policing operation in which officers monitor specific locations that have been identified through crime mapping and analysis or problem-solving processes as places where offences are occurring or are likely to occur.

preventive patrol
A policing operation in which officers randomly monitor areas to discourage crime.

What Do You Think?

Patrol and other policing operations not only target crime directly, but also address society's fear of crime. Why is it important to make people feel safe?

Routine Response

When police are engaged in routine response, they are attending an incident that does not present an immediate threat to public and/or police safety, or property (i.e., low to medium risk). Examples are a traffic collision with no injuries or a report of shoplifting. Routine response enables officers to address and resolve common, everyday incidents that can be handled within a relatively short period of time.

Emergency Response

When police are engaged in emergency response, they are attending an incident that presents an immediate threat to public and/or police safety, or property (i.e., medium to high risk). Most 911 calls require this type of response. Examples are a report of shots fired from a residence or a break and enter in progress at a business. These are less common events that demand immediate attention from the police, who may go to the scene with their vehicle's lights and sirens activated. In such situations, certain legal powers granted to police can expand in order to allow them to execute their duties. For example, police do not require a warrant to enter a residence if they fear for the safety of someone inside (see Chapter 4 for more information on police powers). Emergency response allows police to fulfill their most important role, which is ensuring the public's safety, as well as their own.

Criminal Investigation

A criminal investigation happens after an offence has been committed. Police logically and systematically reconstruct the series of events leading up to and following the incident by gathering evidence; interviewing complainants, witnesses, and suspects; pursuing leads; and documenting their efforts. In most cases, a front-line police officer conducts the entire investigation, calling in specialized units (e.g., Forensics; see Chapter 7 for more information on forensics) only when necessary. In other, more serious cases such as murder or drug trafficking, the investigation is turned over to the specialized units (e.g., Major Crime). Police use a criminal investigation to identify the person or persons responsible for an offence in a manner that best ensures successful prosecution.

Problem solving

Problem solving is a structured process for resolving the issues that form the basis of crime. Police identify and analyze the problem in order to clearly define it, select a response (preferably one that is preventive), evaluate the effectiveness of the solution, and share their results. It enables the police to address crime at its source by either stopping problems from occurring, lowering the incidence of the problems, or reducing their seriousness. Problem solving (as conceptualized by models such as CAPRA and SARA) is the foundational operation for problem-oriented policing and community policing strategies.

Specialized Operations

Security

Security deals with threats against the integrity and safety of a nation, which are typically related to terrorist, extremist, or organized crime activity. It includes national criminal investigations, border integrity, protective policing, critical infrastructure protection, marine security, aircraft protection, and critical-incident management. Security usually falls under the responsibility of agencies that have a federal law enforcement mandate, which in Canada is the RCMP. Some of the work is done by integrated teams (e.g., Integrated National Security Enforcement Team, Integrated Border Enforcement Team) with representatives from the RCMP, other federal partners and agencies, and provincial and municipal police services. Because security relies heavily on intelligence, cooperation and information sharing with other domestic and foreign agencies are critical. As such incidents have the potential to cause significant harm, police employ this operation to prevent them from occurring and to mount a large-scale response should they happen.

What Do You Think?

Twenty-six different police agencies were deployed to the G20 Summit in Toronto. What are the benefits of mobilizing an integrated operation like this to a major event? What are the challenges?

Specialized Teams

Specialized teams (e.g., Emergency Response Team, Major Crime Unit, Explosives Disposal Team, Canine Unit) have advanced knowledge and skills that enable them to respond to unique, medium- to high-risk incidents. Examples of such incidents are an armed suspect barricaded in a residence, the murder of a gas station attendant during an armed robbery, or the delivery of a suspicious package. The teams consist of police officers (and occasionally civilian staff) from within the agency. They are deployed when their specialized abilities are best suited to the successful resolution of an incident, while at the same time ensuring public and police safety. All levels of police agencies (i.e., federal, provincial, and municipal) have various types of specialized teams; however, the resources required for certain teams (e.g., an explosives disposal team) make it prohibitive for smaller agencies to establish their own. In these cases, they will sign agreements with agencies that already have that specialized team, and these agreements allow them to request these services when needed.

Integrated Teams

An integrated team (e.g., Integrated Child Exploitation, Integrated Market Enforcement Team, Integrated Proceeds of Crime) is a specialized service that conducts complex, lengthy investigations into particular local and cross-jurisdictional crimes. The distribution of child pornography, a fraudulent retirement investment scheme, and money laundering are examples of such crimes. Police officers and civilian staff from various federal, provincial, and municipal agencies make up the teams. They not only play an investigational role, but also provide the ability to mobilize large numbers of police officers from within a province and across the country in case of a crisis.

Surveillance

Surveillance is the covert collection of information on individuals or groups by police to combat a wide range of crime. In other words, the information is gathered without the individuals or groups knowing that the surveillance is taking place. It can take the form of physical surveillance, where officers watch and follow a person (or people). Usually, they take photographs or capture video of their observations. The police also use electronic surveillance, such as telephone wiretaps and computer traces, to intercept private communications or remotely monitor individuals. If the surveillance intrudes on a person's privacy (e.g., electronic surveillance, installing a Global Positioning Satellite device on a vehicle, opening mail), police officers in Canada must obtain a warrant issued by a judge of the federal court. The police rely on surveillance to identify an individual, establish patterns of behaviour, identify criminal associates, gather evidence, and advance an investigation.

Human Sources

Human sources (i.e., police informants) are individuals who have timely and relevant information about past or future crimes. Occasionally, they are people who are simply in a position to get close to suspects (e.g., bartenders, restaurant employees, taxi drivers), but more often they are either offenders themselves or have close ties to criminal activity. Police develop relationships of trust with these individuals to cultivate them as human sources and, through conversations or interviews, obtain information in exchange for money or lenient treatment. The identities of human sources are kept confidential to guard their safety, and depending on the nature of the material provided, their names will not appear in legal documents or be disclosed in court. Human sources are usually involved in the early stages of investigations into various types of crime (particularly organized crime) to develop leads.

See also mini chapter 16.7
*Wrongful Convictions and
Jailhouse Informants*

What Do You Think?

Using human sources raises many ethical issues. Should police work with people who, in many instances, are the same people they would be arresting? If a human source is paid or otherwise compensated, how truthful and accurate is the information provided? What if the human source uses money given for information to buy drugs? Should police knowingly place someone at risk for coming forward with information?

Undercover Operations

In undercover operations, specially trained police officers assume another identity to build a rapport with criminals, and then secretly collect information and evidence, or elicit a truthful admission of guilt to an offence. They employ techniques that are at times controversial, such as deception and intimidation. Undercover operations are appropriate for certain high-risk investigations, ranging from homicides, drugs, and the sex trade to organized crime, national security, and financial crimes. They are also used with suspects such as serial killers and contract killers who are at high risk to reoffend and commit other crimes against persons. A particular undercover operation, called "Mr. Big" by the media, has been developed for homicide investigations. It is designed to expose the truth by creating an environment where suspects disclose certain past activities that they may not talk about otherwise. Any admission is carefully evaluated in light of other evidence to validate its reliability.

Crime Mapping and Analysis

Crime mapping is a tool used by analysts to enter data about offences, generate a map illustrating the distribution of those offences, and analyze the

CompStat
A strategic process for collecting, mapping, and analyzing data designed to guide police operations, reduce crime, and ensure the accountability of management in the police agency.

hot spots
Locations that experience a higher than average incidence of crime.

patterns of crime. Geographic information systems are a more sophisticated technology that adds other sets of information, such as demographics (e.g., ages and income levels of residents) and geographical features (e.g., location of residences, schools, and parks) to the crime data. Crime mapping and analysis, as represented by a holistic system such as **CompStat** (Computerized Statistics), gives police an indication as to the type of offences that are being committed, as well as when and where they are occurring (i.e., **hot spots**). Police can also identify trends from this information. This operation is used in a number of ways, from deploying patrols based on predictions of where crime is likely to happen to guiding problem-solving processes in order to prevent offences from taking place at all.

MINI CASE STUDY

Mapping Crime Data

In 2007, the Saint John Police Force in New Brunswick implemented Crimeview software that enabled the agency to merge computer-aided dispatch (CAD) and records management system data into a single map view, creating layers of data (ESRI Canada, 2010). The police force chose to focus on the offences of break and enter and motor vehicle theft, and used the software to create pinpoint maps, hot spot maps, and density maps. Police officers discussed and analyzed the maps at crime-control meetings every two weeks, and developed crime reduction strategies accordingly. Dedicated resources were deployed to problem areas, and the investigative processes and results were assessed. After the implementation of crime mapping and analysis, theft of motor vehicles in the Saint John area dropped by 18 percent, while break and enters decreased by 27 percent. In the future, the police force plans to engage the community in reducing crime by sharing the crime mapping data, as well as to expand the mapping to other serious and frequent offences.

According to the most current report on the matter, Statistics Canada's "Criminal Victimization in Canada, 2009" (Perreault & Brennan, 2010), break and enters and motor vehicle/parts theft were the most commonly self-reported incidents to police in 2009 at 54 percent and 50 percent, respectively. However, 69 percent of all criminal incidents and the majority of sexual assaults (88 percent) were unreported.

What Do You Think?

What do these statistics mean to the utility of crime mapping and analysis?

FIGURE 3.2   Winnipeg Hot Spots

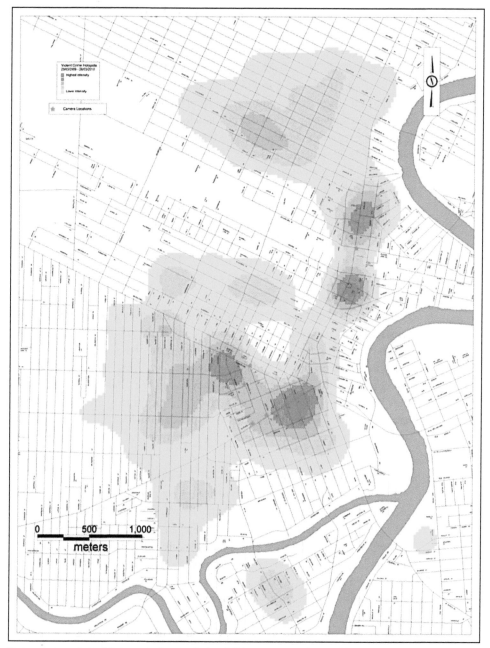

Data maps such as this are used to track the shifting pattern of crime "hot spots" in Winnipeg.

Source: Winnipeg Police Service.

Emerging Operations

Integrated Information Systems

Police information systems house large amounts of data that, for the most part, stay within the jurisdictions of the particular police agencies. Because crime is becoming increasingly sophisticated, interconnected, organized, multi-jurisdictional, and mobile, the sharing of information within and among police agencies is more important than ever. In order to meet this need, police agencies within defined geographical areas are moving to integrated information systems in which they share one dispatch system and one records management system. Such systems increase access to information and improve communication among police, resulting in enhanced public and police safety, effective multi-agency responses to crime, and efficient operational practices. An example is the PRIME-BC computer network in British Columbia, which connects every municipal police agency and RCMP detachment throughout the province and provides instant access to data about offenders and offences to all police agencies.

CCTV Surveillance

Police cannot be everywhere all the time. Instead, they are turning to CCTV (closed-circuit television) cameras to constantly monitor certain public spaces. The video feed is not broadcast, but rather transmitted directly to a receiving location that records the images (no audio is captured). Police do not continuously view the live feed; they watch the taped video only when they need to investigate criminal activity that occurred within range of the cameras. CCTV surveillance is used by police to help them detect, identify, and convict offenders, and to follow the movements of suspects and victims.

Automated Licence Plate Recognition Systems

Vehicles are connected to many types of criminal activity. For example, they can be the target of a crime (e.g., theft), involved in an offence (e.g., hit and run), or the mode of transportation for an offender (e.g., a prohibited driver). The ability for police to quickly locate vehicles of interest is crucial but challenging, given the high volume of vehicles found in most areas and their mobility. Automated licence plate recognition (ALPR) systems are a form of traffic surveillance. Cameras mounted on police vehicles and pattern recognition software read and record licence plates on parked and moving vehicles at a rate of up to 3,000 per hour. The licence plates are checked against a computerized database that only indicates whether or not the marker (i.e., licence plate number) is of interest (i.e., a hit). If it is, the police officer investigates further by running the marker through other operational databases to obtain information about the vehicle. The system logs the licence plate numbers, the location of the vehicles, the type of hit recorded, and the action taken. ALPR assists police in the recovery of stolen vehicles (an offence most commonly committed by youth) and property, and in solving crime that involves a vehicle. It also facilitates the identification of individuals driving while prohibited, suspended, unlicensed, or uninsured.

Facial Recognition Systems

Individuals who have committed or intend to commit criminal acts can easily blend into big crowds, such as those found at airports, sporting events, and concerts. This makes it difficult for police to identify persons of interest. Facial recognition systems are a type of electronic surveillance. A camera or video camera captures a facial image, which is then downloaded into a software program that extracts and compares certain features from the image with a facial database. Pairs of images are grouped as matches or non-matches based on their similarities or differences. Facial recognition systems are primarily used by police at large events to search for potential offenders (e.g., terrorists) who may be there.

What Do You Think?

Because CCTV surveillance (which is already widespread in countries such as Britain and Australia) and facial recognition systems have the capability to track any person's every movement, they are often criticized for their potential to create an Orwellian "Big Brother" state. Critics comment that the government's desire to deter and investigate crime is intruding on citizens' rights to privacy. Is the public's security more important than its privacy? (See also the Jamie Bulger murder, page 348.)

Social Media

All modern policing strategies rely on an effective exchange of information between the police and the community. Social media such as Facebook, Twitter, LinkedIn, and Myspace support two-way communication that is free and reaches a vast number of people. These platforms allow police to engage the community (especially youth) and to seek input into policing problems and priorities and responses, ask for information about offences that have been committed, and advise the public about crime in their area. Social media also help to solve and prevent crime. For example, police can

electronically trace criminal activity through the history of online interactions or learn about issues unfolding in real time (e.g., riots) so that they
can respond quickly and appropriately.

In January 2012, RCMP in Alberta received a tip from a Facebook security officer via the FBI that someone had posted messages on the site
threatening to shoot police officers. The messages were traced to an address
in St. Albert (northwest of Edmonton), and the RCMP was able to arrest
and charge the man responsible before he acted on any of his threats.

Predictive Analytics

Ideally, the primary strategy for police would be predictive policing, in
which criminal activity is prevented by knowing in advance when, where,
and what type of incidents were going to happen and who would be responsible. Predictive analytics is in the early stages of achieving this objective.
Certain types of crime are characterized by identifiable patterns and relationships, both within the criminal activity itself and between it and other
factors (e.g., increased rates of car thefts in the winter when vehicles are left
running). By sorting through massive amounts of policing information (i.e.,
data mining), organizing, and analyzing it, hidden patterns and relationships
can be revealed, or existing relationships confirmed. Predictive analytics is
also able to analyze crime from a behavioural perspective, and identify when
minor crimes may escalate into violence. Tactics, strategies, and policies are
then developed based on all this knowledge. For example, police are able to
create risk and threat assessments (i.e., analytical processes designed to evaluate the likelihood of harm), and deploy resources where they are needed.

Gunfire Alert and Analysis

Using firearms when committing an offence poses the greatest risk to public
and officer safety. The ability of the police to manage and respond quickly to
such incidents is paramount. Gunfire alert and analysis systems are an
acoustical surveillance technology. A collection of microphones or sensors
is set up to cover a defined geographical area that has a historically high
incidence of firearms-related offences. If a gun is fired within this area, the
sound is picked up and transmitted to a computer system that analyzes the
data and displays information about the nature of the incident. Gunfire alert
and analysis systems provide police with real-time reporting of gunfire,
providing detailed reports, including when, where, and how many shots
were fired; the type of weapon used and its relative calibre; and the location
of the shooter. This enables them to respond before receiving calls from the
public and to track such events even when they are unreported.

▶ IN-CLASS EXERCISE
You Are the Police Officer: Part 3

You arrest Susan Medlow and transport her back to the detachment. While searching her, you find a credit card in Mrs. Kovac's name in her jacket pocket. You provide Susan with an opportunity to contact legal counsel and place her in a holding cell. After interviewing her again and obtaining another statement in which she confesses to the crime, you release her on a **promise to appear** in court with the conditions that she remain in the jurisdiction and not contact Mr. and Mrs. Kovac.

Two weeks later, a member from the Integrated Drug Unit contacts you. After executing a drug warrant, the member was searching a local drug dealer's residence and found the dealer's client list. One of the clients was Susan Medlow. The member also seized a blank credit card application that had been mailed to Mrs. Kovac. When he ran computer checks on Susan's and Mrs. Kovac's names, they appeared as links to your credit card fraud investigation. The member advises you that they seized a large quantity of drugs, money, and several firearms from the residence, as well as a debit/credit card skimmer, counterfeit currency, several large bags of shredded paper, and numerous credit cards in different names. The drug unit's investigation has revealed that the dealer is connected to an organized crime group based in Surrey, British Columbia. You contact Mrs. Kovac to advise her of the possibility that her identity may be used in the future and give her tips on how to protect herself against such crime.

Susan appears in court a few months later, pleads guilty to the charges, and is sentenced. You follow up with Mr. and Mrs. Kovac, and find them very pleased with the service they received. You notice, however, that a number of fraud offences have been committed against elderly victims in the detachment area. You decide to implement several community-based initiatives, such as information sessions at seniors' residences and media alerts. Six months later, you run a report from the records management system that indicates the rate of fraud offences has been dropping.

The last part of this case study shows how you, as a police officer, normally conclude an investigation—and where the work of the rest of the criminal justice system begins, as the remaining chapters will illustrate. You determine that laying charges against Susan and protecting Mrs. Kovac from further victimization are the responses that best meet the public interest. Additional information you acquire through an Integrated Drug Unit investigation points to the problems at the foundation of the offences committed by Susan—addiction, the drug trade, and organized crime. These are other problems that need

promise to appear
A form of release from custody whereby the accused agrees, in return for release, to show up at a police station to be fingerprinted and to attend court on specified dates.

to be solved. You assess your handling of the incident and feel it was dealt with appropriately, since Susan has been successfully prosecuted and the clients (Mr. and Mrs. Kovac) are satisfied with your service. Based on other information you acquire and analyze, you immediately tackle another problem by taking action to prevent elderly citizens in the community from being defrauded.

Now that the investigation has ended and you have assessed your perform-ance, you would, ideally, share any lessons learned from your investigation with other police officers. Write down some ways best practices in policing could be shared and be prepared to discuss them in class.

Police Professionalism

Introduction

The citizens of a democratic country grant substantial powers to police:

- the power to restrict freedom through detention or arrest
- the authority to search a person
- the right to use force, including lethal force, when necessary
- the ability to apply discretion.

Police exercise these powers under extremely challenging conditions. Society is changing swiftly and crime is becoming more sophisticated, inter-national, technological, and organized. Although the rates of crime continue to fall in Canada (Brennan & Dauvergne, 2011), Schneider (2004) argues that the impact of crime is increasing as emerging offences such as identity theft and deceitful telemarketing reach further into society. At the same time, the law, and the rights and obligations of police under the law, are becoming more complex (see Chapter 4 for more information on police powers). De-velopments in technology are also transforming the way the police carry out many aspects of their work. Because all these factors place additional de-mands on the police, the level of knowledge and skills they require to perform their jobs is becoming more advanced—and often, they must be able to apply this knowledge and these skills in rapidly evolving, dynamic situations, and make critical decisions within a matter of seconds, or a few minutes at best, based on the information they have on hand at that moment.

Given that these powers carry weighty responsibilities, the public right-fully expects police to act professionally when performing their duties. Professionalism means that police have a conscientious awareness of their role, image, skills, and knowledge in their commitment to quality, client-oriented service. In other words, they must be accountable to the public by ensuring that their job performance and conduct are ethical and beyond reproach. Because police uphold the law, they find themselves in the unique position of being held to a high standard not only while on duty, but also in their personal lives. Police are under greater scrutiny than ever before, as is evidenced by the Dziekański incident at the Vancouver International Airport (see Chapter 4 for a summary of what happened) and the G20 Summit in Toronto (see the Part Two case study for a summary of this event). Any failure in professionalism, accountability, or ethicality and integrity—even by one police officer—casts a shadow on the reputation of all those in law enforcement.

Discretion

Police are given a certain amount of discretion, or flexibility, when enforcing the law. In certain cases, such as murder and domestic violence, they are bound to lay charges and bring the offender to account through the judicial system because the public interest would not be served if they did not do so. However, in other, less serious cases, they can decide whether or not this course of action is in the public's best interest. Police officers make this decision independently when dealing with minor incidents such as speeding or a noise disturbance at a campground. If the incident is more serious, officers make the decision based on input from those who have a vested interest in the outcome, such as the victim or the victim's family, and Crown counsel (i.e., the prosecution). For example, the driver at fault in a collision that resulted in the other driver's death may not be formally charged, or charged with a lesser offence after consulting with Crown counsel, if the victim's family feels that the driver will suffer enough knowing he was responsible for someone's death. Discretion depends on a police officer's judgment, and thus the link to professionalism is clearly evident. The ability to make these subjective decisions effectively relies, in part, on a police officer's accountability, ethicality, and integrity.

Accountability

Accountability is broadly defined as taking responsibility for one's actions. There are two components of police accountability. The police are accountable to the public (their indirect clients in CAPRA), because they have a responsibility to provide information to their communities of interest with respect to their decisions, actions, and results in light of clear, previously agreed-upon understandings and expectations. The police are also accountable to their colleagues, supervisors, and agency, the judicial system, and the various levels of government in that they have a responsibility to provide an account of what they did, why they did it, and what they are doing to improve the performance or results. This means the police must accept the personal consequences of their actions.

Ethical conduct is key to police accountability. Most police agencies have core values to guide the behaviour of their officers and other employees, as well as the agency's mission. Police officers believe that such a system of values is at the foundation of professionalism in policing (Snyman, 2010). Although the complete list varies widely from agency to agency, values such as honesty, compassion, and respect are typically represented. Most agencies also have a code of conduct that outlines the expectations for the professional and personal conduct of its officers (and sometimes other employees), and the consequences for not meeting those expectations. Despite having these references at their disposal, police often encounter situations in which the best decision from an ethical perspective is not always clear, as conflicting values, emotions, and the stress of the job come into play.

Gilmartin and Harris (1998) described the continuum of compromise that police officers face over the course of their careers. Mounting frustration and a lack of control over job processes may result in feelings of victimization. Police officers may deal with these feelings by acting in a manner they would have never thought possible at the beginning of their careers. A developing sense of entitlement or loyalty to one's fellow officers may lead to acts of

---

SIDEBAR

Codes of Conduct

An example of a code of conduct is the one in place for all Ontario municipal police agencies and the Ontario Provincial Police, as detailed in Part V of the *Police Services Act*, Ontario Regulations 123/98. In summary, it states that any chief of police or other police officer commits misconduct if he or she engages in:

- discreditable conduct
- insubordination
- neglect of duty
- deceit
- breach of confidence
- corrupt practice
- unlawful or unnecessary exercise of authority
- damage to clothing or equipment
- consuming drugs or alcohol in a manner prejudicial to duty.

omission (e.g., not completing paperwork) or administrative commission (e.g., drinking on duty), progressing to acts of criminal commission (e.g., falsifying expense claims) over time. Acts of criminal commission are relatively rare. However, other forms of misconduct, such as abuse of power and violating agency procedures, are not uncommon. These situations can come to light in a number of different ways. For example, a police officer may be criminally charged for committing an offence. A member of the public may file a complaint with the local police board or a public complaints commission. A questionable incident may be uncovered through an internal investigation by a police agency's professional standards unit.

Informal and formal disciplinary measures, both internal and external, hold police accountable for their actions. The measures taken depend on the severity of the misconduct. For example, informal discipline is used to address minor problems that can be resolved through something as simple as a conversation between a supervisor and the police officer at fault. Formal discipline, however, ranges from a supervisor documenting the problem in the police officer's personnel file to the police officer being held to account in criminal or civil court. Matters may also be directed through an agency's code of conduct process. In all cases of police misconduct, though, the public is now calling for civilian oversight (Murphy & McKenna, 2012) instead of allowing police to investigate themselves, as has been the traditional practice, which has been seen as potentially subjective and prejudiced in favour of the police.

The Supreme Court of Canada made a landmark decision in *R. v. McNeil* (2009) involving disciplinary measures taken against police officers. This case law holds that records related to findings of serious misconduct on the part of police officers involved in the investigation of an accused fall within the scope of Stinchcombe disclosure (*R. v. Stinchcombe*, 1991). In other words, the police agency must provide information to the prosecution about an officer's misconduct when this misconduct is related to the investigation or could reasonably impact on the case against the accused. Disciplinary records that do not meet these criteria are disclosed only when the accused is able to establish relevance. The requirement to disclose disciplinary issues in the field, or even during training, may severely impact a police officer's ability to participate in certain investigations, depending on the severity and relevance of his or her wrongdoings. For example, a police officer who is found guilty of impaired driving might not be able to conduct impaired driving investigations in the future, since disclosure of the officer's charge may jeopardize successful prosecution of those cases. *R. v. McNeil* is currently being tested in courts across Canada, and its full effect is yet to be determined. (See Chapter 4 for more information on police accountability.)

SIDEBAR

R. v. McNeil

In *R. v. McNeil* (2009), the accused, Lawrence McNeil, was charged with possession of marijuana and cocaine for the purpose of trafficking. The arresting officer, Constable Rodney Hackett of the Barrie Police Service in Ontario, was the primary witness at the trial. After being convicted of the charges but before being sentenced, McNeil learned that Hackett had been engaged in drug-related misconduct that led to internal disciplinary proceedings and criminal charges, both ongoing at the time of his own trial. This revelation led McNeil to appeal his conviction. He requested all documents related to Hackett's misconduct to assist him in preparing an application to introduce fresh evidence at the appeal hearing. Supported by the federal Crown, the Barrie Police Service and the provincial Crown prosecuting Hackett refused to provide the requested documents. The issue of whether or not such records were subject to disclosure was ultimately brought before the Supreme Court of Canada.

Culture and Personality

Police have a distinct culture, characterized by honour, loyalty, and individuality (Dempsey, 1999). It is also marked by a code of silence (Westmarland, 2005)—at times called the "Blue Code," "Blue Wall," or "Blue Line"—that dissuades police officers from reporting one another's misconduct. The culture has evolved to shield them from the day-to-day realities of policing, which are often harsh and unforgiving. Through training and interaction with their colleagues, police officers learn the appropriate behaviour for their culture. For example, they find out that dehumanizing the young victim of a fatal hit and run can help them deal with the emotion of notifying the next of kin, and that being authoritative can de-escalate the behaviour of an assaultive suspect. Their baseline personality is then modified by their socialization within the culture (Twersky-Glasner, 2005), and traits such as cynicism, hostility, secrecy, suspiciousness, and conservatism, among others, emerge. This police personality appears in both their professional and personal lives, and they begin to see themselves as being different from other members of society owing to the powers and authorities they have been given. Police officers develop an "us versus them" mentality, which ultimately separates them from the outside world and societal norms. Research strongly indicates that the police culture and personality is at the root of many issues faced by officers, including misconduct, poor physical health,

The stresses of policing sometimes produce an "us versus them" mentality.

and mental and emotional problems (Harper, Evans, Thornton, Sullenberger, & Kelly, 1999; Gould, 2000; Bannish & Ruiz, 2003).

Professionalization of the Occupation

A growing number of police agencies around the world, such as those in Europe (Paterson, 2011) and Australia (Trofymowych, 2008), require a certain level of higher education as a condition for employment as a police officer. Although this accreditation is occasionally listed as a mandatory prerequisite for applicants, officers typically acquire the necessary credentials through their police training. In contrast, the professionalization of policing is a contentious issue among North American police agencies. In Canada, only Quebec agencies mandate their candidates who do not have a promise of employment from a police department to complete a post-secondary three-year diploma before applying for admission to basic training. Those who already have a promise of employment must still complete a 30-week police technology program before entering basic training. No police agencies offer a college or university accredited diploma or degree as part of their foundational training. In the United States, a mere 1 percent of agencies require potential candidates to have a four-year degree before joining (Reaves, 2010).

North American police agencies are divided on the value of higher education to the occupation of policing. Recent research indicates that there are explicit benefits. For example, an extensive analysis conducted by Aamodt (2004) linked higher education to several positive factors in officer performance and perspective, such as improved academy, field, and patrol performance, reduced days away from work, and fewer formal disciplinary actions. College-educated police officers are less likely to use force (Rydberg & Terrill, 2010) or abuse authority than less educated ones (Telep, 2011). Paterson (2011) also determined that higher education enhances professionalism, accountability, and credibility. Further research needs to be undertaken on whether the concerns raised by North American police agencies—for example, that certain target groups for recruiting have no access to post-secondary education and that educated officers are likely to move to other fields of work—outweigh the benefits. Future decisions about the professionalization of policing will benefit from this type of evidence.

What Do You Think?

Do you think candidates should have a post-secondary diploma or degree as a prerequisite for being hired by a police agency?

Conclusion

As you read in the previous chapter, policing has a long history of tradition and professional practice. The policing strategies and operations you learned about in this chapter are all built upon this foundation. As police officers execute these strategies and operations, they are accountable to the public for the manner in which they carry out their duties and responsibilities.

The next chapter will examine the legal powers of police, and the use of force.

DISCUSSION QUESTIONS

1. Should policing be proactive or reactive?
2. An increasing number of police operations depend on covert (or secretive), coercive, and deceptive techniques. These can range from using unmarked police cars to catch speeding drivers to undercover operatives posing as drug dealers and selling heroin. When are such practices justifiable? Is there a time when they are not?
3. Police officers often face ethical dilemmas in which the core values upheld by their agency collide, and they must choose one core value over another, such as in the following example. Constable Brandon Michaels is called to the scene of a single motor vehicle rollover. Upon arrival, he discovers that the sole occupant of the vehicle is deceased. Unfortunately, it is obvious that the young driver suffered for some time before he died. During the next-of-kin notification, the parents of the young driver ask if their son suffered before passing away. Cst. Michaels simply tells them that a complete investigation of the incident will be conducted over the next few days and avoids speaking about the young driver's suffering. Which two core values are in conflict in this situation? Do you believe Cst. Michaels acted appropriately? Explain your answer.

SUGGESTED FURTHER READINGS

Canadian Association of Chiefs of Police. http://www.cacp.ca

Dempsey, J.S., & Forst, L.S. (2012). *An introduction to policing* (6th ed.). Clifton Park, NY: Delmar.

Gilmartin, K.M. (2002). *Emotional survival for law enforcement: A guide for officers and their families.* Tucson: E-S Press.

Hess, K.M., & Orthmann, C.H. (2011). *Police operations: Theory and practice* (5th ed.). Clifton Park, NY: Delmar.

Police Sector Council. http://www.policecouncil.ca

REFERENCES

Aamodt, M.G. (2004). *Research in law enforcement selection*. Boca Raton, FL: BrownWalker Press.

Bannish, H., & Ruiz, J. (2003). The antisocial police personality: A view from the inside. *International Journal of Public Administration, 26*(7), 831–881. doi:10.1081/PAD-120019322

Braga, A.A., McDevitt, J., & Pierce, G.L. (2006). Understanding and preventing gang violence: Problem analysis and response development in Lowell, Massachusetts. *Police Quarterly, 9*(1), 20–46. doi:10.1177/1098611104264497

Brennan, S., & Dauvergne, M. (2011). Police-reported crime statistics in Canada, 2010. Retrieved from http://www.statcan.gc.ca/daily-quotidien/110721/dq110721b-eng.htm

Carter, D.L., & Carter, J.G. (2009). Intelligence-led policing: Conceptual and functional considerations for public policy. *Criminal Justice Policy Review, 20*(3), 310–325. doi:10.1177/0887403408327381

Connell, N.M., Miggans, K., & McGloin, J. M. (2008). Can a community policing initiative reduce serious crime? A local evaluation. *Police Quarterly, 11*(2), 127–150. doi:10.1177/1098611107306276

Criminal Code, RSC 1985, c. C-46.

Dempsey, J.S. (1999). *An introduction to policing*. Belmont, CA: West Thompson.

Eck, J.E., & Spelman, W. (1987). Who ya gonna call? The police as problem-busters. *Crime and Delinquency, 33*(1), 31–52. doi:10.1177/0011128787033001003

ESRI Canada. (2010). Case study: Police organization uses crime mapping to achieve double digit reduction in crime. Retrieved from http://www.theomegagroup.com/press/articles/saint_john_police_esri.pdf

Gilmartin, K.M., & Harris, J.J. (1998). Continuum of compromise. *Police Chief, 65*(1), 25–28.

Gould, L.A. (2000). A longitudinal approach to the study of the police personality: Race/gender differences. *Journal of Police and Criminal Psychology, 15*(2), 41–51. doi:10.1007/BF02802664

Harper, H., Evans, R.C., Thornton, M., Sullenberger, T., & Kelly, C. (1999). A cross-cultural comparison of police personality. *International Journal of Comparative and Applied Criminal Justice, 23*(1), 1–15. doi:10.1080/01924036.1999.9678629

Heaton, R. (2009). Intelligence-led policing and volume crime reduction policing. *A Journal of Policy and Practice, 3*(3), 292–297. doi:10.1093/police/pap018

Kirby, S., Quinn, A., & Keay, S. (2010). Intelligence-led and traditional policing approaches to open drug markets—A comparison of offenders. *Drugs & Alcohol Today, 10*(4), 13. doi:10.5042/daat.2010.0723

Liou, K.T., & Savage, E.G. (1996). Citizen perception of community policing impact. *Public Administration Quarterly, 20*(2), 163–179.

Mazerolle, L., Soole, D.W., & Rombouts, S. (2006). Street-level drug law enforcement: A meta-analytical review. *Journal of Experimental Criminology, 2*(4), 409–435. doi:10.1007/s11292-006-9017-6

McGarrell, E.F., Freilich, J.D., & Chermak, S. (2007). Intelligence-led policing as a framework for responding to terrorism. *Journal of Contemporary Criminal Justice, 23*(2), 142–158. doi:10.1177/1043986207301363

Murphy, C., & McKenna, P.F. (2012). Police investigating police: A critical analysis of the literature. Retrieved from http://www.cpc-cpp.gc.ca/prr/inv/police/projet-pip-pep-eng.aspx

Paterson, C. (2011). Adding value? A review of the international literature on the role of higher education in police training and education. *Police Practice and Research: An International Journal, 12*(4), 286–297. doi:10.1080/15614263.2011.563969

Perreault, S., & Brennan, S. (2010). Criminal victimization in Canada, 2009. Retrieved from http://www.statcan.gc.ca/pub/85-002-x/2010002/article/11340-eng.htm#a18

Police Services Act, O. Reg. 268/10. (2010). General. Retrieved from http://www.e-laws.gov.on.ca/html/source/regs/english/2010/elaws_src_regs_r10268_e.htm

R. v. McNeil, 2009 SCC 3, [2009] 1 SCR 66.

R. v. Stinchcombe, [1991] 3 SCR 326.

Ratcliffe, J.H., & Guidetti, R. (2008). State police investigative structure and the adoption of intelligence-led policing. *Policing: An International Journal of Police Strategies & Management, 31*(1), 109–128. doi:10.1108/13639510810852602

Reaves, B.A. (2010). Local police departments, 2007. Retrieved from http://bjs.ojp.usdoj.gov/content/pub/pdf/lpd07.pdf

Rosenbaum, D.P., & Lurigio, A.J. (1994). An inside look at community policing reform: Definitions, organizational changes, and evaluation findings. *Crime & Delinquency, 40*(3), 299–314. doi:10.1177/0011128794040003001

Rydberg, J., & Terrill, W. (2010). The effect of higher education on police behavior. *Police Quarterly, 13*(1), 92–120. doi:10.1177/1098611109357325

Schneider, S. (2004). Predicting crime: The review of research. Retrieved from http://www.justice.gc.ca/eng/pi/rs/rep-rap/2002/rr02_7/p6.html

Snyman, R. (2010). The meaning of professionalism in policing: A qualitative case study. *Acta Criminologica, 23*(3), 16–39.

Telep, C.W. (2011). The impact of higher education on police officer attitudes toward abuse of authority. *Journal of Criminal Justice Education, 22*(3), 392–419. doi:10.1080/10511253.2010.519893

Trofymowych, D. (2008). Police education past and present: Perceptions of Australian police managers and academics. *Flinders Journal of Law Reform, 10*, 419–433.

Twersky-Glasner, A. (2005). Police personality: What is it and why are they like that? *Journal of Police and Criminal Psychology, 20*(1), 56–67. doi:10.1007/BF02806707

Weisburd, D., Telep, C.W., Hinkle, J.C., & Eck, J.E. (2010). Is problem-oriented policing effective in reducing crime and disorder? Findings from a Campbell systematic review. *Criminology & Public Policy, 9*(1), 139–172. doi:10.1111/j.1745-9133.2010.00617.x

Westmarland, L. (2005). Police ethics and integrity: Breaking the blue code of silence. *Policing and Society: An International Journal of Research and Policy, 15*(2), 145–165. doi:10.1080/10439460500071721

The Legal Powers of the Police

LEARNING OBJECTIVES

After reading this chapter, students will be able to:

- Discuss the impact of the *Canadian Charter of Rights and Freedoms* on police powers.
- Distinguish between police detention and arrest, and discuss powers given police to detain and arrest suspects.
- Consider the importance of an accused's right to counsel, found in s. 10 of the Charter.
- Understand the common-law and statutory powers relating to search and seizure in Canada.
- Consider the importance of use of force as an option to resolve conflict and understand the legal provisions for the police use of force.
- Understand the National Use of Force Framework and identify and discuss the categories of resistance of suspects, as well as the various force response options available to police officers.
- Identify and discuss accountability and complaints process models for investigating allegations of police wrongdoing.

Introduction

In Canada, there are a number of legislative frameworks that define the roles, powers, and responsibilities of police organizations. In general terms, police officers act on behalf of the government and society to prevent criminal activity, detect and apprehend criminals, preserve the peace, enforce laws, respond to emergencies, assist victims of crimes, and assist in the prosecution of offenders. Indeed, we all rely on the police to maintain law and order and keep us safe.

adversarial system
System of justice in which cases are argued by two opposing sides, the prosecution and the defence, both of which are responsible for fully and forcefully presenting their respective positions; cases are heard and decided by an impartial judge.

There is, however, a conflict that arises in our **adversarial system** of criminal justice between the legal mandate of the police to maintain order and the values and processes that exist in a democracy. For years, Canadians have struggled to balance the competing imperatives of crime control and due process without compromising the rights of the accused and the integrity of the administration of justice. We have sought to preserve basic procedural fairness to accused persons without unduly limiting society's interest in solving crimes and convicting the guilty. Without question, this debate will continue into the future.

As you may recall from Chapter 1, the authors identify five competing models of criminal justice, or normative value positions: crime control, justice, welfare, community change, and restorative justice. On September 20, 2011, the federal government introduced the *Safe Streets and Communities Act* (see the case study in Part Four on page 229), which was an omnibus bill composed of nine measures aimed at improving the safety and security of all Canadians, including:

- eliminating the use of conditional sentences (house arrest) for serious and violent crimes
- imposing mandatory minimum sentences for certain sexual offences
- imposing tougher penalties for specific drug offences, such as the production and possession of illicit drugs for the purposes of trafficking.

Though highly controversial, the Act received royal assent and was proclaimed into force on March 13, 2012.

What Do You Think?

Which of the models of criminal justice does Ottawa's recent initiative fit into? Do you agree with these legislative changes? Do you think they will reduce crime? Will future governments seek to reverse these changes?

Criminal law is far from static. Whether a result of law that has developed through court decisions (i.e., common law) or legislative changes made by federal and provincial governments, the legal landscape in Canada is forever changing. Consequently, police powers are constantly evolving. The introduction in 1982 of the *Canadian Charter of Rights and Freedoms* has undoubtedly affected the way police officers carry out their law enforcement mandate. This chapter will examine the impact of the Charter on the following powers that the police exercise in the course of their duties:

- detention and arrest
- search and seizure
- use of force.

Police Powers to Detain and Arrest

Charter Considerations

The enactment of the Charter has had a profound impact on the legal powers of the police and has placed limits on what officers can do when investigating crime. There are two sections that are particularly important when considering the concepts of arrest and detention. First, s. 9 prohibits state agents, usually the police, from arbitrarily detaining or imprisoning individuals. This means that they must have a valid reason for detaining or imprisoning someone. Second, everyone who has been arrested or detained has the right under s. 10(a) to be informed of the reasons for the detention or arrest, while s. 10(b) entitles persons to be informed of their right to legal counsel and to retain and instruct counsel without delay.

Detention

Contrary to popular belief, the arrest is not the first contact accused persons have with the criminal justice system. Police officers in Canada can detain, question, and search a suspect for investigative purposes before making an arrest. Historically, this has not always been the case, because the common

---

SIDEBAR

Relevant Sections of the Charter

Detention or imprisonment

9. Everyone has the right not to be arbitrarily detained or imprisoned.

Arrest or detention

10. Everyone has the right on arrest or detention
    (a) to be informed promptly of the reasons therefor;
    (b) to retain and instruct counsel without delay and to be informed of that right; and
    (c) to have the validity of the detention determined by way of *habeas corpus* and to be released if the detention is not lawful.

law has been restrictive in granting powers to the police. For example, they did not have the right to detain an individual, only to arrest someone if the officers had reasonable grounds to do so. In more recent years, however, the courts have acknowledged that a natural consequence of the general duties of police officers is the power to enforce the law. This means that the police must have the ability to use force—in detaining, searching, and arresting persons suspected of criminal activity. The police power to detain for investigative purposes has its origins in the "ancillary powers doctrine."

At what point is an individual detained within the meaning of the Charter? "Detention" includes a broad range of encounters between police officers and members of the public. Nevertheless, the police cannot be said to detain within the meaning of the Charter every suspect they stop for investigative purposes. While an individual who is stopped is being detained in the sense that he or she is "delayed" or "kept waiting," it is important to note that the constitutional rights recognized by ss. 9 and 10 are not engaged unless the delay involves significant physical or psychological restraint; the police are not prohibited from interacting with members of the public. However, this situation becomes fundamentally different once officers have specific grounds to connect an individual to a crime. Once there is a link between the person stopped and a recent or ongoing criminal offence, the encounter becomes

---

SIDEBAR

The Ancillary Powers Doctrine

The ancillary powers doctrine is the process through which new police powers can be created by way of common law (also known as case law or precedent). This means that the law is developed by judges through decisions of the courts, rather than through legislative action by Parliament. When delineating the police powers of investigative detention, the Supreme Court of Canada in *R. v. Mann* (2004) stated that the common law should reflect "current and emerging societal needs and values" (para. 17). The court held that police officers may detain for investigative purposes, provided there is a clear connection between the person to be detained and a recent or ongoing criminal offence (para. 34).

What Do You Think?

Consider the role of the trial judge as discussed in Chapter 6. Do you think that judges should be allowed to create police powers, or should such substantive changes to the law be enacted by Parliament and enshrined in statute?

an investigative detention (*R. v. Mann*, 2004). According to the Supreme Court in *R. v. Therens* (1985), a detention occurs when a police officer "assumes control over the movement of a person by a demand or direction which may have significant legal consequence and which prevents or impedes access to counsel" (para. 49). Correspondingly, the duty to inform an individual of his or her s. 10(b) Charter right to retain and instruct counsel is triggered at the outset of an investigative detention. Such detentions are to be brief and they do not impose an obligation on the suspect to answer questions posed by the police (*R. v. Mann*, para. 45).

▶ IN-CLASS EXERCISE
Detention or Not?

Consider the following scenario, and discuss your answers, and reasons for them, as a class:

Locke M. Upp and his dog, Sparky, are out for their daily walk around the neighbourhood. A police officer approaches Upp and tells him that there has been a series of break-ins in the community and that the police are investigating. A backup patrol car arrives during the encounter. One of the officers asks Upp if he has seen anything unusual or suspicious, and requests that he produce some identification.

1. Is this a detention within the meaning of the Charter?
2. Is Locke M. Upp being detained for investigative purposes?
3. What if, during the initial questioning of Upp, officers receive information by radio that includes a detailed description of the suspect and the description matches the appearance of Upp? In this context, is there a legitimate exercise of investigative police powers?

Arrest

The authority police have to make an arrest is granted under different legislation, including federal statutes such as the *Criminal Code* and *Controlled Drugs and Substances Act*, as well as provincial laws such as motor vehicle statutes (e.g., Ontario's *Highway Traffic Act*). Police officers can make an arrest under various circumstances, including to prevent the commission of a criminal offence, to compel the attendance of the accused in court, and to end an offence against public order, such as causing an unnecessary disturbance (i.e., breach of the peace). An **arrest** occurs when a police officer assumes control over the movement of a person by a demand or direction.

When can a police officer make an arrest? If an arrest is justified, and if time permits, the officer can seek an **arrest warrant** by swearing an **information** in front of a justice of the peace (or a judge) alleging that a criminal offence has been committed. If the justice of the peace agrees that there are "reasonable grounds to believe that it is necessary in the public interest," a warrant will be issued directing the police to apprehend the person named in the warrant and bring that individual before a justice of the peace as soon as practicable. Once the warrant has been issued, s. 29 of the *Criminal Code* requires that the arresting officer give notice to named person of the existence of the warrant, advise of the reason for it, and produce it if requested, if it is feasible to do so.

Police officers are exposed to a variety of situations, sometimes requiring them to act quickly. To illustrate: a police officer may observe a suspect committing a criminal act, such as robbery. Therefore, it is not reasonable for the officer to go to a justice of the peace before swearing the information. Is it possible for the police to make an arrest without a warrant?

According to s. 495(1) of the *Criminal Code*, police officers are granted the authority to arrest without a warrant

- a person who has committed an indictable offence or who, on reasonable grounds, they believe has committed or is about to commit an indictable offence;
- a person whom they find committing a criminal offence; or
- a person in respect of whom they have reasonable grounds to believe that a warrant of arrest or committal ... is in force within the territorial jurisdiction in which the person is found.

Section 495(2) imposes a duty on police officers not to arrest a person without a warrant for three types of offences: those found in s. 553 of the *Criminal Code*, hybrid offences, and those punishable on summary conviction. If, however, the officer has reasonable grounds to believe that an arrest is necessary in the public interest for these types of offences, the officer can make an arrest in order to

- establish the identity of the person,
- secure or preserve evidence of or relating to the offence, or
- prevent the continuation or repetition of the offence or the commission of another offence.

A police officer is also authorized to arrest an individual if the officer believes that the person will fail to appear in court.

What are reasonable grounds for making an arrest? In *R. v. Storrey* (1990), the Supreme Court of Canada ruled that the arresting officer must subjectively have reasonable and probable grounds on which to base an arrest without a warrant. That is, a police officer must believe that he or she has the grounds to arrest. Further, the grounds for arrest must be justifiable from an objective point of view. This means that a reasonable person standing in the shoes of the officer would have believed the grounds existed, but it need not amount to a ***prima facie*** case for conviction before making the arrest.

As Griffiths (2013, p. 142) pointed out, in the case of an arrest or an investigative detention, an important threshold in the criminal justice process is crossed. Upon arrest or detention, the police are required to inform suspects promptly under s. 10(a) of the Charter of the reasons they are being arrested, and advise them under s. 10(b) that they have the right to retain and instruct counsel without delay. The latter section imposes the following duties on state authorities when they detain or arrest a suspect (*R. v. Bartle*, 1994, para. 17):

1. the duty to inform persons of their right to counsel without delay as well as the existence and availability of legal aid and duty counsel;
2. the duty to provide detainees with a reasonable opportunity to exercise their right; and
3. the duty to desist from questioning until that reasonable opportunity has been exercised.

Additionally, officers are required by common law to inform detainees of legal aid and duty counsel programs (*R. v. Brydges*, 1990), as well as the existence of a 24-hour 1-800 (toll-free) telephone number that detainees can access to get preliminary legal advice (*R. v. Bartle*, 1994). State authorities are permitted to forgo the second and third duties in urgent and dangerous circumstances. Notably, the person being detained can always relinquish the rights guaranteed by s. 10(b), although the Supreme Court in *Bartle* stated that the standard for **waiver** will be high, especially in circumstances where the alleged waiver has been implicit. If the detainee invokes his or her right and is reasonably diligent in exercising that right, there is a duty on the police to provide the detainee with a reasonable opportunity to contact counsel and to refrain from eliciting evidence until the individual has done so. Failure by the police to fulfill their duties under s. 10 could result in evidence obtained subsequently being excluded under s. 24(2) of the Charter.

prima facie
Legal presumption meaning "on the face of it" or "at first sight." Refers to a matter that appears to be self-evident from the facts. The term denotes evidence that, unless contested, would be sufficient to prove a particular fact in issue; the evidence need not be conclusive.

waiver
The giving up of a right. May be done expressly, or it may be implied from the circumstances.

Under what circumstances can a police officer enter a private dwelling to arrest someone? In *Eccles v. Bourque et al.* (1975), the Supreme Court of Canada held that police officers could enter a private dwelling to make an arrest pursuant to an arrest warrant. Two decades later, Canada's highest court ruled in *R. v. Feeney* (1997) that, absent **exigent circumstances**, police officers are prohibited from entering private dwellings without authorization. In response to this decision, Parliament introduced what is now s. 529(3) of the *Criminal Code*, which permits police officers to enter a private dwelling without a warrant for the purpose of arresting a suspect in exigent circumstances. According to s. 529.4(3), officers must announce their presence before entering, unless they have reasonable grounds to believe that the announcement would place someone in imminent danger of bodily harm or result in the loss of evidence.

exigent circumstances
Situations in which people are in imminent danger of bodily harm or death, in which there is risk of imminent loss or destruction of evidence, or in which a suspect will escape.

Search and Seizure

As early as the 17th century, the common law has recognized the importance of, and has placed a high value on, the security and privacy of the home (*Semayne's Case*, 1604). And since the introduction of the *Canadian Charter of Right and Freedoms*, "The emphasis on privacy in Canada has gained considerable importance" (*R. v. Feeney*, 1997, para. 42). There are both common-law and statutory powers that authorize the police to search individuals and places and to seize evidence for purposes of prosecution. Section 8 of the Charter provides that all Canadians have the right to be secure against unreasonable search or seizure. Such protection was first considered by the Supreme Court of Canada in *Hunter et al. v. Southam Inc.* (1984). Mr. Justice Dickson, writing for a unanimous court, said that the protection entrenched in s. 8 is very broad in its scope and is intended to prevent unjustified state intrusions into the privacy of individuals. In other words, it prohibits unreasonable searches.

Minimum Standards

The court established what are known as "constitutional minimum standards"—a framework within which to evaluate the constitutionality of legislation authorizing search warrants. Unauthorized searches (without search warrant or wiretap authorization) are generally and presumptively unreasonable under s. 8. Where it is feasible, and if there is time to do so, police officers need to satisfy these minimum requirements:

1. have prior authorization (e.g., search warrant or wiretap authorization) (*Hunter et al.*, p. 110);

2. have authorization from a person who is capable of acting judicially—that is, in a neutral and impartial manner (e.g., justice of the peace or judge) (p. 112); and
3. have reasonable grounds to believe, sworn upon oath by the individual seeking the authorization, that an offence has been committed and that there is evidence to be found at the place of the search (pp. 114–115).

The standard is high. There must be a "credibly based probability"—that is, the items sought are likely to be found—rather than mere suspicion. Importantly, if a search is authorized by law (through a search warrant, wiretap authorization, or exemptions under common law or legislation), it still has to be carried out in a reasonable manner.

Technique for Investigating Marijuana Grow Operations

The police, however, cannot perform an illegal search in order to gather evidence to obtain a search warrant. For example, in *R. v. Kokesch* (1990), the police conducted a **perimeter search** of the accused's property on the basis of a suspicion that he was growing marijuana, but without reasonable and probable grounds for believing that narcotics would be found on the premises prior to conducting the perimeter search.

The Supreme Court of Canada found that the warrantless search of the yard violated s. 8 of the Charter and the evidence was accordingly excluded under s. 24(2). Likewise, the court has also found that the "knock on" technique constitutes a search and violates s. 8 as well (*R. v. Evans*, 1996). This tactic involves a police officer approaching a dwelling house and knocking on the door in hopes that when the occupant opens it, sufficient evidence (i.e., olfactory, or smell) will be immediately apparent to support an arrest or an application for a warrant. The knock-on technique goes beyond that which is authorized by law and is now considered an illegal search.

perimeter search
A search of the outside of a dwelling house and its surroundings; used as a method of acquiring sufficient information on which to base a search warrant application to search inside the house.

Search by Warrant: Criminal Code

The general authority for issuing search warrants is found in s. 487 of the *Criminal Code*.[1] Before issuing a warrant, a justice (i.e., a provincial court judge or justice of the peace) must be satisfied that there are reasonable grounds to believe that there will be evidence with respect to the commission of an offence found at the place of the search. The details that must be provided to the justice are set out in an **information to obtain a search warrant (ITO)**. The test in reviewing a decision to issue a warrant is whether "there was reliable evidence that might reasonably be believed on the basis of which

information to obtain a search warrant (ITO)
A document prepared and sworn by the person seeking a search warrant (usually a police officer) specifying the offence alleged, the place(s) to be searched, and the specific item(s) to be seized.

the authorization could have issued" (*R. v. Morelli*, 2010, para. 40). The Supreme Court of Canada's decision in *Morelli* made clear that courts will not tolerate misleading or incomplete ITOs. Lastly, s. 29(1) of the *Criminal Code* states that everyone who executes a warrant must have it with him or her "where it is feasible to do so, and to produce it when requested to do so." This statutory provision complements the rights afforded persons upon arrest or detention under s. 10 of the Charter.

Taking Bodily Substances for DNA Analysis

What is the scope of the law regarding the taking of bodily substances for DNA analysis? Prior to the 1995 amendments to the *Criminal Code*, the search and seizure of bodily samples was not authorized by either statutory or common law. Therefore, police officers used the "scavenger method" to obtain DNA samples by searching for discarded tissues and cigarette butts (Brockman & Rose, 2011, p. 177). As noted in *R. v. Stillman* (1997), police cannot take hair samples, dental impressions, or buccal (cheek) swabs without prior judicial authorization. These types of searches are deemed to be highly invasive and contravene the principles of fundamental justice pursuant to s. 7 of the Charter (para. 51). Special provisions now exist for obtaining forensic evidence: blood samples are covered in s. 256 of the *Criminal Code*, while DNA and bodily impression warrants are found in ss. 487.04 to 487.091.

The interception of our private communications by means of electronic surveillance is also covered under our right not to be subjected to unreasonable search and seizure. Police officers must obtain prior judicial authorization either under s. 184.2 of the *Criminal Code*—to intercept communications with the consent of one of the parties (participant surveillance)—or under s. 186—to intercept private communications without the consent of either party (third-party surveillance). In the latter context, judicial authorization is sought by an application made under s. 185 and is accompanied by an affidavit—a written statement of facts sworn under oath. Under s. 186(1), before the authorization is granted, the affiant—usually a police officer— must demonstrate what is referred to as "investigative necessity." The requirements of s. 186(1) coincide with the constitutional requirements under s. 8 of the Charter (*R. v. Unger*, 1993). Failure to comply with these requirements would render the interceptions (communications) unlawful.

If an application to obtain the authorization fails to demonstrate that a warrant is a necessary part of the police investigation, or if the evidence disclosed in the officer's affidavit filed in support of the request is falsified, evidence obtained as a result could be excluded pursuant to s. 24(2) of the Charter. If authorization is properly obtained, it must, as with a search warrant, be reasonably executed and must be done in a reasonable manner (*R. v. Joseph*, 2000, p. 136).[2]

Search Without Warrant: Legislation and Common Law

There are, however, some searches authorized by legislation or common law that are reasonable under s. 8 without authorization (no need for a search warrant). There are numerous statutory powers that allow for warrantless searches. Section 117.02 of the *Criminal Code* authorizes a peace officer to conduct a warrantless search of persons, vehicles, or any place or premises other than a dwelling house for weapons or ammunition, "where the conditions for obtaining a warrant exist but, by reason of exigent circumstances, it would not be practicable to obtain a warrant." Warrantless searches or entries into private dwellings are permitted in limited exigent circumstances (see s. 529.3 of the *Criminal Code* and s. 11(7) of the *Controlled Drugs and Substances Act*). To illustrate, police officers are authorized to forcibly enter a private dwelling in response to an emergency 911 call. They have a duty to find out the reason for the call and have the power, derived as a matter of common law from their duty, to enter the dwelling to verify that there is in fact no emergency (*R. v. Godoy*, 1999, para. 23). Lastly, it should be noted that there are numerous provincial statutes and other federal statutes that allow for search and seizure without authorization.

Search During Investigative Detention: No Fishing Expeditions

As explained above, the Supreme Court of Canada in *Mann* (2004) found that the police have the authority to detain persons for investigative purposes. The Court also considered the extent to which police officers could search a person held in an investigative detention. According to Justice Iacobucci, for the majority, "Where a police officer has reasonable grounds to believe that his or her safety or that of others is at risk, the officer may engage in a protective pat-down search of the detained individual" (para. 45). While a pat-down search incidental to an investigative detention may be justified, this common-law power does not authorize a "fishing expedition"; the police cannot go through pockets to obtain evidence. As previously discussed, police must advise the individual of the reason for the detention, as well as the person's rights under s. 10 of the Charter. While the threshold test to conduct a protective search as outlined in *Mann* is "reasonable grounds," Latimer (2007) points out that, where the alleged offence being investigated involves firearms, the threshold appears to be reasonable suspicion for protective searches incident to an investigative detention. In any event, search powers during investigative detention are different from those following an arrest.

Searching Incident to Arrest

Another common-law search-related power is a search incidental to arrest; that is, the power of a police officer to search a person who is taken into custody (and the immediate surrounding area) without warrant. Police officers do not need reasonable grounds to conduct this type of search, but they first need reasonable grounds to make the arrest. In other words, for the search to be lawful, the arrest itself must be lawful. A search incidental to arrest is not mandatory and must be for a valid purpose, such as to secure or preserve evidence, ensure the safety of the officer or the suspect, and prevent escape (*Cloutier v. Langlois*, 1990, p. 186). The search cannot be conducted in an abusive fashion and must be carried out in a reasonable manner. In *R. v. Golden* (2001), the Supreme Court of Canada in a 5–4 majority held that, if a search incident to a lawful arrest involves a strip search, the police must have "reasonable and probable grounds justifying the strip search in addition to reasonable and probable grounds justifying the arrest" (para. 99).

Doctrine of Plain View

The police also retain the common-law power to seize items under the plain view doctrine. In the context of search and seizure, this doctrine provides that objects discernible by a police officer who is legally in a position to observe them can be seized without a search warrant and are admissible as evidence. To illustrate, if a police officer lawfully stops a motorist for a traffic violation (e.g., speeding) and, while approaching the vehicle, sees a firearm on the backseat, the police officer has reasonable grounds to search inside the vehicle and seize the firearm, even though that offence has nothing to do with the traffic violation. Additionally, while the law related to search and seizure prevents unjustified state intrusions into the privacy of individuals, s. 489(2) of the *Criminal Code* allows police officers who are executing a search warrant to seize evidence of an offence that is not mentioned in the warrant. It is not a power to search, but rather a power to seize items in plain view.

Consent Searches

Police officers are authorized to conduct warrantless searches when an individual voluntarily consents to the search, thereby waiving the constitutional protections afforded them. Fairness demands that the individual appreciates the potential legal consequences of agreeing to the search. The person consenting must truly understand that the police may use anything uncovered in a search in a subsequent prosecution. In *R. v. Wills* (1992), the Ontario

Court of Appeal provided the following guidelines for establishing whether voluntary consent was given (para. 69):

- there was consent, expressed or implied;
- the person had the authority to give the consent;
- the consent was voluntary and was not the product of police oppression, coercion, or other external conduct, which negated the freedom to choose;
- the person was aware of the nature of the search being requested;
- the person was aware of his or her right to refuse to permit the police to engage in the search; and
- the person was aware of the potential consequences of giving the consent.

In essence, the consent must be real and voluntary. The person searched must have sufficient awareness to have waived constitutional rights against search and seizure. The degree of awareness of the consequences of the waiver of the s. 8 right required of an accused in a given case will depend on its particular facts. The Supreme Court of Canada later approved of these guidelines for consent in *R. v. Borden* (1994).

Police Use of Force

In recent years, the use of force by Canadian police officers has attracted considerable media and public attention. Several incidents involving police wrongdoing have been featured prominently in headline news stories, including those in which individuals have died while in police custody and where deadly force was used. Since most people have little direct contact with the criminal justice system, popular media and journalistic reports are a fertile source of information and education on topics such as police use of force. Indeed, these reports of police wrongdoing are sensationalized and often critical of the actions of the police. Sometimes, such incidents of police wrongdoing/misconduct warrant close scrutiny and censure; other times, however, the allegations are without foundation. As Walma and West (2001, p. 59) observe, "Public scrutiny always enjoys the benefit of hindsight, sober reflection, and in some cases additional information." It is important to keep in mind that police officers can quickly find themselves in dangerous and unpredictable situations and have little time to assess a threat or possible threat, determine an appropriate response, and defuse the situation.

Nevertheless, these narratives undoubtedly have an effect on public attitudes toward the police, the criminal justice system, and government more

Police must act quickly under pressure, but "public scrutiny always enjoys the benefit of hindsight."

generally. Moreover, negative perceptions of the police and the use of force to resolve conflict have eroded public confidence in the administration of justice. This damage has placed a burden upon the integrity, prestige, and reputation of the law enforcement profession. The resulting public indignation is illustrated in a 2009 Angus Reid public opinion poll indicating that, while over a third of Canadians maintained a positive opinion of the Royal Canadian Mounted Police (RCMP), a majority of respondents in British Columbia (61 percent) said their confidence in the national police force had worsened. The decline in confidence followed on the heels of numerous allegations of police wrongdoing, including several incidents of police-involved deaths. The tragic death of Robert Dziekański (see the mini case study on page 113 in this chapter) triggered an outcry against police violence and police use of force. This case has led to considerable discussion at all levels of civic discourse about the conflict of interest present in police investigating themselves, as well as concerns regarding the impartiality of investigators. The topic of police investigating police, as well as policy reform in this area (e.g., establishment of independent, civilian-led investigative agencies), will be addressed later on in this chapter.

The Use of Force

use of force
Amount of effort required by police to compel compliance by an unwilling subject.

The **use of force** is a defining feature of the police, and officers are granted the authority to use force, including deadly force, to assist them in their broad law enforcement mandate (i.e., crime control and public order) (Bittner, 1970; Manning, 1977). Though it is fundamental to police work, the level of force employed should be guided by the principles of proportionality, necessity, and reasonableness. If a police officer uses excessive force in the course of his or her duties, it could amount to a violation of the suspect's right to life, liberty, and security of the person under s. 7 of the Charter. If an agent of the state (e.g., a police officer) violates an individual's rights and freedoms guaranteed under the Charter, the accused may seek a remedy under s. 24(2) or in civil court.

See also mini chapter 16.2
*Section 1 of the Charter:
The Oakes Test*

According to Murphy and McKenna (2007, p. 5), there are a number of situational, structural, and symbolic qualities unique to police work, such as danger, risk, authority, and conflict. Police officers are exposed to a variety of scenarios while carrying out their enforcement duties that range from rather benign to highly charged, risky, and potentially dangerous situations. When an officer responds to an incident, he or she is continuously assessing the risk to determine the appropriate level of intervention. If the use of force is necessary, the level of force should correspond to the level of resistance by the individual.

Robert Dziekański

Source: Paul Pritchard.

Read the following case and ask yourself:

1. Were the officers' actions proportional, necessary, and reasonable in the circumstances?

2. Do you feel that the use of force in this context was excessive?

In October 2007, Robert Dziekański, a 40-year-old construction worker, emigrated from Poland to join his mother, Zofia Cisowski, in Kamloops, British Columbia. He arrived at the Vancouver International Airport on October 13, 2007, following a long flight. He and his mother had arranged to meet at the baggage carousel in the international terminal. Unbeknownst to either of them, the baggage area for international arrivals was a secured area where his mother was not allowed to enter. Dziekański was eventually cleared through a primary customs inspection by a Canadian border services officer and referred to the customs secondary area for further processing, which is standard procedure for someone who doesn't speak English and is immigrating to the country. For the next six hours, however, Dziekański's whereabouts remained unclear, though he was seen several times wandering around the customs and baggage area for international arrivals. Dziekański was eventually escorted by another border services officer to the immigration secondary area after having completed a secondary customs examination. Once Dziekański's immigration procedures were done, he wandered back and forth between the public area of the international arrivals terminal and the International Reception Lounge.

For reasons that have not been adequately explained, Dziekański remained in the international arrivals area for almost 12 hours, growing increasingly confused and visibly agitated. Among other things, he was fatigued from the flight and anxious to see his mother, who was waiting for him in the public waiting area. Speaking no languages other than Polish, he was unable to communicate effectively with bystanders and airport security personnel, and efforts to calm him down were unsuccessful. He threw a wooden table against a set of glass doors in the International Reception Lounge and smashed a computer. Four RCMP officers arrived on the scene and moved into the secure area where Dziekański was holed up. One officer quickly used a conducted energy weapon (CEW—i.e., a Taser) against Dziekański five times, who, after being subdued and handcuffed, died shortly thereafter.

Although provincial Crown prosecutors decided not to lay charges against the police officers involved in the incident, the BC government established a commission of inquiry and appointed Thomas Braidwood, a former appeal court justice, to head up the commission. The first phase of the inquiry (see Braidwood, 2009) examined the police use of conducted energy weapons, and the second phase (see Braidwood,

2010) focused on the circumstances surrounding the death of Dziekański. From the first report came numerous recommendations, including appropriate training and retraining on the proper use of CEWs, restricting their use to circumstances where a suspect's behaviour is imminently likely to cause bodily harm, and avoiding the repeated deployment of a CEW on a suspect in a single encounter. Additionally, Mr. Justice Braidwood suggested that the RCMP be required to comply with the policies and procedures with respect to CEWs applicable to provincially regulated law enforcement agencies.

In his second report, released in June 2010, Mr. Justice Braidwood was critical of the conduct of the police officers involved, suggesting that the tragic outcome could have been prevented. He recommended the establishment of an independent, civilian-based investigative agency to investigate police-involved deaths and incidents causing serious harm. In October 2011, the BC legislature introduced amendments to the *Police Act*, creating an Independent Investigation Office (IIO).

Sources: Braidwood (2009); Braidwood (2010).

discretion

The decision-making process and judgment police officers use when determining how best to deal with a situation they encounter. Other branches of the criminal justice system, including the courts and corrections, also have discretionary powers that can influence the outcome of cases.

Significantly, no system of laws or regulations prescribes how police officers should react in every possible scenario they might encounter in the field. Therefore, **discretion** plays a vital role in policing and permeates all aspects of the job. Decision-making responsibilities with respect to the use of force are important for the resolution of problems and disputes. Prominent factors influencing a police officer's discretion to take action include legal factors such as the seriousness of the crime and the strength of the evidence, as well as non-legal factors such as social class, sex, age, the characteristics of the neighbourhood, and the demeanour of the individual. As the seriousness of a police incident increases, the amount of discretion an officer can exercise decreases correspondingly. Indeed, police officers exercise a considerable amount of discretion in how to best resolve situations, and do so with little oversight or accountability for the decisions they make (MacAlister, 2012, p. 2).

Frameworks Justifying the Use of Force

Unquestionably, police have a duty to administer and enforce the law. As alluded to in the introduction, this duty entails, among other things, investigating alleged offences, apprehending offenders, and protecting life and property. It is reasonable that police officers should be granted special powers to use force, including deadly force, in meeting these obligations. The authority to use force comes from a number of sources, including the common law and various statutes (e.g., the *Criminal Code*, provincial and territorial police acts, and firearms regulations). The duties of the RCMP also originate from common law and are set out in s. 18 of the *Royal Canadian Mounted Police Act*. This Act states, among other things, that it is the duty of its members (i.e., peace officers) to engage in "the apprehension of criminals and offenders and others who may be lawfully taken into custody."[3]

The primary legal justification for the use of force, however, is found in s. 25 of the *Criminal Code*:

> Every one who is required or authorized by law to do anything in the administration or enforcement of the law ... is, if he acts on reasonable grounds, justified in doing what he is required or authorized to do and in using as much force as is necessary for that purpose.

This is a fairly broad and complicated provision. Subsection 1 creates a legal justification for individuals, including police officers, to use as much force as is necessary in the administration and enforcement of the law provided their actions are required or authorized and they act on reasonable grounds. Importantly, s. 25(3) places a limit on the powers granted in s. 25(1) by prohibiting force intended or likely to cause death or grievous bodily harm unless the officer has an **objectively reasonable** belief that the amount of force used is necessary for self-protection, or for safeguarding another person under the officer's protection, from death or grievous bodily harm.

However, s. 25(4) permits the police to use force that is intended or likely to cause death or grievous bodily harm to prevent a suspect from fleeing a lawful arrest (with or without a warrant), provided all the following requirements of the provision are met:

- The arrest must be lawful.
- The offence must be serious enough that the person could be arrested without warrant.
- The officer must reasonably believe the force is necessary to protect the officer or others from "imminent or future death or grievous bodily harm."
- The escape cannot be prevented by "reasonable means in a less violent manner."

Criminal offences for which no arrest warrant is required or for which a warrantless arrest is legal include:

- indictable offences
- persons escaping from lawful arrest
- persons whom a police officer finds committing a criminal offence.

objectively reasonable
Where a person's thoughts or actions, measured by the "objective standard" used in courts to establish criminal responsibility, are deemed to be those that a reasonable person would have in a similar situation.

Although s. 25 authorizes the police to use force, including lethal force, police officers who use force that is objectively excessive—that is, not reasonable under the circumstances—are subject to criminal liability under s. 26 of the *Criminal Code*. If the actions of the officer are found to be unreasonable or excessive, he or she may be criminally charged with assault pursuant to s. 265 of the *Criminal Code*. Similarly, if a police officer causes the death of a person in circumstances that are found not to meet the requirements of s. 25(3), (4), or (5), that officer may be charged with homicide.

Indeed, police officers are justified in using force if they act on reasonable grounds and use only as much force as is necessary. Notwithstanding that fact, the use-of-force provisions found in s. 25 are problematic because it is difficult to ascertain how much force is "reasonable" or "necessary." In an effort to clarify the level of force that is appropriate in the possible scenarios officers might encounter in the field, various police agencies have developed a "use of force model" to help guide them. These models serve as a standardized guideline, and they outline the various actions to consider in situations requiring the use of force.

Models of Police Use of Force

As you read the following, it is important to keep in mind that models are simplified ways of explaining complex processes, such as police use of force.

In Canada, models depicting use of force by police officers first appeared in the 1980s. While they proved helpful for training purposes, many concerns arose from their use, including the number of models in existence, inconsistent vocabulary/terminology, and varying approaches to the use of force by police agencies. As noted by Hoffman, Lawrence, and Brown (2004), these earlier models were generally rigid and represented a linear progressive decision-making process. Linear models were based on the assumption that all situations were unidirectional, following a path from soft approaches to intermediate weapons, culminating with use of lethal force. Research and experience demonstrated, however, that a linear approach did not reflect the dynamic nature of real-life police situations as effectively as the appropriate use-of-force response options did (p. 3).

Given the criticisms associated with linear models, law enforcement agencies subsequently developed versions that took into account the situations police officers encounter in their day-to-day activities. In 1993, Ontario developed the Ontario Use-of-Force Options Model, which "integrated both force options and a generic decision-making process summarized as 'assess-plan-act'" (Hoffman et al., 2004). The success of the Ontario model prompted a number of other provinces and the RCMP to follow suit.[4] In

April 1999, 65 use-of-force experts and trainers from Canada and the United States were brought together at the Ontario Police College to develop the National Use of Force Framework (NUFF). The CACP endorsed this national initiative in November 2000 as a framework from which law enforcement agencies across Canada could develop sound procedures and protocols for their own use-of-force standards (Braidwood, 2009, p. 94).

The National Use of Force Framework presented in Figure 4.1 is a standardized approach to conflict situations and represents the process by which an officer assesses, plans, and responds to a given situation.[5] Unlike the unidirectional linear models, this framework provides an element of

FIGURE 4.1   National Use of Force Framework

The officer continuously assesses the situation and acts in a reasonable manner to ensure officer and public safety.

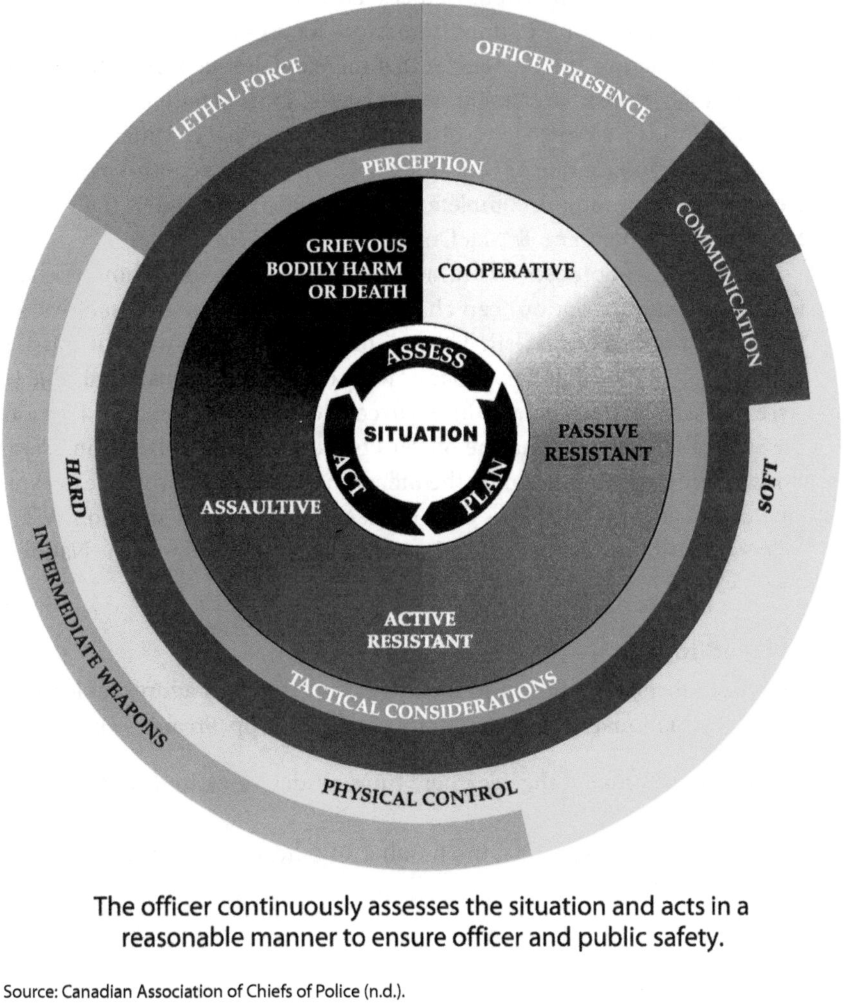

Source: Canadian Association of Chiefs of Police (n.d.).

proportionality between the situation and the police response. As discussed above, earlier models did not reflect the true nature of many real-life situations and assumed that police incidents progressed directly from minimal force to lethal force. In reality, situations may not follow this progression at all (MacAlister, 2010). For example, a situation may start out extremely violently without any buildup. Others may start out intensely, but de-escalate to where persons involved become cooperative. For this reason, linear models have been criticized for requiring an officer to move through the incremental progression one step at a time. This limits the use-of-force options available by restricting the tactical options when responding to a level of resistance/threat exhibited by a suspect. A unidirectional model also restricts the police officer's ability to de-escalate a given situation and resort to lower-level force options even though the circumstances have been reassessed.

Importantly, the force options framework focuses on the dynamic nature of a police situation and recognizes that there are unique factors that influence the officer's risk assessment. For example, some situations will require the use of little or no force to resolve conflict (i.e., verbal commands and the proximity of a police officer will suffice), whereas police control of combative situations may require complete incapacitation of the subject (i.e., deadly force) (Alpert, Dunham, & MacDonald, 2004, p. 475).

The assessment process is continuous and helps to "explain how a behaviour (and response option) can change from cooperative to assaultive (or from communication to lethal force) in a split-second without passing through any of the other behaviour or force options" (Hoffman et al., 2004). Assessing a situation requires officers to consider three factors: the situation, the subject's behaviour, and the officer's perception and tactical considerations. These components guide the officer in determining whether to escalate, de-escalate or, when possible, to disengage from the situation. What follows is an abbreviated examination of the key components of the National Use-of-Force Framework report.

A. The Situation

When an officer responds to an incident, he or she must address at least six different situational conditions (Braidwood, 2009, pp. 96 and 97):

1. Environment: the weather, time of day, location, and physical position.
2. Number of subjects: the number of officers versus the number of subjects.

3. Perception of subject's abilities: the subject's size, strength, and emotional state, proximity to weapons, and whether the subject is under the influence of drugs and/or alcohol.
4. Prior knowledge of subject: criminal history and reputation.
5. Time and distance: the level of threat to public safety, availability of cover, imminent arrival of backup, and ability to increase the distance.
6. Potential attack signs: possible physical behaviours that may give clues as to the subject's intentions (e.g., ignoring the officer, aggressive verbalization, refusing to comply with a lawful request, invasion of personal space, and hiding or fleeing).

Importantly, police incidents need to be scrutinized on a case-by-case basis, taking into account the situational factors, the behaviours of the individuals, the perceptions of the officers, and tactical considerations inherent in each context.

B. Subject's Behaviour

Under this model, there are five categories of resistance of individuals and associated behaviours:

1. Cooperative: the subject is compliant and responds positively to the officer's verbal commands.
2. Non-cooperative: the subject is non-compliant with the officer's lawful requests or commands. There is little or no physical resistance (e.g., failure to follow directions, refusal to leave the scene, taunting police officers).
3. Resistant: the subject actively resists an officer's lawful direction and uses non-assaultive physical action to resist or escape an officer's control (e.g., attempting to escape custody by fleeing).
4. Combative: the subject exhibits active and hostile resistance to an officer's lawful requests and attempts, threatens, or applies physical force with the intent to cause injury or resist (e.g., kicking, punching).
5. Showing the potential to cause grievous bodily harm or death: the subject's behaviour is threatening and the officer reasonably believes the subject's actions are intended to, or likely to, cause grievous bodily harm or death to the public or the officer (e.g., use of a firearm or knife).

C. Officer's Perceptions and Tactical Considerations

There are five categories of force response options that are available to police officers. The objective of the use-of-force model is to guide officers in their assessment of the situation, select a level of force that is appropriate to the circumstances, and to act in a reasonable manner to ensure officer and public safety. Given the dynamic nature of any situation, the force options selected may change at any point.

1. Officer presence: the presence of an officer, or visible signs of authority such as a uniform or marked police car, may change a subject's behaviour.
2. Communication: the use of verbal and non-verbal communication to control and/or resolve the situation.
3. Physical control: any physical technique, not involving the use of a weapon, is used to gain control. "Soft" techniques include joint locks, restraining techniques, and handcuffing. "Hard" techniques include empty-hand strikes such as punches, kicks, and strategic application of pressure (e.g., choke hold).
4. Intermediate weapons: these are less lethal weapons (not intended to cause serious injury or death), which include impact weapons (e.g., police baton, Taser) and aerosols (e.g., tear gas, pepper spray).
5. Lethal force: this involves the use of any weapons or techniques that are intended to, or are reasonably likely to, cause grievous bodily harm or death.

Although police officers are guided by the philosophy that the most successful police intervention is the one that results in the least amount of harm, police-related incidents involving the use of force "are typically dynamic, rapidly evolving, and often extremely violent in nature" (Butler & Hall, 2008, p. 142).

Police Wrongdoing and Accountability

For years, various accountability and complaints-process models have been employed in different jurisdictions around the world to investigate alleged police wrongdoing. As Table 4.1 illustrates, they range from marginal independence to complete independence by non-police agencies (MacAlister, 2012, p. 158). Throughout most of Canada, such allegations have historically been investigated by other police officers. These investigations have typically been conducted by Internal Affairs or Professional Standards units within the police organization directly involved in the alleged wrongdoing—

with investigative oversight by police officers from a neighbouring agency on occasion.

What Do You Think?

Should police agencies be investigating themselves? Do you agree with the underlying philosophy that police officers are in the best position to judge the actions of other officers taken in the field? Are police officers able to conduct impartial and neutral investigations into misconduct of their own?

Such was the case with the RCMP until 2010, when the agency announced a new national policy directive that would see all serious police-related incidents forwarded to outside agencies (Royal Canadian Mounted Police [RCMP], 2010).

Today, this internal investigative process remains prevalent among municipal police agencies in Quebec, New Brunswick, Prince Edward Island, and Newfoundland and Labrador, and in those jurisdictions that employ the RCMP (MacAlister, 2012, p. 158).

TABLE 4.1   Investigating Alleged Police Wrongdoing

Internal	Investigations carried out by officers from within the same agency
Quasi-internal	Investigations carried out by the same agency with investigative oversight by officers from another police agency
Hybrid-quasi internal	Investigations carried out by police from a nearby police agency
Hybrid	Investigations carried out by police from a nearby police agency under civilian oversight and/or control
Hybrid-quasi-external	Investigations carried out by a civilian-led agency using seconded police
Quasi-external	Investigations carried out by a civilian agency using seconded and civilian investigators
External	Investigations carried out by a civilian agency that is led and staffed by non-police civilians

Source: MacAlister (2010).

The underlying philosophy behind self-investigations is that police officers are the only persons who have the requisite expertise to undertake such investigations. This argument, however, has been shown to be unsound. In 2007, the Commission for Public Complaints Against the RCMP (CPC) initiated an inquiry into public concerns regarding the impartiality of RCMP members conducting criminal investigations into the activities of other RCMP members in cases involving serious injury or death. The CPC analyzed a total of 28 randomly selected cases alleged to have resulted in sexual assault, serious injury, or death between 2002 and 2007, taking into account the following criteria:

- conduct
- policy compliance
- timeliness
- line management
- level of response.

In its final report, *Police Investigating Police: Final Public Report* (2009), the CPC found that more than two-thirds of the cases were handled inappropriately. Although the commission recommended legislative, policy, procedural, and structural changes to improve criminal investigations into RCMP members, the report fell short of proposing a genuine independent civilian investigation model. Instead, the CPC recommended that other police agencies be used to investigate cases of police-involved deaths and other serious injury cases. The RCMP accepted these recommendations in early 2010 (RCMP, 2010).

The notion of police investigating themselves undoubtedly gives rise to legitimate concerns about conflict of interest, as well as concerns regarding the impartiality of investigators. As Mr. Justice Braidwood noted in his 2010 report (p. 411):

> Many members of the public perceive that the investigators may allow loyalty to fellow officers to interfere with the impartial investigative process. This perception, even if not justified in a given case, can lead to public distrust and an undermining of public confidence in the police.

Over the past 20 years, concerns over a perceived lack of objectivity and legitimacy have led to calls for reform and for the establishment of an independent regulatory framework to investigate incidents of alleged police misconduct. And, in an era of increased accountability, jurisdictions in some provinces have mandated civilian-led agencies to investigate incidents of police-related deaths and serious injuries. One of the central features of this regulatory framework is that impartial civilians who are independent of any police service or organization undertake these investigations; it is a civilian-managed and civilian-run process (MacAlister, 2010, p. 37).

In response to concerns about the police investigating themselves, Ontario has established the Special Investigations Unit (SIU). In existence since 1989, the SIU is a civilian oversight body charged with investigating incidents involving death and serious injury of members of the public arising in the course of police work. The SIU "seeks to protect the fundamental human rights of all its citizens by ensuring that those charged with enforcing the laws and advancing public safety remain accountable should they violate those rights" (Adams, 2003, p. 9). Similar civilian-led investigative bodies were recently established in Alberta (the Alberta Serious Incident Response Team), Manitoba (Independent Investigative Unit), and Nova Scotia (Serious Incident Response Team).

Over the past decade, British Columbia has witnessed a number of high-profile cases involving serious allegations of police misconduct, including several police-involved deaths. Notwithstanding these allegations, the province has been slow to react to the legislative developments in other jurisdictions. Though calls for far-reaching reforms of the police complaints and investigation process emerged as early as 1994, the BC government is only now implementing those recommendations. In May of 2011, BC's minister of justice and attorney general, Shirley Bond, introduced Bill 12 into the Legislative Assembly to amend the *Police Act* in order to create an Independent Investigation Office (IIO).

Accountable to the Ministry of Justice, the IIO is mandated to investigate all police-related incidents occurring throughout the province of British Columbia that involve the serious injury or death of an individual. This agency's jurisdiction also extends to alleged contraventions of a "prescribed provision" in federal or provincial legislation. The IIO has jurisdiction over both municipal police and the RCMP operating in the province.[6] A civilian director heads this new investigative organization, and while the legislation allows for the hiring of former police officers as investigators, the goal is that within five years none of the investigators working in the unit will have a background in policing. The overall aim of the IIO is to create more accountability, oversight, and transparency of police incidents that result in death or serious injury, as well as to enhance public confidence in policing.

Conclusion

The enactment of the *Canadian Charter of Rights and Freedoms* has had a profound impact on our adversarial system of criminal justice. Indeed, the legal rights provisions set out in ss. 7–14 of the Charter protect individuals from abuses of state power throughout the criminal investigative process, while ensuring fairness during subsequent legal proceedings. Passage of the Charter was a watershed moment in human rights and civil liberties history. It also marked a dramatic transformation in the Canadian legal landscape, with a shift away from crime control and the perceived needs of law enforcement to an emphasis on due process values and the rights of individual citizens. On the one hand, some have argued that the police have become constrained by legislation, which has limited the powers police officers seemingly require to effectively carry out their law enforcement mandate. On the other hand, the Charter can be seen as a system of procedural checks and balances, among other things, that has influenced police decision-making processes and how police officers approach law enforcement more generally. Essentially, the police are not given carte blanche during criminal investigations, but, as we have seen throughout this chapter, there is common-law authority as well as statutory provisions granting the police powers to carry out their duties effectively, including more intrusive investigative techniques where there are reasonable grounds to deploy them.

The Charter's passage has dramatically transformed Canada's legal landscape.

As Gérald Lafrenière (2001, p. 1) points out in a paper prepared for the Senate Special Committee on Illegal Drugs:

> It is clear that the arrival of the Charter and the individual rights and freedoms that it protects has allowed the courts to play an even greater role in defining permissible boundaries of police conduct. In determining whether police conduct is acceptable, one is generally forced to weigh conflicting interests. First, there are the individual's interests, including the interest of being free from state intrusion. Second, there are the state's interests, including protecting society from crime. Because these interests generally conflict, it can sometimes be difficult to agree on where the line should be drawn in relation to police conduct.

Since the inception of the Charter 30 years ago, the courts have sought to delicately balance the competing interests of the state and the individual. This has not been an easy task, as Canada's highest court "has taken inherently conflicting positions in cases that pit police investigative powers against Charter rights" (Stribopoulos, 2005, para. 6). This approach highlights the key issues and tensions inherent in the competing models of criminal justice alluded to in Chapter 1.

There is no doubt that the police require powers to maintain law and order in our society. Both Parliament and the courts have recognized the difficulty in detecting crime, enforcing the law, and protecting society while, at the same time, safeguarding individuals from abuses of state power. The struggle to find a compromise between competing imperatives such as the rights of the individual and the integrity of the administration of justice is sure to continue in years to come.

DISCUSSION QUESTIONS

1. What sections of the Charter have an effect on the law regarding detention and arrest in Canada?
2. On what grounds can a police officer stop an individual for an investigative detention? Provide an example of a situation that might be considered a detention and circumstances that would not be viewed as a detention for investigative purposes.
3. Under what circumstances can a police officer arrest someone without a warrant?
4. It's garbage day and you have placed your trash cans at the edge of your residential property for collection. Can a police officer reach a few inches over the property line in order to retrieve items from the cans? Is this a breach of your s. 8 Charter right to be secure against unreasonable search or seizure? If the police seize incriminating evidence from your trash cans, should that evidence be excluded in accordance with s. 24(2) of the Charter?
5. Should evidence that has been improperly or illegally seized by the police during a search be automatically excluded from trial?
6. Police officers are authorized to conduct warrantless searches when an individual voluntarily consents to the search. What are the guidelines for establishing whether voluntary consent was given?
7. What is the National Use of Force Framework?
8. What are two criticisms of the linear, unidirectional models depicting the use of force?

NOTES

I would like to thank Joan Brockman and David MacAlister for their valuable comments and suggestions on an earlier draft of this chapter.

1. Section 487.1 allows a person seeking a search warrant to obtain one by means of telecommunication where it is impracticable for the peace officer to appear personally to make the application.
2. See Keenan and Brockman (2010) for an analysis of how wiretap authorizations are obtained in undercover operations, such as the Mr. Big investigative technique.
3. See *R. v. L.S.L.* (1991).

4. The RCMP uses the Incident Management Intervention Model (IM/IM), which is similar to the one represented here.
5. In addition, Griffiths (2013, p. 147) notes how the model "provides police administrators and judicial review personnel with an objective framework for analyzing use-of-force situations."
6. Section 38.01 of the *Police Act* defines "officer" and "police service" as including the RCMP.

SUGGESTED FURTHER READINGS

Braidwood, T. (2010). *Why? The Robert Dziekanski tragedy*. Vancouver: Braidwood Commission on the Death of Robert Dziekanski.

Brockman, J., & Rose, V.G. (2011). *An introduction to Canadian criminal procedure and evidence* (4th ed.). Toronto: Nelson.

Cameron, J. (1996). *The Charter's impact on the criminal justice system*. Scarborough, ON: Carswell.

Davies, W.H. (Commissioner). (2011). *Alone and cold: Criminal Justice Branch response—Davies commission inquiry into the response of the Criminal Justice Branch (B.C.)*. Victoria: Davies Commission.

Griffiths, C.T. (2013). *Canadian criminal justice: A primer* (4th ed.). Toronto: Nelson.

Hoffman, R., Lawrence, C., & Brown, G. (2004). Canada's national use-of-force framework for police officers. *The Police Chief, 71*, 125–141.

Kennedy, P. (2009). *Police investigating police: Final public report*. Ottawa: Commission for Public Complaints Against the RCMP.

Wood, J. (2007). *Report on the review of the police complaint process in British Columbia*. Victoria: Government of British Columbia.

REFERENCES

Adams, G.W. (2003). *Review report on the Special Investigations Unit reforms prepared for the Attorney General of Ontario by the Honourable George W. Adams, Q.C.* Toronto: Ministry of the Attorney General.

Alpert, G.P., Dunham, R.G., & MacDonald, J.M. (2004). Interactive police-citizen encounters that result in force. *Police Quarterly, 7*, 475–488.

Bittner, E. (1970). *The functions of police in modern society*. Washington, DC: Government Printing Office.

Braidwood, T. (2009). *Restoring public confidence: Restricting the use of conducted energy weapons in British Columbia*. Vancouver: Braidwood Commission on the Death of Robert Dziekanski.

Braidwood, T. (2010). *Why? The Robert Dziekanski tragedy*. Vancouver: Braidwood Commission on the Death of Robert Dziekanski.

Brockman, J., & Rose, V.G. (2011). *An introduction to Canadian criminal procedure and evidence* (4th ed.). Toronto: Nelson.

Butler, C., & Hall, C. (2008). Police/public interaction: Arrests, use of force by police, and resulting injuries to subjects and officers—A description of risk in one major Canadian city. *Law Enforcement Executive Forum*, 8, 141–157.

Canadian Association of Chiefs of Police (CACP). (n.d.). National use of force model. Retrieved from http://www.cacp.ca/media/aboutus/ policyguidelines/10/National_Use_of_Force_Framework.pdf

Davies, W.H. (Commissioner). (2011). *Alone and cold: Criminal Justice Branch response—Davies commission inquiry into the response of the Criminal Justice Branch (B.C.)*. Victoria: Davies Commission.

Griffiths, C.T. (2013). *Canadian police work* (3rd ed.). Toronto: Nelson.

Hoffman, R., Lawrence, C., & Brown, G. (2004). *Canada's national use-of-force framework for police officers*. Document no. 575175. Alexandria, VA: International Association of Chiefs of Police. Retrieved from http://www.policechiefmagazine.org/magazine/index.cfm?fuseaction =display_arch&article_id=1397&issue_id=102004

Keenan, K.T., & Brockman, J. (2010). *Mr. Big: Exposing undercover investigations in Canada*. Halifax: Fernwood.

Lafrenière, G. (2001). Police powers and drug-related offences. Prepared for the Senate Special Committee on Illegal Drugs. Ottawa: Library of Parliament. Retrieved from http://www.parl.gc.ca/Content/SEN/Committee/371/ille/ library/powers-e.htm

Latimer, S. (2007). The expanded scope of search incident to investigative detention. *Criminal Reports*, 48, 201.

MacAlister, D. (2010). *Police-involved deaths: The failure of self-investigation final report*. Vancouver: British Columbia Civil Liberties Association.

MacAlister, D. (2012). Policing the police in Canada: Alternative approaches to the investigation of serious police wrongdoing. In D. MacAlister (Ed.), *Police-involved deaths: The need for reform* (pp. 158–191). Vancouver: British Columbia Civil Liberties Association.

Manning, P.K. (1977). *Police work: The social organization of policing*. Cambridge, MA: MIT Press.

Murphy, C., & McKenna, P. (2007). *Rethinking police governance, culture and management*. Ottawa: Public Safety Canada. Retrieved from http://www.publicsafety.gc.ca/rcmp-grc/_fl/eng/rthnk-plc-eng.pdf

Royal Canadian Mounted Police (RCMP). (2010). *RCMP announces new policy on external investigations*. Retrieved from http://www.rcmp-grc.gc.ca/ news-nouvelles/2010/02-04-external-externe-eng.htm

Stribopoulos, J. (2005). In search of dialogue: The Supreme Court, police powers and the Charter. *Queen's Law Journal*, 31, 1–74.

Walma, M.W., and West, L. (2001). *Police powers and procedures*. Toronto: Emond Montgomery.

Legislation

Canadian Charter of Rights and Freedoms, part I of the *Constitution Act, 1982*,
    being Schedule B to the *Canada Act 1982* (UK), 1982, c. 11.
Controlled Drugs and Substances Act, SC 1996, c. 19.
Criminal Code, RSC 1985, c. C-46.
Highway Traffic Act, RSO 1990, c. H.8.
Police Act, RSBC 1996, c. 367.
Royal Canadian Mounted Police Act, RSC 1985, c. R-10.
Safe Streets and Communities Act, SC 2012, c. 1.

Cases

Cloutier v. Langlois, [1990] 1 SCR 158.
Eccles v. Bourque et al., [1975] 2 SCR 739.
Hunter et al. v. Southam Inc. (1984), 14 CCC (3d) 97 (SCC).
R. v. Bartle, [1994] 3 SCR 173.
R. v. Borden, [1994] 3 SCR 145.
R. v. Brydges, [1990] 1 SCR 190.
R. v. Evans, [1996] 1 SCR 8.
R. v. Feeney, [1997] 2 SCR 13.
R. v. Godoy, [1999] 1 SCR 311.
R. v. Golden, [2001] 3 SCR 679.
R. v. Joseph, [2000] BCJ No. 2800.
R. v. Kokesch, [1990] 3 SCR 3.
R. v. L.S.L., [1991] SJ No. 30 (QB).
R. v. Mann, [2004] 3 SCR 59.
R. v. Morelli, [2010] 1 SCR 253.
R. v. Stillman, [1997] 1 SCR 607.
R. v. Storrey, [1990] 1 SCR 241.
R. v. Therens, [1985] 1 SCR 613.
R. v. Unger (1993), 83 CCC (3d) 228 (BCCA).
R. v. Wills, 70 CCC (3d) 529 (Ont. CA).
Semayne's Case (1604), 5 Co. Rep. 91a.

PART THREE
The Law, Courts, and Procedures

Robert Pickton

Karla O'Regan

A padlocked gate at Robert Pickton's BC pig farm
Source: PNG Library.

Few Canadian crimes have been as gruesome and horrifying as those of Robert Pickton. In 1998, the *Vancouver Sun* began to publish reports of missing women in a Vancouver neighbourhood known as the Downtown Eastside. This region, sometimes referred to as Canada's "poorest postal code," is notorious for its epidemic levels of drug use and trafficking, as well as for its poverty, its sex trade, and its criminal violence. It is also well known for the many forms of social activism that flourish there, including the community-based policing efforts of a specialized Vancouver police team known as the "Odd Squad," chronicled in the film *Through a Blue Lens* (1999). The *Sun*'s news coverage revealed that more than 60 women were missing. It identified many of them as sex trade workers, some as having drug addiction problems, and more than half as being Aboriginal. The media coverage raised serious questions about the effectiveness of Canada's criminal law and its enforcement.

In early 2002, police responded to a tip that a pig farmer, Robert Pickton, had a collection of illegal firearms on his farm in Port Coquitlam, BC. While executing a search warrant for the firearms, police discovered a series of personal items belonging to some of the missing women, including an asthma inhaler, some running shoes, and a necklace. Police used this evidence to obtain a second search warrant that enabled officers to investigate Pickton's farm further. In the course of this search, they uncovered human remains that matched the DNA of many of the missing women. Pickton was subsequently charged with 27 counts of first-degree murder. Forensic teams were sent out to the farm to excavate and search for further evidence. Their discoveries more aptly resembled a horror film than reality. There were severed hands and feet, jawbones, and skulls, some of them buried, some in freezer buckets, and others decomposing in garbage pails. Forensic evidence also suggested that Pickton had used his butchering equipment on the farm to dispose of the bodies, grinding them with pork meat, in some cases, for resale, and, in other instances, using them for pig feed (Cameron, 2007). The forensic investigation of the Pickton farm took more than two years and encompassed a huge geographic area; it concerned the deaths of almost 50 victims and involved interviewing more than 1,000 witnesses, making it the largest forensic inquiry in Canadian history.

During Pickton's preliminary inquiry, evidence was presented that in 1997 he had been charged with attempted murder after stabbing a female sex worker whom he had taken back to the farm with him; she subsequently escaped. The Crown later **stayed** this charge after determining that the victim, because of her drug addiction problems, would not be a credible witness. However, when Pickton was arrested on this charge, the clothes and rubber boots he had been wearing that night were seized into evidence. In 2004, during preparatory investigations for Pickton's first-degree murder trial, forensic testing was performed on these items. This testing revealed the DNA of two of the missing women. Although Pickton's lawyer attempted to have this evidence excluded from the trial, the judge allowed its admission. The judge did allow an application by Pickton's defence team to **sever the counts** in his indictment from 27 to 6. He did so on the grounds that one of the victims listed in the indictment ("Jane Doe") could not be identified (only one rib bone and half a skull were found by forensic teams) and that a trial for 26 first-degree murder charges would go on too long for a jury to reasonably consider. Pickton's trial proceeded on six counts of first-degree murder for the victims whose evidence was most similar. In December 2007, a jury convicted Pickton of six counts of second-degree murder, and he was

stayed In the context of a legal case, this term refers to a "stay" of proceedings, which means that the court has effectively "paused" or suspended the case. A stay can be for a particular time period (e.g., until a witness can be found) or for an indefinite period. The Crown may start the proceedings again at any time, provided the time limit for doing so has not expired. In law, this time period is called a "statute of limitations." In criminal law, there is no such limitation on indictable offences. Where a stay of proceedings has been granted, the accused is free to go (until such time as the case is begun again—if it ever is).

severance In criminal law, "severance" refers either to the "cutting away" of some charges from a multi-count indictment or to the separation of defendants in a joint trial so that each accused has to proceed with her case individually.

sentenced two days later to 25 years in jail with no possibility for parole—the maximum available sentence.

The Pickton case enables us to put in context many of the issues discussed in the following chapters, including the difference between charges of first- and second-degree murder. Pickton's lawyers attempted to argue that either someone else had committed the murders or that Pickton had not acted alone, raising the question of "reasonable doubt" with respect to his criminal responsibility. Chapter 5 will help you to think about these defences in greater detail; it examines the history of Canadian criminal law with a view to showing how offences are classified, what types of defences are available to an accused, and what discretionary powers key decision-makers in Canada's criminal law can exercise during a criminal trial. Often, when criminal cases are reported in the news, readers have the impression that offenders have benefited from a "technicality." Certainly, many people felt that this was the case when Pickton's charges were dropped from 27 to 6. This came about during the preliminary inquiry, when it was decided that a 27-count indictment would be too onerous on a jury and would thereby interfere with the "interests of justice." Chapter 6 examines these matters of criminal procedure—for example, the preliminary inquiry, the jury-selection process, and some of the Charter rights often raised during a criminal trial—in greater depth, with a view to showing how these "technicalities" are the bedrock for many of the civil protections that make Canada one of the world's leaders in human rights. The media's coverage of the Pickton case focused largely on the discoveries made by forensic teams, and this aspect of the case will help illustrate Chapter 7's discussion of forensic science and evidence collection. Chapter 8 will provide the necessary background for thinking critically about Pickton's sentence and the factors the court needed to consider when determining it.

The Pickton case highlighted a number of legal, procedural, and forensic technicalities, but it also drew attention to what criminologists might term the "extralegal" components of Canada's criminal justice system. All of Pickton's victims and each of the more than 60 missing women from Vancouver's Downtown Eastside were sex-trade workers, and many of them were Aboriginal. News reports of the growing numbers of victims and the public commentary on these reports underscored the great vulnerability of these marginalized women. Many charged that the failure of police to adequately investigate these disappearances was linked to systemic forms of racism and sexism (Jiwani & Young, 2006). In its *Review Report* (2010) of the case, the Vancouver Police Department characterized the investigation as a failure in certain respects. The police report also acknowledged that sex-trade workers had suffered multiple incidents of prejudice during the course of the investigation. However, unlike many critics of the case, the Vancouver police dismissed the idea that bias was behind the investigation's missteps.

The Pickton case renewed debates about the criminalization of prostitution. It exposed the very real dangers of a prohibited sex trade that forces individuals to work in isolated areas where they are vulnerable to violence and abuse. These dangers were recognized in the 2012 landmark Ontario Court of Appeal case *Bedford v. Canada*, which ruled that a number of the *Criminal Code*'s prohibitions against prostitution were unconstitutional. Similarly, the stereotypes associated with prostitution and drug use can further marginalize these victims, moving incidents of violence and abduction outside the attention of police, community activists, and social outreach programs.

What Do You Think?

1. A lot of public debate occurred when Pickton's indictment was severed, leaving him to stand trial for only 6 of the 27 murders with which he was originally charged. One of the main reasons the indictment was severed was that 27 counts were thought to be too onerous on a jury. Using the information you learn in Chapter 6 as a guide, do you agree with this decision? What other options were available to the Crown?

2. Chapter 7 discusses the collection of forensic evidence. What specific challenges do you think the Pickton case created for forensic teams? Imagine that you are a member of the forensic unit sent to the Pickton farm to collect evidence. What are some of the first things you would do or need to know upon arriving?

3. Does the fact that all of Pickton's victims were poor, shared a gender and an occupation, and suffered social discrimination for their addictions and racial backgrounds suggest that further inquiries are needed into how the criminal law, the police, the court system, and the media respond to (or ignore) these "extralegal" factors?

REFERENCES

Barna, L. (Executive Producer). (2010). *Pig farm* [documentary film]. Toronto: CTV.

Cameron, S. (2007). *The Pickton file*. Toronto: Knopf Canada.

Jiwani, Y., & and Young, M.L. (2006). Missing and murdered women: Reproducing marginality in news discourse. *Canadian Journal of Communication*, 31(4), 895–917.

LePard, D. (Deputy Chief Constable). (2010). *Missing women investigation review*. Vancouver: Vancouver Police Department.

The History and Structure of Criminal Law

LEARNING OBJECTIVES

After reading this chapter, students will be able to:

- Understand the key concepts, rules, and principles that structure Canadian criminal law.
- Understand the governmental institutions that create and administer criminal law and how these institutions relate to each other.
- Understand how criminal law and process develop in relation to changing social values, needs, and expectations.
- Appreciate how collective historical experience with diversity and cooperation inform responses to contemporary challenges.
- Constructively apply these conceptual and analytical tools when engaging with particular cases and issues.

Introduction

To properly understand the history and structure of Canadian criminal law, it is necessary to distinguish between criminal *law* and criminal *process*. Substantive criminal law is based in common—or judge-made—law, the *Criminal Code* (and other statutes), and the Constitution. Through the judgments of trial and appeal (or appellate) courts, substantive criminal law crystallizes into *doctrine*, providing judges with a rich variety of time-honoured rules and principles to be applied to each new case.

Criminal process, by contrast, describes the social and political *contexts* within which government and non-government actors collectively produce and administer **substantive criminal law**. Criminal process involves such matters as the composition and jurisdiction of criminal courts; the respective roles of judges, juries, and lawyers; the legislative process; the means by

substantive criminal law
Statutory and common law that prohibits undesirable conduct and that prescribes punishment for specific offences.

which judges review the constitutionality of criminal law statutes; and how local communities bring their values, interests, and expectations to bear on official decision making.

Although in some sense fixed and predetermined, substantive criminal law assumes its full meaning only when it is interpreted and applied in concrete social and historical settings (Roach, 2009, p. 3). The unique facts of a case, changing moral perspectives, media coverage, and community involvement all influence how laws are produced and administered. Equally, however, **precedent**, logic, and constitutional principles such as individual rights, procedural fairness, and the rule of law affect the speed and direction of legal change. If constructed properly, substantive criminal law can both keep pace with changing social contexts and remain anchored in fundamental values that deserve to be protected and promoted.

precedent

In common-law legal systems, an authoritative rule or principle established in a prior case that subsequent courts are obligated to apply in future cases.

The purpose of this chapter is to provide a brief overview of the history and structure of criminal law, showing that courts, Parliament, and local communities collectively shape legal doctrine and process to better reflect enduring democratic values. The chapter begins with an introduction to the social and political context of pre-Confederation criminal law and process, focusing on the three primary sources of criminal law. What follows is a discussion about pre-Confederation criminal law and how it is linked with common law; the codification of criminal law in the post-Confederation era; and criminal law and process in the Charter era. As you read through it, keep in mind the Pickton case study that preceded this chapter, and how the issues raised therein can be examined in terms of the broader themes discussed in this chapter.

Criminal Law in Historical Context

As mentioned, there are three primary sources of criminal law:

- the Canadian Constitution
- the *Criminal Code* and other statutes enacted by Parliament
- the common law.

These sources are hierarchically structured, with the Constitution standing as the supreme law of the land, overriding any law with which it conflicts. Statutes prevail over **common law** and are currently the sole source of criminal offences. The common law is judge-made law rooted in the historical customs of local communities as well as in principles of reason inherited from medieval courts, or "assizes," in England (Blackstone, 2001).

common law

Law that is developed by judges when deciding cases, rather than through legislative enactments.

The importance of these sources of criminal law has varied significantly over the years. The Constitution was created through an act of British Parliament only in 1867, as part of Canadian Confederation, which saw various colonial governments and territories integrated into the Dominion of Canada. Before Confederation, there was no autonomous national government effectively controlling the vast expanses of what would ultimately become Canada. In fact, between the 16th century and most of the 19th century, political and legal authorities were divided among several governments, including England, France, and other European powers; colonial governments; informal settler communities; and indigenous nations. Within such a context, there could be no single constitution or uniform set of criminal laws applicable across the land.

However, the absence of both a national constitution and criminal code did not mean that there was no criminal law. Local communities created their own customs and norms in relative autonomy from outside political influences. Indigenous nations, for example, had developed sophisticated political and legal orders long before Europeans arrived in North America. Cast in oral rather than written form, indigenous criminal law was nonetheless remarkably similar to European criminal law in form and in substance (Llewellyn & Hoebel, 1941). These communities administered criminal justice through recognized judicial, legislative, and policing authorities, and employed legal concepts held in common by many European nations. Similarities in substantive law covered such areas as the classification of criminal offences (e.g., homicide, theft, assault), criminal defences (e.g., provocation, mistake of fact, extreme intoxication), and sentencing principles (e.g., deterrence, rehabilitation, restitution).

Settlers brought with them European legal traditions as they established colonies. Those from New France, for example, relied on French legal traditions, as well as the moral and religious authority of the Catholic Church up to and even following their conquest at the hands of the British in 1763 (Hay, 1981). Similarly, British settlers relied on the principles and processes of English criminal law. British colonies were officially constituted by "letters patent," written instructions issued by the Crown, that outlined what substantive laws would be binding and how the criminal justice system would be administered (Mewett & Manning, 1994, pp. 3–33). Colonies were authorized to establish their own legislatures, which were responsible to those eligible to vote. Legislatures quickly began issuing distinctive criminal laws and processes designed to suit local conditions. British nationals who occupied unsettled territory, meanwhile, were considered to be governed by English common law and statutory law wherever they travelled, so that such law preceded the consolidation of complete political power in remote regions (Mewett & Manning, 1994, p. 3).

Canadian Provinces

Although it stood as a guiding framework for the development of local laws within each colony, European criminal law was quickly replaced or radically altered by local laws. Legislators in Nova Scotia, for example, modelled their criminal legal order on English criminal law statutes as they stood in 1497, but largely ignored statutory law enacted after this date (Brown, 1989, p. 57). Local courts, however, would refer to developing English law when deciding cases, thus contributing to a highly pluralistic legal order rooted in local and European legislative provisions. New Brunswick did almost nothing to codify its substantive criminal law, leaving this task to courts for much of its early history (Brown, p. 51). Populated by Loyalists who fled the United States following the American Revolution, New Brunswick's courts and lawyers borrowed heavily from American statutory and common law, although its legislature did consolidate its criminal laws in conformity with English law in the mid-19th century (Brown, pp. 42, 49–50).

The provinces of Upper Canada (Ontario) and Lower Canada (Quebec) similarly used English law as a guiding framework that was frequently adjusted to suit local conditions. The Parliament of Upper Canada, established in 1791, did not issue any statutes regarding substantive criminal law until 1800, at which point it incorporated English criminal law as it stood in 1792. Given its rich and diverse cultural history, Lower Canada was able to rely on an intricate blend of English, French, and North American law. English-speaking residents had control over Parliament and the courts, ensuring that English common and statutory law would be used for criminal prosecutions—a practice the British Parliament officially sanctioned through the *Quebec Act of 1774*. However, *les Canadiens* (descendants of French colonists who populated New France) rarely interacted with official laws and institutions. Owing to various factors—linguistic barriers; exclusion from the legal profession, the judiciary, and other important positions; distrust of English officials; and a preference for French perspectives on crime—*les Canadiens* pursued informal means of administering criminal justice, such as through traditional religious authorities and unofficial tribunals (Hay, 1981).

In 1841, Britain merged Upper Canada and Lower Canada into a united Province of Canada. It stipulated that the laws of the two jurisdictions would continue "in those Parts of the Province of *Canada* which now constitute the said Provinces respectively" (*Union Act, 1840*). Unlike Lower Canada, Upper Canada had made significant changes to both substantive criminal law and to penal codes, much as Nova Scotia and New Brunswick had. The result was that the bases of criminal liability, criminal process, and sentencing varied greatly within a single jurisdiction. Consequently, an accused could receive a comparatively light sentence, or even be acquitted, depending on where the trial was held, not on what the individual had done.

Canada's geographic size and location also inhibited the creation of a uniform criminal legal order. Unlike indigenous criminal law, English criminal law is primarily written. The costs and risks associated with shipping statutes, consolidated law books, and case law spanning five centuries of English history across the Atlantic were prohibitive, so only a few wealthy legislators, lawyers, and judges could keep up with developing English law. In the absence of well-stocked law libraries, practitioners in provinces such as New Brunswick and Upper Canada found it cheaper and easier to purchase law books from the United States. Others chose to focus on small but growing case law generated by the decisions of local courts, which greatly simplified legal education, but also reduced general knowledge of developing English law. For similar reasons, the majority of lawyers in these provinces had little to no formal training in traditional English (continuing) educational or professional institutions, such as the Inns of Court, located in London, England. Consequently, each colony not only chose for itself what to criminalize, but also how to organize and structure the criminal process, including the selection and training of criminal lawyers, and the composition and jurisdiction of courts (Brown, 1989).

In sum, the division of political authority and geographic realities meant that pre-Confederation criminal law was highly decentralized and fragmented. This is not to say it was dysfunctional or ineffective. On the contrary, these origins helped contribute to principles of respect for regional, linguistic, and ethnocultural diversity that have come to characterize Canadian multiculturalism. They also reaffirmed the important connections between criminal law and community values and identities. Still, by the 19th century, the British government was keen to consolidate its power and to contain the expansionist tendencies of revolutionary America. Slowly but surely, it began the process of Confederation, with criminal law standing as one of the most potent symbols of its power and a means of cultivating national unity.

Criminal law was a potent, unifying tool in the process of Confederation.

Balancing Unity and Diversity in Law

Pre-Confederation Criminal Law and the Common-Law Ideal

For at least two reasons, the common law was just the sort of approach that was called for in this pluralistic historical context. First, it is rooted in strong claims about the universality of those principles that constitute substantive criminal law. In fact, the common law is so called precisely because it contains legal principles held by virtually all communities (Blackstone, 2001). Many hoped that the logic of the common law could be used to tether diverse

FIGURE 5.1   Hierarchy of Courts

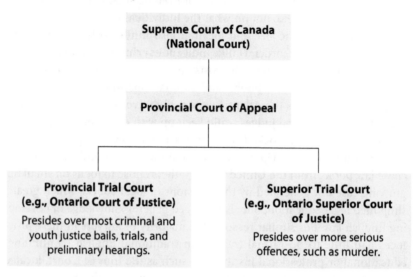

Canadian legal orders into a uniform, national legal system, much as it was supposed to have done among the Irish, Scottish, Welsh, and English in Britain (Pollock, 1912). Second, since common law is judge-made law, its operation would require a functioning, national court system. This, in turn, would help harmonize the criminal processes of the various political communities. But could the common law achieve these goals?

Essentially, common law is a body of law rooted in judicial decisions rather than legislative or constitutional provisions. One of the cardinal principles of common law is that it is unfair to treat similar cases differently. This principle helps to ensure that the law is relatively fixed and predetermined—that is, it ensures the rule of law. In theory, uniformity is achieved through the operation of *stare decisis*, which is the legal principle that judges are obliged to respect the precedents established by earlier decisions. *Stare decisis* is enforced by appellate courts; they review the decisions of lower trial courts and their rulings are considered to be binding. Thus, if a lower court refuses to follow precedent or makes an error interpreting past decisions, appellate courts can correct the error.

stare decisis
A legal principle by which judges are obliged to respect and apply legal principles established by prior decisions.

rule of law
The principle that all political authority must be exercised in accordance with fixed and predetermined legal rules and principles.

The Rule of Law

The **rule of law** is a legal maxim that requires political power to be exercised in accordance with pre-existing legal principles and rules. It stipulates that no person—not even the socially, politically, or economically powerful—is above the law. It also ensures a certain measure of equality between the governed and those doing the governing. On the one hand, clear, fixed, and predetermined rules enable us to know what our rights and obligations are ahead of time, so that we may adjust our behaviour accordingly. On the other hand, government officials must give notice to citizens that a law will be changed and that it is being done for public, rather than personal, reasons. To protect the rule of law, there are judicial institutions, such as courts, that are authorized to settle disputes about the content, scope, and applicability of legal rules. The following is a list of some of the principles associated with the rule of law:

- Laws should be prospective rather than retroactive.
- Laws should be stable and resistant to frequent or arbitrary change, especially by individual state officials.
- There should be clear rules and procedures for making laws.
- The independence of the judiciary is to be guaranteed.
- Principles of natural justice should be observed, particularly those concerning the right to a fair hearing.
- Courts should have the power of **judicial review** to ensure that the government complies with the law.
- Courts should be accessible to the public.
- The discretion of law enforcement and crime prevention agencies should be exercised in accordance with fixed and pre-determined rules.

judicial review
The process by which judges scrutinize laws, policies, and governmental practices to ensure their consistency with the Constitution, including the *Charter of Rights and Freedoms*.

What Do You Think?

In looking at the principles associated with the rule of law, can you think of any examples where socially, politically, or economically powerful individuals have received different treatment on any one of these principles within the Canadian court system? How did this happen?

Basic Principles of Common Law

One of the most enduring myths associated with common law is that judicial decisions derive their authority from universal principles of reason that are illuminated by the particular facts of a case (Blackstone, 2001). Common-law reasoning is in this sense "inductive"; that is, judges' collective experiences working through recurring social problems gradually produce a small set of reasonable and sustainable solutions in the form of decisions. These decisions then stand as precedent, or authoritative guides, for judges faced with

The Structure of Canada's Courts

Each province and territory in Canada has, accordingly, a "provincial" or "territorial" court that presides over most criminal and youth justice bails, trials, and preliminary hearings. Within Ontario, for example, this court is known as the Ontario Court of Justice; in British Columbia, it is known as the British Columbia Provincial Court. Despite differences in name, the overall structure and function of all provincial courts are the same. Each province, on the advice of a judicial appointments advisory committee, appoints judges to these courts.

More serious criminal matters (murder, international crime, and so on) are directed to "superior" courts that are administered by each province. Ontario's is the Ontario Superior Court of Justice, whereas British Columbia refers to its superior court as the British Columbia Supreme Court. Each province also has an "appellate" court that hears appeals from both provincial and superior courts. The decisions of these appellate courts are binding on all courts within a province, but not on courts in any other province or jurisdiction. So, for example, the Ontario Court of Appeal can overrule decisions of the Ontario Superior Court of Justice, but not those of the BC Supreme Court. The federal government appoints judges to superior and appellate courts in all provinces.

The Supreme Court of Canada is the highest court in the land and the final court of appeal. As a national court, its decisions are binding throughout all provinces and territories. The Supreme Court is composed of judges appointed by the prime minister and is looked to as a source of guidance, clarity, and innovation in the Canadian criminal justice system. (See also Figure 5.1 on page 140.)

Source: Supreme Court of Canada, www.scc-csc.gc.ca.

similar problems in the future. Much as in science, the accumulation of decisions can be used to create general theories of justice that help us understand the world within which we live and how to make it better (think back to Chapter 1, in which the main models and philosophies of justice were described).

And so the British considered the common law indispensable to constructing a unified Canada out of disparate colonies. Crafted out of universal principles, the common law could be transplanted from England to North

America and still operate according to the same essential logic; the colonies would be part of one overarching system. To ensure this, colonies were to establish a court system and a legal profession predicated on common-law principles and institutions. Moreover, the decisions of local courts could be appealed to appellate courts in England, which helped enhance coherence between colonial and English jurisprudence. In 1875, Canada created the Supreme Court of Canada and sought to abolish appeals to English courts. In 1926, however, the Judicial Committee of the Privy Council—one of the highest courts in Britain—ruled that its authority to review the decisions of Canadian courts could not be removed by an act of Canadian Parliament. The Supreme Court of Canada's status as the court of last resort for criminal matters took effect in 1933, after Britain passed the *Statute of Westminster,* 1931.

An example of uniformity can be found in the common-law principle that no one may be punished for criminal acts unless he or she is morally blameworthy (Coke, 1809)—a fact to be determined during the course of a fair and public trial. This principle is secured through the two basic elements of a criminal offence: the ***actus reus*** and ***mens rea***. *Actus reus* describes the guilty act or omission that often (but not always) causes harm to a victim (*R. v. Malmo-Levine*, 2003). *Mens rea* describes the guilty mind or the intentional element of an offence. Within common-law systems, the *mens rea* is what distinguishes criminal conduct from accidents or behaviour that is simply dangerous or harmful. For example, it would be a simple accident if you took someone's watch home with you, thinking that it is yours. By contrast, if you pick up the watch and take it home because it is worth more than yours, then you have committed a crime. The difference does not lie in the *actus reus* or the harm caused to the victim, since the act and the loss are the same in both examples. The difference is that in the latter case, you have engaged in anti-social behaviour by choosing or intending to flout community values that underpin the idea of property. Others would then rightly worry about future thefts and becoming victims.

Criminal law is concerned not only with what an offender has done to a victim, but what the intention of the act was and how this conduct may harm, disrupt, or diminish fundamental social values (Stephen, 1883, pp. 78–79). The protection and promotion of these values is what makes criminal law such an important part of national unity and identity.

It might seem that the two elements of a criminal offence ensure uniformity in criminal law, since there exists a limited class of prohibited acts and public values. **Culpable homicide**, for example, occurs when one person causes the death of another human being (*Criminal Code*, s. 222). Surely

actus reus
The guilty act or external element of a criminal offence—that is, those actions and omissions that are prohibited by criminal law. If *actus reus* is proven beyond a reasonable doubt in combination with *mens rea*, an accused may be held criminally responsible for his or her conduct.

mens rea
The guilty mind or intentional element of a criminal offence—that is, what an accused knew or ought to have known about the consequences of prohibited conduct. If *mens rea* is proven beyond a reasonable doubt in combination with *actus reus*, an accused may be held criminally responsible for his or her conduct.

culpable homicide
Causing the death of another person, directly or indirectly, by any means; defined in s. 222 of the *Criminal Code* and divided into categories— murder, manslaughter, or infanticide.

homicide is homicide, whether it happens in Ontario, Nova Scotia, or Quebec. Indeed, in many cases it is easy to determine whether someone caused the death of another. But at other times, the matter is not so simple. Suppose a man stabs another man, causing a non-fatal wound to the leg. The victim's friends then drop him in the mud while carrying him to the hospital, where he receives improper medical treatment and dies a week later. Who caused the death in this scenario? Was it the accused, the victim's friends, or the negligent doctor? Perhaps two or even all three caused the death. There is no clear answer to be found in the technical words "causes the death of another human being," although we can imagine a range of policy factors to

---

SIDEBAR

Causation

The challenging issues raised by causation are clearly illustrated in the case of *R. v. Reid* (2003). The accused, Joey Reid and Michael Stratton, had engaged in a fight with the deceased after a night of excessive drinking with a group of mutual friends. During the fight, one of the accused caused the deceased to lose consciousness after applying a firm chokehold. Although the group had called 911, a bystander began improperly administering CPR, which resulted in vomit entering the deceased's lungs. Medical experts testified that death was caused by asphyxiation, which itself was caused by the CPR. All were in agreement that the physical traumas suffered during the fight were unquestionably not the direct cause of death. Indeed, expert testimony established that, in most cases, people who lose consciousness due to chokeholds of this nature regain consciousness within several minutes and do not suffer lasting negative effects. Still, the accused were convicted of manslaughter on the grounds that their unlawful assault was a "significant contributing factor" in the victim's death.

The Nova Scotia Court of Appeal overturned this verdict and ordered a new trial, finding that the principles of causation were not adequately conveyed to the jury. Ordinarily, the test of causation for manslaughter would be whether the accused's actions were a significant contributing cause of death. In the court's view, however, the jury in this case ought to have been instructed to consider whether the administration of CPR constituted an "intervening act" sufficient to break the chain of causation between the fight and the victim's accidental death. That is, the jury should have been asked to consider whether the CPR could be viewed as a natural or foreseeable consequence of the unlawful assault, or whether it interrupted the chain of events that would ordinarily have occurred in such a situation.

What Do You Think?

In what ways did the judge use extra-legal materials to make a judgment? What theoretical models discussed in Chapter 1 would be helpful in thinking about this case?

consider, including denouncing assault with a deadly weapon and ensuring that medical treatment is administered properly. When the letter of the law is silent, judges must fill in the gaps using extra-legal materials, including their personal reactions to the facts of the case, assessments of the credibility of witnesses, policy considerations, and public opinion.

Mens Rea: A Look at the Law, Women, and Changing Values

Matters become even more complicated when considering *mens rea*. To recall, *mens rea* helps determine whether someone's actions reflect deviant choices and character traits. What counts as deviant or morally blameworthy conduct depends in large part on what a community's values are at any given time, as well as on the personal views of judges and jurors. Since these values change from time to time and from place to place, criminal law will change as well. One useful way of examining these changes is by considering cases involving women. Historically, for example, the common-law offence of rape carried a marital exemption, such that husbands were granted unlimited sexual access to their wives' bodies. At law, wives were not permitted to refuse to consent. Thus, husbands who intentionally forced their wives to have sexual intercourse with them were not seen to exhibit "deviant" conduct, and were therefore not punished. What is more, women were regarded as "morally underdeveloped," and so their testimony alone could not lead to a finding of guilt; there had to be other supporting evidence (Tang, 1998).

See also mini chapter 16.4 Intimate Partner Violence and Specialized Courts

Matters were not helped much by the fact that provincial law societies systematically excluded women (as well as Aboriginals, racial and religious minorities, and the poor) from the legal profession (Backhouse, 2003). Not only were women prevented from being lawyers, they were often excluded from the judicial bench and were prevented from serving as jurors. The sorts of values to which substantive criminal law responded, therefore, were those of dominant social, economic, and political groups (McInnes & Boyle, 1995; Sheehy, 1989).

Criminal Law Defences

Implied Consent and Mistake of Fact

Criminal law's patriarchal, discriminatory qualities are also visible in the doctrine of "implied consent" and the "mistake of fact" defence as it is applied in cases of sexual assault. The latter raises a reasonable doubt as to whether the defendant possessed the knowledge necessary to form *mens rea*. In the context of a sexual assault, for example, an accused (typically a man) could plead innocent on the grounds that he held an honest but

MINI CASE STUDY

"No Means No"

In *R. v. Ewanchuk* (1998), the accused (Steve Ewanchuk of Edmonton) engaged in sexual touching within the confines of a trailer despite the complainant repeatedly saying no. At trial, the accused successfully invoked the mistake of fact defence on the grounds that the complainant's attire and failure to leave the trailer constituted implied consent. On appeal, Justice John McClung stated that the accused's conduct was "less criminal than hormonal," and that the complainant "did not present herself to Ewanchuk or enter his trailer in a bonnet and crinolines." (Somewhat ironically, Justice McClung's grandmother was Nellie McClung, one of Canada's most celebrated champions of women's rights.)

The Supreme Court of Canada overturned these decisions and firmly rejected the validity of "implied consent" on the grounds that recklessness, wilful blindness, or negligence in confirming consent in contexts of ambiguity is as morally blameworthy as intentionally or knowingly committing sexual assault. Followed by a comprehensive *Criminal Code* amendment, *Ewanchuk* (1999) gave legal form to the "no means no" principle, requiring that any honest but mistaken belief as to consent be reasonable. Practically, this means the accused must hear "yes" before proceeding with sexual activity. Significantly, it was not until women were appointed to the Supreme Court of Canada that progress was made in this area, highlighting again the interrelationship between criminal process and substantive criminal law.

mistaken belief that the complainant (usually a woman) consented. This kind of defence suggests that the harm caused by the sexual assault was purely accidental or inadvertent, rather than intentional. Relying on patriarchal, misogynistic perspectives, judges and jurors might acquit rapists because a victim was dressed provocatively, was involved in the sex trade industry, led a promiscuous lifestyle, or in any way implied consent—factors that could even invalidate a complainant's express communication of non-consent.

So, romantic narratives about the common law as a great unifying force must be qualified. Although an ideal worth striving for, the common law did not, and indeed could not, integrate the legal orders of various colonies into a holistic legal system or ensure that they were consistent with English common law. Varying widely, the common law of each political community reflected local conditions and values, some of which were used to justify injustice and oppression. Criminal law had to wait for genuinely national values and a strong national government to emerge before it could be uniformly produced and administered.

The Codification of Criminal Law

Despite high hopes for the common law, pre-Confederation criminal law was highly decentralized, fragmented, and capricious. Following Confederation, Britain granted the federal government exclusive constitutional authority to create and amend substantive criminal law under s. 91(27) of the *Constitution Act, 1867* (formerly entitled the *British North America Act*). One of its first objectives was to make criminal law so simple and clear that citizens could easily understand it and judges could not use it as a platform for their personal or political views—an objective championed on ethical grounds by Jeremy Bentham in early 19th-century Britain (Couyoumdjian, 2008). Unlike Britain, Canada followed Bentham's initiative by collecting, consolidating, and restating all pre-Confederation criminal law within a comparatively small collection of statutes. This process of effectively writing down the previously unwritten common law is called "codification."

Two fundamental principles found within the newly enacted *Constitution Act, 1867* facilitated codification: **parliamentary sovereignty** and **federalism**. Parliamentary sovereignty is a democratic principle that stipulates that Parliament is supreme to all other governmental institutions, including the executive and the judiciary. That is to say, Parliament has exclusive authority to alter legal rights and obligations, and statutory law therefore overrides any common law with which it conflicts. Parliamentary sovereignty is closely related to the values of representative democracy and the rule of law, ensuring that laws are produced by elected representatives who are accountable to the voting public, and that political power is exercised in accordance with clear and publicly accessible rules. By taking law-making authority out of the hands of an unelected (and therefore not accountable) judiciary, the federal government hoped to lay the foundations for fixed and predetermined laws, the authorship of which ultimately rested with citizens.

Federalism similarly draws strength from the tenets of representative democracy. It describes a system of government in which sovereignty is constitutionally divided among a central, or federal, government and constituent political units, such as provinces or states. Dividing power in this way enables local governments to issue laws and policies that better suit local culture, values, and conditions. At the same time, federalism helps local communities pursue common social, political, and economic interests through the central government (Robinson & Simeon, 1999). Federalism accordingly strikes a balance between national unity and regional, linguistic, and ethno-cultural diversity.

The federal government's rising power following Confederation, however, challenged the provinces' historically exclusive control over substantive

parliamentary sovereignty
The principle by which Parliament is supreme over all other governmental institutions.

federalism
A system of government in which all political authority is divided among a central, national, or federal government and regional political units, such as provinces.

criminal law and criminal process. Foreseeing conflict, the British government granted provinces exclusive or shared constitutional authority over most phases of criminal process, including the structure and organization of courts (although the appointment of judges fell under federal authority); the establishment, maintenance, and management of prisons; and policing (*Constitution Act, 1867*, ss. 92(4), (6), (8), and (14)). The legal profession continued to be regulated by provincial law societies, and, crucially, the prosecutions of most criminal offences were initiated and conducted by provincial Crown counsel. The Constitution gave provinces the substantive power to issue "regulatory laws," which were used to prohibit inherently risky, harmful, or dangerous conduct (Roach, 2009, p. 194). Regulatory law has evolved to include such matters as pollution; the manufacture, storage, and transportation of dangerous substances; and various driving offences. Section 92(15) of the Constitution gave provinces the power to use imprisonment as punishment for violating regulatory offences.

The *Constitution Act, 1867* did not, therefore, deprive provinces of the power to establish and maintain community values through the regulation of conduct, even though their power to pass criminal laws was taken away. Moreover, the *Criminal Code* stipulated that criminal law rooted in pre-

TABLE 5.1   Federal and Provincial Powers: The Constitution Act, 1987 and the Division of Criminal Justice Powers

Federal powers (s. 91)
- Substantive criminal law (e.g., *Criminal Code* and associated statutes);
- Criminal procedures to be used in trial and pretrial proceedings;
- The establishment, maintenance, and management of penitentiaries;
- The structure and organization of the Royal Canadian Mounted Police; and
- The appointment (and payment) of judges to the Supreme Court, federal courts, superior courts, and courts of appeal in all provinces and territories.

Provincial powers (s. 92)
- Regulatory laws covering all matters of a local or private nature (e.g., *Highway Traffic Act*, *Employment Standards Act*);
- The imposition of punishment by fine, penalty, or imprisonment for the violation of regulatory laws;
- The establishment, maintenance, and management of public and reformatory prisons in and for the province;
- Municipal and provincial institutions, including municipal and provincial police forces;
- The appointment (and payment) of judges to provincial (trial) courts; and
- The administration of justice, including the constitution, maintenance, and organization of provincial, superior, and appellate courts.

Confederation common law remained in force, unless it was inconsistent with federal legislation. Contempt of court is one such law. This common-law offence enables judges to imprison people who have disobeyed or disrespected a court's authority by failing to maintain silence or a respectful attitude, failing to obey a subpoena, or wilfully disobeying a process or order of the court. Pre-Confederation statutory law also remained in force until 1955, while English law in force in provinces following Confederation remains valid to this day, unless inconsistent with federal legislation (*Criminal Code*, s. 8(2)). Finally, as noted earlier, judges sitting in provincial courts had to take into consideration a wide range of social values when interpreting criminal offences. The codification of the criminal law constrained, but could not eliminate, judges' interpretive discretion, which was still to be exercised in such ways as to respond to local needs, values, and conditions. This role continues to be influenced by the views offered by provincial Crown prosecutors on the meanings and purposes of *Criminal Code* provisions, as well as on sentencing.

Within this favourable constitutional context, Parliament passed Canada's first *Criminal Code* in 1892. Although a step in the right direction, the objective of simplifying the criminal law was only partially realized. First, the *Criminal Code* is not the only source of criminal law in Canada. There are a number of other statutes in operation, including the *Controlled Drugs and Substances Act*, the *Firearms Act*, the *Youth Criminal Justice Act*, and the *Crimes Against Humanity and War Crimes Act* (see sidebar).

Second, some provincial statutes regulate behaviour that is also prohibited by criminal law (these are commonly referred to as **quasi-criminal law**). The *Highway Traffic Act*, for example, regulates matters such as speeding or driving with open liquor—conduct that may expose one to prosecution for such criminal offences as dangerous driving or driving while impaired. Similarly, the *Child and Family Services Act* allows for state interventions where parents or legal guardians are unable or unwilling to care for their children—conduct that may also trigger criminal charges such as failure to provide the necessities of life.

quasi-criminal law
Law that performs some of the same functions as criminal law (e.g., punishment, denunciation, protecting law and order) but through different procedures.

Third, courts retained the authority to create and modify common-law offences until 1953, at which point Parliament expressly decreed that persons could only be convicted of statutory offences (with the sole exception of the common-law offence of contempt of court, s. 9(a) of the *Criminal Code*). Finally, criminal legislation is subject to judicial interpretation, no matter how clearly it may be worded. Courts accordingly must still resolve disagreements about the content, scope, and applicability of legal rules and principles; a role that invites the imposition of judges' personal and political views.

SIDEBAR

The Crimes Against Humanity and War Crimes Act

The *Crimes Against Humanity and War Crimes Act* (CAHWCA) is an especially interesting example of a criminal law statute, because it gives domestic legal effect to international criminal law. Under this Act, Canadian courts are authorized to assume jurisdiction over crimes against humanity, war crimes, genocide, and any other crime recognized under international law, even if the crime took place in another country and did not involve any Canadian citizens—a power referred to as "universal jurisdiction." The CAHWCA also allows courts to assume jurisdiction over international crimes committed within Canada or abroad by Canadian citizens and state officials. This suggests that international law can take its place alongside the common law, statutes, and the Constitution as a source of criminal law in Canada.

In 2009, Désiré Munyaneza, a Rwandan national with permanent resident status in Canada, became the first person charged and convicted under the CAHWCA. After being recognized by members of the Rwandan diaspora in Toronto, Munyaneza was prosecuted in Quebec. The Quebec Superior Court found him guilty of genocide, war crimes, and crimes against humanity during the Rwandan genocide, and sentenced him to life imprisonment with no possibility of parole for 25 years.

Thus, criminal law remained considerably complex and fragmented into the 21st century, cutting across a wide range of federal, provincial, and English statutes, compounded by enduring common-law concepts and judges' contextualized interpretations of legislative language. At the same time, the democratic rhetoric associated with codification obscured continuing systemic social, political, and economic inequalities. Women, and racial and religious minorities were denied the franchise (that is, not allowed to vote in elections) throughout much of the 20th century, while invisible minorities such as homosexuals were denied social and political recognition. The result was a *Criminal Code* that not only did not reflect the values or interests of many Canadians, but was used—much as the common law had been used—to legitimize systemic injustices and human rights abuses. Improvements were made, but much more work had yet to be done.

Criminal Justice and the Charter of Rights and Freedoms

On April 17, 1982, the *Constitution Act, 1982* entered into force, signalling Canada's complete political and legal independence from Britain. Including some of the provisions found within previous constitutional documents, the *Constitution Act, 1982* included one enormously important addition: the *Charter of Rights and Freedoms*. The Charter imposes serious restraints on the government's capacity to create and administer criminal law by guaranteeing a wide range of rights and freedoms, including the right to life, liberty, and security of the person; the right to equality and non-discrimination; the right to be free from unreasonable search and seizure; and the right against arbitrary arrest and detention.

Section 52 of the Constitution states:

> The Constitution of Canada is the supreme law of Canada, and any law that is inconsistent with the provisions of the Constitution is, to the extent of the inconsistency, of no force or effect.

This provision puts principles of respect for human dignity and rights alongside parliamentary sovereignty and federalism as one of the three pillars of the Canadian Constitution. This means that a law or police practice that violates the Charter will no longer have any authority, even if it is based in valid legislation, official government policy, or common law. Courts may also consider international human rights instruments when interpreting the content and scope of Charter rights (Hudson, 2008). In fact, many of the Charter's provisions were modelled after international human rights treaties, partly to enhance compliance with Canada's international legal obligations and partly to reinforce the country's international image as a leader in human rights (Bayefsky, 1992).

The Charter is given effect principally through judicial review, a process through which courts scrutinize the merits of legislative and police actions against legal and moral standards. The power of judicial review is rooted within s. 24 of the Charter, which stipulates that the judiciary is responsible for enforcing the rights it guarantees, sometimes by excluding evidence that has been gathered in ways that violate these fundamental principles of justice—a topic explored in greater detail in the next chapter. In some respects, running counter to the codification movement, the Charter has given courts the authority to alter or even strike down laws created by democratically elected officials. Some support this expanded role, believing that the independence and impartiality of the courts make them strong candidates to be the protectors of unpopular groups and minorities (Roach, 2001; Dworkin, 1977). This view certainly finds support in Canada's history of actively excluding minorities from the political process. Critics say that s. 24 unravels the democratic gains made during the codification movement, giving judges the final say on challenging political issues that are best left to representative institutions (Mandel, 1994; Bakan, 1997).

These problems are made worse by the fact that many of the Charter's provisions are vague and open to interpretation. Section 2(b), for example, protects our "freedom of thought, belief, opinion and expression." Given this wording, how might we approach criminal laws prohibiting the wilful promotion of hatred against an identifiable group? On the one hand, freedom of expression could be interpreted literally, in which case laws restricting expression of any sort would have to be declared unconstitutional. On the other hand, hate speech laws protect victims of hatred, and help to protect and promote public values associated with equality and non-discrimination. In light of this consideration, hate speech laws may be justified because the public values of equality and non-discrimination outweigh the accused's interest in unconstrained and arguably low-value expressive activity (Medjuck, 1992). As with common-law elements of criminal offences, the law itself is silent on which of these interpretations is to be preferred. It is not at all clear why unelected judges, rather than legislators, should have the last word on such issues.

What Do You Think?

Consider the Pickton case study on page 131. What types of tensions do you see the Charter creating in the Pickton case? Do you believe individual rights should be protected over societal interests, or do you think the right balance was struck? Can you imagine how this case might have been dealt with in an earlier time—such as the 1970s (before the Charter existed), or 100 years ago? What social values have changed that might affect the context in which a case like this is considered?

Defenders of the Charter say that courts do not have the last word in such matters. Rather, the Charter structures "dialogue" among courts, Parliament, police, and other institutions as to how best to pursue pressing and substantial objectives (Roach, 2001; Hogg & Bushell, 1997). Section 1, for example, states that rights and freedoms may be limited if Parliament can prove that such limits are demonstrably justified in a free and democratic society. At this stage, Parliament would explain to judges how a disputed law that limits the rights of an accused does so both as minimally as possible, and toward the twin ends of protecting victims and promoting values of human dignity. In most cases, Charter challenges do not result in legislation or important police powers being invalidated. Rather, courts, Parliament, and law enforcement agencies find ways to harmonize the interests of all three main stakeholders of criminal justice: the accused, the victims, and the public. To the extent that Parliament and the police have an obligation to protect victims and promote fundamental values, courts tend to allow reasonable limits on the rights of accused, or at least offer suggestions as to how a law or practice may be modified to achieve its ends without restricting rights more than is necessary.

Sometimes courts will use the Charter to modify and improve the common law. For example, courts continue to exercise their common-law authority over criminal defences—mechanisms that enable an accused to justify or excuse conduct that would otherwise be criminal on the grounds that the action was either morally right (i.e., justified) or morally involuntary (i.e., excusable) (Roach, 2009, pp. 293–295). Self-defence, for example, justifies the use of force if a person reasonably believes she or he is facing an attack and has no safe avenue of escape (*R. v. Pétel*, 1994). Historically, accused were held to the standard of a "reasonable man" in such cases. In *R. v. Lavallee* (1990), the Supreme Court ruled that equality requires that this objective standard incorporate all of an accused's relevant personal characteristics, including sex, gender, and relationship with the attacker.

MINI CASE STUDY

R. v. Lavallee

A modified objective standard was used to acquit a woman in an abusive relationship after she shot her husband in the back of the head. Some (mostly male) judges and jurors had a hard time understanding how shooting someone from behind could be interpreted as self-defence, especially when the accused could have left the relationship at any time (*R. v. Lavallee*, 1988). Led by the Supreme Court's first female judge, Bertha Wilson, the court relied on expert testimony in finding that the accused suffered from **battered woman syndrome**, and that this explained how she could have reasonably foreseen an imminent attack when others could not, as well as how she could not have seen a safe avenue of escape (Willoughby, 1989; Crocker, 1985).

Applying a modified objective standard in this case enhanced equality, but this approach can sometimes have unintended effects. For example, a **modified objective standard** is used in "provocation" defences, in which a person found guilty of murder is convicted of the lesser offence of manslaughter on the grounds that the victim's "insulting" or "wrongful" acts would have caused a reasonable person to lose self-control. The defence of provocation has long been used to reduce the punishment handed out to husbands who kill their wives for perceived disobedience. In *R. v. Thibert* (1996), the Supreme Court adopted the perspective of a husband "faced with the breakup of his marriage" in finding that the accused acted reasonably when he shot and killed the person with whom his wife was having an affair; this, despite the fact that a woman's choice to leave her husband can hardly be deemed an act for which murder is an appropriate response. Provocation has since been used, albeit unsuccessfully, in a number

Battered woman syndrome (or battered person syndrome) was first studied by American psychologist Lenore Walker, who investigated the reasons why people often stay in abusive relationships. In 1979, after interviewing more than 1,500 abused women, Walker published the results of her research. She found that almost all abusive relationships involved a similar pattern of violence (which she described as the "cycle of violence"). This research allowed for the development of the legal defence of battered woman syndrome, which considers how this cycle of violence can affect an abused person's level of fear and perception of imminent threat—key factors of a court's assessment of self-defence. Battered woman syndrome has been used successfully in a number of cases in Canada, Australia, New Zealand, and the United States in which abused spouses killed their abusers.

A **modified objective standard** is used when a court changes the objective standard by which an accused's behaviour is judged. The modified standard allows the court to consider the specific characteristics of the accused and his or her circumstances at the time of the offence. The objective standard generally used is that of the "reasonable person." That is, in order to determine whether or not the accused acted reasonably, the court asks what a reasonable person would have done in the same situation. Where the modified objective standard is used, as in *Lavallee*, the court instead asks what a reasonable battered woman would have done in the same situation.

of cases where accused have argued that murdering their wives was an appropriate cultural response to perceived dishonour (*R. v. Humaid*, 2006; *R. v. Ly*, 1987). In particular, it was argued that Charter rights associated with equality and multiculturalism require courts to take into account the accused's cultural beliefs and attitudes about gender roles when applying the provocation defence. Consequently, the modified objective standard can create tensions between respect for an accused's cultural rights and the individual rights of a victim.

What Do You Think?

1. Although domestic violence can occur between partners of any gender, the majority of victims are women. The *Lavallee* case has been celebrated as an achievement in gender equality. How do you think the law's acceptance of battered woman syndrome increases equality for women?

2. Do an Internet search for "battered woman syndrome" and read about some of its key factors (e.g., the abused partner believes the violence is her fault). How might these factors influence the decisions a person might make in an abusive situation? Are these factors important for courts to consider when assessing reasonableness?

3. What do you think about the legal system's use of the modified objective standard? Is it ever valid to consider the personal characteristics of the accused? What "tensions" do you think it creates between the rights of the accused and those of the victim? What role does the Charter play in this potential conflict?

Conclusion

The history of Canadian criminal law and process has been one of gradual democratization. Ultimately rooted in the Canadian Constitution, criminal law and process have come to reflect enduring democratic values associated with parliamentary sovereignty, federalism, and human dignity. Although not always realized in practice, these values owe their origins to the ideals of English common law and to the delicate balance struck between national unity and regional, linguistic, and ethnocultural diversity. Highly pluralistic and decentralized, pre-Confederation law effectively protected and promoted the health and well-being of primarily immigrant communities. Post-Confederation criminal law was transformed to promote the effectiveness and ambitions of a new federal government, helping to cultivate a developing national identity. Dividing constitutional authority over criminal law and criminal process eased this evolution, with provinces retaining significant influence over the interpretation and application of federal criminal law.

The *Charter of Rights and Freedoms* continued this tradition, shoring up deficiencies in our political processes. Courts have since reclaimed their historic role as one of the primary agents of criminal justice, alongside Parliament. Built around both national and international values associated with human dignity, the Charter has been designed to benefit the true stakeholders of criminal justice: the accused, the victims, and the public. This is achieved by ensuring that criminal process is structured in a fair, inclusive, and impartial way, and that criminal law is consistent with basic moral standards. Although there is much work yet to do, the foundations of a praiseworthy criminal justice system have been established.

▶ IN-CLASS EXERCISE

In *R. v. Keegstra* (1996), the Supreme Court reviewed the constitutionality of criminal laws prohibiting hate speech. Section 319(2) of the *Criminal Code* states:

> Every one who, by communicating statements, other than in private conversation, wilfully promotes hatred against any identifiable group is guilty of
> (a) an indictable offence and is liable to imprisonment for a term not exceeding two years; or
> (b) an offence punishable on summary conviction.

This provision was used to arrest, charge, and prosecute James Keegstra, an anti-Semitic high school teacher. Keegstra taught his classes that Jewish people were responsible for depressions, anarchy, chaos, wars, and revolution. According to Keegstra, Jews "created the Holocaust to gain sympathy" and, in contrast to the open and honest Christians, were said to be deceptive, secretive, and inherently evil. Keegstra expected his students to reproduce his teachings in class and on exams, and were given poor grades if they did not.

Keegstra argued that hate speech laws unjustifiably infringed his Charter right to freedom of expression in s. 2(b), which states:

Everyone has the following fundamental freedoms
(b) freedom of thought, belief, opinion and expression …

The government replied that the Charter protects equality, human dignity, and multiculturalism, as well as freedom of expression, and that hate speech laws are designed to protect the rights of victims as well as important public values. For those reasons, it argued, the laws are justified, if not necessary, in a free and democratic society.

Exercise Questions

1. In what ways would you say freedom of expression is "fundamental"?
2. Does this freedom apply to speakers only, or can it be interpreted to protect the rights and interests of the audience or the public at large?
3. How does the justifiability of hate speech laws shift when you adopt the perspective of the accused? The victim? The public?

DISCUSSION QUESTIONS

1. In *R. v. Reid* (2003), the Nova Scotia Court of Appeal ordered a retrial, finding that the jury was not properly instructed on the principles of causation. If you were a member of the jury, how would you decide the case in light of the Court of Appeal's clarifications? Would you say the accused's actions in this case were a "significant contributing cause" of the victim's death? If so, was the improper administration of CPR an intervening force sufficient to acquit the accused of a homicide offence?
2. Unlike the United States, Canada chose to establish a uniform, national body of criminal law that applies across all provinces and territories. How have we balanced centralization with continuing respect for linguistic, regional, and ethnocultural diversity?
3. In what ways does the domestic implementation of international criminal law fit into the broader historical context of Canadian

criminal law and process? Is it appropriate for Canadian courts to convict foreign nationals for international crimes committed outside of Canada?

4. The "reasonable person" (formerly the "reasonable man") standard has become an integral part of criminal justice in the Charter era, particularly in the context of self-defence, provocation, and mistake of fact defences. To what extent should courts consider an accused's personal characteristics in determining the reasonableness of the individual's beliefs and behaviour? In what ways might this approach impact uniformity in applying the criminal law, and is this a good or a bad thing?

SUGGESTED FURTHER READINGS

Brown, D.H. (1995). *The birth of a criminal code: The evolution of Canada's justice system*. Toronto: University of Toronto Press.

Cameron, J., & Stribopoulos, J. (Eds.). (2008). *The Charter and criminal justice: Twenty-five years later*. Markham, ON: LexisNexis.

Klineberg, J. (2003). Anger and intent for murder: The Supreme Court decision in R. v. Parent. *Osgoode Hall Law Journal, 41*(1), 37–73.

Medjuck, S. (1992). Rethinking Canadian justice: Hate must not define democracy. *University of New Brunswick Law Journal, 41*, 285–294.

Shaffer, M. (1997). The battered woman syndrome revisited: Some complicating thoughts five years after R. v. Lavallee. *University of Toronto Law Journal, 47*, 1–34.

REFERENCES

Backhouse, C. (2003). Gender and race in the construction of "legal professionalism": Historical perspectives. Retrieved from http://www.lsuc.on.ca/media/constance_backhouse_gender_and_race.pdf

Bakan, J. (1997). *Just words: Constitutional rights and social wrongs*. Toronto: University of Toronto Press.

Bayefsky, A. (1992). *International human rights law: Use in Canadian Charter of Rights and Freedoms litigation*. Toronto: Butterworths.

Blackstone, W. (2001). *Commentaries on the laws of England*. W. Morrison (Ed.). London: Cavendish.

Brown, D.H. (1989). *The genesis of the Canadian Criminal Code of 1892*. Toronto: University of Toronto Press.

Coke, E. (1809). *The first part of the institutes of the laws of England*. London: L. Hansard & Sons.

Couyoumdjian, J.P. (2008). An expert at work: Revisiting Jeremy Bentham's proposals on codification. *Kyklos, 61*(4), 503–519.

Crocker, P. (1985). The meaning of equality for battered women who kill men in self-defense. *Harvard Women's Law Journal, 8*, 121.

Dworkin, R. (1977). *Taking rights seriously*. Cambridge, MA: Harvard University Press.

Hay, D. (1981). The meaning of the criminal law in Quebec, 1764–1774. In L.A. Knafla (Ed.), *Crime and criminal justice in Europe and Canada* (pp. 77–110). Waterloo, ON: Wilfrid Laurier University Press.

Hogg, P.W., & Bushell, A. (1997). The Charter dialogue between courts and legislatures. *Osgoode Hall Law Journal, 35*(1), 75–124.

Hudson, G. (2008). Neither here nor there: The (non-)impact of international law on judicial reasoning in Canada and South Africa. *Canadian Journal of Law and Jurisprudence, 21*(2), 321–354.

Llewellyn, K., & Hoebel, E.A. (1941). *The Cheyenne way: Conflict and case law in primitive jurisprudence*. Norman, OK: University of Oklahoma Press.

Mandel, M. (1994). *The Charter of Rights and the legalization of politics in Canada*. Toronto: Thompson Educational Publishing.

McInnes, J., & Boyle, C. (1995). Judging sexual assault law against a standard of equality. *University of British Columbia Law Review, 29*, 341.

Medjuck, S. (1992). Rethinking Canadian justice: Hate must not define democracy. *University of New Brunswick Law Journal, 41*, 285.

Mewett, A.W., & Manning, M. (1994). *Criminal law* (3rd ed.). Toronto: Butterworths.

Pollock, F. (1912). *The genius of the common law*. New York: Columbia University Press.

Roach, K. (2001). *The Supreme Court on trial: Judicial activism or democratic dialogue*. Toronto: Irwin Law.

Roach, K. (2009). *Criminal law* (4th ed.). Toronto: Irwin Law.

Robinson, I., & Simeon, R. (1999). The dynamics of Canadian federalism. In J. Bickerton & A.-G. Gagnon (Eds.), *Canadian politics* (3rd ed.) (pp. 239–262). Peterborough, ON: Broadview Press.

Sheehy, E.A. (1989). Canadian judges and the law of rape: Should the Charter insulate bias? *Ottawa Law Review, 21*, 741.

Stephen, J.F. (1883). *A history of the criminal law of England*. London: Macmillan.

Tang, K. (1998). Rape law reform in Canada: The success and limits of legislation. *International Journal of Offender Therapy and Comparative Criminology, 42*, 258–270.

Willoughby, M.J. (1989). Rendering each woman her due: Can a battered woman claim self-defense when she kills her sleeping batterer? *Kansas Law Review, 38*, 169.

Legislation

*An Act to Give Effect to Certain Resolutions Passed by Imperial Conferences Held in the
Years 1926 and 1930* (UK) ("*The Statute of Westminster*"), 22 & 23 Geo. V, c. 4.
Child and Family Services Act, RSO 1990, c. 11.
Constitution Act, 1867 (UK), 30 & 31 Vict., c. 3.
Constitution Act, 1982, being Schedule B to the *Canada Act 1982* (UK), 1982, c. 11.
Controlled Drugs and Substances Act, SC 1996, c. 19.
Criminal Code, RSC 1985, c. C-46.
Firearms Act, SC 1995, c. 39.
Highway Traffic Act, RSO 1990, c. H.8.
The Union Act, 1840, statutes of Great Britain (1840), 3-4 Vict., c. 35.
War Crimes and Crimes Against Humanity Act, SC 2000, c. 24.
Youth Criminal Justice Act, SC 2002, c. 1.

Cases

R. v. Ewanchuk (1998), 57 Alta. LR (3d) 235 (CA).
R. v. Ewanchuk, [1999] 1 SCR 330.
R. v. Humaid (2006), 81 OR (3d) 456 (CA).
R. v. Keegstra, [1996] 1 SCR 458.
R. v. Lavallee (1988), 52 Man. R (2d) 274 (CA).
R. v. Lavallee, [1990] 1 SCR 852.
R. v. Ly (1987), 33 CCC (3d) 31 (BCCA).
R. v. Malmo-Levine; R. v. Caine, 2003 SCC 74, [2003] 3 SCR 571.
R. c. Munyaneza, [2009] RJQ 1432.
R. v. Pétel, [1994] 1 SCR 3.
R. v. Reid, 2003 NSCA 104.
R. v. Thibert, [1996] 1 SCR 37.

Criminal Procedure and Evidence

LEARNING OBJECTIVES

After reading this chapter, students will be able to:

- Understand the basic concepts of criminal procedure law.
- Identify the criminal justice theoretical models that predominate in criminal procedure.
- Recognize the role of criminal justice professionals in Canadian criminal procedure.

Introduction

Two of the competing perspectives analyzed in Chapter 1 underlie Canadian criminal procedure law: crime control and due process. Both schools of thought have influenced different aspects of procedural law. For example, the exclusion-of-evidence rule (discussed below) as it applies in Canada tends to give police officers some discretion and considerable power to investigate and respond to crime. This is a crime-control measure, which can be clearly seen when compared with the rules of evidence followed in other Western societies that tend to be more severe and considerably limit the powers of police officers. The fact that the Crown prosecutor has a very high standard of proof and that a jury has to be unanimous to return a guilty verdict are examples of the influence of due process. This is so because both approaches have dominated at different times without prevailing in the ultimate debate, and both have attracted the attention of criminal lawmakers and society.

Overview of the Criminal Justice Process

Criminal procedure in Canada operates in stages at three levels. At each level, there are specific criminal justice officials that have been entrusted with diverse responsibilities. They interact with one another to ensure that the criminal justice process transitions smoothly throughout each level and ultimately results in the successful completion of a given criminal case. The three levels are:

1. the police investigation
2. the prosecution's analysis
3. the criminal court process.

Basically, this means that a police investigation must first take place before the prosecution has the ability to analyze the case, and the prosecution must first analyze the case before it can be brought to the level of the criminal court process.

Police Investigation

First and foremost, the criminal process begins with the commission of a criminal offence; that is, an individual must first violate a prohibition set out in a criminal statute. The criminal justice system must then become aware of this violation—in most cases, offenders go unnoticed and are consequently not subject to the criminal process. Once a criminal offence comes to the attention of the criminal justice system, three further steps must first be chronologically satisfied before the criminal trial process can be carried out. The individual who committed the crime must be:

- correctly arrested
- accurately identified
- appropriately charged.

Arrest

Once a crime has been committed, the police must first determine who is responsible for the offence in question. If officers were not present when the offence happened, it is common for them to interact with the public and/or gather physical evidence directly connected to the alleged criminal activity. In other words, the police carry out the investigative process. For example, consider a situation where the police have received a report that an assault has occurred; they were not present when it was committed. The police officers will then generally go directly to the location where the assault took place and collect evidence that will lead to the identification of the person who committed the assault. This will involve speaking to the victim and/or eyewitnesses who were there when the assault occurred. The process can be lengthy, but it ultimately results in police narrowing down or identifying a potential suspect, which then leads to the arrest of that suspect. (See also the discussion of police powers in Chapter 4.)

It is important to keep in mind that, in order for the arrest to be valid, the police must respect the suspect's legal rights that are protected by the

Canadian Charter of Rights and Freedoms. Otherwise, they will not be legally permitted to take the suspect into custody. The Charter also grants everyone the right to not be arbitrarily detained or imprisoned. An arrest can be made only to:

- prevent a crime from being committed
- terminate a breach of peace
- compel a person to attend trial.

The police need a warrant to arrest, except in the following circumstances:

- They have caught a person in the act of committing an offence.
- They have **reasonable grounds** for believing that a person has committed an indictable offence.
- They have reasonable grounds for believing that a person is about to commit an indictable offence.

reasonable grounds
The required basis for arrest; more than a hunch or mere suspicion.

In all these situations, the arrest must be **necessary in the public interest**.

Once the suspect is taken into custody, the police are responsible for making sure that the suspect they have arrested is in fact the individual who committed the crime; for example, the assault in the hypothetical case described above. To do this, the police must have evidence that directly connects the suspect with the crime in question. In the assault example, the most likely step is that police ask an eyewitness to come to the police station to identify the person who was witnessed committing the assault. Generally, the police do this by providing a lineup of people, one of whom is the suspect, while the

necessary in the public interest
One of the criteria that an arrest must meet if it is made without a warrant; defined in *R. v. Mann* (2004) as "reasonably necessary in light of all the circumstances."

Police arresting a suspect during a raid targeting gangs in Abbotsford, BC.
Source: Vancouver Sun/Police handout.

others are known to be innocent. If the eyewitness, or multiple eyewitnesses, identifies the suspect, this is generally sufficient evidence for the police to conclude that the suspect they have in custody is in fact the individual who committed the crime. Police officers can also interview the suspect. The Charter contains some protections against possible police abuse (this issue is discussed in more detail in Chapter 4). The police must inform suspects that they have a right to remain silent and that any statement made to the police may be used against them in a court of law.

Charge

Once the police conclude that the suspect committed the crime, they have to decide whether or not to charge the individual with the offence. Continuing with our assault example, the police would have sufficient evidence to charge the suspect with assault. Once the charge is laid, however, it is the Crown that has the final say as to whether the charge proceeds. This is an essential step because if the Crown decides that the case should not proceed, the suspect is free to go and the criminal process will not continue. However, if the Crown agrees with the charge and the supporting evidence, the case will proceed through the court system; the suspect is then referred to as the "accused." This is significant because once a suspect is charged with a crime, it does not mean that the person is a criminal; it just means that the individual is accused of committing the crime.

Once a suspect is charged with a crime, it does not necessarily mean that he or she is a criminal.

SIDEBAR

Severance of Accused and Counts

When there are many accused or a single accused and charges, the prosecution generally tries all accused and all charges together, such as when several people are accused of the joint commission of an offence. An accused may request that he or she be tried separately on one or more of the counts and or separately from the other accused. The court may order the severance of the accused and counts when the interest of justice so requires; for example, a joint trial will be unfair to the accused. As was discussed in the Pickton case study, not all of the cases of missing women were prosecuted.

What Do You Think?

Recall the discussion in Chapter 5 regarding the rule of law. In what way(s) does the concept of severance of accused and counts jeopardize the principles associated with the rule of law? Who benefits by having all of the charges dealt with together?

There are two other types of written statements that may also be involved during charging: an **information** and an **indictment**.

The Prosecution's Analysis

The decision to proceed rests on the prosecution's analysis. It is the second essential part of the criminal process because it is ultimately the deciding factor as to whether or not a case is heard in criminal court. The Crown must follow a two-tiered test to determine whether or not to prosecute:

1. The evidential test—namely, whether there is sufficient **admissible** evidence to provide a realistic prospect of conviction.
2. The public interest test—namely, whether it is in the public interest to prosecute.

The public interest test recognizes that the resources needed to conduct a criminal trial are limited. So, the Crown must decide to proceed on only those cases that are worthy of prosecution. But in making these decisions, the Crown must analyze a multitude of factors, which vary from case to case. Some of these factors may include the accused's background, any mitigating circumstances, the attitude of the victim, and the availability of alternatives to prosecution. The only exception to the public interest test is domestic violence cases, where Crown prosecutors have no discretion and are obligated to proceed to trial.

information
A written statement, given by the police or a private citizen to a magistrate, that describes in ordinary language the alleged offence for which a warrant or summons is required, and that may be substantiated on oath.

indictment
A written accusation that sets out the charges against an accused person for a serious indictable offence.

admissible
Allowable as evidence in a case.

What Do You Think?

Consider the Pickton case study at the beginning of this part. Would you say that the prosecutorial decisions that were made in that case were in the public interest?

Hybrid Offences

Crimes are classified as indictable offences, summary convictions, or hybrid offences. Indictable offences are the most serious crimes and are subject to a wide range of sentences—the most severe of which is life imprisonment. These offences include murder, manslaughter, robbery, and aggravated sexual assault. Summary convictions, meanwhile, include minor offences that are punishable by a fine of no more than $2,000 and/or a maximum term of imprisonment of six months. Examples of summary convictions are trespassing at night, causing a disturbance, and taking a motor vehicle without the owner's consent.

Hybrid offences constitute the majority of offences in Canada. They include assault, impaired driving, child pornography, sexual assault, and criminal harassment. For hybrid offences, the Crown prosecutor has to decide whether to prosecute these offences as indictable offences or summary convictions, taking into consideration the circumstances surrounding the offence and the background of the accused.

According to federal policy, procedure by indictment is reserved for the most serious cases. The factors that the prosecution has to take into account are the following:

- Whether the facts alleged make the offence a serious one.
- Whether the accused has a lengthy criminal record.
- The sentence that will be recommended by the attorney general in the event of a conviction.
- The effect that having to testify at both a preliminary inquiry and a trial may have on victims or witnesses.
- Whether it would not be in the public interest to have a trial by jury.

Preliminary Inquiry

Trials are held at either the provincial court level or superior court level. For summary conviction offences, the trial will automatically remain in provincial court. For most indictable offences, the accused is given the option to choose to have a trial at either the provincial (with no preliminary hearing) or superior court (after a preliminary hearing) level. In the case of former capital indictable offences (such as murder and treason), however, the accused has no choice: a preliminary hearing will be automatically conducted and the trial will be held in superior court.

prima facie

Legal presumption meaning "on the face of it" or "at first sight."

A preliminary inquiry is basically a hearing to determine whether or not the prosecution has, **prima facie**, sufficient evidence against the accused; that is, if the evidence were to be believed on the face of it, the accused would be found guilty. All preliminary inquiries occur at the provincial court level. The prosecution is given the opportunity to present the evidence to the judge (e.g., present eyewitness statements and/or physical evidence from the crime scene), and defence counsel can cross-examine witnesses and make arguments about the evidence. It is then up to the judge to decide whether or not the case should proceed to trial at the superior court level.

The accused, generally upon consultation with his or her defence counsel, can issue one of the following "peremptory pleas":

1. Pardon: The accused has been convicted of the same *Criminal Code* offence in a prior criminal case.

2. *Autrefois acquit*: The accused has been acquitted of the same *Criminal Code* offence in a prior criminal case.
3. *Autrefois convict*: The accused has been convicted of the same *Criminal Code* offence in a prior criminal case.

The end of the preliminary inquiry marks the end of the pretrial criminal process. Before we move on to the criminal trial process, consider the following hypothetical example, which will help summarize the above discussion and add some perspective.

A man has assaulted another man in Ontario. The Ontario Provincial Police (OPP) become aware of the assault and begin to investigate. After the police arrest the man, or suspect, whom they believe to be the individual who committed the assault, they bring in eyewitnesses to confirm this belief. Once the eyewitnesses positively identify the man, he is charged with assault. Remember, if the prosecution decides not to prosecute the person—namely, for the assault in this case—the criminal process is over, and the man will be free. However, let's assume the Crown prosecutor decides to proceed with the case. The man, who is now identified as the accused, proceeds through the Ontario Court of Justice (OCJ), which is the formal name for the provincial court.

The Criminal Court Process

Disclosure

A fundamental right in Canadian criminal procedure is disclosure. Disclosure derives from the right of the accused to make full answer and defence. The prosecution is obliged to turn over all relevant evidence in its possession. In *R. v. C. (M.H.)* (1991), the Supreme Court of Canada held:

> There is a general duty on the part of the Crown to disclose all material it proposes to use at trial and especially all evidence which may assist the accused even if the Crown does not propose to adduce it.

However, this obligation is not absolute. The Crown has discretion with respect to the timing of disclosure and the justified withholding of information. That said, disclosure must begin prior to trial, and is usually triggered by a request from the defence. The Crown prosecutor must also continue to hand over new evidence as it is discovered. The obligation is also subject to the limitation that the accused has no right to information that is absolutely irrelevant to the case, such as information that may be contained in the private records of victims and witnesses.

The purpose of disclosure is twofold: (1) to ensure that the accused knows the case to be met and is able to make full answer and defence; and (2) to encourage the resolution of facts at issue, including, where appropriate, the entering of guilty pleas at an early stage in the proceedings.

The information to be disclosed need not qualify as evidence; that is, it need not pass all of the tests concerning admissibility. It is sufficient if the information is relevant, reliable, and not subject to some form of privilege.

Privilege

Privilege is a legal right to keep certain kinds of communication confidential. While there are some exceptions, communications of this kind, generally speaking, cannot be disclosed and are inadmissible in court. Examples of privilege are communications between attorney and client, doctor and patient, priest and penitent, and spouses.

The attorney–client privilege is considered a fundamental civil and legal right. The courts recognize three preconditions for the existence of this privilege:

1. a communication between the attorney and the client
2. communication that entails the seeking or giving of legal advice
3. communication that is intended to be confidential by the parties.

Exceptions to this privilege include communication that is itself criminal. Note that this privilege belongs to the client, not the lawyer. The lawyer "merely acts as a gatekeeper, ethically bound to protect the privileged information that belongs to his or her client" (*Lavallee, Rackel, & Heintz v. Canada (Attorney General); White, Ottenheimer, & Baker v. Canada (Attorney General); R. v. Fink*, 2002).

The litigation privilege is a kind of immunity given for certain acts and statements taken in connection with the litigation process. According to the Supreme Court, in *Blank v. Canada (Justice)* (2010), the purpose of the litigation privilege is

> based upon the need for a protected area to facilitate investigation and preparation of the case for trial by the adversarial advocate. [It creates a] "zone of privacy" in relation to pending or apprehended litigation. Once the litigation has ended, the privilege to which it gave rise has lost its specific and concrete purpose—and therefore its justification.

In general, a spouse of the accused may only be a competent witness for the defence. But when the accused is charged with certain listed offences, such as sexual assault or incest (*R. v. Hawkins*, 1996), the spouse can be called as a witness for the prosecution without the consent of the person charged.

The physician–patient privilege is limited by the risk to public safety. To ascertain the existence of this risk, courts must objectively consider the following factors:

- whether there is a clear risk to an identifiable person or group of persons.
- whether there is risk of serious bodily harm or death.
- whether the danger to public safety is imminent.

Exceptions to the medical privilege should be restricted to information that is necessary and closely connected to the protection of public safety.

What Do You Think?

What are some other types of privilege, and what might their limitations be?

Bail Provisions

A criminal trial, subject to safeguards and formalities, is a relatively lengthy process. Since the accused is considered innocent until proven guilty in a court of justice, the accused, as a general rule, should be free until convicted. However, the accused may be held in custody in certain circumstances. A bail hearing is conducted to determine whether the person will remain in custody for the court proceedings or be released. Otherwise, they are taken to a holding facility to await the trial. Bail serves two purposes: (1) to ensure or secure the accused's appearance in court; and (2) to relieve the accused of imprisonment and the government of the burden and cost of keeping the accused in prison while pending trial.

The Charter guarantees everyone the right to not be denied reasonable bail without just cause. The Supreme Court interpreted that this right includes two distinct elements; namely, the right to reasonable bail and the right to not be denied bail without just cause. "Reasonable bail" refers to the terms of bail. Thus, the amount of bail and the restrictions imposed on the accused's liberty while on bail must be reasonable. "Just cause" refers to the right to obtain bail. Thus, bail must not be denied unless there is just cause to do so. The just cause aspect of s. 11(e) of the Charter sets out the grounds under which bail is granted or denied. At a bail hearing, the presiding justice must order an accused to be released (except where the charges are murder or treason), unless the Crown prosecutor can show cause as to why the accused should be held in custody pending trial. The only grounds for denial of bail are to

- ensure the accused's attendance in court
- protect the public
- maintain confidence in the administration of justice.

Recently, there has been some reform to bail resulting from the nature of serious crime. On December 15, 2010, Bill C-464 (bail reform) became law in Canada. It added a clause to s. 515(10)(b) of the *Criminal Code* giving courts the power to deny bail to someone accused of a serious crime who is deemed a potential danger to children under the age of 18.

In most cases, the onus rests with the prosecution to show cause why the accused should not be released. In some situations, the burden is switched—the accused must show cause why he or she should not be detained. In *R. v. Pearson* (1992), the Supreme Court upheld the constitutionality of this reverse onus of proof. Release may either be on an undertaking, which involves only a signature, or on a recognizance, where money or other security can be forfeited if the accused does not attend court or breaches any conditions imposed. The Charter guarantees that the amount of money be within the accused's reach. Most defendants are released on a recognizance; that is, they are released into their own care or the care of another. A person who comes forward to take responsibility for the accused while on release is called a "surety" or "guarantor."

What Do You Think?

What is the impact on a trial when an accused appears in court from detention rather than from the community where he has been released on his own recognizance? Are there situations in which an individual should be held in pretrial detention because of his or her life circumstances (e.g., poverty, unemployment, no familial ties)? How do these factors influence the trial?

Trial Procedure

Anatomy of the Criminal Trial

The criminal trial ultimately results in the accused's conviction or acquittal. The Crown presents its case first, calling witnesses and asking them questions—"examination in chief"—and producing all relevant evidence. (In jury trials, there are opening statements by both the prosecution and defence.) The defence can then cross-examine the witnesses. If a new issue arises in cross-examination or if there is some uncertainty, the Crown prosecutor may re-examine the witness. As a general rule, new facts cannot be introduced in re-examination (*R. v. Moore*, 1984).

After the Crown rests its case, defence counsel can ask for the charges to be dismissed if there is not sufficient evidence to prove an element of the offence. If there is enough evidence, defence counsel has the option to not call evidence or to call its witnesses and produce other evidence. The Crown prosecutor will then cross-examine the witnesses and counsel will have the right to re-examine them if necessary.

After resting its case, the defence will make the closing arguments, followed by the Crown. If the defence did not call any witnesses, the prosecutor will make the closing arguments first. Where jury trials are concerned, this arrangement has been criticized because closing last seems to give an advantage, given that jurors tend to remember what was said last.

After both sides have made their closing arguments, the judge will decide whether to find the accused guilty or not guilty. If the accused is found guilty, the judge will either sentence the individual right then and there, or put it over for sentencing. If the case has been tried before jurors and a judge, the judge will "charge" the jurors; that is, sum up the case and instruct the jurors as to the law they have to apply. After deliberating, the jurors will render a verdict (see below); the sentence is imposed by the judge in a separate hearing without jurors.

Jury Selection

Under s. 11(f) of the Charter, any person charged with an offence that carries a term of imprisonment of five years or more has the right to be tried by jury. All other offences are heard by judge alone. The manner in which jurors are chosen depends on provincial rather than federal law. In general, jurors have to be Canadian citizens who have attained the age of majority. The sheriff calls prospective jurors to make up a panel.

The judge may excuse any juror from jury service for reasons of (a) personal interest in the matter to be tried; (b) relationship with the judge, the Crown prosecutor, the accused, the counsel for the accused, or a prospective witness; or (c) personal hardship or any other reasonable cause.

Twelve jurors are then selected following a procedure where the defence and the prosecution may challenge prospective jurors. Challenges are either "peremptory" or "for cause." The former allows either side to challenge a prospective juror for no reason. Each has a certain number of peremptory challenges depending on the offence. For example, for high treason or first-degree murder, there are 20 peremptory challenges for each side; for most other offences, there are 12.

Challenges for cause are unlimited. Section 638 of the *Criminal Code* spells out the grounds for challenges for cause. They include those situations where the prospective juror

- is not indifferent between the Queen and the accused (i.e., is not neutral);
- has been convicted of an offence for which he was sentenced to a term of imprisonment exceeding 12 months;
- is not a Canadian citizen;
- is physically unable to perform properly the duties; or
- does not speak the official language of Canada that is the language of the trial.

Challenges for cause may not be used to either over- or underrepresent a certain class in society or as a fishing expedition in order to obtain personal information about the jurors.

What Do You Think?

A number of television shows have dramatized the use of high technology and psychological profiling to weed out potential jurors. Do you think that the cost of using such techniques is justifiable for jury trials? Who would benefit from such procedures?

The Verdict

In jury trials, jurors must be unanimous in their decision. The Supreme Court of Canada clarified what this meant:

> This does not mean that the jurors are obliged to agree, but that only a unanimity of views shall constitute a verdict bringing the case to an end. The obligation is not to agree but to co-operate honestly in the study of the facts of a case for its proper determination according to law. (*Latour v. The King*, 1951)

hung jury
A jury that is not able to reach a unanimous verdict; that is, not all jurors can agree that the accused is guilty.

If the jurors cannot reach a unanimous decision (known as a **hung jury**), a mistrial is declared and the prosecution has the right to begin a new trial before the same court with a new jury. In the event the new trial also ends in a mistrial, the prosecution still has the opportunity to file for a new trial until a unanimous verdict is reached. In practice, Crown prosecutors generally refrain from retrying a case more than once, so as not to violate **double jeopardy** guarantees. Unlike those cases tried only by a judge, where the

double jeopardy
The constitutional right not to be tried again for an offence for which there was a previous conviction or acquittal.

judge has to provide reasons for the verdict, jurors do not have to offer reasons of their decision.

Evidence

The sources of evidence are primarily judge-made through common-law rules, and some statutes, particularly the *Canada Evidence Act*, which codifies many of the earlier common law.

Judges are considered to have "principled flexibility"; that is, they have discretion to act within some general principles that govern evidence. These principles are:

- Relevance, which refers to evidence that has any tendency in reason to prove a fact at issue in a proceeding. A fact is relevant if it has probative value; that is, the fact is capable of proving or has the tendency to prove something.
- Finality, which mandates judges to eventually put a final stop to the case.
- Efficiency, which mandates judges to make good use of time and resources.
- Fairness, which requires that the prosecution and the defence have equal access to justice and that the fact finder be protected from prejudicial evidence.

Burden of Proof

The prosecution has the burden of proof, which means it has to convince the trier of fact of the guilt of the accused. The Crown must prove every element of the crime—for example, the *actus reus* and *mens rea*—beyond a reasonable doubt. This is inextricably intertwined with the presumption of innocence. This standard of proof is generally considered to imply that the trier of fact has to be around 95 percent certain of the guilt of the accused. This standard differs from the one used in civil proceedings—referred to as "preponderance of evidence," which simply requires the trier of fact to be more than 50 percent convinced. In some situations, there is a reverse onus of proof. For example, it is presumed under the law that every person is sane. Therefore, for a finding of "not criminally responsible by reason of mental disorder," it is the accused who must prove, by preponderance of evidence, that he or she is insane. Further, before any defence can be introduced before a jury, it must have an air of reality. If so, the judge may admit the defence, which will then be pondered by the trier of fact; namely, that same judge or the jury. Also, judges have to consider a possible defence even if defence

The Crown must prove every element of the crime beyond a reasonable doubt.

counsel failed to raise it before the jury, but there must be something specific that suggests the existence of the defence.

Means of Evidence

Evidence is classified according to its purpose and type (see also coverage of evidence in Chapter 7 on forensics). According to the purpose, evidence can be considered "demonstrative," "illustrative," "direct," or "circumstantial."

- *Demonstrative evidence*, such as video surveillance, stands on its own.
- *Illustrative evidence* is used by a witness to show something—for example, maps, photographs, and images generated by satellite global positioning systems.
- *Direct evidence* supports a proposition directly at issue in a case—for example, fingerprints at a murder scene in a criminal trial.
- *Circumstantial evidence* can be used to infer a conclusion—for example, a sighting of the accused in the neighbourhood at the time of the offence.

Unlike other common-law jurisdictions where direct evidence has priority over circumstantial evidence, in Canada, both circumstantial and direct types of evidence have the same value.

Evidence is classified as (1) real evidence, which consists of all tangible evidence, which is physical objects such as tape recordings, computer printouts, or photographs; (2) documentary evidence, which is any printed relevant information; and (3) testimonial evidence, which is evidence given *viva voce* by a witness in the form of answers to posed questions.

viva voce
A statement made
orally to the court.

Witnesses

Although the police may have interviewed certain individuals during the investigation phase, the prosecution and the defence can call any individual to testify at trial, whether these individuals were questioned before or not. Witnesses are classified as either lay or expert. Before being declared as experts by a judge, witnesses must qualify based on their knowledge, skills, experience, or education. Expert witnesses give testimony based on their scientific, technical, or other specialized knowledge. The purpose of such testimony is to assist the trier of fact in understanding the evidence or to determine a fact in issue. Expert witnesses, as opposed to lay witnesses, may give an opinion if it is based on sufficient facts or data and is the product of reliable principles and methods.

Objections

The judge controls what witnesses can hear. Both the prosecution and the defence may object to questions. An objection can be "sustained" or "overruled" by the judge. If sustained, the witness must refrain from answering the question.

Exclusion of Evidence

Canada follows a somewhat restrictive approach to the exclusion of evidence obtained against the law. Section 24 of the Charter prescribes that where a court concludes that:

> evidence was obtained in a manner that infringed or denied any rights or freedoms guaranteed by this Charter, the evidence shall be excluded if it is established that, having regard to all the circumstances, the admission of it in the proceedings would bring the administration of justice into disrepute.

Thus, the Charter implicitly authorizes courts to admit evidence illegally obtained if the contravention is not be so serious as to bring the administration of justice into disrepute. Further, it is the accused who has the burden of proving that evidence was obtained in violation of his or her rights and that such a violation would bring the administration of justice into disrepute.

The courts consider a number of factors when determining how the admission of illegally obtained evidence will affect the fairness of the trial, including the following:

- *The nature of the trial.* The trial is a key part of the administration of justice and its fairness is a major source of the repute of the system.
- *The nature of the Charter violation.* The more serious the Charter violation, the more severe the disrepute that will result if the evidence is admitted.
- *The effect of excluding the evidence.* Any exclusion of evidence essential to a charge because of a trivial breach of the Charter would result in an acquittal and would bring the administration of justice into varying degrees of disrepute directly proportionate to the seriousness of the charge. The more serious the offence, however, the more damaging an unfair trial would be to the system's repute.

Appeals

In the case of a conviction (i.e., a finding of guilt) or an acquittal (i.e., a finding of not guilty), the criminal case can proceed to the appellate court level. For example, if the accused is found not guilty, the Crown has the right to appeal the criminal case. By contrast, if the accused is given a guilty verdict, the accused has the right to appeal. The appellate courts function in a hierarchal ordering, and only hear issues of law; that is, facts or evidence from a trial court are not dealt with in an appellate court. The first level of appellate courts comprises the provincial appellate courts; there is one within each province (see Figure 5.1 in Chapter 5, The History and Structure of Criminal Law). The Court of Appeal for Ontario (frequently referred to as the Ontario Court of Appeal) is the appellate court in the province of Ontario. The second and final level of the appellate courts is the Supreme Court of Canada. Basically, appeals from the trial courts are generally processed through the provincial appellate courts, and decisions of the provincial appellate courts, if appealed, are then processed through the Supreme Court.

SIDEBAR

Questions of Law Versus Questions of Fact

People are often confused over the exact meaning of these two terms:

Questions of law pertain to legal principles, rules, and tests.

For example, whether the offence of criminal harassment requires intentional *mens rea*.

Questions of fact pertain to what actually took place in the course of the crime.

For example, whether the accused was present at the crime scene.

The Right to Appeal in the Pickton Case

This news item appeared in November 2009, following Pickton's 2007 murder conviction:

> The Supreme Court of Canada has broadened the scope of an appeal by convicted serial killer Robert Pickton, giving him more grounds to argue his conviction should be overturned.
>
> As usual, the high court gave no reasons for its decision, which was released online on Thursday morning.
>
> Pickton lost a previous appeal in June when the B.C. Court of Appeal issued a split ruling upholding his conviction, saying the mistakes made by the trial judge were not serious enough to warrant a new trial.
>
> But because that ruling was a split decision, Pickton won the right to an automatic appeal to the Supreme Court of Canada, but only by using the arguments put forward by the dissenting B.C. Court of Appeal justice.
>
> Following Thursday's decision, Pickton's lawyers will now be able to make arguments based on what the majority found, allowing them to argue in broader terms why the conviction should be overturned.
>
> Pickton was sentenced to life in prison with no parole for at least 25 years after a sensational trial in 2007. The one-time pig farmer was convicted in the murders of six prostitutes, but was charged in 20 other deaths, as well.
>
> Source: CBC (2009).

What Do You Think?

What do you think of the court's decision?

▶ IN-CLASS EXERCISE AND DISCUSSION QUESTIONS

1. A police officer sees an Aboriginal woman walking on the street. The officer has a hunch that the woman has illegal drugs and arrests her. After a search, he finds the woman has cocaine and methamphetamine.

   a. Is the arrest legal? Why or why not?

   b. What are the requirements for a valid arrest?

2. John steals a chocolate bar from a grocery store. The store manager sees him. The store manager stops John and points to a sign on the

store wall, which reads "For your protection: In order to bring you low prices and efficient customer service, shoplifters will be prosecuted." The manager tells John that he will be prosecuted.

   a. Is the store manager right? Explain your answer.

   b. If you were the prosecutor, would you proceed with the case against John?

   c. What test would you apply in deciding whether or not to prosecute John? How would you apply it?

3. A police officer arrests Alex for murder. He tortures Alex until he confesses to the murder. Alex begs the officer to let him call a lawyer and to receive medical attention. The officer denies both requests.

   a. Was the confession obtained legally? Explain your answer.

   b. If you were the judge, would you admit the confession into evidence? What test would you apply? How?

   c. Which criminal justice model predominates in the police officer's conduct?

   d. Which criminal justice model predominates in the judge's conduct?

4. Ian is an 18-year-old man who lives in a small community where everybody knows each other. Ian gropes Sally, an 18-year-old woman, while they are on a bus. Sally complains and calls the police. Ian is arrested for sexual assault.

   a. Under s. 271 of the *Criminal Code*, sexual assault is a hybrid offence; that is, it may be prosecuted as either an indictable offence or a summary conviction. If you were the prosecutor, would you try Ian on a summary conviction or an indictable offence? Why?

   b. Suppose that Ian was prosecuted for an indictable offence. If you were his defence counsel, would you choose to have the case heard before a judge alone or a judge and jury? Why?

5. Rob has been charged with exposure contrary to s. 173 of the *Criminal Code* for having urinated in a public park in the presence of children. Rob appears before the court for his bail hearing.

   a. Suppose you are the judge. Would you grant or deny bail? Why?

   b. What test would you apply? How?

   c. What constitutional rights does Rob have?

NOTE

I would like to thank Mike Storozuk and Denise Marcil for their help in the preparation of this chapter.

SUGGESTED FURTHER READINGS

Coughlan, S. (2012). *Criminal procedure* (2nd ed.). Toronto: Irwin Law.

Gold, A.D. (2007). *Halsbury's laws of Canada: Criminal procedure*. Markham, ON: LexisNexis.

Paciocco, D.M., & Stuesser, S. (2011). *The law of evidence* (6th ed.). Toronto: Irwin Law.

Paciocco, D.M., Tanovich, D.M., & Skurka, S. (1997). *Jury selection in criminal trials: Skills, science, and the law*. Toronto: Irwin Law.

Penney, S., Rondinelli, V., & Stribopoulos, J. (2011). *Criminal procedure in Canada*. Markham, ON: LexisNexis.

REFERENCES

Blank v. Canada (Justice), 2010 FCA 183.

Canadian Charter of Rights and Freedoms, part I of the *Constitution Act, 1982*, RSC 1985, app. II, no. 44.

CBC. (2009, November 26). Supreme Court broadens Pickton's grounds for appeal. CBC News. Retrieved on May 11, 2012 from http://www.cbc.ca/news/canada/british-columbia/story/2009/11/26/bc-supreme-court-pickton-appeal.html

Latour v. The King, [1951] SCR 19.

Lavallee, Rackel & Heintz v. Canada (Attorney General); White, Ottenheimer, & Baker v. Canada (Attorney General); R. v. Fink, [2002] 3 SCR 209, 2002 SCC 61.

R. v. C. (M.H.), [1991] 1 SCR 763.

R. v. Hawkins, [1996] 3 SCR 1043, 11 CCC (3d) 129, 2 CR (5th) 245.

R. v. Mann, 2004 SCC 52.

R. v. Moore (1984), 15 CCC (3d) 541 (Ont. CA).

R. v. Pearson, [1992] 3 SCR 665.

Forensic Science and Forensic Psychology

LEARNING OBJECTIVES

After reading this chapter, students will be able to:

- Name the founders of both forensic science and forensic psychology.
- Know the basics about crime scene investigations.
- Understand the role of forensic scientists working in a forensic laboratory.
- Understand how real-life DNA analysis compares with the media myth.
- Understand the role of the forensic psychologist.
- Understand the importance of studying eyewitness testimony.
- Understand the basic difference between police profiling and profiling done by psychologists.
- Understand the forensic psychologist's role as an expert witness.
- Understand the contributions of forensic psychology to police training.

CHAPTER OUTLINE

Introduction

Television programs such as *CSI* and *Bones* have generated considerable public interest in forensic science. Similarly, movies such as *Silence of the Lambs*, *Manhunter*, and *Mindhunters*, and television programs such as *Criminal Minds* have generated interest in forensic psychology and criminal profiling. Unfortunately, these productions offer poor portrayals of the real-life work of both disciplines. The objective of this chapter is to demystify the real work done by forensic scientists and forensic psychologists.

Forensic Science

Modern forensic science has its origins in the works of a number of 19th-century scientists, but the contributions of two French scientists in particular are worthy of special attention: Alphonse Bertillon (1853–1914) and Edmond Locard (1877–1966). Bertillon is best known for the development of what we now know as mug shots and crime scene photography. He was the first to use a combination of photography with **anthropometry**. His system relied on cross-referencing full-length body photographs of known criminals with precise measurements of their bodies. These measurements included height, head length and breadth, length of the middle finger, tattoos, scars, the length of the left foot, the length of the forearm from the elbow to the end of the middle finger, and reach. This gradually evolved into the modern mug shot. Offender identification previously depended almost entirely on unreliable eyewitness descriptions. Bertillon also introduced the practice of photographing objects at the crime scene. He photographed crime scene objects from ground level and from above, and was the first to place measuring scales next to objects being photographed. This allowed for more accurate recording of crime scenes, including the position of the body relative to other objects, any injuries to the body, and any other evidence, such as footprints, stains, and signs of forcible entry. This was a major advance over the previous practice of using hand-drawn sketches.

Locard, a pupil of Bertillon, made an even more significant contribution to forensic science. As the director of the first crime laboratory in France in the early 1900s, he proposed what is now known as **Locard's exchange principle**. The importance of this principle is clear. If an offender comes into contact with objects at a crime scene, then the offender would leave traces of that contact on the objects. Gathering **trace evidence** is now standard practice.

Securing the Crime Scene

In most situations, the first responders to a crime scene are uniformed officers. It is their responsibility to secure the crime scene to ensure that it is not disturbed until a more experienced investigator, typically the lead investigator, arrives. The lead investigator will then assume responsibility for controlling the crime scene as well as investigating the crime. Only those persons authorized to conduct the investigation will be allowed access to the scene. Nothing can be moved or removed from the crime scene without the lead investigator's permission.

First responders must also call for medical assistance for any injured person at the scene and must record statements made by any victims. Any

anthropometry
The science of measuring the size, weight, and proportions of the human body in criminal cases.

Locard's exchange principle
States that whenever objects come in contact with one another, there will be an exchange of material between them.

trace evidence
Evidence such as blood or other body fluids (e.g., saliva, semen), fingerprints, hair, teeth marks, fibres from clothing or carpets, flakes of skin left under fingernails, or dirt left on clothing or shoes.

MINI CASE STUDY

Crime Scene and Evidence Logging Issues in the O.J. Simpson Case

Failure to secure a crime scene and/or failure to log evidence gathered at a crime scene can have a major impact on the outcome of the case. For example, in the controversial 1995 trial of former NFL superstar O.J. Simpson (who was tried on two counts of murder following the deaths of his ex-wife Nicole Brown Simpson and her friend Ron Goldman), the defence team argued that several errors had been made with respect to blood evidence found at the crime scene. First, blood samples were taken at the crime scene on June 13, 1994, the day *after* the murders. Photographs were also taken of the general location of the crime scene and of the specific locations where blood evidence was found. The photos taken on June 13 of a gate at the crime scene did not show any evidence of bloodstains. However, photos taken on July 3 showed bloodstains on the gate. When asked about the discrepancy, the person responsible for collecting the evidence offered no explanation. It was also revealed that the lead investigator had not immediately logged into evidence a sample of Simpson's blood obtained at his residence the day after the murders. After receiving the vial of blood in an unsealed envelope, the detective went to the crime scene, which was some distance away, with the blood sample. Only several hours later did he give it to the investigator, who later claimed to have found samples of Simpson's blood on the gate. This contributed to the defence claim that evidence was planted at the crime scene. That claim was further supported by evidence showing that more than 1.5 millilitres of the Simpson blood sample taken at his residence had disappeared. These errors may have contributed to the not guilty verdict in this case (Thompson, 1996).

potential witnesses must also be identified. The fire department, the gas company, or anyone else needed to eliminate hazards found at the scene must also be called. If an offender is present, the offender should be taken into custody. If a body is found, the coroner's office must also be called to examine the body *in situ* (in its original place).

The Role of Crime Scene Investigators

After the crime scene has been secured, the real work of crime scene investigation begins. In Canada, major crimes such as murder or rape are investigated by **identification officers** (often referred to as "ident officers"). Minor crimes, such as break-ins or other property crimes, are investigated by **scene of crime officers (SOCOs)**; in other countries they may be called "criminalists," or "crime scene investigators." Until recently, the RCMP required officers to have a minimum of seven years on the job before they

identification ("ident") officers
Police officers who are given specialized forensic training to investigate major crimes.

scene of crime officers (SOCO)
Usually police officers, but in rare cases may be civilian members who have taken similar training to investigate minor crimes.

could apply to become ident officers. They would then complete a two-year apprenticeship. More recently, an officer may begin training as an ident officer after only three years, but the training period has been extended to four years. Other police services have similar training requirements.

The ident officer's job is to collect the evidence, ensuring that every piece of evidence collected at the scene is logged and the location from where it was taken is photographed. Ident officers are trained to collect fingerprints, footprints, tire markings, fibre, hair, any biological evidence (e.g., blood, saliva, semen) found at a major crime scene. They may also collect cigarette butts, plastic bags, paint smears or chips, soil samples, tool marks, petroleum products (in arson cases), and any object that may have been used as a weapon. Ident officers rarely, if ever, question suspects or become involved in any other aspects of the investigation. Their job is to collect the evidence from the crime scene and turn that evidence over to the scientists working in the forensics laboratories.

When collecting evidence, ident officers must follow strict protocols. For example, when collecting biological evidence (Saferstein, 2011), officers must:

1. use gloves when taking samples and change gloves each time a new sample is taken;
2. collect "substrate samples" (these are control samples of what are believed to be uncontaminated surfaces near the point where physical evidence has been collected);
3. use clean, disposable forceps, discarding used forceps after collecting each piece of evidence; and
4. place all evidence in appropriate containers, with each piece of evidence placed in its own container, usually a plastic bag or some other sterile container.

Failure to follow these protocols could seriously jeopardize an investigation.

The Role of Forensic Laboratories

Forensic specialists working in forensic laboratories receive more sophisticated training than do ident officers. To work in one of the six RCMP forensics laboratories (Halifax, Ottawa, Winnipeg, Regina, Edmonton, and Vancouver), applicants must have at least a four-year bachelor of science in an appropriate science discipline. Some of the people who do this work have more advanced degrees: MSc or PhD. Similar requirements are in place for anyone working at provincial forensic analysis facilities. These laboratories are where scientists analyze all forensic evidence collected at a crime scene. They analyze any ballistic evidence, samples of drywall containing trace

Poor Evidence Handling in the O.J. Simpson Case

The murder trial of O.J. Simpson provides another example of how poor handling of forensic evidence undermines a prosecution. At trial, the defence team argued that sloppy handling of blood samples taken at the crime scene rendered the DNA test results null and void. According to the defence, "criminalists" (the term used in California for ident officers) failed to follow written protocols for handling blood evidence. Blood samples found at the crime scene were taken with wet cotton swabs and left in plastic bags in a hot truck on a sunny day: DNA deteriorates in moist, hot conditions. The defence argued that the resulting deterioration in the blood evidence rendered it unreliable. They also argued that the errors indicated that the criminalists were poorly trained (Thompson, 1996). These errors may have further contributed to Simpson's acquittal.

In an attempt to counter defence arguments about the accuracy of DNA testing, the prosecution had all forensic evidence tested in duplicate at two separate laboratories. Although this strategy was successful in one way (the defence did not contest the accuracy of any of the tests), it allowed the defence to focus almost exclusively on the issue of "tampering" and whether the evidence that was collected at the scene was reliable from the beginning.

What Do You Think?

What other pros and cons can you see to the practice of replicating DNA testing in criminal cases?

elements of blood, paint scrapings taken from a hit-and-run victim, blood samples for traces of drugs or poisons, as well as clothing, carpet, or other fibres found at the scene. They also analyze tool marks left on doors or windows to gain entry into a house or building, or bite marks left on a body. Like ident officers, forensic laboratory workers never become involved in the other aspects of criminal investigations.

Similar to improper crime scene procedures, improper laboratory handling of evidence can jeopardize an investigation and can lead to defence challenges of the evidence at trial. Looking again at the Simpson case, the defence team was able to argue that blood evidence was mishandled in the lab. A lab worker had spilled some of Simpson's blood sample. According to the defence argument, that person then transferred the blood sample onto other pieces of evidence, including the glove allegedly belonging to Simpson, as well as the cotton swatches of blood evidence taken from the crime scene (Thompson, 1996). These mistakes may also have contributed to Simpson's eventual acquittal.

DNA Evidence and Offender Identification

DNA profiling is predicated upon the finding that, in the human genome, DNA segments are arranged in repeating patterns, known as "tandem repeats." Although these patterns are inherited from parents and, as such, members of the same family may have similar patterns, each individual has a unique pattern. It is these patterns that DNA analysis uses to make a match between DNA found at a crime scene with a suspect's DNA.

The most common forms of DNA profiling are restriction fragment length polymorphisms (RFLP), polymerase chain reaction (PCR), short tandem repeats (STR), and mitochondrial DNA analysis (mtDNA) (Saferstein, 2011). RFLP profiling was the first method to be widely accepted within the scientific community. Typically, this test can take several weeks to complete. It has fallen into disfavour largely because of the time it takes to obtain results and because it requires relatively large sample sizes, approximately 24 millimetres. This is the test that was used to analyze semen stains on the dress of Monica Lewinsky during the impeachment of US President Bill Clinton (Saferstein, 2011). Using PCR typing, scientists can create millions of copies of the sample DNA, making it possible to analyze samples as small as one-billionth of a gram. This makes it a more desirable method in criminal investigations where small sample sizes may be all that is available. Because it can be used to analyze DNA found in the nucleus of cells, STR profiling is currently the most common form of DNA profiling. Its scientific advantage is that it allows scientists to more easily distinguish one DNA sample from another. Its limitation is that it is difficult to get a profile of a male DNA sample more than three days after a sexual assault. It is also difficult to get a profile of a male sample if it is mixed with a significantly larger female sample. So much confidence is placed on DNA analysis that it has been called the "gold standard" of forensic science.

One of the more common misconceptions about DNA testing is that it **reasonable doubt** can establish guilt or innocence beyond the legal standard of **reasonable** The standard of belief **doubt**. Although DNA identification may be superior to other forms of beyond which the identification, it is not foolproof. As indicated in reference to the O.J. Simpson prosecution must prove its trial, and in numerous other cases, DNA evidence can be and will continue case to obtain a criminal to be challenged in cases where there is evidence that the DNA samples have conviction; in other words, not been handled or processed according to established protocols. Further, the defendant's guilt must it is no substitute for conducting a thorough police investigation using be proven to the extent more conventional investigative techniques. For example, with respect to that "no reasonable person" the identification of serial killers, it has been shown that while DNA analysis could have a "reason- plays an important role in obtaining convictions, it plays a less important able doubt" about it. role in identifying offenders (White, Lester, Gentile, & Rosenbleeth, 2011). Serial killers are more likely to be identified as a result of information obtained from witnesses, including any survivors.

The Paul Bernardo Case

The time needed to analyze DNA samples is much longer than depicted on television. At best it takes a few days, but it can take a week or more depending on the quality of the DNA sample and the volume of samples to be tested. Delays in analyzing samples occur because the labs are often overburdened. For example, during the investigation of a series of rapes in Scarborough, Ontario that began in 1987, Paul Bernardo was asked to provide DNA samples (hair, blood, and saliva) on November 20, 1990 (CBC News, 2010). Testing of the samples did not begin until December 1992. The testing was de-

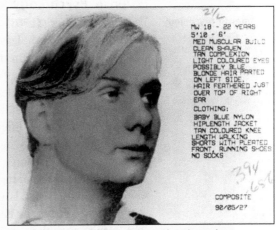

Composite sketch of Paul Bernardo released by police during rape investigations.

layed because the police had collected so many DNA samples that the lab could not analyze them in a timely fashion. As a result, Bernardo was free to commit more crimes, including the murders of two teenage girls in June 1991 and April 1992. This case sparked significant improvements in the speed at which DNA is analyzed. However, while testing is now completed much more quickly, delays resulting from overworked labs still occur (Galloway, 2007). Further, there are numerous examples of investigations that could not be resolved using DNA because testing failed to provide useable analysis. Consequently, other investigative methods must be used. Same-day, overnight, or even same-week DNA testing is an investigator's dream, not a reality.

What Do You Think?

Many of the beliefs that people have about forensic evidence—including its collection, the speed with which test results can be obtained, and the information that it can provide—are heavily influenced by television dramas like *CSI* or *Criminal Minds*. In some cases, these beliefs can lead jurors to question the validity of forensic evidence during a trial if the evidence does not seem as convincing or as definitive as it does on television. In other cases, these beliefs can lead jurors to place too much faith in forensic science, believing crimes are "solved" in a laboratory. Many wrongful conviction cases in North America have been linked to faulty or tainted DNA evidence. What other effects do you think media representations of forensic evidence might have on the actual operations of the criminal justice system?

Forensic Psychology

forensic psychology
The application of psychological research, methods, theories, and practices to a task faced by the legal system (Wrightsman & Fulero, 2005, p. 2).

Hugo Münsterberg (1863–1916) is often said to be the founder of **forensic psychology**. He was at least one of the first to show that psychology could play an important role in the legal system.

Arguably, his most significant contributions were to the study of eyewitness testimony and the psychology of false confessions. In his most famous book, *On the Witness Stand*, Münsterberg (1908) showed that eyewitnesses to the same event may have different memories of the event. For example, after witnessing someone moving quickly through a room carrying an object with one hand and talking on a cellphone, one person might say he saw a man carrying a briefcase seemingly talking to himself, while another might say she saw a woman carrying a large purse and talking on a cellphone. Münsterberg also observed that many false confessions are the result of offenders fearing that, even though they are innocent, the evidence against them is sufficient for a conviction. Other false confessions might be the result of mere fatigue. After a prolonged interrogation, an individual might confess because the person is simply too exhausted to offer further resistance. In support of the latter claim, Münsterberg used the example that some of the confessions in the infamous Salem, Massachusetts witch trials of 1692 were undoubtedly given by men and women suffering from sleep deprivation and fatigue brought on by prolonged, continuous, and arduous questioning.

Hugo Münsterberg

By contemporary standards, much of Münsterberg's work was methodologically flawed. His lab procedures were crude and his claims of scientific validity were exaggerated. Nonetheless, he stands out as a champion of applying scientific method to understanding how memory works and how to apply that knowledge. He was the first to use psychological perspective and method in the assessment of key issues in the legal system.

The Role of Forensic Psychology

In the years since Münsterberg championed the application of psychology and scientific method to the legal system, forensic psychology has undergone significant development. Modern forensic psychology investigates a wide range of activities. The list of pursuits includes:

- assessing the psychology of police recruits
- detecting offender deception during questioning
- assessing children as potential witnesses
- determining the risk of offenders to reoffend
- assessing the sanity of an accused

- assessing the reactions of victims
- studying jury behaviour.

Several aspects of forensic investigation are discussed in this chapter.

Psychology and Police Training

The involvement of forensic psychologists in police training begins with pre-hiring interviews. These interviews are usually the first stage in the recruitment process. An important part of the interview and screening process is to determine the psychological suitability of applicants to perform police work. For example, the RCMP interview focuses on self-awareness, flexibility, problem-solving skills, self-control, self-discipline, communication skills, the ability to act as a team player, and the ability to identify and meet client needs (Royal Canadian Mounted Police, 2012). The interview may also include taking one or more psychological tests. The most commonly used tests include **cognitive ability tests**, **personality tests**, and **situational tests** (Pozzulo, Bennell, & Forth, 2012).

There is some evidence that certain cognitive ability tests are better than others. For example, Bertua, Anderson, and Salgado (2005) showed that tests measuring general cognitive abilities are better predictors of potential job performance than are cognitive ability tests measuring specific abilities. While both types of test are useful assessment tools, questions arise regarding the lack of standardized criteria for assessing recruits (Dantzker, 2011). There is concern interviewer biases may inadvertently become part of the questioning and that this could result in some potential recruits from minority groups being overlooked (McMurray, Karim, & Fisher, 2010). One Canadian study by Hausdorf, LeBlanc, and Chawla (2003) found that some cognitive ability tests may screen out potential minority recruits because of biases built into the design of the testing instrument. These biases can range from gender and race to ethnicity and class.

The most commonly used personality tests are the Minnesota Multiphasic Personality Inventory (MMPI) and the MMPI-2. Both these test have been considered the gold standard for assessing personality since the early 1940s. The MMPI, however, has come under increased scrutiny, because it was not intended as a recruitment tool (Pozzulo et al., 2012); for more than 30 years, it has been known that the MMPI is unable to detect some psychological disorders (Gass, Russell, & Hamilton, 1990). More recently, Baer and Miller (2002) observed that the MMPI-2 is also ineffective when attempting to distinguish between honest and fake responses. This creates obvious problems when trying to recruit or train police officers.

cognitive ability tests
Tests designed to measure reasoning, perception, memory, verbal and written language skills, mathematical ability, and problem solving.

personality tests
Standardized tests used to measure personality characteristics or discover personality disorders that might affect a person's ability to perform a specific job.

situational tests
Tests that present applicants with hypothetical job-related scenarios and ask them to identify appropriate responses from a list of alternatives.

Because of these problems with the MMPI and MMPI-2, other techniques have been adopted. The California Psychological Inventory (CPI) is used to measure personality characteristics such as dominance, sociability, and flexibility. One recent study comparing the MMPI and the CPI found that the latter was better able to predict officer performance than was the MMPI (Varela, Boccaccini, Sogin, Stump, & Caputo, 2004). The CPI is also better able to assess interpersonal skills, such as the ability to interact with the community, other officers, and supervisors.

The intent of situational tests is to make the simulations as realistic as possible. They may include simulations of domestic disputes, foot patrols, crime scene investigations, officer-down scenarios, or hostage-taking scenarios. Simulations have long been part of police recruit training, and are being increasingly used as a training tool for even more experienced police officers (Seymour, Stahl, Levine, & Ingram, 1994). However, Bennell, Jones, and Corey (2007) found that training scenarios are sometimes narrowly focused on testing a particular situation and do not offer a sufficient variety of scenarios, thus potentially limiting their effectiveness.

What Do You Think?

Critiques of the usefulness of police training scenarios generally focus on the narrowness of the scenarios (i.e., because they present only one issue) and the effect that the scenarios can have on police officers' confidence to deal with highly complex and volatile situations. Do you agree? What might be some of the advantages of these situational tests?

Psychological Profiling

offender profiling
The process of using all available information about a crime, a crime scene, and a victim in order to compose a profile of the unknown perpetrator (Ainsworth, 2001, p. 7).

Offender profiling is often incorrectly assumed to have been created by the FBI's Behaviour Science Unit (BSU) in the early 1970s (Ressler, Burgess, & Douglas, 1988). Psychologists had been offering their services as profilers for several decades before the BSU started its training program (Canter, 2000). The BSU training program was the first by a police agency. Other police agencies, including the RCMP in Ottawa, soon followed. Trainee police profilers are usually experienced officers who are given specialized training that enables them to combine their police experience with knowledge in psychology, criminology, sociology, and conflict resolution.

Although there are some former FBI profilers who claim that their profiles have identified particular offenders (Douglas, 1995), there is little independent empirical evidence to support the claim. It is often said that the type of profiling done by the police is more art than science (Holmes & Holmes, 2009). Canter (2000) has even suggested that it amounts to little more than informed speculation since it lacks empirical support.

According to Holmes and Holmes (2009), psychological profiling makes several assumptions about the crime scene and the offender. It assumes that the crime scene reflects the personality of the offender, that the offender will commit the crime in a manner that is peculiar to that offender, that the of-fender will not change his or her personality, and that the profile will be of assistance to investigators. Canter prefers the term **investigative psychology** because of the great reliance upon scientific method.

Canter says investigative psychology focuses on the classification and description of criminals and their activities, showing the connection be-tween the offenders' criminal activity and their everyday lives. Ainsworth (2001) adds that it is easy to forget that criminals are not engaged in crimi-nality all day, every day. Most spend the largest portion of their daily lives doing ordinary things. Someone who commits an uncaring, selfish crime is likely to be an uncaring, selfish person in his or her everyday life.

investigative psychology
Field of study that takes the scientific discipline of psychology—its principles, theories, and empirical findings—and applies it to investigations and the legal process.

Eyewitness Testimony

While Münsterberg may have initiated the psychological study of eyewitness testimony, contemporary psychologists have developed this specialization into a mature research area. The accuracy of eyewitness testimony is vital to any police investigation and eventual court proceeding. As the memory experiment in the class exercise (below) suggests, memory is not always accurate. There is potential for an offender to be misidentified through eyewitness testimony, and some accused persons have been wrongfully convicted based on false memory. Memory can be influenced by such things as self-confidence, social influences from peers or other witnesses, or even verbal or non-verbal communication from a police officer prior to or during identification lineups. Leach, Cutler, and Wallendael (2009) found that fac-tors such as faulty instructions given by the police to an eyewitness, the motivation of an eyewitness to make an identification, and the mood of an eyewitness at the time of the identification compared with the person's mood at the time of the criminal event all have an impact on the accuracy of eye-witness testimony. Eyewitness testimony can also be influenced by the wording of questions, which may suggest that a specific answer is wanted. In other cases, such as the one in the memory experiment, the witness may have had only a brief moment to view the events, and the lack of viewing time may affect his or her memory. Both defence lawyers and Crown pros-ecutors may deliberately attempt to confuse witnesses.

See also mini chapter 16.7
Wrongful Convictions and Jailhouse Informants

▶ IN-CLASS EXERCISE
Memory Experiment

The instructor should connect to the Internet and go to the following web-site: www.psychology.iastate.edu/~glwells/theeyewitnesstest.html. Once at the website, click "here" to observe the video. (If any student has previously viewed this experiment, ask that student not to say what he or she observed.)

1. Have the entire class view the brief video *once*. It is important that students view the video without talking to anyone else.
2. After viewing the video, return to the main page and click on "click here" to observe the suspect lineup.
3. After viewing the suspect lineup, but before clicking on any of the suspect numbers, ask the students to record their suspect choices without discussing them with anyone else.
4. Next, ask the class to say who chose suspect 1, 2, 3, 4, 5, or 6. *Do not click on any suspect number yet.* Keep a rough tally of how many students identified suspect 1, how many suspect 2, and so on.
5. Discuss the following questions with the class:
   - Why did you select that suspect as the offender?
   - If you did not select an offender, why not?
   - What do you think influenced your decision?
6. Now click on the suspect numbers to reveal the suspect. Discuss the response shown on the screen when a suspect number is pressed.
7. Discuss the implications of this experiment for such issues as the reliability of eyewitness testimony and wrongful convictions.

A key task for forensic psychologists, therefore, is to identify optimal conditions for conducting police lineups. There have been numerous studies suggesting ways in which the police can improve their interviewing and lineup techniques. One Canadian study recommended that police should use a standard method for instructing witnesses participating in a lineup (Kaschuk, 2011). The study found that failure to use standard instructions can have a negative impact on the results of the lineup. The memory experiment above included viewing a photo lineup for which you were given no instructions. You were not told that the suspect might not be present, and all the photos were shown to you at once. Studies suggest that this is not the best practice. For example, Sporer (1993) found that it was best to show the photos to the witness one at a time, rather than all at once.

Keep in mind that a key objective for forensic psychologists studying eyewitness testimony is to test and retest the issues that arise from reliance upon eyewitnesses. It is important to know how police lineups are conducted and how to obtain optimal results from lineups. It is also important to know the extent to which children may be relied upon as eyewitnesses. Serious questions have been raised about the validity of recovered memories of childhood sexual abuse (MacMartin & Yarmey, 1999). Not all recovered memories are real.

Police Interrogations and Confessions

Forensic psychologists are often asked to give advice with respect to police interrogations and false confessions. As a consultant, the forensic psychologist's client may be the defence trying to illustrate how a police interrogation produced a false confession, or a police department seeking to improve its interrogation practices to reduce false confessions. On rare occasions, the forensic psychologists may act as a "friend of the court" to offer advice to the judiciary with respect to issues related to false confessions. Regardless of who the client is, the task is to offer advice based on research.

False confessions may be voluntary, compliant, or coerced (Kassin, 2008). Some individuals will voluntarily confess to a crime they did not commit. They do so because they feel a need to be punished for some real or imagined transgression, or they may wish to protect a loved one who actually committed the crime. According to Kassin, these confessions are the least likely to be investigated by forensic psychologists because they are so easily detected by the police. "Compliant confessions" are a form of coerced confession. They occur when an innocent person admits to the crime to reduce the stress of the interrogation. Individuals may also confess if they have been led to believe that they will get a recommendation for a reduced charge or lighter sentence. Another form of coerced confession occurs when the suspect comes to believe that he or she actually committed the crime. These are called "coerced internal confessions." The person may actually not trust his or her own memories of the events and become vulnerable to external pressure during interrogation (Kassin, 2008).

In some cases, a person may not trust his or her own memories of events.

Kassin, Drizin, Grisso, Gudjonsson, and Redlich (2010) found that a common factor in coerced confessions, whether compliant or internalized, is the confrontational nature of police interrogations. During an interview, most police interrogators in North America use the "Reid technique." This technique depends on the interrogator interpreting the truthfulness of a suspect's statements using the suspect's verbal and non-verbal reactions to questioning. It involves using psychologically manipulative methods, such as sleep deprivation and false statements about the evidence police have, and/or making promises of leniency in return for a confession. These strategies contribute to the making of false confessions. Kassin (2008) pointed out that the assumptions upon which the Reid technique is based have never been adequately tested and remain unproven.

Kassin et al. (2010) argued that replacing the Reid technique with some other form of interrogation would help reduce the number of false confessions. They pointed to interrogative methods employed in England, where the Reid technique is not used. To reduce the number of false confessions, the police are advised to limit interrogations to no longer than four hours, to refrain from making false statements about the evidence in their possession, and to eliminate promises of leniency if the offender confesses.

Expert Testimony

Most forensic psychologists would agree that providing expert testimony in court is a difficult task. In most cases, the client is either the defence or the prosecution. Wrightsman and Fulero (2005) observed that this poses difficulty for both the court and forensic psychologists. An expert witness is supposed to offer evidence based on his or her professional expertise and is not supposed to be an advocate for either side in the case. Nonetheless, they are often seen as advocates because they are being asked to testify for either the defence or the prosecution. On rare occasions, they may be asked by the court to express an opinion. For this reason, the courts and forensic psychologists have been attempting to set guidelines for the admissibility of expert testimony.

The standard for admissibility of expert testimony in Canada is the four-part Mohan criteria (Wilansky, 2002), which states:

1. The evidence must be logically *relevant* to the case at hand and must not be prejudicial.
2. The evidence must meet the *necessity criteria*, meaning it must be knowledge which neither the judge nor the jury could be expected to know; it must be expert knowledge, not general knowledge.
3. The evidence must not be subject to any previous *exclusionary rules* or decisions. This means that if it has already been determined that evidence about an accused's character has been ruled inadmissible, then any testimony related to that character would not be permitted unless the accused raised the issue in defence.
4. The person giving the evidence must be recognized as an expert by the judge based on that person's experience or specialized training and education.

Determining Insanity

Providing expert testimony to establish whether the accused is legally insane is one of the most difficult tasks a forensic psychologist may be asked to perform. The legal rules for judging insanity vary from country to country and are based on legal—and not necessarily psychological—criteria. In Canada, the criteria were established in the *Criminal Code* in 1892 by application of the **McNaughton rule**. Essentially, a person could not be convicted of a crime if at the time of the offence the individual had some form of mental defect or "disease of the mind" that made the person incapable of knowing that what he or she was doing was wrong. Under this rule, an accused found to be insane was declared "not guilty by reason of insanity." This provision remained in effect until 1991, when the *Criminal Code* was amended so that an accused found unfit to stand trial was declared "not criminally responsible on account of mental disorder" (NCRMD).

When assessing the sanity of a defendant in Canada, it is common practice to use the Rogers Criminal Responsibility Assessment Scale. This instrument has five scales with 30 items each. Despite the rigour of the scale, determining sanity is still a challenge. There is no set point on the scale that says above the line someone is sane and below the line someone is insane. It is a judgment made by those doing the evaluation. Despite popular misconceptions, this defence is rarely used and is rarely successful. In most cases where it is successful, both the prosecution and the defence agree before the trial begins that the accused meets the NCRMD standard (Pozzulo et al., 2012). Courtroom battles pitting one against the other are rare in Canada.

As noted by Kramer and Gagliardi (2009), it is often difficult for the psychologist to determine whether the behaviour being exhibited by the accused is real or feigned. An accused may also have deliberately feigned past symptoms. For this reason, Kramer and Gagliardi recommended multiple assessment tools when making a diagnosis. Other researchers have suggested that the fact that the accused is usually assessed long after the time when the act was committed also makes it difficult to determine the individual's state of mind at the time of the act (Ferguson & Ogloff, 2011).

McNaughton rule

Rule stipulating that a person cannot be convicted of a crime if, at the time of the offence, he or she had a mental defect or disease of the mind that made him or her unaware of the nature of his or her actions, or incapable of knowing that the act was wrong.

Conclusion

This chapter has provided overviews of both forensic science and forensic psychology. The activities and training of the people involved differ significantly, but they have a common purpose. They are both dedicated to using scientific methods to collect and analyze data.

The work of forensic science begins with the securing of the crime scene, to ensure that only authorized people enter it and that all evidence is carefully logged. From there, the work goes to the forensic laboratory, where the data, including any samples of bloodstains, fibres, and other evidence gathered at the scene, are processed and analyzed using strict protocols. While often portrayed in the media as something that can be done in a matter of hours, DNA analysis in real life can take weeks or even months to complete.

Forensic psychology has many and varied tasks ranging from helping the police to develop better training techniques, to providing expert testimony on an offender's sanity, to assessments of the accuracy of eyewitness testimony. While media portrayals often depict forensic psychology as a virtually infallible bank of knowledge, real-life forensic psychology is not so simple. There are significant ongoing debates and controversies that require repeated and frequent studies to update and refine the knowledge base.

DISCUSSION QUESTIONS

1. Discuss possible reasons why the public is often given misleading portrayals of both forensic science and crime scene investigations. What are the consequences of these misleading portrayals?
2. Discuss the implications for the advancement of forensic science of the battles waged in courts between defence lawyers and prosecutors about the reliability of DNA evidence.
3. Discuss the implications of the differences between police offender profiling and investigative psychology.

SUGGESTED FURTHER READINGS

Anderson, G.S. (2007). All you ever wanted to know about forensic science in Canada but didn't know who to ask! Ottawa: Canadian Society of Forensic Science. http://www.csfs.ca/contentadmin/UserFiles/File/Booklet2007.pdf

Chisum, W.J., & Turvey, E.B. (2000). Evidence dynamics: Locard's exchange principle and crime reconstuction. *Journal of Behavioral Profiling, 1*(1). http://www.profiling.org/journal/vol1_no1/jbp_ed_january2000_1-1.html

Cole, S.A., & Dioso-Villa, R. (2009). Investigating the "CSI effect" effect: Media and litigation crisis in criminal law. *Stanford Law Review, 61*(6), 1335–1373.

Hickey, E.W. (2006). *Serial murderers and their victims* (4th ed.). Belmont, CA: Thompson Wadsworth.

Holmes, R.M., & Holmes, S.T. (2009). *Profiling violent crimes: An investigative tool* (4th ed.). Thousand Oaks, CA: Sage.

Saferstein, R. (n.d.). Documenting a crime scene. http://www.videojug.com/interview/documenting-a-crime-scene-2. (This website contains video material explaining how and why a crime scene is secured and the types of evidence collected.)

Wells, G. (n.d.). http://www.psychology.iastate.edu/~glwells/homepage.htm. (This website of a leading expert on eyewitness testimony includes videos and other useful resources.)

Your Amazing Brain. (n.d.). Are you a good eyewitness? http://www.youramazingbrain.org/testyourself/eyewitness.htm (A test of your memory skills similar to the in-class memory experiment.)

REFERENCES

Ainsworth, P. (2001). *Offender profiling and crime analysis*. Cullompton, UK: Willan.

Baer, R.A., & Miller, J. (2002). Underreporting of psychopathology on the MMPI-2: A meta-analytic review. *Psychological Assessment, 14*(1), 16–26.

Bennell, C., Jones, N.J., & Corey, S. (2007). Does the use of force simulation training in Canadian police agencies incorporate principles of effective training? *Psychology, Public Policy, and Law, 13*(1), 35–58.

Bertua, C., Anderson, N., & Salgado, J.F. (2005). The predictive validity of cognitive ability tests: A UK meta-analysis. *Journal of Occupational and Organizational Psychology, 78*(September), 387–409.

Canter, D. (2000). Offender profiling and criminal differentiation. *Legal and Criminological Psychology*, 23–46.

CBC News. (2010, June 17). *Key events in the Bernardo/Homolka case*. Retrieved from http://www.cbc.ca/news/canada/story/2010/06/16/f-bernardo -homolka-timeline.html

Dantzker, M.L. (2011). Psychological preemployment screening for police candidates: Seeking consistency if not standardization. *Professional Psychology: Research and Practice, 42*(3), 276–283.

Douglas, J. (1995). *Mind hunter*. New York: Pocket Books.

Ferguson, M., & Ogloff, J.R. (2011). Criminal responsibility evaluations: Role of psychologists in assessment. *Psychiatry, Psychology and Law, 18*(1), 79–94.

Galloway, G. (2007, March 31). Backlog haunts Canada's top forensic lab: Fraser. Retrieved from http://www.theglobeandmail.com/news/national/ article753078.ece

Gass, C.S., Russell, E.W., & Hamilton, R.A. (1990). Accuracy of MMPI-based inferences regarding memory and concentration in closed-head-trauma patients. *Psychological Assessment: A Journal of Consulting and Clinical Psychology, 2*(2), 175–178.

Hausdorf, P.A., LeBlanc, M.M., & Chawla, A. (2003). Cognitive ability testing and employment selection: Does test content relate to adverse impact? *Applied HRM Research, 7*(2), 41–48.

Holmes, R.M., & Holmes, S.T. (2009). *Profiling violent crimes: An investigative tool* (4th ed.). Thousand Oaks, CA: Sage.

Kaschuk, N. (2011). Toward a proper and complete instruction for photo lineups: Preserving the probative value of identification evidence. *Canadian Criminal Law Review, 16*(1), 1–11.

Kassin, S.M. (2008). The psychology of confessions. *Annual Review of Law and Social Science, 4*, 193–217.

Kassin, S.M., Drizin, S.A., Grisso, T., Gudjonsson, G.H., & Redlich, A.D. (2010). Police-induced confessions: Risk factors and recommendations. *Law and Human Behavior, 34*(1), 3–38.

Kramer, G.M., & Gagliardi, G.J. (2009). Forensic evaluation of insanity: Assessing valid symptom report in defendants with major mental disorder. *Journal of Forensic Psychology Practice, 9*(1), 92–102.

Leach, A.-M., Cutler, B.L., & Wallendael, L.V. (2009). Lineups and eyewitness identification. *Annual Review of Law and Social Science, 5*, 157–178.

MacMartin, C., & Yarmey, A.D. (1999). Rhetoric and the recovered memory debate. *Canadian Psychology, 40*(4), 346–358.

McMurray, A.J., Karim, A., & Fisher, G. (2010). Perspectives on the recruitment and retention of culturally and linguistically diverse police. *Cross Cultural Management: An International Journal, 17*(2), 193–210.

Münsterberg, H. (1908). *On the witness stand.* Garden City, NY: Doubleday.

Pozzulo, J., Bennell, C., & Forth, A. (2012). *Forensic psychology* (3rd ed.). Toronto: Pearson Canada.

Ressler, R.K., Burgess, A.W., & Douglas, J.E. (1988). *Sexual homicide: Patterns and motives.* Lexington, MA: Lexington Books.

Royal Canadian Mounted Police. (2012, February 1). Preparatory guide for the regular member selection interview. Retrieved from http://www.rcmp-grc .gc.ca/recruiting-recrutement/htm-form/prep-interview-entrevue-eng.htm

Saferstein, R. (2011). *Criminalistics* (10th ed.). Upper Saddle River, NJ: Prentice Hall.

Seymour, G., Stahl, J.M., Levine, S., & Ingram, J.L. (1994). Modifying law enforcement training simulators for use in basic research. *Behavior Research Methods, Instruments, and Computers, 26*(2), 266–268.

Sporer, S.L. (1993). Eyewitness identification accuracy, confidence, and decision times. *Journal of Applied Psychology, 78*(1), 22–33.

Thompson, W.C. (1996). DNA evidence in the O.J. Simpson trial. *University of Colorado Law Review, 67*(4), 827–858. Retrieved from http://phobos.ramapo .edu/~jweiss/laws131/unit3/simpson.htm

Varela, J.G., Boccaccini, M.T., Sogin, F., Stump, J., & Caputo, A. (2004). Personality testing in law enforcement employment settings. *Criminal Justice and Behaviour, 31*(6), 649–675.

White, J.H., Lester, D., Gentile, M., & Rosenbleeth, J. (2011). The utilization of forensic science and criminal profiling for capturing serial killers. *Forensic Science International, 209*(1), 160–165.

Wilansky, P. (2002). *Does Mohan matter in child sexual abuse cases?* (Doctoral dissertation). Retrieved from ProQuest Dissertations and Theses http://www.proquest.com (AAINQ72019).

Wrightsman, L.S., & Fulero, S.M. (2005). *Forensic psychology.* Belmont, CA: Thomson Wadsworth.

Sentencing

LEARNING OBJECTIVES

After reading this chapter, students will be able to:

- Compare the purpose, principles, benefits, and limitations of sentencing in Canada.
- Identify and discuss the principles of sentencing as outlined in Canada's *Criminal Code*.
- Understand the sentencing process, including how judges make sentencing decisions.
- Comment on the involvement of victims of crime in the court process.
- Comment on the various specialized types of sentences.
- Discuss the effectiveness and limitations of the various alternatives to sentencing.
- Comment on the recent changes to sentencing in Canada.
- Discuss the impact of mandatory minimum sentences.

CHAPTER OUTLINE

Introduction

> The determination of a just and appropriate sentence is a delicate art which attempts to balance carefully the societal goals of sentencing against the moral blameworthiness of the offender and the circumstances of the offence, while at all times taking into account the needs and current conditions of and in the community. (*R. v. M. (C.A.)*, 1996)

Sentencing in Canada has remained fairly consistent since formalized courts, at both the federal and provincial levels, were established shortly after Confederation in 1867. Once an accused person is convicted (found guilty) of a crime, the court must decide on an appropriate **sentence**. Sentencing is one of the most challenging and controversial aspects of our justice system. The public has strong opinions about it, the media reports its perspective, and the written law has its framework. In addition to all of that, there are the individuals affected by the crime—victims and offenders—who also have a broad range of religious, social, cultural, and moral

sentence
A judicial determination of the legal sanction to be given to a person who has been convicted of an offence. For example, Joe is sentenced to pay a fine of $100.

values and views. These are people whose lives will be forever changed, as was shown in the Part One case study.

Theoretical Principles of Sentencing

Sentencing involves handing out a punishment to the convicted offender, taking into consideration that an appropriate sentence can deter the individual from committing future crimes or rehabilitate the person. Sentencing raises a number of questions. Should the sentence support the state's aim to maintain order in society? Will this sentence deter other potential offenders from committing crimes? Does the sentence acknowledge society's support in rehabilitating this offender? Answers to these questions may seem straightforward at first, but in reality they are complex. What is an "appropriate" sentence, and who defines it? How can we be certain that this punishment will indeed prevent future crimes? How do we know if convicted offenders can be rehabilitated? And what is the overriding purpose of sentencing—to protect society, or to rehabilitate or punish offenders? Moreover, judges can still exercise their discretion in most instances. And regardless of how long or tough sentences may be, offenders will in most cases eventually get out of prison, which raises further questions, such as: Did the time in prison prepare the offender to **reintegrate** into the community and become a productive member of society?

*See also mini chapter 16.8
Capital Punishment*

reintegrate
Returning offenders to society as law-abiding and productive citizens.

Deterrence

The concept of deterrence plays a key role in sentencing—to deter not only the individual offender from committing future crimes, but potential offenders as well. This crime-control approach is based on protecting society through the prevention of criminal acts. According to this theory, laws are effective when the fear of getting caught and going to jail is real and certain; you might think twice about stealing your neighbour's car. But if the causes underlying your choice to steal that car involve poverty and a lack of opportunity for work, any law in place may not deter you from committing that crime. That counterargument acknowledges the larger responsibilities society has for the welfare of all of its citizens. Think about it: Canada's *Criminal Code* has 467 sections of laws and more than ten additional acts, yet many people break those laws every single day.

But laws and appropriate sentences are meant to control deviant behaviour. There are two types of deterrence: specific and general. *Specific* deterrence is meant to discourage the offender from committing future crimes, while *general* deterrence is meant to discourage all other potential offenders from committing crimes. That is, if the sentence is severe enough, it will deter others from committing similar criminal acts.

But how long should that sentence be? If a sentence is too lenient, it might send the message that sentencing is not to be feared. If it is too harsh, the message might be that the justice system is not fair, which in turn might actually encourage more criminal activity. For example, if the minimum sentence for armed robbery is ten years in jail, robbers might decide to kill their victims, because they would be able to identify them.

What Do You Think?

Recall the case that begins Part One of this book, and the sentence you had suggested for the offender. Try to consider your sentence in terms of deterrence: In what ways, if any, does it reflect a particular theory of deterrence? Was it specific or general?

Selective Incapacitation

The concept of selective incapacitation is based on the idea that if someone is removed from society, that person will no longer be a threat. The belief is that by removing or restricting an offender's freedom, it makes it almost impossible for the individual to commit another crime.

While both the incapacitation and deterrence theories focus on punishing offenders for the express purpose of protecting society, incapacitation favours much longer sentences. This approach is generally taken with offenders with lengthy criminal histories. Long prison sentences are considered a good idea because removing habitual or career offenders from society for an extended period of time is thought to decrease the overall crime rate. Some research supports this (Ehrlich, 1975, p. 402), but the fact is, approximately 90 percent of offenders are eventually released from prison. A study by Zedlewski in 1987 concluded that for every $1 spent on incarcerating an offender, there is a $17 saving to society in terms of social costs (such as insurance premiums for businesses and taxes to pay police). Critics, however, believe this philosophy is flawed, since it cannot provide the cause–effect between punishing a robber to life imprisonment and reducing the overall crime rate. Incapacitating criminals only protects society while that offender is in prison. Offenders will be released eventually from prison, and some research supports the position that after offenders have served their prison terms, they may actually be more predisposed to committing further crimes (as cited in Clear, 1994).

Rehabilitation

The rehabilitation concept takes the approach that many offenders can be treated in humane ways and, once released, they will lead crime-free lives. Communities, individuals, and the state all have a role in repairing the harm done by an offender's actions. Programs and case management are then designed to "correct" the behaviour and personality of offenders, in the hope that what was once learned can be unlearned and that new coping behaviours can be established. The basis for this approach is rooted in the belief that offenders have many layers—that is, they are not "just" criminals—and that their social and psychological experiences (lack of education, living in poverty, or enduring childhood abuse) have influenced criminal thinking and decision making. Therefore, treatment is necessary in order to prepare them to return to society as law-abiding citizens. Since every offender is different and the accompanying social and psychological issues are also different, the type and length of treatment should also vary. Advocates of rehabilitation-based sentencing believe that prisons should have a variety of programs available to assist the variety of offenders housed within.

The success of such rehabilitation programs is the subject of much debate. Many argue against spending valuable resources on programming in prison, while others believe in its inherent success, especially when programs and offender needs are matched effectively (Andrews et al., 1990, p. 400).

What Do You Think?

In the case study that begins Part One, consider the offender: At this stage in his life, what programs would you recommend that could successfully support his rehabilitation in prison?

Retribution

Another principle of sentencing found in s. 718 of the *Criminal Code* is retribution. This principle is tied into the justice model discussed in Chapter 1 where offenders should be punished no more or no less severely than their actions warrant; that is, the severity of the sentence should depend on the seriousness of the crime (not the seriousness of the individual). The belief is that all punishments should be equally and fairly given to each person convicted of the same crime. The focus here is on the *crime* committed rather than on any attributes of the individual. For example, John is convicted of assault with a prior history of assault; the justice model suggests that he should be given the same sentence as Joe, who has also been convicted of assault and has a prior history of assault. However, if John has a history of addiction, is Aboriginal, and is young, he would most likely be given a different type of sentence (or a longer one) than Joe, whose history includes corporate crimes and domestic abuse. In theory, the sentence imposed should be based on the crime committed, but in reality, that is often not the case.

Retribution is not concerned with treatment or reducing the crime rate (crime prevention). It focuses on an offender's past behaviour as the basis for sentencing, not on the offender's likelihood for future criminal activity or the protection of society. The principle of retribution is informed by the justice model, which maintains that while sentences are determinate (will eventually end), they should be shorter rather than longer. For example, justice advocates would support a sentence of seven years for assault with a weapon (including community-based sentences) with no opportunity to apply for parole (or early release), in contrast to supporters of deterrence or incapacitation, who would prefer a longer sentence also with no opportunity to apply for parole.

Restorative Justice

The restorative justice approach focuses on repairing the harm that has been done as a result of the criminal act. This theory recognizes that crime causes harm that can be felt by an individual, a business, and/or a community, and is harmful to the offender as well. It is believed that by repairing this harm—emotional or material—offenders will understand the consequences of their actions and be deterred from committing more crimes; the community and its members will be healed and therefore able to live without fear. This approach is about bringing people together to respond to crime, and those responses should not punish or rehabilitate the offender, but instead put conditions in place for repairing as much of the harm caused by the crime as possible. The restorative justice approach is reflected in two of the sentencing principles outlined in s. 718 of the Code: s. 718(e), which requires judges to consider how the sentence will provide reparations to the victim and community; and s. 718(f), which requires that sentences promote a sense of responsibility in offenders for the harm their crimes have done.

Maximum punishments for all crimes are supported, although minimum punishments are not; judicial discretion is valued and preference is given to a wide range of sentences that may better fit the offender and individual or community harmed. This means that sentences such as fines, community service (e.g., repairing the broken store window caused by the break-in), compensation, reconciliation, and apologies are favoured over imprisonment for many crimes.

What Do You Think?

How might these principles of sentencing (deterrence, selective incapacitation, rehabilitation, retribution, and restorative justice) be considered with respect to the theoretical models of criminal justice outlined in Chapter 1 (crime control, justice, welfare, community change, and restorative justice)?

How Does a Judge Decide on a Sentence?

Regardless of whether the offender was found guilty by a judge or by a jury, it is the judge presiding over the trial who decides on an appropriate sentence. Sentences can include periods of incarceration, probation, a fine, and/or a conditional sentence, among others. Ideally, the same trial heard in different courtrooms by different judges should result in the same or similar sentences. But in reality, judicial decision means judicial discretion—the judge decides what is appropriate. This creates "disparity." **Disparity** is the notion that differences in treatment and outcomes exist, not necessarily due to intentional prejudice, but as a result of a judge's beliefs and philosophies. This disparity has caused concern and has led to demands that judicial discretion be controlled, as with mandatory minimum sentences. Currently, judges have great discretion in terms of how to sentence an individual convicted of a crime that does not have a mandatory minimum period of incarceration. For example, Bob, convicted of sexual assault, could be sentenced to 18 months in prison, while Sam could be sentenced to two years probation for the same crime. Because the offenders appeared before a different judge, the disparity in sentencing would appear to be based on each judge's sentencing beliefs. Prime Minister Harper's Bill C-10 aims to eliminate judicial discretion and disparity for several crimes. Although there is logic behind the premise, it cannot be ignored that what led Bob and Sam to commit these crimes could be very different circumstances (e.g., addiction, being a survivor of abuse), which, if not addressed with treatment, could lead to repeat offending regardless of incarceration.

disparity
In a legal context, the difference or inconsistency among judges with respect to sentencing.

SIDEBAR

What Are the Numbers?

Canada's recorded population for 2010 was 34,108,752. The number of people who identified themselves as being from at least one of the country's Aboriginal groups was 824,341, meaning approximately 2.4 percent of the population are Aboriginal. However, they make up approximately 18.5 percent of Canada's prison population.

Admissions of Aboriginal offenders to correctional facilities for 2010 included **remand** custody (21 percent), provincial and territorial sentenced custody (27 percent), federal custody (18 percent), probation (18 percent), and conditional sentences (20 percent).

Sources: Statistics Canada (2011a); Indian and Northern Affairs Canada (2011); Office of the Correctional Investigator (2006); Calverley (2010).

remand
The holding of an accused in custody while he or she waits for trial or sentencing (as opposed to being granted bail, which would allow the individual to live in the community while awaiting trial).

Judges' sentencing decisions are based on a variety of factors. It is true that the judge must sentence a convicted person according to the terms set out in the *Criminal Code* for that offence, but in many cases, there is leeway.

Judicial Discretion

The Canadian Criminal Justice Association (CCJA) has recommended that sentences "be based on individual contextual factors relating to each offence, rather than legislated minimums that result in ineffective, expensive, and unduly harsh periods of incarceration" (CCJA, 2006). In this light, the discretion of individual judges is an important factor.

In 1996, Bill C-41 came into force. According to the Supreme Court of Canada, this was the most comprehensive reform of the law of sentencing in Canadian history. Set out in s. 718 of the *Criminal Code*, the amendment clarified how sentences should be decided and delivered. It also lists six principles of sentencing, intended to guide judges in each sentence they hand down:

a. To denounce unlawful conduct;
b. To deter the offender and other persons from committing offences;
c. To separate offenders from society, where necessary;
d. To assist in rehabilitating offenders;
e. To provide reparations for harm done to victims or to the community; and
f. To promote a sense of responsibility in offenders, and acknowledgment of harm done to victims and to the community.

Mandatory Minimum Sentences

Twenty-nine offences in the *Criminal Code* carry a mandatory minimum sentence of imprisonment. The majority (19) of these sentences were introduced in 1995, with the enactment of Bill C-68, with emphasis on crimes of repeat violent offenders, and crimes involving firearms. (For a table setting out mandatory minimum sentences under the *Criminal Code*, see www.emp.ca/cj.)

Currently, minimum sentences in Canada can be broken down into four principal categories:

1. The first is a mandatory life sentence imposed upon conviction for three offences: treason, first-degree murder, and second-degree murder.
2. The second consists primarily of firearms offences.
3. The third pertains to repeat offenders.
4. The fourth is for hybrid offences. Hybrid offences give Crown prosecutors the option to treat the offence as either "summary" or

"indictable." For summary offences, the punishments are less severe and there is no mandatory minimum sentence. Prosecutors decide how to proceed based on the seriousness of the crime, the offender's history, the harm done to the victim, and whether the offender has taken any steps toward rehabilitation since arrest.

There are several sentences that carry a mandatory minimum—the theoretical basis of which is deterrence and the protection of society. These sentences are "prescribed," which means that a judge has no discretion. Concerns have been raised that mandatory minimums could lead to unfair sentencing in cases where public interest and individual mitigating circumstances could support a more lenient sentence. An example is the Robert Latimer case (see the mini case study).

So far we've seen that a judge must take into consideration

- the sentencing limits of the summary or indictable offence
- the seriousness of the crime
- a sentencing philosophy
- whether the offender can be rehabilitated.

Later in the chapter we will discuss the impact on the victim. For discussion of mandatory minimum sentences under the *Safe Streets and Communities Act*, see the Part Four case study.

Aggravating and Mitigating Circumstances

Judges must also consider whether there were any other circumstances present during the commission of the crime or relevant to the offender's criminal lifestyle before sentencing. Such circumstances include whether the offender was acting in self-defence, or was under the influence of drugs or alcohol, or was in a position of trust over the victim. These "aggravating" or "mitigating" circumstances may be presented to the judge in a "presentence report."

aggravating circumstances
Elements in the crime or in the life circumstances of an offender that may permit a judge to sentence the offender to a longer term in prison before being eligible to apply for parole or conditional release.

Aggravating circumstances can often result in a more severe sentence than would be imposed in a case without such circumstances or in contrast to the average sentence length for this crime. This means that despite the general parameters of a sentence (mandatory minimum and maximum), if any one or more of these circumstances were present during the commission of the offence, the judge may choose to increase the sentencing penalty. Such circumstances could be:

- the offender was in a position of trust and authority over the victim
- there was premeditation and planning

Robert Latimer

The Robert Latimer case (*R. v. Latimer*, 2001) is one of the most famous in Canadian history, and sparked a fierce national debate on the issue of euthanasia, sometimes called "compassionate homicide" or "mercy killing." Here is a timeline of the case:

- October 1993: Robert Latimer, a Saskatchewan farmer, kills his severely disabled 12-year-old daughter, Tracy, by placing her in his pickup truck and asphyxiating her with exhaust fumes. He initially tries to hide his actions, but later admits to poisoning his daughter and is charged with first-degree murder.
- Fall 1994: Latimer admits during his trial that he killed Tracy, but suggests his actions were justified and not criminal because he wanted to put an end to the chronic pain that she suffered.
- November 1994: Latimer is convicted of second-degree murder. The judge has no choice in sentencing because this offence carries a mandatory sentence of life in prison, and requires offenders to serve a minimum of ten years in jail before applying for parole. Latimer appeals his conviction.
- July 1995: The Saskatchewan Court of Appeal upholds the conviction (that is, the conviction remains as is).
- October 1995: It is revealed that the Crown prosecutor interfered with the jury by asking them about their beliefs pertaining to religion, abortion, and mercy killing, which leads to a further appeal.
- November 1996: The Supreme Court of Canada hears the appeal.
- February 1997: The Supreme Court orders a new trial.
- November 1997: The jury in the second trial finds Latimer guilty of second-degree murder and recommends that he be eligible for parole after one year, which goes against the mandatory minimum sentence set out in the *Criminal Code*.
- December 1997: The trial judge gives Latimer a "constitutional exemption" to the mandatory minimum sentence of ten years and imposes a sentence of one year in custody followed by one year to be spent in the community. The Crown appeals this sentence.
- November 1998: The Saskatchewan Court of Appeal sets aside the constitutional exemption and upholds the mandatory minimum sentence.
- February 1999: Latimer appeals to the Supreme Court of Canada.
- January 2001: The Supreme Court upholds Latimer's life sentence with no possibility of parole for ten years.

What Do You Think?

Should the *Criminal Code* be revised so that judges can consider exceptions to minimum terms of incarceration in certain cases, such as Robert Latimer's? What consequences might this have?

- the offender used force or a weapon
- there was injury to the victim
- there was high financial or personal value of the stolen or damaged property or goods
- the victim was a youth or a vulnerable person, such as a senior citizen or someone with a developmental disorder.

"Non-offence factors" could also affect the type and length of sentence. An offender with a long criminal record may receive a harsher sentence than a first-time offender for the same offence. The judge would consider how much time has passed between the offender's last conviction (sometimes called the **gap principle**), and whether the offence was committed while the offender was out on bail or on probation, or on some form of conditional release, such as parole. Also weighing against the offender may be whether or not the offender interfered with the police investigation, lied to the police, escaped from lawful custody, or gave a false identify.

Mitigating circumstances are factors that may make the sentence more lenient. Such circumstances would mitigate a sentence—that is, provide reasonable explanations for how and why the offence occurred. These are not considered excuses to avoid criminal responsibility; they are considered practical elements that speak to the fact that people are fallible, have complex histories, and may be dealing with a variety of issues that can influence decision making. Here are some circumstances that might be taken into consideration:

- the accused was acting in self-defence
- the accused was intoxicated or has a history of addiction
- there was no premeditation
- the crime was of financial need rather than greed
- there are mental health issues that may reduce decision-making capabilities
- the accused is a person under age 18 (s. 718.01)
- the accused is Aboriginal (s. 718.2(e))
- the accused is a senior with a short life expectancy because of a chronic or terminal illness.

Under s. 718.2, a judge is required to consider several factors when determining an appropriate sentence and to consider whether the "sentence should be increased or reduced to account for any relevant aggravating or mitigating circumstances relating to the offence or the offender" (Department of Justice Canada, 2005, para. 4), without ignoring evidence that the

gap principle
A principle whereby a judge, when deciding on an appropriate sentence for a repeat offender, considers how much time has passed since the offender's last conviction.

mitigating circumstances
Elements in the crime or in the life circumstances of an offender that may permit a judge to sentence the offender more leniently.

SIDEBAR

Determining the Sentence

The following passage from s. 718.2 of the *Criminal Code* presents several considerations that a judge must take into account when determining a sentence:

a) a sentence should be increased or reduced to account for any relevant aggravating or mitigating circumstances relating to the offence or the offender, and without limiting the generality of the foregoing,

i. evidence that the offence was motivated by bias, prejudice or hate based on race, national or ethnic origin, language, colour, religion, sex, age, mental or physical disability, sexual orientation, or any other factor, or

ii. evidence that the offender, in committing the offence, abused the offender's spouse or child, or

iii. evidence that the offender, in committing the offence, abused a position of trust or authority in relation to a victim;

iv. evidence that the offence was committed for the benefit of, at the direction of or in association with a criminal organization, or

v. evidence that the offence was a terrorism offence

shall be deemed to be aggravating circumstances;

b) a sentence should be similar to sentences imposed on similar offenders for similar offences committed in similar circumstances;

c) where consecutive sentences are imposed, the combined sentence should not be unduly long or harsh;

d) an offender should not be deprived of liberty, if less restrictive sanctions may be appropriate in the circumstances; and

e) all available sanctions other than imprisonment that are reasonable in the circumstances should be considered for all offenders, with particular attention to the circumstances of aboriginal offenders.

offence was motivated by prejudice, that the offender was in a position of trust, or other such points (see the sidebar "Determining the Sentence").

Sections 718.01 and 718.02 state that offences involving child abuse, assaulting a police officer, or intimidation of anyone involved in the justice system should also encourage consideration of the above objectives. Further, section 718.1 requires that the sentence must be proportionate to the gravity of the offence and the degree of responsibility of the offender; that is, the sentence given for an offence should not be extreme—basically, the "eye for an eye" philosophy: the offence and the sentence must match.

The sentence must be proportionate to the gravity of the offence.

Section 718.2(e) is another element of sentencing that was amended to address the overrepresentation of Aboriginals in prison. Continually debated, this sentencing section was upheld by the Supreme Court of Canada in *R. v. Gladue* (1999) (discussed in detail in Chapter 12). The court held that where a term of incarceration would normally be imposed, judges must consider the unique circumstances of Aboriginal people in deciding whether or not imprisonment is absolutely necessary. Judges must consider:

1. the systemic factors that may have contributed to the criminal behaviour of the Aboriginal people; and
2. the specific sentencing procedures and sanctions that may be more appropriate. These may include such things as restorative justice and healing practices (Griffiths & Cunningham, 2003, p. 201).

However, in subsequent cases (*R. v. Wells*, 2000), the Supreme Court of Canada has held that s. 718.2(e) should not have an impact on the fundamental duty of sentencing—that judges should impose a sentence that is appropriate for the offence and the offender (Griffiths & Cunningham, 2003, p. 202).

What Do You Think?

Section 718.2(e)

Section 718.2(e) of the *Criminal Code* sets out guidelines for judges in determining sentences:

- It requires that judges consider sanctions other than imprisonment.
- It states that incarceration is to be considered a last resort for everyone, and particularly for Aboriginal offenders.
- It encourages the development and use of restorative justice programs.
- It supports the right of Aboriginal offenders to have the opportunity to participate in culturally based programs and special sentencing provisions.

How should these considerations be regarded when sentencing Aboriginal or non-Aboriginal offenders? What are some of the benefits to these considerations in the overall system of justice? What are some of the limitations?

If requested, a "pre-sentence report" can be prepared by a probation officer to help the judge determine an appropriate sentence for an offender. It outlines the offender's background and the context of the crime, giving the judge a better sense of the person being sentenced. A probation officer's pre-sentence report about the offender could include details relating to:

- previous convictions
- gang activity
- vulnerability of the victim
- multiple criminal incidents
- use or threatened use of a weapon
- brutality
- employment record
- rehabilitative efforts since the offence was committed
- disadvantaged background
- guilty plea and remorse
- length of time to prosecute or sentence the offender
- good character.

What Do You Think?

In the Part One case study, many mitigating and aggravating factors would be present in the pre-sentence report on the offender. How much weight should the judge place on those factors when determining a sentence?

Victims

Victim Impact Statements in Sentencing

Judges may invite any victims of the crime to prepare a statement detailing how the crime has impacted their lives, work, health, and relationships. In 1988, prompted by the United Nations Declaration of Basic Principles of Justice for Victims of Crime, all Canadian ministers of justice agreed to adopt a uniform policy statement of victims' rights that would be used to guide their legislative and administrative initiatives in the area of criminal justice (Canadian Resource Centre for Victims of Crime, 2006).

See also mini chapter 16.3
Victims' Rights

Advocates argue that making victims part of the court system would recognize their impact and status in court proceedings (Hall, 1991). This is the only opportunity victims have to address the court directly and share their personal perspectives. Throughout the trial process, the victim may be called to the stand as a witness and give testimony in response to questions asked by the Crown prosecutor and by defence counsel, but the victim is not permitted to talk freely. A victim impact statement, therefore, offers the victims a sense of ownership, allowing them to finally tell their side of the story, as we saw in the Part One case study. These statements may assist the judge in determining an appropriate sentence. Opponents of this argue that expanding victims' rights would challenge the very basis of our adversarial legal system and bias proceedings.

What Do You Think?

How may the victim impact statement in the Part One case study have affected the sentencing process?

Types of Sentences

Not Criminally Responsible

A finding of not criminally responsible (NCR) means that even though an accused person is found guilty of committing the crime, the individual lacks the *mens rea* necessary to be found criminally responsible. Reasons that can affect *mens rea* include mental illness or disease, including episodes of psychosis. The accused will therefore typically serve a period of incarceration in a forensic mental hospital.

Absolute and Conditional Discharges

If the court imposes an "absolute discharge," the offender is found guilty of the offence, but is not convicted. The offender cannot be subsequently charged and retried for this offence, and if he or she commits another crime, the record of discharge can be used against him or her in court. If after one year there have been no new charges or convictions, the record of an absolute discharge will be removed from CPIC (Canadian Police Information Centre, www.cpic-cipc.ca).

For a "conditional discharge," the offender is found guilty but, as with an absolute discharge, is not convicted. However, he or she is required to follow certain rules for a specified length of time, as set out in a probation order. Once that period has passed, the discharge becomes absolute, but if the offender does not follow the rules or commits a new offence during this time, the offender can be convicted and sentenced for the original offence.

Suspended Sentence

With a suspended sentence, a conviction is entered after the offender is found guilty, but the judge "suspends" the passing of sentence for a fixed period either with or without a probation order. If no further offences are committed by the offender during this period, there will be no sentence (JURIST Canada, 2012).

Fines

At the discretion of the judge, fines can stand alone as a sentence or be combined with other types of sentences, such as probation or incarceration. The fine is the most frequently used sentencing option in Canada (in 2008–9, 30 percent of guilty cases resulted in a fine, down from 38 percent in 2000–1: Thomas, 2010). Fine payments go directly into governmental coffers, which in turn pay for various judicial services and resources, whereas proceeds from restitution orders are directed at the victims of the crime.

Any person convicted of an offence (except where the offence has a minimum term of imprisonment) can receive a fine. For summary conviction offences, the maximum fine is $5,000; for indictable conviction offences, there is no limit. Judges will also normally impose a 15 percent victim-fine surcharge. This money goes into a victims' fund to pay for programs for all victims of crime (John Howard Society, 1999, p. 4).

Intermittent Sentence

When a judge sentences an offender to prison for 90 days or less, s. 732 of the *Criminal Code* allows the judge to order that the time be served "intermittently." This means that the offender could serve the prison sentence on weekends. When not in custody, the offender must comply with the conditions set out in a probation order (John Howard Society, 1999, p. 6).

Conditional Sentence

A conditional sentence is a prison sentence that is served in the community. Time in prison is suspended as long as the offender obeys the rules imposed by the court and under the supervision of a probation officer. A conditional sentence can be given as an alternative to incarceration for sentences of less than two years, but not all offenders are eligible, such as those convicted of an offence that has a mandatory minimum prison sentence. All conditional

deterrence
Disincentive to commit a crime; an effect of arrest and incarceration.

denunciation
A condemnation or criticism of another's actions.

rehabilitation
The treatment of offenders in order to prevent future criminal activity.

orders have mandatory conditions, and may also include optional conditions (Canadian Bar Association, 2011), including:

- a "no contact order" to ensure that the offender has no contact with a particular person or does not visit a particular place
- a weapons prohibition order to prevent the offender from having any firearms or other weapons
- an order for the offender to give a sample of DNA for the DNA National Data Bank
- a compensation order allowing the person whose property was damaged to sue the offender in civil court
- driving prohibitions.

What Do You Think?

Consider the Ouimet report's findings that longer-term sentences don't work in a universal way. Think back to the case study at the beginning of Part One, or the *Proulx* case study, below. What might the effects of long-term incarceration in these cases be?

Mandatory Conditions

Mandatory conditions for an offender serving a conditional sentence are that the person must:

- keep the peace and be of good behaviour;
- appear before the court when required to do so;
- report to a supervisor by a specified date (usually within two working days) and thereafter when required by the supervisor and in the manner directed by the supervisor;
- remain within the jurisdiction of the court unless written permission is obtained from the court or the supervisor to go outside of that jurisdiction;
- notify the court, the supervisor, or the probation officer in advance of any change of name, address, or employment.

Optional Conditions

The court can include any other reasonable conditions it feels are appropriate; for example:

- not to use drugs or alcohol
- not to own, possess, or carry a weapon
- perform up to 240 hours of community service within a one-year period
- attend a treatment program approved by the province.

If an offender breaks any rules imposed by the court, the suspension of the prison sentence can be cancelled and the offender required to serve the remainder of the sentence in prison.

Probation

Probation is a sentence that is served in the community and is another type of alternative to incarceration (such as are conditional sentences). A probation order could also follow a period of incarceration—a combination of different **dispositions**. While on probation, the convicted person must follow specific conditions set by the judge for a specified time period under the supervision of a probation officer. All probation orders have a set of mandatory conditions and judges have the discretion of adding further conditions that may reflect the particular offending behaviour. Offenders who break any of the conditions of their probation order may be charged with "Breach of Probation" and subject to a term of imprisonment of up to two years (for more on probation, see Chapter 11).

disposition

The specific sanction imposed by a judge in sentencing a person who has been convicted of an offence. For example, Joe is sentenced to imprisonment; the disposition is four years.

MINI CASE STUDY

R. v. Proulx

R. v. Proulx (2000) is another key case in Canadian history that has influenced sentencing. Here, the Supreme Court's judgment pertained to conditional sentences. In this case, after drinking at a party, the 18-year-old accused decided to drive home some friends in a vehicle that was mechanically unsound. He drove erratically for 10 to 20 minutes, sideswiped one car, and crashed into another. One of the passengers in the accused's car was killed, and the driver of the second car was seriously injured. The accused pleaded guilty to dangerous driving causing bodily harm and dangerous driving causing death. The trial judge sentenced him to 18 months in jail. Proulx appealed, resulting in the Manitoba Court of Appeal substituting the jail time for a conditional sentence. Another appeal was submitted, this time by the Crown, which resulted in the Supreme Court restoring the original jail sentence. The court explained that the original sentence was not unfit and that the trial judge did not commit any error that would justify overturning the jail sentence in favour of a conditional sentence (Department of Justice Canada, 2011b).

Electronic Monitoring

One way of controlling correctional costs and promoting safe reintegration of offenders into society is the electronic monitoring (EM) of offenders, an alternative to imprisonment. They are typically sentenced to remain in their homes and their whereabouts are monitored by an electronic device that is strapped around their ankle. Research on the effectiveness of such programs has been inconsistent, with very little evidence to show that EM reduces the likelihood of offenders returning to crime (Public Safety Canada, 1999, pp. 1 and 2), most likely because it does not address the causes of offending.

Restitution

Restitution involves the offender paying the victim to cover expenses resulting from the crime, such as property loss or damage. The amount of restitution is equal to the replacement value of the property. In cases where someone is injured, the restitution may cover medical bills and lost income (John Howard Society, 1999, p. 4). The belief is that "repayment" of the harm done needs to occur in order for the accused to "learn" from their mistakes, although judges recognize that money cannot replace the harms done. However, offenders are often unable to financially meet the expectations of the restitution order.

Alternative Measures Program

Under provincial jurisdiction, a variety of possibilities exist as an alternative to court for persons alleged to have committed minor offences. The Crown decides whether to take this route, and with the accused's acknowledgment of guilt, the accused will be referred to community corrections. The goals of the program are:

- to prevent the individual from getting a criminal record
- to stop the criminal behaviour
- to promote community involvement
- to foster community awareness through participation.

There are six programs within this mandate: fine option, institutional fine option, community work service, pre-trial release, probation and conditional sentence supervision, and temporary absence program (Solicitor General and Public Security Government of Alberta, 2011).

Fine Option Program

Offenders sentenced to pay fines may participate in the fine option program, which allows them to pay off their fines through community work service. They can perform this service in lieu of, or in addition to, the cash payment of fines. The compensation rate is set at minimum wage standards for adults and typically involves some type of community service.

Institutional Fine Option

Offenders who are unable to or refuse to pay the fine may be eligible to "work off" the fine by remaining in a correctional facility. When they have earned enough credits to satisfy the fine, they are released (John Howard Society, 1999, pp. 4 and 5). The period of imprisonment is based on the following calculation:

$$\frac{\text{the unpaid amount of the fine} + \text{the costs \&}}{\underset{\text{8 hours per day}}{\text{(divided by)}}} \times \begin{array}{l}\text{the provincial} \\ \text{minimum hourly wage}\end{array}$$

Imprisonment

Imprisonment involves taking away an offender's freedom and incarcerating him or her in either a provincial or federal correctional facility, depending upon the length of the sentence. Imprisonment is the most serious sentencing option available in Canada and is intended as a last resort to be used only when a judge considers less restrictive alternatives to not be suitable. For summary conviction offences, the maximum term of incarceration is six months. For indictable conviction offences, the term varies by offence: some carry a minimum sentence of incarceration, and others carry the maximum sentence possible, which is life imprisonment (John Howard Society, 1999, p. 6).

Dangerous Offender Designation

Under s. 753 of the *Criminal Code*, the Crown can apply to the court to designate an individual a dangerous offender. Any person convicted of a serious personal injury offence (e.g., sexual offences, homicide offences) and who poses a danger to the life, safety, or physical/mental well-being of others, may qualify. This section allows the court to sentence those offenders to an indefinite period of incarceration (i.e., a life sentence); after serving seven years, the offender is eligible for a parole review every two years (John Howard Society, 1999, p. 7). (See Chapter 12 for more detailed discussion of the dangerous offender designation.)

Long-Term Offender Designation

Section 753.1 describes those offenders who may be subject to a long-term offender application by the Crown, which is any person who meets the following criteria:

- It would be appropriate to impose a sentence of two years or more for the offence.
- There is a "substantial risk" that the offender will reoffend.
- There is a reasonable possibility of eventual control of risk in the community.

Substantial risk exists when (1) the offender has been convicted of one of a list of sex offences, and (2) the offender:

- shows a pattern of repetitive behaviour, of which the current conviction forms a part, that shows a likelihood that the offender will cause death or injury to other people or inflict severe psychological damage on other people, or
- by conduct in any sexual matter including that involved in the current conviction, has shown a likelihood of causing injury, pain or other evil to other people in the future through similar offences.

If the court designates long-term offender status, the offender will be given a sentence of imprisonment of at least two years, followed by a period of supervision in the community not exceeding 10 years.

What Do You Think?

What sentence or combination of sentences would you give the offender in the Part One case study? Based on what you know, should the Crown apply for dangerous offender designation?

Appealing a Sentence or a Conviction

Once a trial has ended and an accused has been convicted (found guilty), there is the possibility of an appeal, which can be filed by either the Crown prosecutor or defence counsel. The finding of guilt (conviction) or innocence (acquittal) can be appealed, as can the sentence. But not everything can be appealed, and there are certain rules that must be followed. There have to be "grounds" for appeal, which involve questions of law, questions of fact, or both. For example, appealing a conviction means that the convicted person believes that there was a procedural error (question of law) in the trial, evidence presented was not correct, or new evidence was discovered (questions of fact)—any of which resulted in the offender being found guilty. Appealing the sentence means that the convicted person believes the sentence is too harsh or is unconstitutional. Most appeals originate from the defence, but the Crown prosecutor can appeal a sentence (believing it to be too lenient) or appeal the acquittal of an accused person (Griffiths & Cunningham, 2003, p. 167).

Once an appeal has been filed, the convicted person may be released from jail on bail until the appeal is heard. A judge must consider this request and consider factors such as the merit of the appeal to ensure that frivolous appeals do not take up the court's time. The Court of Appeal has five possible options when hearing an appeal on conviction (Government of Canada, 2005):

1. Decide not to hear the appeal.
2. Hear the appeal and dismiss it (not support its continuing on).
3. Substitute the conviction with a lesser offence that was originally included upon arrest, which could possibly reduce the sentence. For example, Joe was arrested and charged with robbery, theft over $5,000, and assault with a weapon. He was found guilty and sentenced to serve ten years for the robbery. Joe's appeal is heard and the Court of Appeal substitutes the ten-year sentence for robbery with a four-year sentence for assault with a weapon.
4. Direct that the offender be acquitted.
5. Order a new trial.

Specialized Courts and Sentencing Processes

Aboriginal Healing Circles

See also mini chapter 16.5 *Restorative Justice in Focus: Sentencing Circles*

Aboriginal culture reflects a belief that all living things—people, animals, and nature—are interconnected. Circles, being inherently inclusive and non-hierarchical, represent respect, equality, continuity, and interconnectedness. Healing circles have proven to be a very useful tool for addressing criminal behaviour within Canadian Aboriginal communities. They support the process of healing for offenders, victims, and their families, as well as give people a means to reclaim their cultural traditions. Aboriginal teachers use them to illustrate aspects of the indigenous community over time, including the effects of colonization. Healing circles have also been adopted within criminal justice systems as an alternative or additional sanction to address the harms caused by criminal behaviour to both the offenders and the victims. After a finding or admission of guilt, the court invites interested members of the community to join the judge, prosecutor, defence counsel, police, social service providers, and community elders, along with the offender and the victim, and their families and supporters, to meet in a circle to discuss the offence, the factors that may have contributed to it, sentencing options, and ways of reintegrating the offender into the community. The circle allows individuals who offend and their community to work together to heal together, in the belief that each person has a role and responsibility in that process. (See Chapter 12 for further discussion about Aboriginal issues, and see Chapter 16 for an extensive entry on sentencing circles.)

What Do You Think?

What place would Aboriginal healing circles have in the sentencing of the offender in the Part One case study? Could a circle have helped him sooner?

Drug Courts

Drug treatment courts (DTC) aim to reduce crimes committed as a result of drug dependency. They do so through court-monitored treatment and community service support for offenders with drug addictions. The first DTC opened in Toronto in 1998; to date, there are seven other courts in operation across Canada. The principles of DTC recognize that not all criminal behaviour is inherently bad, but rather, is a symptom of an individual's addiction. By diverting drug-dependent offenders from the correctional system, more effective measures can be implemented, in the belief that future criminal activity will be deterred. Participants must appear regularly in court, and successfully complete all ordered sanctions. Programming and court staff work with community partners to address participants' other needs, such as safe housing, stable employment, and job training, which can also impact criminal behaviour. Once the participant gains social stability and demonstrates control over the addiction, either the criminal charges are "stayed" (meaning a judgment is suspended or postponed) or the offender receives a non-custodial sentence (such as house arrest). If unsuccessful, the offender will be sentenced as part of the regular court process. (See Chapter 12 for further discussion about drug issues.)

Domestic Violence Court

Domestic or family violence courts have been established in several provinces across Canada since as early as 1990. These courts address the nature of violence that occurs within the family, as opposed to violence between strangers or casual acquaintances. Many unique dynamics exist within the context of family violence, such that a high proportion of victims will often recant their earlier testimony or are reluctant victims and witnesses. Because of these realities, alternatives were needed. The primary objectives of domestic violence courts (DVC) are generally to:

- provide mechanisms designed to respond to the unique nature of family violence;
- improve the response of the justice system to incidents of spousal abuse by decreasing court processing time;
- facilitate early intervention for those who act violently toward family members;
- provide appropriate support to victims, including children;
- increase offender accountability; and
- divert criminal justice expenditures.

In a DVC program, teams of specialized personnel who are educated and trained about the dynamics and realities of family violence work together to create a program of support and accountability for the accused. Teams often include expert police, lawyers, and judges, victim assistance programs, probation services, and partner agencies that deliver psychological or social treatment. By working together, teams ensure that priority is given to the safety and needs of domestic assault victims and their children, and to the prevention of future victims.

See also mini chapter 16.4 Intimate Partner Violence and Specialized Courts

Current Issues in Sentencing

Safe Streets and Communities Act

The *Safe Streets and Communities Act* (2012) follows a deterrent approach, in the belief that "getting tough" through harsher sentencing will deter crime. However, statistical evidence shows that violent crime is at an all-time low in Canada. By 2011, the national crime rate had fallen to its lowest level since 1973. The police-reported crime rate, which measures the overall volume of crime, continued its long-term downward trend in 2010, declining 5 percent from its 2009 level. (This trend is clearly visible in the figure on page 13 of Chapter 1.) At the same time, the Crime Severity Index, which measures the seriousness of crime, fell 6 percent. Further, approximately 40 percent of police-reported crime in Canada comes from two relatively less serious offences: thefts under $5,000 and mischief (Statistics Canada, 2009, p. 8; 2011b).

Additionally, research elsewhere (California, Arizona, and Texas) has demonstrated the shortcomings of this "tough on crime" approach.

Public Opinion

The sentencing process has frequently attracted widespread public criticism either for being too lenient on certain offenders or for needing more emphasis on rehabilitation. Nationwide surveys over the past 20 years have repeatedly shown that most Canadians believe that sentences should be more severe, particularly for violent offenders (Roberts & Birkenmayer, 1997, pp. 459–482). Yet, a public opinion poll conducted in 2008 revealed that violence, gun crimes, and the justice system were not major concerns. Among voters loyal to three major parties (Liberal, Conservative, NDP), the results were the same: justice concerns were considered "the most important" by only about 2.5 percent of people within each party.

What Do You Think?

Public opinion often favours tough sentences for sexual offences, despite evidence that questions their effectiveness. If mandatory minimum sentences such as those in the *Safe Streets and Communities Act* had been in place prior to the crime in the Part One case study, do you think that may have deterred or prevented the crime?

Why do you think so many Canadians support "tough on crime" policies, despite the relatively low levels of crime today?

Conclusion

Sentencing in Canada is one of the most complex and controversial aspects of our criminal justice system. Judges must make crucial decisions that will restrict an individual's rights, and they must do so by considering many different elements of the person, the case, the context, and more. When determining a sentence, judges are also guided by the principles in the various models of our justice system: deterrence, rehabilitation, selective incapacitation, and justice. Changes are ahead for Canada and its judicial approach to sentencing. With government intervention, certain issues with our sentencing system are being revised, such as bringing in more mandatory minimum sentences, which will reduce a judge's options when sentencing someone. This change is favoured by some, criticized by others. We will have to wait for its long-term consequences to be revealed in order to make our own judgment. However, an ongoing concern in sentencing is the over-representation of Aboriginals within our correctional system and the need for an increase in victims' voices within the sentencing process.

► IN-CLASS EXERCISE

Present a short case—one with an incident and victim similar to those in the Part One case study, or perhaps a less emotionally charged case. Have students in small groups identify and discuss the mitigating and aggravating factors, as well as the five other elements a judge considers (s. 718, etc.) to decide on an appropriate sentence using the *Criminal Code*. Bring the small groups together and present each group's decision and decision-making process to the class as a whole to discuss and debate.

DISCUSSION QUESTIONS

1. What are some of the arguments for mandatory minimum sentences? What are some arguments against them?
2. How do the media influence public opinion on sentencing? How do the media influence decisions made by judges?
3. What are the benefits of victim impact statements? What are the limitations?
4. What aspects of our criminal justice system would you change and why?
5. Compare and contrast the sentencing options of absolute discharge and suspended sentence. When should neither be used?

6. What are the benefits of s. 718.2(e) of the *Criminal Code*? What are its limitations?

7. What might be some positive consequences of the *Safe Streets and Communities Act*? Negative consequences?

SUGGESTED FURTHER READINGS

Aboriginal Healing Circles and Aboriginal Practices with Offenders in Canada

The Healing Circle. http://www.iisd.org/7thgen/healing_circle.htm

Correctional Service of Canada. http://www.csc-scc.gc.ca/text/prgrm/abinit/challenge/11-eng.shtml

Drug Treatment Courts

Department of Justice Canada. http://www.justice.gc.ca/eng/news-nouv/nr-cp/2005/doc_31552.html

Domestic Violence and Family Violence Courts

Public Health Agency of Canada. http://www.phac-aspc.gc.ca/ncfv-cnivf/EB/eb-Mar-2009-eng.php#article

REFERENCES

Andrews, D.A., Zinger, I., Hoge, R., Bonta, J., Gendreau, P., & Cullen, F. (1990). Does correctional treatment work? A clinically relevant and psychologically informed meta-analysis. *Criminology, 28*, 393–404.

Calverley, D. (2010). Adult correctional services in Canada, 2008/2009. *Juristat, 30*(3). Catalogue No. 85-002-X. Ottawa: Statistics Canada. Retrieved from http://www.statcan.gc.ca/pub/85-002-x/2010003/article/11353-eng.pdf

Canadian Bar Association. (2011). British Columbia Branch. Conditional sentences, probation and discharges. Retrieved from http://www.cba.org/bc/public_media/criminal/203.aspx

Canadian Criminal Justice Association (CCJA). (2006). *Brief to the Standing Committee on Justice, Human Rights, Public Safety and Emergency Preparedness*. Position paper. Retrieved from http://www.ccja-acjp.ca/en/c10en.html

Canadian Resource Centre for Victims of Crime. (2006). Victims' rights in Canada. Retrieved from http://www.crcvc.ca/docs/vicrights.pdf

Clear, T. (1994). *Harm in American penology: Offenders, victims, and their communities*. Albany, NY: State University of New York Press.

Department of Justice Canada. (2005). Backgrounder: Expanding drug treatment courts in Canada. Retrieved from http://www.justice.gc.ca/eng/news-nouv/nr-cp/2005/doc_31552.html

Department of Justice Canada. (2011a). Mandatory sentences of imprisonment in common law jurisdictions: Some representative models. Retrieved from http://www.justice.gc.ca/eng/pi/rs/rep-rap/2005/rr05_10/a.html

Department of Justice Canada. (2011b). Research and Statistics Division. *The changing face of conditional sentencing.* Retrieved from http://www.justice .gc.ca/eng/pi/rs/rep-rap/2000/op00_3-po00_3/p5_1.html

Ehrlich, I. (1975). The deterrent effect of capital punishment: A question of life and death. *American Economic Review, 65,* 397–417.

Government of Canada. (2005). *Canada's system of justice.* Ottawa: Department of Justice Canada.

Griffiths, C.T., & Cunningham, A.H. (2003). *Canadian criminal justice: A primer* (2nd ed.). Toronto: Nelson Thomson Canada.

Hall, D.J. (1991). Victim voices in criminal court: The need for restraint. *American Criminal Law Review, 28,* 233–266.

Indian and Northern Affairs Canada. (2011). *Registered Indian population by sex and residence 2010.* Ottawa: Government of Canada. Retrieved from http://www.aadnc-aandc.gc.ca/DAM/DAM-INTER-HQ/STAGING/texte-text/ai_rs_pubs_sts_ni_rip_rip10_rip10_1309289046808_eng.pdf

John Howard Society of Alberta. (1999). Sentencing in Canada. Retrieved from http://www.johnhoward.ab.ca/pub/pdf/C33.pdf

JURIST Canada: The Legal Education Network. (2012). Canadian legal research. Retrieved from http://jurist.law.utoronto.ca/

Office of the Correctional Investigator. (2006). Backgrounder: Aboriginal inmates. Retrieved from http://www.oci-bec.gc.ca/rpt/annrpt/annrpt20052006info -eng.aspx

Parole Board of Canada. (2010). History of parole in Canada. Retrieved from http://www.pbc-clcc.gc.ca/about/hist-eng.shtml

Parole Board of Canada. (2011). Parole decision-making: Myths and realities. Retrieved from http://www.pbc-clcc.gc.ca/infocntr/myths_reality-eng.shtml

Public Safety Canada. (1999). *The electronic monitoring of offenders.* Research summaries 4(3). Retrieved from http://www.publicsafety.gc.ca/res/cor/sum/_fl/cprs199905-eng.pdf

R. v. Gladue, [1999] 1 SCR 688.

R. v. Latimer, [2001] SCR 3.

R. v. M. (C.A.) (1996), 46 CR (4th) 269 (SCC).

R. v. Proulx, [2000] 1 SCR 61.

R. v. Wells, [2000] 1 SCR 207.

Roberts, J.V., & Birkenmayer, A. (1997). Sentencing in Canada: Recent statistical trends. *Canadian Journal of Criminology, 39*(4), 459–482.

Safe Streets and Communities Act, SC 2012, c. 1.

Solicitor General and Public Security Government of Alberta. (2011). Adult programs. Retrieved from http://www.solgps.alberta.ca/PROGRAMS _AND_SERVICES/CORRECTIONAL_SERVICES/COMMUNITY _CORRECTIONS/Pages/adult_programs.aspx

Statistics Canada. (2009). Canadian Centre for Justice Statistics. *Gender differences in police-reported violent crime in Canada, 2008*. Catalogue No. 85F0033M. Ottawa: Author. Retrieved from http://www.statcan.gc.ca/pub/85f0033m/85f0033m2010024-eng.pdf

Statistics Canada. (2011a). *Canada at a glance 2011*. Catalogue No. 12-581-XIE. Ottawa: Author. Retrieved from http://www.statcan.gc.ca/pub/12-581-x/12-581-x2011000-eng.pdf

Statistics Canada. (2011b). Police-reported crime statistics. *The Daily*. (2011, July 21). Retrieved from http://www.statcan.gc.ca/dai-quo/index-eng.htm

Thomas, J. (2010). Adult criminal court statistics, 2008/2009. *Juristat, 30*(2). Catalogue No. 85-002-X20100031135. Retrieved from http://www.statcan.gc.ca/pub/85-002-x/2010002/article/11293-eng.htm

PART FOUR
Corrections

Safe Streets and Communities Act

Karla O'Regan

Minister of Justice Rob Nicholson introducing the *Safe Streets and Communities Act*, September 20, 2011

Source: Department of Justice.

How many times have you heard governments vow to "get tough" on crime or "declare war" on drugs, on vandalism, or on some other criminal behaviour? Vows and declarations of this kind are often part of election platforms, and sometimes—despite the vast amount of research and expert opinion (largely from criminal justice scholars) suggesting that they are both costly and ineffective—they lead to major legislative reform initiatives. "Cracking down on crime" makes for good politics. Instead of responding to actual crime-report data, this approach caters to the public's fear of crime. And it appeals to crime-control philosophies (such as deterrence or retribution) that posit crime as the deliberate choice of a rational individual rather than an event driven by socio-economic conditions and the offender's circumstances and characteristics. In short, it positions crime as an individual's act rather than a wider social problem.

What Do You Think?

Which of the crime-control philosophies explored in Chapter 1 does the "get-tough" view best demonstrate? How might each of the other models discussed view the *Safe Streets and Communities Act*?

The *Safe Streets and Communities Act* (SSCA), a piece of legislation that the Conservative government tabled in September 2011 (Bill C-10) and made law in March 2012, exemplifies one of these "get-tough" approaches to crime control. This statute is a collection of legal amendments that substantially changes how Canada deals with criminal offenders. Composed of nine smaller bills, each of which failed to pass when introduced by the Conservatives during their minority rule, the SSCA creates a number of new criminal offences, significantly restricts the use of conditional sentencing (eliminating it entirely for some offences), and establishes harsher sentencing principles for young offenders. It also increases mandatory minimum sentences while broadening the scope of offences to which such mandatory minimum sentences apply. These mandatory minimum sentences eliminate a judge's discretion when sentencing an offender and can often lead to unjust penalties, particularly when the mandatory sentences involve long periods of incarceration and the offenders suffer from substance abuse and/or mental health issues that cannot be adequately treated under the conditions of ordinary incarceration.

The SSCA also removes one of the key principles governing the treatment of offenders within the Correctional Service of Canada (CSC). Section 4 of the *Corrections and Conditional Release Act* (CCRA), like the sentencing principles found in s. 718 of the *Criminal Code*, lists ten principles meant to inform the CSC's decisions about the incarceration, rehabilitation, and reintegration of offenders. One prescription is

> that the Service use the least restrictive measures consistent with the protection of the public, staff members and offenders.

The SSCA has eliminated this guideline concerning "least restrictive measures." Instead, it lists the "protection of society" as the "paramount" consideration in the treatment of offenders.

As early as 2007, the Conservatives offered justifications for removing this principle; then minister Stockwell Day released a report on corrections issues entitled *A Roadmap to Strengthening Public Safety*. Day's report argued

---

Mandatory Minimum Sentences: The Case of Mrs. B

One of the more controversial offences to which a mandatory minimum sentence applies is the production and cultivation of marijuana. The discretion of a judge has been removed in these cases, which now involve a mandatory one-year jail term for the offender found guilty. A recent case involving a 67-year-old grandmother demonstrates the dangers of these mandatory sentences. Mrs. B had neglected to file the paperwork that her family physician had given her to fill out so that she could receive a licence to produce medical marijuana. Lacking this licence, she was charged with producing and cultivating a prohibited substance, and she was convicted. The judge gave her a conditional seven-month sentence that allowed her to serve her time in the community rather than in prison. Had this case been heard after the SSCA came into force, Mrs. B would be serving time in one of our provincial correctional facilities.

that this principle—that is, the principle of using the least restrictive measures possible for offenders—"has been emphasized too much by staff and management of CSC, and even by the courts in everyday decision-making about offenders" (2007, p. 16). This principle, according to Day's report, has created an "imbalance" within correctional services by putting the onus on the government to justify using more severe measures against offenders, when it is offenders who ought to be required to justify their access to "privileges." The Conservative position is that prisoners should earn their access to programs and services and that corrections officers should no longer be required to use the least punitive measures when disciplining and controlling inmates.

Some of the previous chapters in this book have looked at the inherent tension in Canada's criminal justice system between the state's interest in protecting the public and each individual's right to privacy and freedom from state intervention. Seen from this perspective, criminal procedure is an enterprise that seeks to balance these two competing interests. Often, finding this balance means establishing protections for the accused person—an individual who stands alone against the power of the state. Robert Cover (1986, p. 1601) describes the scope of the state's power over the individual in the following way:

> Legal interpretation takes place in a field of pain and death. This is true in several senses. Legal interpretive acts signal and occasion the imposition of violence upon others: A judge articulates her understanding of a text, and as a result, somebody loses his freedom, his property, his children, even his life.

Given the state's near-absolute power of dispensation over the individual, it is difficult to characterize the legislative checks on this power (e.g., the restrictions on how and why persons should be incarcerated) as "privileges." It has been argued (Jackson & Stewart, 2010, p. 2) that "prison is the acid test of our commitment to human rights" because "there is no other government activity in a democratic society that entails as much power over individual citizens' freedom as prison." This point seems even stronger when we consider the reality of life in prison. Conservative criticisms of correctional policies often feature rosy images of prison life—the privileged inmate watching TV in a country-club setting. The reality is otherwise. In an op-ed piece in the *New Yorker* magazine (2012), writer Adam Gopnik describes prison as a "trap for catching time," where life is "mostly undramatic—the reported stories fail to grab us, because, for the most part, nothing *happens*." This is not to suggest that, because life behind bars is mundane and routinized, its effects are insignificant. Charles Dickens visited a number of prisons while travelling in America, and he commented on the extraordinary trauma that the human mind and body sustain while incarcerated. In an 1842 note, he remarked:

> I believe that very few men are capable of estimating the immense amount of torture and agony which this dreadful punishment, prolonged for years, inflicts upon the sufferers. ... I hold this slow and daily tampering with the mysteries of the brain, to be immeasurably worse than any torture of the body: and because its ghastly signs and tokens are not so palpable to the eye and sense of touch as scars upon the flesh; because its wounds are not upon the surface, and it extorts few cries that human ears can hear; therefore I the more denounce it, as a secret punishment which slumbering humanity is not roused up to stay.

The following chapters describe the modern incarceration experience and the difficulties it poses for all concerned. Among the most challenging tasks of the criminal justice system is to assess the offenders as they enter correctional facilities while providing adequate programming for them while they are incarcerated. The Office of the Correctional Investigator reported in 2010 that the suicide rate for inmates is seven to eight times higher than for other Canadians. In a ten-year period (1998–2008), over 100 inmates committed suicide in federal penitentiaries. The incidence of self-harm and self-mutilation is also on the rise. The recent call to close three federal penitentiaries as well as a secure mental health treatment facility in Kingston will likely lead to the exacerbation of existing problems in the management and control of inmates.

Offenders pose unique health and security challenges when they enter correctional facilities, and—as Chapter 9 demonstrates, in discussing jail as a closed environment—they frequently develop further problems while incarcerated. Despite the valiant efforts of correctional staff and service providers, incarceration remains the least effective means of reducing **recidivism**

Recidivism is a term used among criminologists and criminal justice scholars to describe the act of repeating criminal behaviour. An offender who reoffends after being released from a correctional service is said to *recidivate*. A great deal of the research conducted in criminal justice fields is aimed at reducing the recidivism among criminal offenders. By a common measure, the success rate of correctional programs correlates negatively with their recidivism rate. A number of studies have shown that the longer and more severe a correctional sentence, the greater the degree of recidivism and the more severe the offence(s) subsequently committed.

among offenders (Smith, Goggin, & Gendreau, 2002). This fact has led to interest in and exploration of non-carceral alternatives for offenders. Chapter 10 explores these alternatives in detail, showing how the successful reintegration of offenders into the community is a key consideration in risk assessment and management. These issues continue to play a major role for corrections workers even after offenders have done their time. Often, as discussed in Chapter 11, the public's reaction to conditional release programs and parole eligibility is even more hostile than its reaction to incarceration sentences. Each offender enters the system with a different identity and personal narrative, and these variances in background, age, race, gender, language, health, offence, and personality traits create unique challenges for the correctional system, as outlined in Chapter 12.

The challenges associated with corrections that are explored in this section of the book can create a sense of helplessness. It is hard not to become overwhelmed with the complexity of issues and wonder whether *anything* works. This is usually where political platforms are forged on corrections issues, leading to wide-scale reform measures that aim to offer a "quick fix" at high costs to the taxpayer and the correctional system. This is particularly so when these initiatives rely on myths about what tactics do work and how crime happens.

See also mini chapter 16.1 "Nothing Works" Revisited

The SSCA, for instance, recommends adult sentences for young offenders who are convicted of certain violent offences—a proposal that flies in the face of almost all criminal justice research on youth at risk (as you'll read about in this text's next section.) This Act also increases the length and scope of mandatory minimum sentences, although research has shown that these mandatory minimums come at the expense of much-needed discretion from police, Crown attorneys, judges, and correctional staff; these sentences ultimately put more people in prison, for longer periods of time. When coupled with research on the systemic forms of discrimination already existing in the criminal justice system, the problems of overpopulation and overrepresentation within Canada's prison systems are escalated to levels of human rights violations. This is perhaps best summarized in the title of a now famous book by Jeffrey Reiman (1979), *The Rich Get Richer and the Poor Get Prison*. Adam Gopnik (2012), writing about the American prison system, speaks to this danger when he writes:

> For a great many poor people in America, particularly poor black men, prison is a destination that braids through an ordinary life, much as high school and college do for rich white ones. More than half of all black men without a high-school diploma go to prison at some time in their lives. Mass incarceration on a scale almost unexampled in human history is a

fundamental fact of our country today—perhaps the fundamental fact, as slavery was the fundamental fact of 1850. In truth, there are more black men in the grip of the criminal-justice system—in prison, on probation, or on parole—than were in slavery then. Over all, there are now more people under "correctional supervision" in America—more than six million—than were in the Gulag Archipelago under Stalin at its height.

Sadly, Canada is not much different from the United States. Despite the lowest crime rates in nearly four decades and a number of provisions (such as s. 718.2(e) of the *Criminal Code*, explored in Chapter 9) specifically aimed at decreasing the proportion of Aboriginal offenders in the prison population, Canada still imprisons a great deal more Aboriginal offenders than it does offenders from other backgrounds. In 2008–9, Aboriginal youth accounted for only 6 percent of all youth in Canada, yet represented 27 percent of youth remanded and 36 percent of youth admitted to sentenced custody (Calverley, Cotter, & Halla, 2010).

What Do You Think?

Think back on your work reviewing the case study that opened this book. The offender in that case had committed a horrible crime even after serving multiple sentences of imprisonment for previous offences. Recidivism is a particular concern in his case. Would you, as the judge in that case, have preferred a mandatory minimum sentence or do you feel your discretion was a valuable tool in reaching a decision that would best speak to the sentencing principles in s. 718 of the *Criminal Code*?

Try to keep that opening case study and the changes effected by the *Safe Streets and Communities Act* in your mind as you read through the following chapters and think about the correctional sentences and services that Canada employs. There is much to keep in mind as we consider how the criminal justice system should do its job, but, as Jane Barker notes at the conclusion of Chapter 12, "it is imperative that we not forget the people themselves."

REFERENCES

Calverley, D., Cotter, A., & Halla, E. (2010). Youth custody and community services in Canada. *Juristat, 30*(1). Retrieved from http://www.statcan.gc.ca/pub/85-002-x/2010001/article/11147-eng.pdf

CSC Review Panel. (2007). *A roadmap to strengthening public safety*. Ottawa: Public Works. Retrieved from http://www.publicsafety.gc.ca/csc-scc/cscrprprt-eng.pdf

Doob, A., & Cesaroni, C. (2001). The political attractiveness of mandatory minimum sentences. *Osgoode Hall LJ, 39*(2/3), 287–304.

Gopnik, A. (2012). The caging of America. *The New Yorker*, January 30. Retrieved from http://www.newyorker.com/arts/critics/atlarge/2012/01/30/120130crat_atlarge_gopnik

Safe Streets and Communities Act, SC 2012, c. 1. Retrieved from http://laws-lois.justice.gc.ca/eng/AnnualStatutes/2012_1/FullText.html

Smith, P., Goggin, C., & Gendreau, P. (2002). *The effects of prison sentences and intermediate sanctions on recidivism: General effects and individual differences*. Ottawa: Public Works.

Sprott, J.B. (2001). *Background for the YCJA: Report on data prepared for the Department of Justice Canada*. Ottawa: Public Works.

Tousaw, K. (2011, October 29). Targeting Mrs. B. *Toronto Star*. Retrieved from http://www.thestar.com/opinion/editorialopinion/article/1078042--targeting-mrs-b

Institutional Corrections

<table>
<tr>
<td>

LEARNING OBJECTIVES

After reading this chapter, students will be able to:

- Describe the responsibilities of the two adult correctional systems in Canada.
- Describe the differences between jails/detention centres, correctional centres, and penitentiaries.
- Identify the reasons why an offender is assessed as a maximum-, medium-, or minimum-security offender.
- Explain key principles used to guide risk assessments.

</td>
<td>

CHAPTER OUTLINE

</td>
</tr>
</table>

Introduction

Canada has three distinct correctional systems (youth, adult provincial/territorial, and federal), with each operating custodial facilities (closed custody, detention centres, jails, and penitentiaries) where people are held in custody for a variety of reasons, such as awaiting trial or serving a sentence imposed by a court. It is often confusing for the general public to distinguish between these facilities, but it is important to understand the different role each of these facilities has within the Canadian criminal justice system. The focus of this chapter is limited to adult custodial facilities, while Chapters 13 and 14 will discuss the youth criminal justice system.

Jurisdiction

Provincial and territorial adult correctional systems are responsible for operating jails and detention centres, as well as correctional facilities, which involves supervising offenders serving custodial sentences up to two years less a day. Jails and detention centres generally hold people on **remand** awaiting trial or sentencing, awaiting transfer to federal institutions, or serving very short sentences—usually no more than 60 days. Correctional facilities operated by the provinces/territories supervise people sentenced up to two years less a day. The federal system (Correctional Service of Canada,

remand
The holding of an accused in custody while he or she waits for trial or sentencing.

or CSC), meanwhile, is responsible for supervising offenders serving custodial sentences ranging from two years to life and/or indeterminate sentences. Institutions operated by CSC are generally referred to as penitentiaries.

The *Corrections and Conditional Release Act* (CCRA) is the key piece of legislation authorizing CSC to operate custodial facilities to house offenders serving federal sentences, whereas the *Ministry of Correctional Services Act* is the key piece of legislation authorizing the Ontario government to operate provincial correctional institutions.

The Goals of Correctional Systems

The two key goals of correctional systems are to correct problematic behaviour and to protect the public. In examining the two mission statements below, it is clear that rehabilitation and community safety are the key priorities. CSC's mission statement is as follows:

> The Correctional Service of Canada, as part of the criminal justice system and respecting the rule of law, contributes to public safety by actively encouraging and assisting offenders to become law-abiding citizens, while exercising reasonable, safe, secure, and humane control. (CSC, 2007, para. 2)

The mission of the Ontario Ministry of Community Safety and Correctional Services (MCSC) is as follows:

> The Ministry is committed to enhancing community safety through effective supervision, care, custody, and intervention as well as influencing the behavioural change and reintegration of inmates/offenders into Ontario communities. (MCSC, 2010, p. 2)

▶ IN-CLASS EXERCISE

Look at the provincial legislation for adult corrections in the jurisdiction in which you live. Does it include a mission statement that indicates what services are provided and what they are meant to accomplish? If there is no mission statement, what guidance is given?

Protection of the Public: Myth or Reality?

When a parent corrects a child for problematic behaviour, the goal is to generally stop the problematic behaviour by imposing a consequence to help underscore the need to change the behaviour. The criminal justice system assumes a parental role within society to address criminal behaviour using two key concepts—specific and general deterrence. When a judge imposes a sentence, the goal is to send a direct message to the individual that the behaviour is not acceptable (specific deterrence), and at the same time discourage other members of the community from the same behaviour (general deterrence). Serving time in jail is a state-sanctioned consequence for criminal behaviour, with the idea that being removed from the community will help offenders know their actions will not be tolerated by society and that they need to change if they want the privilege of freedom and living within the community.

Institutions are considered key instruments of **social control** and public safety. There is a real sense of security felt by a community when someone convicted of a violent offence is sentenced to a period of incarceration. With incarceration comes the assumption that the individual is not able to commit further crimes and that the person will learn a lesson. In Canada, most offenders are serving determinate sentences and will be released from prison at the completion of their sentence or during their sentence on some type of conditional release. The release of offenders can be a source of concern for the community, especially given the media sensationalism that sometimes accompanies the release, depending on who the offender is. Also contributing to a community's anxiety is the failure of the correctional systems to better educate the public about correctional interventions, about decision-making and supervision practices, and about the resources that are available to manage released offenders—such as correctional programs, halfway houses, and day reporting centres. Increased transparency would also help gain public confidence. Given the poor communication and educational practices of the correctional systems, it is reasonable for communities to have many concerns about the offenders being released. Stories about offenders successfully completing their sentences, making significant changes in their lives, and never reoffending do not make the headlines. Instead, we have stories about violent recidivism that create a sense of fear and concern that the system does not work.

social control
Informal influences (e.g., disapproving frown from a parent) and formal influences (e.g., laws, regulations) on a person's behaviour.

Some suggest that the reason people commit crimes or reoffend is because the penalties are not harsh enough. This belief is at the core of the recent legislative and policy changes to lengthen and create stiffer penalties in Canada. Both provincial/territorial and federal levels of government have adopted these changes despite contrary evidence that harsher sentences and longer periods of incarceration do not reduce crime rates (Cullen & Gendreau, 2000; Spohn & Holleran, 2002). There is often a disconnect between research and public policy that is beyond the scope of this chapter, but it is important to note that social policies are not always based on empirical evidence, despite the fact that the governments often fund researchers to conduct the very studies that demonstrate the ineffectiveness of harsher sentences.

An Overview of Incarceration in Canada

Rates of Incarceration

In 2009, Canada's incarceration rate was 117 per 100,000, which, although considerably lower than that of the United States, which is 760 per 100,000, is still considered problematic, given that the rate increased by 1 percent in the 2008–9 fiscal year. The increase in the incarceration rate is not due to increases in people being sentenced, but rather reflects a trend present in Canada since the mid-1990s that involves an increase in the number of people being remanded in custody (Statistics Canada, 2009). Those remanded in custody have not yet been proven guilty of an offence, yet they are separated from friends and family, not able to work, and pay taxes. This is a worrisome trend and reflects the "law and order" philosophy that Canada seems to be adopting, despite the negative results experienced by the United States, which adopted this approach years ago and is now slowly moving away from it.

Types of Institutions

Maximum-security institutions are characterized by high static security systems, such as perimeter walls or fences; mobile perimeter patrols; armed guard posts, both outside and within the penitentiary; electronic security systems; electronic doors and locks; metal detectors; restriction of movement; urine testing; frequent searches, including the use of drug-detecting dogs; and frequent head counts of inmates. Dynamic security strategies are also relied on, which include the interaction of correctional staff with offenders, the provision of correctional programs and supervised employment opportunities, and the availability of positive and productive leisure activities. Significantly, people remanded in custody do not have access to programs, work or training opportunities, or activities that offenders sentenced to a jail term have access to. Jails and detention centres are generally operated as maximum-security institutions, given that little may be known about the accused awaiting trial. This suggests that careful supervision and limiting freedom of movement are needed to help ensure the safety of all offenders and staff.

Medium-security institutions have many of the same security features as maximum-security institutions, but there is greater freedom of movement for inmates. The majority of federal offenders are classified as medium security (Public Safety Canada, 2010).

Minimum-security institutions are significantly different from maximum-security institutions, in that they do not have the same static security systems. There are usually no armed security posts, but careful supervision is maintained. The living conditions are generally more comfortable, characterized by less rigid schedules and more freedom of movement, except at night; the dress code for offenders is often more relaxed, as well.

Multi-level institutions are those consisting of several different security levels within one facility. Most penitentiaries that house female offenders are multi-level institutions. There are small units that are maximum security, while others operate as medium- or minimum-security facilities.

Male and Female Facilities

Correctional systems are often criticized for the lack of attention and resources directed toward female offenders, as well as for the lack of gender-specific **assessment** instruments, programs, and institutions (Van Gundy, 2012). In part, the historically lower arrest rates, convictions, and custodial sentences imposed for female offenders explain this deficiency. However, with the recent increase in female arrests, convictions, and custodial sentences (Barker, 2009), along with pending legislation that will likely increase incarceration rates and lengthen periods of incarceration, women's prisons will become significantly taxed, owing to their limited number. The incarcerated female offender population differs from its male counterpart in several key ways (see Chapter 12 for a more extensive discussion about female offenders). In general, female offenders tend to have less extensive criminal histories, are serving shorter sentences, have lower rates of violent offences, and have higher rates of mental health needs than male offenders (Barker, 2009; Van Voorhis, Wright, Salisbury, & Bauman, 2010).

One key difference between male and female facilities is that most if not all institutions that house female offenders are operated as multi-level or maximum-security institutions. This is due to how few women are incarcerated compared with men in Canada. There are significant challenges for correctional staff in appropriately addressing the risk and needs of all inmates in multi-level institutions. For example, minimum-security female offenders experience more freedom of movement and have more access to visitors, services, and activities than do the maximum-security offenders in the multi-level institution, but minimum-security offenders in a multi-level institution have more restrictions than do inmates in a minimum-security prison. This may have a negative impact on the rehabilitative process and increase the challenges these women face when released back into the community. It may also increase the possibility of low-risk offenders being negatively affected by those who have stronger anti-social attitudes and values. In contrast, male offenders sentenced to periods of incarceration are generally imprisoned in single-level security institutions, where security procedures and services can specialize in addressing their risk levels, rather

assessment
The process by which professionals such as doctors, social workers, and correctional staff gain insight into a person's behaviour and situation; usually the first step toward developing an intervention plan.

than having to be all things to all offenders housed in the facility. Institutions that house female offenders are modelled after male institutions despite the known differences as to what would best facilitate the correctional practice for female offenders (Van Gundy, 2012).

The five newer federal penitentiaries for women located across Canada are better designed than the former Prison for Women in Kingston, Ontario, but given the complexity of the offender population within each of these facilities, there are still many challenges to overcome. For example, institutions that restrict human interaction do not help to facilitate the relationship needs of female offenders. Many of those with mental health needs cannot be managed in the lower-security wings of the institutions and are therefore often housed in maximum-security or segregation units that significantly reduce their ability to interact with others. Institutions that facilitate companionship and that are highly interactive tend to help to assist with the rehabilitation process, especially for female offenders (Van Gundy, 2012).

Costs of Incarceration

There is a high cost associated with incarceration, and as more people are incarcerated for longer periods, the costs to society will only increase. For example, during the 2008–9 fiscal year, the cost to house a male offender in a federal maximum-security penitentiary for one year was approximately $147,000, compared with $93,000 to house a male offender in either a medium- or minimum-security penitentiary. In comparison, the cost to incarcerate a woman in a federal penitentiary was about $203,000 per year—regardless of the security level, given that women's penitentiaries operate as multi-level facilities (Public Safety Canada, 2010).

A life sentence means that an offender will spend the rest of his or her life incarcerated unless the offender is released to the community on parole. Therefore, if an offender at age 25 is sentenced to life and the average lifespan is approximately age 75 for men, the government will be responsible for all costs associated with the housing, supervision, food, clothing, and health care of this offender for the next 50 years. That means it will cost you the taxpayer approximately $7 million to house one male offender in maximum security for the length of his life sentence. Now, multiply this by the number of offenders serving life sentences. It can be argued that this is money well spent because it ensures the safety of the community, but limited evidence exists to confirm that lengthy periods of incarceration reduce crime and recidivism. Perhaps, investing some of the money dedicated to incarceration into alternative responses to crime that have the support of empirical evidence would prove to be a more effective use of public funds.

Traditional Versus Modern Institutions

Older institutions such as Kingston Penitentiary (recently slated for closure) and the Toronto Jail (known as the "Don Jail") were designed with little consideration given to how housing large numbers of offenders in small areas might affect their mental and physical health. The living areas were essentially rows of cells built upon more rows of cells, making it very easy for the spread of contagious illnesses. Traditional institutions, particularly maximum- and medium-security ones, were designed to limit interaction between staff and offenders. Most have security posts located outside of the inmate living areas (the range). The officers patrol the range at various intervals, but the majority of time is spent supervising from a distance behind glass or secure barrier. Newer-style institutions tend to use a more interactive and direct supervisory approach. Older-style institutions often have rigid schedules, and offenders have little opportunity to make decisions for themselves, so that they become very dependent on the "system"—often referred to as being institutionalized. Jails and detention centres continue to follow this more traditional approach; however, correctional centres and penitentiaries are designed to facilitate the development and maintenance of life skills.

Around 1996, the Ontario government made a decision to close small jails and build large regional detention centres to lower the costs associated with incarceration and to address the fact that many facilities were overcrowded and poorly designed, and presented multiple health and safety risks to staff and offenders, and therefore required costly renovations (Standing Committee on Prison Conditions, 2006). As can be imagined, there are a few significant issues related to this decision, including increased hardship on families and the offender, given that it might no longer be possible for visits if it is too far and too costly for the family to travel to the regional detention centre. There are now also added costs involved with transporting the accused to court and back to the detention centre for court proceedings,

Toronto's notorious Don Jail, which opened in 1865, crammed inmates into closely packed, unsanitary cells and limited their communication with staff. Today, jails are designed to facilitate positive interactions and skills development.

Source: Peter Power/Globe and Mail.

despite new initiatives to reduce costs by using video appearances; there may be longer waiting times for an offender to receive needed services, as well.

Other provinces and territories also face the high costs of maintaining and renovating older facilities as well as the need to expand their capacity to deal with an increasing remand population and with more custodial sentences being imposed. In Edmonton, for example, a new remand centre is currently being built.

Like the Ontario government, the federal government also faces the challenge of aging institutions, and a number of significant renovations have taken place in the past decade to modernize and expand the capacity of existing penitentiaries, given that recent legislative changes are likely to bring an increase in the penitentiary population. The designs of newer penitentiaries allow offenders more opportunities to develop and maintain life skills than traditional institutions did. For example, offenders in many medium- and minimum-security penitentiaries are responsible for their own food choices and preparation, rather than being served prepared meals from an established menu.

Security Classification

Section 30 of the CCRA and s. 17 of the *Corrections and Conditional Release Regulations* establish three key criteria to be used by CSC staff when determining whether a federal offender should be housed in a maximum-, medium-, or minimum-security penitentiary: escape risk; risk to public safety in event of escape; and level of supervision required within the institution to ensure the safety of other offenders and staff. A "security classification assessment" is completed by a federal parole officer when an offender is admitted to the penitentiary, and a yearly review of the classification is completed. The security classification includes reviewing the nature of the offence(s) that the offender is serving a sentence for; determining whether there are any outstanding charges; assessing the offender's behaviour when in custody to date (remand, previous sentences); reviewing the criminal history, personal and social history, health (physical and mental) history and needs of the offender; assessing the risk of violent behaviour; and determining whether there is evidence of the offender continuing to be involved in criminal activity. Therefore, an individual who is considered a high risk to escape, poses a high risk to public safety in event of an escape, and requires close monitoring to ensure safety and security in the institution would be classified as a maximum-security offender.

The pieces of legislation governing provincial and territorial institutions contain very similar criteria to those used by CSC to determine the security classification of offenders serving time within their correctional facilities.

▶ IN-CLASS EXERCISE

You Be the Institutional Parole Officer

Would you classify this offender as a maximum-, medium-, or minimum-security offender based on the case summary below? Be prepared to explain your decision.

Review the correctional programs available at women's penitentiaries (Hint: Correctional Service of Canada's website will be a good source to consult). What institutional programs would you recommend for Rita? Be prepared to explain your decision.

What could you do as Rita's institutional parole officer to help facilitate her maintaining a positive parenting relationship with her son while she is incarcerated?

Do you think Rita will become involved in criminal activity again after her release? Be prepared to support your position.

Rita is a 36-year-old first-time non-violent federal offender serving a three-year sentence for possession of narcotics. She has no criminal history or any outstanding charges. She is a single parent with a four-year-old son. At the time of the offence, she was experiencing significant financial difficulties, so when she was approached by a friend of a friend and offered a chance to earn $5,000 by storing some cocaine in her home, she agreed. While waiting for trial, she was supervised on bail without incident for 15 months. Rita does not have a history of substance abuse, and the motivation behind her crime was financial. She does not have any extended family, and her son's father refuses to take responsibility for his child; as a result, her son is in foster care. She expresses great regret for her actions and takes responsibility for her poor decision making. Since arriving at the institution two weeks ago, Rita has demonstrated an ability to follow rules. She has expressed an interest in upgrading her education, because she hopes this will help her secure more stable and higher-paying employment upon release.

Assessment of Offenders

Offenders who receive a federal sentence are transported from a provincial facility to a federal reception or assessment unit for a comprehensive intake assessment. In Ontario, the assessment unit for male offenders is in Millhaven Institution in Bath; for female offenders, it is in Grand Valley Institution in Kitchener. The assessment process involves examining all available documents about the offender's family background, peers, substance abuse, criminal history, previous periods of incarceration or community supervision, employment and education, and medical and mental health history. Offenders are interviewed and required to complete a computerized assessment as well. The purpose of the assessment process is not only to determine the security classification, but also to develop a correctional plan that identifies the interventions needed to address the risk factors for criminal behaviour. It is important to understand that some risk factors cannot be changed (e.g., age at first arrest, previous criminal convictions); these are often referred to as **static risk factors**. There are many risk factors that can be changed (e.g., criminal associates, attitudes, employment, substance abuse), and these are often referred to as **dynamic risk factors**, or **criminogenic needs**. To manage static risk factors, supervision strategies are used to reduce the risk these factors present. For example, within custodial settings, those who are high risk are supervised more closely than those who are low risk; within the community, special conditions such as curfews are imposed to restrict the offender's movement during the time frames in which previous crimes were committed. To address dynamic risk factor(s), services such as substance abuse treatment programs are provided to help reduce or stop the behaviour, which in turn lowers the risk of recidivism.

static risk factors
Risk factors associated with criminal history that cannot be changed (e.g., age at first arrest).

dynamic risk factors (or criminogenic needs)
Factors such as substance abuse and negative peers that contribute to an individual's criminal behaviour but are possible to change.

The Risk-Need-Responsivity Model

Clinical judgments made by mental health and correctional professionals about an offender's risk to reoffend are not as accurate as predictions based on actuarial instruments (structured instruments that use existing statistical evidence). For example, Bonta, Law, and Hanson (1998) found that the correlation with recidivism predicted by clinical judgment was very small (0.03) for offenders with mental health disorders, but quite robust (0.39) for predictions made using actuarial instruments. CSC and many other correctional systems around the world use the **risk-need-responsivity (RNR) model** to guide correctional assessment and intervention strategies. It was developed by three Canadian researchers, Andrews, Bonta, and Hoge.

risk-need-responsivity (RNR) model
Assessment and rehabilitation theory that suggests it is possible to accurately predict the likelihood that someone will reoffend and to effectively intervene to reduce the risk.

The *risk principle* indicates that an offender's risk to reoffend can be predicted and reduced if the level of service provided matches the risk level of the person (Andrews & Bonta, 2006). For example, a multi-recidivist violent offender with a ten-year addiction to heroin—the direct reason for the criminal behaviour—is at higher risk to reoffend than a first-time non-violent offender who imported drugs for financial gain. The correctional interventions and programs used to assist these two offenders need to be matched to their respective risk levels.

Researchers have demonstrated that placing someone in an intensive program when the risk level is low can actually increase the person's risk to reoffend (Andrews et al., 1990; Lowenkamp, Latessa, & Holsinger, 2006). An offender who smokes the occasional "joint" is not going to relate to others who are daily heroin or cocaine users, and so this mismatch of treatment services will result in the offender being less interested in participating in additional treatment if the first experience was negative. This is also a waste of valuable resources because more services and costs were spent than were needed for the casual-use offender. Additionally, there is the risk of increasing the offender's level of drug use if he or she is exposed to those with much higher levels of use. A maximum-security offender requires more intensive supervision and interventions to help reduce the risk of continued criminal activity than does a first-time non-violent offender. The cost of housing an offender in maximum security is staggering, so only those who require it should be there. Additionally, housing low-risk offenders in a maximum-security unit increases the risk of continued criminal activity, given that they are associating with others who have entrenched criminal attitudes, values, and longer histories of criminal behaviour ("the contagion effect").

Housing low-risk offenders in a maximum-security unit increases the risk of continued criminal activity ("the contagion effect").

The *need principle* refers to addressing the specific factors that are directly related to the offender's criminal behaviour as having the most impact on reducing recidivism (Andrews & Bonta, 2006; Andrews, 2012). Gendreau, Little, and Goggin (1996) identified some of the key criminogenic risk factors associated with recidivism.

The top three criminogenic need factors were found to be anti-social support, anti-social personality, and anti-social cognitions. These findings highlight the importance of identifying and assessing the key people of influence within an offender's life. On one hand, very positive, pro-social people who are supporting the offender may help to reduce the likelihood of recidivism; on the other hand, negative associates who possess anti-social values and attitudes and engage in criminal behaviour will be a significant risk factor. Correctional staff need to work with offenders to help them understand the role associates, friends, and possibly even family members can play in their criminal behaviour, and to help them create strategies for developing a more pro-social group of people to associate with. Further highlighting this importance is the fact that Andrews and Bonta also identified social supports for crime as a key criminogenic need area, along with anti-social personality pattern, pro-criminal attitudes, substance abuse, family and marital relationships, employment history, and educational achievement. Like the risk principle, the need principle requires that the level of service match the extent of the need in order to have meaningful results (Andrews & Bonta, 2006). Addressing needs not directly linked to criminal behaviour has little impact on recidivism and is therefore not a good investment of resources. It is imperative that comprehensive assessments are completed in order to establish the need areas and match the need with the treatment.

The *responsivity principle* refers to the need to match service delivery and methods with the offender's learning style and his or her cultural and religious background in order to have the highest potential for reducing the likelihood of continued criminal behaviour (Andrews & Bonta, 2006; Andrews, 2012). There is a significant body of research that indicates **cognitive-behavioural strategies** are more effective than other approaches, especially those that are non-structured (Andrews & Bonta, 2006).

It is recognized that at times there may be reasons to stray from what the RNR model suggests in individual cases; sometimes there are circumstances that suggest the standard practice would not be helpful. This is acknowledged by the "professional discretion principle." However, significant caution must be exercised before straying from the other principles. For example, if an offender is referred to multiple treatment programs to address multiple needs, it may be necessary to prioritize which need to address first, which to address second, and so on. It would be inappropriate for an offender to be involved in several high-intensity treatment programs at the same time. There may also be certain circumstances that suggest an alternative approach may be required, or that the timing of the intervention needs to change. For example, if an inmate is diagnosed with cancer and requires chemotherapy, it would be unwise to put him or her in an intensive treatment program for anger management while undergoing invasive and intensive medical treatment fraught with many uncomfortable side effects.

The RNR model provides clear guidelines for correctional staff about assessment, treatment strategies, and the general environment that enhances the likelihood of reducing recidivism.

cognitive-behavioural strategies
Strategies, based on the theory that our thoughts, perceptions, and interpretations of the world influence our behaviour, that help us change the way we perceive or interpret a situation, which in turn changes how we behave.

Offender Population Profile

In 2008, approximately 36,921 people were incarcerated in either a penitentiary (13,286) or a provincial/territorial institution (23,635), with the majority in provincial/territorial institutions (13,486) being held on remand. Women serving federal sentences account for about 6 percent of the total federal population. The median age of the federal offender population at admission to federal penitentiaries is 33 years of age, and an increase in the number of offenders admitted to federal custody in their thirties and forties has been noted (Public Safety Canada, 2010); this may simply be a reflection of Canada's aging population. The offender population is aging, and this poses significant issues for correctional officials in terms of how best to meet the increasing health-care needs of aging offenders. Additionally, concerns such as protection of older offenders from potential threats from other offenders and mobility issues require changes in how institutions are physically structured and operated.

Of particular concern is the overrepresentation of Aboriginal offenders involved in the criminal justice system and the fact that the proportion of Aboriginal offenders kept in custody is higher than for non-Aboriginal offenders. Even though the Aboriginal population represents about 3 percent of the total Canadian population, approximately 18 percent of the total federal offender population is Aboriginal. Further exacerbating this situation is the fact that a higher proportion of Aboriginal offenders are incarcerated (21 percent) than those supervised in the community (14 percent) (Public Safety Canada, 2010). These statistics underscore the need for a serious examination of the circumstances of Aboriginal people in Canada and of existing policies within the criminal justice system for addressing systemic bias.

Federal offenders serving a life or indeterminate sentence make up about 23 percent of the total federal population, and 69 percent of the total federal population have been convicted of a violent offence (Public Safety Canada, 2010).

Chapter 12 explores offender population profiles in detail.

What Do You Think?

In what ways do prisons accommodate the needs of older offenders? Are prison cells retrofitted for wheelchair accessibility? What are the implications of such mobility devices for security classifications within the penitentiary system?

Correctional Programs

The offender population is increasing in its complexity, which is challenging the resources of the correctional system and staff. For example, there has been a dramatic increase in the number of offenders experiencing mental health problems, as well as an increase in those associated with criminal gangs, those with serious substance abuse problems, and those with extensive histories of criminal behaviour (CSC, 2009). These increases all pose challenges to correctional staff from two perspectives: how to ensure the safety of offenders and staff; and how best to address the issues that brought the offender into conflict with the law.

A range of evidence-informed programs—such as anger management, violence prevention, substance abuse, life skills, education and job training—

are available to address the treatment needs of offenders within both provincial correctional centres and federal penitentiaries. It is essential that offenders be matched with the appropriate treatment services to address their risk and need levels, in keeping with the RNR model (Cullen & Gendreau, 2000). After the comprehensive assessments are completed upon an offender's admission to custody, case management plans are developed on the basis of the intake assessment results; they identify both the need and risk levels and the most appropriate correctional programs to address them. In addition, health-care professionals (doctors, nurses, psychologists, psychiatrists, and social workers) provide essential treatment to address offender needs.

The ability to participate in educational, treatment, employment, recreational, and spiritual programs and activities helps to ensure that offenders have an opportunity to learn different behaviours and lifestyle activities to help prepare them for a positive reintegration into the community and a reduced likelihood of recidivism.

MINI CASE STUDY

Tommy

Tommy is a 57-year-old repeat federal offender who has spent the majority of the last 40 years incarcerated in traditional-style institutions. In an interview, he talked about how every time he had been released from jail, he found himself overwhelmed and extremely lonely because he felt his "family" was at the institution, and that he would find a way to "come home." What was particularly interesting was that he considered *the staff* to be his family. He described how he has known some staff members for more than 30 years, and knew them when they were, for example, correctional officers, and how some are now unit managers, or the deputy warden. Their professional and genuine care for him as a client was the first time he had experienced others being concerned for his welfare, which he fully appreciated, given that he had not enjoyed the luxury of a support system in the community.

Discussion Questions

1. Do you think institutional staff should be "cold and distant" toward offenders to prevent offenders from becoming dependent on staff for guidance and encouragement? Explain your answer.

2. How can facilities be structured differently to reduce the institutionalization of offenders?

3. What type of planning and assistance do you think is required to ease the transition from institution to community upon release?

SUGGESTED READINGS

Andrews, D.A., & Bonta, J. (2006). *The psychology of criminal conduct* (4th ed.).
    Newark, NJ: LexisNexis/Matthew Bender.
Carlson, L.W. (2001). *Breakfast with the devil.* London, ON: Insomniac Press.
Conover, T. (2000). *Newjack: Guarding Sing Sing* (1st ed.). New York: Vintage Books.
Correctional Service of Canada. Educational resources. http://www.csc-scc.gc.ca/
    education/er-rp-eng.shtml
Statistics Canada. (2009). Adult and youth correctional services: Key indicators.
    The Daily (2009, December 8). Retrieved from http://www.statcan.gc.ca/
    daily-quotidien/091208/dq091208a-eng.htm

REFERENCES

Andrews, D.A. (2012). The risk-need-responsivity (RNR) model of correctional
    assessment and treatment. In J.A. Dvoskin, J.L. Skeem, R.W. Novaco, &
    K.S. Douglas (Eds.), *Using social science to reduce violent offending*
    (pp. 127–156). New York: Oxford University Press.
Andrews, D., Zinger, I., Hoge, R., Bonta, J., Gendreau, P., & Cullen, F. (1990). Does
    correctional treatment work? A clinically relevant and psychologically
    informed meta-analysis. *Criminology, 28,* 369-404.
Andrews, D.A., & Bonta, J. (2006). *The psychology of criminal conduct* (4th ed.).
    Newark, NJ: LexisNexis/Matthew Bender.
Barker, J. (2009). A "typical" female offender. In J. Barker (Ed.), *Women and the
    criminal justice system: A Canadian perspective* (pp. 63–87). Toronto:
    Emond Montgomery.
Bonta, J., Law, M., & Hanson, R.K. (1998). The prediction of criminal and violent
    recidivism among mentally disordered offenders: A meta-analysis.
    Psychological Bulletin, 123, 123–142.
Correctional Service of Canada. (2007). Mission statement. Retrieved from
    http://www.csc-scc.gc.ca/text/organi-eng.shtml
Corrections and Conditional Release Act, SC 1992, c. 20.
Corrections and Conditional Release Regulations, SOR/92-620.
Cullen, F.T., & Gendreau, P. (2000). Assessing correctional rehabilitation: Policy,
    practice and prospect. *Criminal Justice, 3,* 109–175.
Gendreau, P., Little, T., & Goggin, C. (1996). A meta-analysis of the predictors of
    adult offender recidivism: What works! *Criminology, 34,* 575–607.
Gopnik, A. (2012). The caging of America. *The New Yorker,* January 30. Retrieved
    from http://www.newyorker.com/arts/critics/atlarge/2012/01/30/120130crat
    _atlarge_gopnik
Lowenkamp, C.T., Latessa, E., & Holsinger, A. (2006). The risk principle in action:
    What have we learned from 13,676 offenders and 97 correctional programs?
    Crime & Delinquency, 51, 1–17.

Ministry of Community Safety and Correctional Services. (2010). *Results-based plan briefing book 2010–11*. Retrieved from http://www.mcscs.jus.gov.on.ca/english/publications/RbP1011/RbP201011.html#vision

Public Safety Canada. (2010). *Corrections and conditional release statistical overview: Annual report 2010*. Ottawa: Public Works and Government Services of Canada.

Reiman, J.H. (1979). *The rich get richer and the poor get prison: Ideology, class and criminal justice*. Boston: Allyn and Bacon.

Spohn, C., & Holleran, D. (2002). The effect of imprisonment on recidivism rates of felony offenders: A focus on drug offenders. *Journal of Criminology, 40*(2), 329–357.

Standing Committee on Prison Conditions. (2006). *The superjails in Ontario*. Toronto: John Howard Society.

Statistics Canada. (2009). Adult and youth correctional services: Key indicators. Retrieved from http://www.statcan.gc.ca/daily-quotidien/091208/dq091208a-eng.htm

Van Gundy, A. (2012). Gender and corrections. In R. Muraskin (Ed.), *Women and justice: It's a crime* (5th ed., pp. 344–353). Upper Saddle River, NJ: Prentice Hall.

Van Voorhis, P., Wright, E.M., Salisbury, E., & Bauman, A. (2010). Women's risk factors and their contributions to existing risk/needs assessment: The current status of a gender-responsive supplement. *Criminal Justice and Behavior, 37*, 261–288. doi:10.1177/0093854809357442

Community Corrections

Introduction

Social problems such as poverty, limited resources for struggling families, family violence, child abuse, high unemployment rates, gang involvement, and substance abuse are all contributing factors to criminal behaviour. Crime most often begins in the community; therefore, it makes the most sense to provide services within the community to help people who are considered "at risk" of coming in conflict with the law or who have already come in conflict with the law. "Community corrections" is a term that refers to a wide range of sanctions and interventions used by the criminal justice system to respond to and prevent criminal behaviour. The purpose of community corrections is to assist offenders in making positive changes in their lives that will help them become crime-free; to reduce crime; and to promote community safety. The focus of this chapter is on community sanctions: probation, intensive supervision, conditional sentence, and community service. The essential role of non-governmental organizations such as St. Leonard's Society, the John Howard Society, the Elizabeth Fry Society, and the Salvation Army in supporting the goals of reducing crime and increasing community safety is also briefly examined. The focus in the following chapter is on how gradual release programs such as halfway houses and parole are designed to assist in crime reduction, community safety, and the safe reintegration of offenders returning to the community. In combination, these two chapters provide an overview of community corrections in Canada.

Community Sanctions: A Good Idea?

The question of whether to incarcerate someone or to allow someone to serve his or her sentence entirely in the community is not easily answered. Personal knowledge or experience often influences a person's opinion. For example, a veteran probation and parole officer (PPO) may be very supportive of community **sanctions** (i.e., sentences) because of first-hand knowledge of supervisory practices, success rates, and so forth. However, a victim may not be supportive of a community sanction given his or her recent victimization, and limited knowledge and confidence that the offender will be adequately supervised. In addition, the media have an influential role regarding public perceptions about corrections, the police, and the justice system. Newspapers need to make a profit. Unfortunately, the more sensational, intriguing, and horrific the circumstances of a crime, the more papers are sold. As a result, facts are often presented in highly inflammatory ways, and this creates an illusion that community correctional **interventions** such as probation do not work. That false impression, combined with misinformation by some reporters who are not well informed about the law, results in public fear and confusion. Political platforms also tend to influence public opinion, even though politicians are supposed to be representing their constituents. The goal of politicians is to gain public support for their policies, so statistics and isolated cases are often used in a way to solicit support for the "cause," such as tougher sentences.

There are several key points related to community corrections that are often ignored in public debates and media coverage. For example, social conditions within the community are contributing factors to criminal behaviour. Yes, individuals are responsible for their conduct, but it is essential to understand the behaviours within a particular offender's environmental context. Given that social conditions are unlikely to dramatically change, it is critical that offenders learn how to adaptively cope within their environment. That does not mean that advocating for significant social change, such as policies and practices to eliminate poverty, is not necessary. However, serving a sentence in the community provides an opportunity for the offender to learn how to handle situations in a manner that will not result in harm to others and society. Although offenders receive treatment in jail, many have difficulty transferring these newly acquired skills to the "real world" when they are released back into the community unless there are

sanction
A penalty, such as a fine, probation, or incarceration, imposed on someone found guilty of a criminal offence.

interventions
Various strategies, such as treatment programs, job training, or upgrading education, used to help an offender learn alternatives to criminal behaviour.

good follow-up interventions available. Community sentences help with this reintegration because offenders are receiving help and learning new skills within their environment. There is a higher success rate of changing the behaviour of offenders when community rehabilitation programs are involved than when offenders are removed from their communities to either prisons or closed treatment facilities for a period of time (Andrews, Zinger, Hoge, Bonta, Gendreau, & Cullen, 1990). Significant reductions in recidivism are realized within community settings when the three key principles of the risk-needs-responsivity (RNR) model are used (Andrews & Bonta, 2006; for a review of the RNR model, see Chapter 9). Despite the available research findings, community corrections and supervision remain undervalued and not utilized to their maximum potential in Canada.

An additional benefit of holding individuals accountable for their criminal behaviour but at the same time allowing them to remain in the community is that it allows them to maintain their responsibilities such as employment, parenting, contributing to family finances, and paying taxes (Alarid, Cromwell, & Del Carmen, 2008). There are offenders who are incarcerated who could instead be safely managed in the community, and there are offenders who pose too much risk to community safety and therefore require a period of incarceration followed by a gradual, carefully supervised transition back to the community.

▶ IN-CLASS EXERCISE
Community-Based Corrections

1. Do you think that all persons convicted of a crime should serve a portion of their sentence in an institution? Explain your answer.
2. Identify and discuss three reasons why community-based corrections should be used more extensively in Canada than they are currently.
3. Identify and discuss three reasons why community-based corrections should not be used more extensively in Canada.

Probation

Probation is the most common sanction imposed by the courts in Canada (Thomas, 2004), and is a sentence that is completed within the community. Judges consider three key factors when deciding whether probation would be appropriate:

probation
A sentence that is served within the community and that often comes with certain restrictions and conditions, such as regularly checking in with a probation and parole officer.

- the nature and seriousness of the offence
- the risk to community members if the person is allowed to serve the sentence in the community
- individual circumstances, such as substance abuse (Anderson, 2001).

In Canada, the maximum length of a probation sentence is three years. A probation order can be attached to a jail sentence so long as the period of incarceration does not exceed two years. It can also be used on its own or in combination with fines, community service, or suspended or intermittent sentences. The provincial correctional system is responsible for supervising people on probation (Griffiths, 2010). The majority of people sentenced to probation are female offenders. In 2008–9, there were about 99,000 people on probation in Canada. Interestingly, the percentage of people being sentenced to probation was 3 percent higher in 2008–9 than in the previous year (Calverley, 2010). It will be interesting to closely monitor whether the *Safe Streets and Communities Act* (2012) will reduce the use of community sanctions such as probation, given that this legislation recommends harsher sentences and minimum sentences.

People with mental health problems are more vulnerable to becoming involved with the criminal justice system.

As with other branches of the correctional system, many offenders who receive community sentences have mental health problems. This is partly due to the dehospitalization policy decisions made in the 1960s within Canada and elsewhere around the world (Sealy & Whitehead, 2004). Although it is not necessary (in most cases) to have people with mental disorders hospitalized or otherwise separated from society, it is necessary to provide services to address their health needs. Those experiencing mental health problems are more vulnerable to becoming involved with the criminal justice system because the health system has failed to provide adequate supports and services. As society continues to stigmatize those with mental health needs, the number of people with mental health problems involved in the criminal justice system will increase. PPOs are often provided with few resources to assist offenders with these problems. Such offenders require access to mental health professionals, stable housing, social supports, employment, or training programs.

Probation Conditions

People sentenced to a period of probation are subject to a variety of rules. Some of the standard rules that offenders must follow while on probation include keeping the peace and being of good behaviour, appearing before the court as required, and notifying the probation officer before changing addresses or places of employment. Other conditions imposed by the judge are directly related to the individual offender and the issues determined to be linked to the person's criminal behaviour, which is in keeping with the RNR model discussed in Chapter 9 (Griffiths, 2010). The most frequently imposed additional conditions are to abstain from alcohol and drugs, to attend counselling, and not to associate with specified people (Johnson, 2006).

For example, if an offender's substance abuse has been identified as a **criminogenic risk factor**, conditions to abstain from drugs and to attend substance abuse treatment might be imposed by the judge. The PPO would then be responsible for referring the person to the appropriate program that matches the level of need in keeping with the RNR model. Additionally, the PPO is responsible for ensuring that the offender attends the treatment program and for monitoring his or her progress.

Another possible criminogenic risk factor might be the offender's associates. If that is the case, a non-association condition might also be imposed. This condition is much harder for the PPO to enforce than the first example, because the PPO cannot be everywhere at all times; but the condition does serve as a reminder to the offender that negative associates are not helpful when he or she is trying to maintain a positive lifestyle. Often it is during the course of a police investigation that an offender is discovered to be violating this condition. Police officers report all contact with persons on probation to PPOs; however, sometimes the timeliness of this information being shared can be problematic. For example, if a police officer during a shift comes in contact with a probationer under non-criminal circumstances, reporting this to the PPO may be delayed if the officer is then dispatched immediately to a serious call that requires considerable time to resolve. Additionally, the police officer may then not be on duty again for several days. This is not a case of the police officer being irresponsible, but just the reality of how delays in communication can happen.

Another way that PPOs find out about offenders violating the non-association condition is through community partners, known as **collateral contacts**. A PPO develops a network of contacts such as family members, other professionals, and community members to assist with supervising an offender. These people provide information to the PPO about the offender's behaviour in the community. One of the biggest challenges facing offenders in the community is isolation. Many struggle with loneliness if they have previously only associated with negative peers and are now not allowed to associate with this group. That may be a key reason why some choose to violate this non-association condition. It is imperative that if this condition has been imposed, the offender is assisted in developing a positive, pro-social (as opposed to anti-social) network of friends.

criminogenic (or dynamic) risk factors
Factors contributing to an individual's criminal behaviour that are possible to change, such as substance abuse or negative peers. If change occurs, the risk for continued criminal behaviour is reduced.

collateral contacts
People on whom probation and parole officers rely to assist in supervising offenders and confirming information provided by offenders.

As one can imagine, being subjected to numerous conditions may create great demands on a probationer's time. For example, if someone is required to work or attend school full time in addition to attending a treatment program in the evening three times a week, plus report to the PPO once per week, it may be difficult to do all these things and fulfill personal obligations, such as helping to maintain the family residence and equally sharing in parenting duties. Considerable attention needs to be paid to whether the conditions are feasible for that person's circumstances, or whether the system is, in such cases, simply setting the person up for failure.

Violation of Probation Order

Failure to comply with a probation order may result in the offender being charged with a breach of probation. When a violation occurs, it is generally the PPO's responsibility to assess the situation and make a decision whether to charge the offender with a breach of probation (violations regarding such conditions as curfews, associates, and using intoxicating substances are sometimes determined by police officers). A conviction for breaching probation may result in an additional sanction being imposed by the court. The judge may impose a jail sentence, a second probation order, and/or additional conditions. If a person is convicted of new offences while already on probation as a result of a suspended sentence or conditional discharge, the Crown attorney may ask the court to revoke the probation. In the case of a conditional discharge, the court may revoke the discharge, convict the person of the original charge, and impose the sentence that normally would be given when a discharge is not granted. In the case of a suspended sentence, the court may now impose the appropriate sentence. Therefore, much is at stake for someone who has difficulty complying with probation conditions.

Probation and Parole Officer Responsibilities

PPOs fulfill a vital role within community corrections. They wear many hats, as they complete assessments and prepare pre-sentence reports to assist judges in making sentencing decisions, while also supervising people on probation or provincial parole.

Pre-Sentence Reports

As mentioned above, pre-sentence reports are prepared by PPOs and are used by judges to help determine the most suitable sanction when a person is found guilty of an offence. A pre-sentence report contains information about the offender's criminal behaviour, criminal history, and social circumstances.

PPOs interview the offender, family members, friends, and employers (past and present), and review official police and correctional files in order to prepare a comprehensive document. A pre-sentence report generally includes a summary of the individual's personal family history, education, employment history, associates, community supports, and identifies criminogenic (dynamic) and **static risk factors** (Griffiths, 2010). In addition, recommendations for possible conditions to include are made for the judge's consideration should a probation order be imposed. The judge reviews this report in conjunction with the information gained during the trial to determine the best response to the criminal behaviour. If a custodial sentence is imposed, the institutional staff also use the pre-sentence report, as do supervising PPOs to help develop the best supervision and intervention plan. Given the importance of these reports, PPOs must have exceptional interviewing, assessment, and writing skills. In some probation offices, the work is divided so that some PPOs specialize in completing pre-sentence reports, while others focus on supervising probationers. In other offices, every PPO's workload combines both preparing pre-sentence reports and supervising probationers.

static risk factors
Risk factors associated with criminal history that cannot be changed (e.g., age at first arrest).

Supervision

PPOs enforce the rules and monitor offenders' compliance with their probation orders. For example, if a person is required to attend treatment, the PPO needs to confirm and monitor the offender's attendance and progress in treatment. Bonta, Rugge, Scott, Bourgon, and Yessine (2008) concluded that PPOs focus too much on enforcement and not enough on principles of effective correctional practices as outlined in the RNR model. Their findings highlight the "push–pull" between research evidence on the one hand and departmental policies and standards on the other. Their findings also highlight the need for different departmental priorities and training practices of PPOs.

PPOs often need to be counsellors, referral agents, life-skills coaches, mediators, and more. They are expected to know more today about risk assessment, human behaviour, effective interventions, and community resources than they were 20 years ago. Many, with minimal additional training, are also involved in facilitating programs for offenders in several locations. This requires that candidates for PPO positions need to have extensive knowledge and skills prior to being hired. Bracken (2003) conducted a study that involved asking PPOs in Manitoba and in the United Kingdom what they considered to be the essential knowledge and skills of PPOs. Three key abilities were identified by both groups:

1. Coping with offender emotions.
2. Interpersonal communication skills.
3. Interviewing skills.

In addition, knowledge of community resources was also identified as being essential for PPOs to possess. Without this knowledge, PPOs might spend a lot of time investigating what treatment programs are available for those they are supervising.

What Do You Think?

The idea of an offender being sentenced to probation is not always supported by members of the community, politicians, or victim service groups. Some think serving a sentence in the community is a "slap on the wrist" and ineffective in reducing recidivism. How do you feel about a sentence of probation? Explain your answer.

Intensive Supervision

In the 1970s, the philosophy of corrections began to place more emphasis on punishment, and an increase in enhanced intensive supervision strategies started to occur. These would involve an ever-expanding list of conditions (e.g., the number of contacts with the PPO or other correctional staff per week); more restrictive conditions, such as a curfew; and more limitations on activities within the community. In the 1990s, observers began to conclude that the standard probation and parole practices were inadequate for the majority of offenders, because there was too much emphasis on surveillance and not enough on rehabilitation (Taxman, 2008). This realization led to more enhanced practices being developed, although the level of accountability, and the increased surveillance and enforcement by PPOs continued. However, the increased frequency of contact between offenders and supervisors did not increase quality, but rather increased the detection of minor technical violations that typically were not observed when there was less contact (Petersilia & Turner, 1993). The number of persons supervised by an individual PPO did decrease, to allow for these increased surveillance and enforcement tasks.

Given the increased supervision standards PPOs had to follow and the greater emphasis on rules and conditions, the supervisory relationship between probationer and officer became even more structured, and less of a helping relationship characterized by counselling. A primary reason for reducing caseloads was to ensure better monitoring in combination with more time to provide counselling and guidance to offenders. Ideally, if probationers saw the PPO as a source of support rather than just as an enforcer of the rules, they might in fact disclose issues they are troubled with in order to receive assistance, which could reduce the risk of recidivism. The key role of PPOs was case management, making referrals, and monitoring compliance of conditions (Taxman, 2008). Some intensive supervision strategies coupled increased surveillance with targeted treatment intervention programs. Evaluations of intensive supervision programs that incorporated treatment showed almost a 22 percent reduction of recidivism, but surveillance-oriented intensive supervision alone tended to have no impact (Aos, Miller, & Drake, 2006). Currently, more attention is being given to the quality of the professional relationship between the PPO and probationer, in the belief that this relationship itself can be used for more than supervisory purposes: it can also be an intervention.

Electronic Monitoring

Electronic monitoring is a newer resource available to assist with monitoring offenders' compliance with their supervision conditions. In both Ontario and British Columbia, judges who impose a conditional sentence order decide whether it is necessary for the offender to wear the electronic monitoring device. This decision is made by parole board members when they are releasing an offender into the community on **parole**. Electronic monitoring devices are usually attached to the ankle and use GPS technology to monitor the person's location 24 hours per day, seven days per week. These devices are considered to be tamper-resistant and quite reliable, although issues such as a power outage, severe storms, and subways can interfere with tracking. Electronic monitoring can assist authorities to ensure a person is at home when required to be by curfew. What cannot be determined is what the individual is doing at that particular location. For example, the person may be at home as required, but could be selling drugs, abusing a child, associating with people the offender is not to be in contact with, or conspiring to commit a crime. Therefore, electronic monitoring on its own is not effective for ensuring community safety and compliance with conditions; other supervisory techniques are also required to ensure community safety (Bonta, Wallace-Capretta, & Rooney 2000).

parole
An early conditional supervised release from a custodial sentence. A person on parole has served a portion of the sentence within an institution.

Electronic monitoring makes sense for higher-risk offenders, but it cannot be the only supervisory technique used for them, given its limitations. Electronic monitoring did not have a significant impact on recidivism in the study conducted by Bonta et al. (2000), but these researchers did observe a high completion rate of community supervision orders without incident when such monitoring was used. In Canada, it is used more often with lower-risk offenders than with high-risk ones. This is counter to Andrews and Bonta's risk-needs principles, which suggest offenders with the highest risk and need profile should receive the most intensive supervision and treatment, and those with the lowest risk and need profiles should receive minimal supervision and interventions. Interestingly, Correctional Service of Canada recently stopped using electronic monitoring after completing an evaluation of its pilot project. The program was cancelled due to the inconclusive findings of multiple research studies about its effectiveness.

Conditional Sentences

conditional sentence
A sentence served in the community and supervised by probation and parole officers. Offenders are required to abide by a number of conditions that, if breached, may result either in additional conditions to comply with or in incarceration.

Introduced in Canada in 1996, **conditional sentences** are also served in the community. They are only imposed when a judge is satisfied that the risk to the public is not too great. Offenders with a history of breaching court or supervision orders are typically not given conditional sentences. These sentences usually have strict conditions similar to those in probation orders and are supervised by PPOs, but the offenders are not on probation. Violations of conditional sentence orders can be dealt with in a variety of ways by the judge. The options range from taking no action to adding conditions to incarceration (Griffiths, 2010).

Community Service Orders

community service order
An order imposed by the court requiring the offender to complete up to 240 hours of volunteer work.

The premise behind **community service orders** is to provide offenders an opportunity to, in a practical way, give back to the community that their crimes have harmed; often these orders are used in combination with probation orders. Many community agencies are willing to allow offenders to complete their community service hours at their locations. Some offenders may help at the local food bank, sorting donated food and packing food hampers; others may work at a community centre cleaning the building, while still others may give talks about the dangers of drinking and driving.

Community Partnerships

non-governmental organizations
Organizations that provide social services to community members who are not adequately addressed by governmental social service programs.

PPOs rely heavily on **non-governmental organizations** (NGOs) to provide services to address both criminogenic and non-criminogenic need areas. These organizations often receive contracts from correctional departments to provide a service, such as a treatment program, to offenders. Other programs and services offered by NGOs are funded from sources such as United Way, private donations, corporate donations, and government contracts from departments other than corrections. Mandates of correctional departments have increasingly focused on funding only programs concerned with risk factors directly linked to criminal behaviour, which has in turn increased the difficulties NGOs experience in providing services to the broader need areas. This narrower focus has created more demand for creative ways to assist offenders who have problems that need to be addressed, but do not fall within the mandate of the probation office. NGO agencies such as the Elizabeth Fry Society, the John Howard Society, St. Leonard's Society, the Salvation Army, and Operation Springboard provide many services to people in conflict with the law or at risk of being involved with the justice system. Services range from offering institutional programming, **halfway houses**, and treatment programs such as anger management and substance abuse, to assisting with employment and housing.

halfway house
A residential setting within the community that is staffed by professional workers who support offenders released on parole with the process of returning to the community.

Additionally, some agencies also act as advocates and play a key role in ensuring that correctional officials and departments are held accountable. The John Howard and Elizabeth Fry societies are known for their advocacy work. Many progressive changes to both institutional and community correctional practices are as a result of effective advocacy and research. For example, the Elizabeth Fry Society was instrumental in challenging and bringing to light professional misconduct that occurred at the now closed Prison for Women in Kingston, Ontario. The John Howard Society is well known for its advocacy work and focus on ensuring humane conditions for people involved in the criminal justice system. Each of these NGOs also strives to educate the general public about the issues within the criminal justice system. These organizations work toward helping to improve conditions within the community to help reduce the very conditions within the community that contribute to criminal behaviour.

▶ IN-CLASS EXERCISE
You Be the Probation and Parole Officer

Read the following case of Tran, then refer to the discussion questions that follow. As you read, consider the issues discussed in the preceding chapter, and how you might respond to them as a PPO.

Current Offence

Tran was 20 years of age at the time of his arrest. He was charged with possession of a controlled substance for the purpose of trafficking. He pleaded not guilty but was ultimately found guilty by the court. During the presentence interview with Tran, he adamantly denied being in possession of the drugs, but seemed resigned to the fact that he had been found guilty and displayed some anxiety about what sanction the judge was going to impose at his next court date. Tran indicated that while he has used drugs occasionally, he is not dependent, despite his mother's claims to the contrary. He stated that he was interested in completing his high school diploma and becoming a professional welder.

Previous Criminal History

Tran has no prior convictions or arrests.

Family History

The writer interviewed Tran's mother to gain insights into his personal development. His mother raised Tran on her own with little support since the time he was two years of age. During her marriage to Tran's father, he was abusive to her. She was afraid that his father would become abusive toward Tran, which is why she ended the marriage. Tran's parents are his only relatives in Canada. He did have sporadic supervised contact with his father during his childhood. Tran stopped all contact with his father when he turned 18. His father had been invited to contribute to this report, but he refused.

Tran moved out of his family home when he was 17, because he did not want to follow his mother's rules, such as letting her know where he was, and doing simple chores such as taking out the garbage, mowing the lawn, and shovelling the snow.

Tran's mother is very disappointed that her son has become involved in criminal behaviour, but is not surprised it happened. She is hopeful that he will see how his friends have had a negative impact on his life. She is willing to allow him to return home to live, but he must be willing to follow her rules, which include not using drugs or bringing drugs into her home, or associating with his friends who use drugs.

Education and Employment

He was a good student during grade school but was frequently truant from high school and dropped out in grade 11. Tran's mother advises that he had been a very dedicated student until he started high school. She says he developed friendships with some questionable peers who she believes were a negative influence. She noticed that after forming these relationships, Tran began losing interest in school, and started skipping classes, smoking marijuana, and drinking alcohol; he became secretive about his whereabouts and was quite disrespectful toward her.

Tran has held many part-time positions as an unskilled labourer in the construction industry, and as a dishwasher and short-order cook for a variety of restaurants.

DISCUSSION QUESTIONS

The following questions pertain to the in-class exercise above.

1. What are the static and criminogenic risk factors present?
2. What additional conditions would you recommend that the judge consider imposing if Tran is sentenced to probation? Explain your rationale.
3. You have been assigned to supervise Tran during his probation. What areas of his life would you consider important to monitor and why? How would you monitor these areas?
4. What do you think Tran's risk to reoffend is? Why? How can you intervene as his probation officer to help reduce his risk to reoffend?

SUGGESTED FURTHER READINGS

Andrews, D.A., & Bonta, J. (2006). *The psychology of criminal conduct* (4th ed.). Newark, NJ: LexisNexis/Matthew Bender.

Bonta, J., Ruggee, T., Scott, T., Bourgon, G., & Yessine, A.K. (2008). Exploring the black box of community supervision. *Journal of Offender Rehabilitation, 47*(3), 248–270. doi:10.1080/10509670802134085

Bracken, D. (2003). Skills and knowledge for contemporary probation practice. *The Journal of Community and Criminal Justice, 50*(2), 101–114. doi:10.1177/0264550503502001

Taxman, F.S. (2008). To be or not to be: Community supervision déjà vu. *Journal of Offender Rehabilitation, 47*(3), 209–219. doi:10.1080/1050967080213

REFERENCES

Alarid, L.F., Cromwell, P., & del Carmen, R. (2008). *Community-based corrections* (7th ed.). Belmont, CA: Wadsworth/Cengage.

Anderson, J. (2001). Probation. In J.A. Winterdyk (Ed.), *Corrections in Canada: Social reactions to crime* (pp. 81–101). Toronto: Pearson.

Andrews, D.A., & Bonta, J. (2006). *The psychology of criminal conduct* (4th ed.). Newark, NJ: LexisNexis/Matthew Bender.

Andrews, D.A., Zinger, I., Hoge, R.D., Bonta, J., Gendreau, P., & Cullen, F.T. (1990). Does correctional treatment work? A clinically relevant and psychologically informed meta-analysis. *Criminology, 28*(3), 369–404.

Aos, S., Miller, M., & Drake, E. (2006). *Evidence-based public policy options to reduce future prison construction, criminal justice costs, and crime rates.* Washington State Institute of Public Policy Report No. 06-10-1201. Olympia, WA: Washington State Institute for Public Policy.

Bonta, J., Wallace-Capretta, S., & Rooney, J. (2000). Can electronic monitoring make a difference? An evaluation of three Canadian programs. *Crime & Delinquency, 46*(1), 61–75.

Bonta, J., Ruggee, T., Scott, T., Bourgon, G., & Yessine, A.K. (2008). Exploring the black box of community supervision. *Journal of Offender Rehabilitation, 47*(3), 248–270. doi:10.1080/10509670802134085

Bracken, D. (2003). Skills and knowledge for contemporary probation practice. *The Journal of Community and Criminal Justice, 50*(2), 101–114. doi:10.1177/0264550503502001

Calverley, D. (2010). Adult correctional services in Canada, 2008/2009. *Juristat, 30*(3). Catalogue No. 85-002-X. Ottawa: Statistics Canada. Retrieved from http://www.statcan.gc.ca/pub/85-002-x/2010003/article/11353-eng.pdf

Griffiths, C.T. (2010). *Canadian corrections* (3rd ed.). Toronto: Nelson.

Johnson, S. (2006). Outcomes of probation and conditional sentence supervision: An analysis of Newfoundland and Labrador, Nova Scotia, New Brunswick, Saskatchewan and Alberta, 2003/2004 to 2004/2005. *Juristat, 26*(7). Catalogue No. 85-002-XIE. Ottawa: Statistics Canada.

Petersilia, J., & Turner, S. (1993). Research in brief. *Evaluating intensive supervision probation/parole: Results of a nationwide experiment*. Washington, DC: National Institute of Justice.

Safe Streets and Communities Act, SC 2012, c. 1.

Sealy, P., & Whitehead, P. (2004). Forty years of deinstitutionalization of psychiatric services in Canada: An empirical assessment. *The Canadian Journal of Psychiatry, 49*(4), 249–257.

Taxman, F.S. (2008). To be or not to be: Community supervision déjà vu. *Journal of Offender Rehabilitation, 47*(3), 209–219. doi:10.1080/10509670802134036

Thomas, M. (2004). Adult criminal courts statistics, 2003/04. *Juristat, 24*(12). Catalogue No. 85-002-X. Ottawa: Statistics Canada.

Conditional Release in Canada

<table>
<tr>
<td>

LEARNING OBJECTIVES

After reading this chapter, students will be able to:

- Explain some of the key assumptions that underlie conditional release in Canada.
- Identify the types of conditional release that are used in the federal correctional system.
- Describe the nature of community supervision and the level of freedom of the person under supervision.
- Discuss how conditional release contributes—or does not contribute—to lower rates of reoffending after a person is released from prison.
- Identify and discuss the major controversies surrounding conditional release.

</td>
<td>

CHAPTER OUTLINE

</td>
</tr>
</table>

Introduction

This chapter describes the nature of conditional release programs in Canada and examines whether they can deliver the promise of reducing the frequency of crimes committed by prisoners after release while at the same time reducing the number of people incarcerated, along with the related costs of their incarceration.

There are numerous conditional release laws, regulations, programs, and practices in Canada today. It is beyond the scope of this chapter to address them all. Instead, this chapter will discuss some of the key questions and issues that conditional release gives rise to, such as:

- What assumptions underlie conditional release?
- What types of conditional release are used?
- What is community supervision like?
- Do conditional release programs reduce crime?
- What are the controversies that surround conditional release?

The focus of this chapter will be on the federal correctional system, which deals with those sentenced to prison for two or more years. Sentences of less than two years are handled by the provinces and territories, and while their prison admissions far outnumber those of federal penitentiaries (252,433 compared with 8,594 in 2007–8, for example) (Calverley, 2010, p. 17), their conditional release measures and practices vary greatly from each other. As such, space limitations here prevent a discussion of those systems in detail.

What Is Conditional Release?

conditional release
Release from prison before the expiry of the sentence subject to requirements set by the releasing authority.

As the term implies, **conditional release** describes the circumstances under which individuals are released from prison before the full expiry of their sentence ("warrant expiry date"). Conditional release requires that the person live under restrictions, participate in programs, and report to a supervisor. The release restrictions placed on someone serving a life or indeterminate sentence apply until the individual dies, because those sentences never expire. The nature of the programs, restrictions, and intensity of supervision differs between individuals and may change over time, but every person can be returned to prison at any time and for any reason that makes the Parole Board of Canada think that the person's risk of committing another crime has increased. Conditional release is intended to reduce recidivism (reoffending) by addressing the *risks* that the person presents through supervision and restrictions while also addressing the person's *needs* through appropriate treatment, programs, and support.

Does Conditional Release Undermine Punishment?

For some, the notion of early release conflicts with what they consider to be the "just" punishment imposed by the court. They find it difficult to understand that someone serving a federal prison term might be released before the full sentence has been served.

Conditional release, while better than prison, still greatly restricts a person's liberty. Except in unusual circumstances and when ordered by the court, there is no provision that would allow for prisoners to serve their entire sentence in the penitentiary and then be released conditionally under community supervision.

The laws of sentencing coexist with the laws of conditional release—one does not trump the other. This means that the sentence, although often expressed in terms of years, is not in fact an exact prescription for how it will be served. Rather, the sentence is a set of limits on the punishment. The length (anywhere from a matter of days to life) and the maximum permitted

> ## SIDEBAR
>
> ## Purpose of the Correctional System
> ### Section 3 of the Corrections and Conditional Release Act
>
> 3. The purpose of the federal correctional system is to contribute to the maintenance of a just, peaceful and safe society by
>   (a) carrying out sentences imposed by courts through the safe and humane custody and supervision of offenders; and
>   (b) assisting the rehabilitation of offenders and their reintegration into the community as law-abiding citizens through the provision of programs in penitentiaries and in the community.

intervention (e.g., fine, probation, community service, imprisonment) are specified. The purpose of corrections in Canada is set out in the *Corrections and Conditional Release Act* (CCRA; 1992).

The purpose of the correctional system is to ensure that the sentence handed down by the court is carried out and to help prepare prisoners for their release back into the community. It is important to note that only the courts can determine the punishment and set the maximum term of loss of freedom. It is not the role of the correctional system to determine the punishment, so it is not mentioned as a purpose in the CCRA.

There are a number of principles that guide the Correctional Service of Canada in how it administers the sentence. One of those principles relates to the degree to which authorities can use **coercive measures**. Referred to as the principle of "least restrictive measures," it states:

> 4(d) that the Service use the least restrictive measures consistent with the protection of the public, staff members and offender.

Abiding by this principle has been of crucial importance since its adoption as part of the CCRA in 1992.

Since the inception of the penitentiary in North America at the beginning of the 19th century, the management of prisoners has depended primarily on the use of force and coercion to maintain control. Initially, the authorities relied entirely on measures such as the "silent system," hard labour, floggings, and isolation and other forms of deprivation, all with a smattering of religious instruction, in the belief that these measures would reform prisoners by making them "penitent" (hence the name "penitentiary"). Instead, prisoners were more likely to become broken, humiliated individuals driven

coercive measures
Measures that use force or threats of punishment to make an individual comply with the orders of a person in authority.

to insanity, self-mutilation, and suicide (Jackson, 2002). It slowly became clear that relying entirely on force and intimidation to maintain control was of limited effect and created circumstances that were inhumane and counterproductive. Prison officials came to recognize that the most powerful motivator for the vast majority of prisoners was the prospect of earlier release from custody.

In 1868, Canada introduced a system of "remission" through which prisoners could reduce their time in custody by up to one-third through good behaviour. While this practice of granting remission for good behaviour, or the absence of bad behaviour, was abolished in the federal correctional system in 1969, it is still a significant feature of provincial and territorial prisons today.

A few decades later, in 1899, *The Ticket of Leave Act: An Act to Provide for the Conditional Liberation of Convicts* first introduced a form of conditional release referred to as a "ticket of leave." The *Parole Act* of 1959 abolished the ticket of leave, replacing it with "parole," which became the responsibility of the newly created National Parole Board. The Act also set out the purpose of parole and the criteria for release. In 1992, the laws relating to all forms of conditional release were revised and included in the CCRA.

Types of Conditional Release

gradual release

The process by which a convict moves from higher levels of security through lower levels and eventually into the community under conditional release.

Conditional release is part of, but not the same as, **gradual release**. Gradual release involves reducing the security and related controls imposed on a person throughout the sentence. This process typically begins well before any form of conditional release. A person is assessed at the beginning of the sentence for placement in a prison that is geared to the level of security and availability of programs considered appropriate. Assessments are conducted throughout the length of the sentence. Typically, imprisonment will start out at a maximum or medium security facility. With time, appropriate behaviour, and program participation, a person might be moved to a place with lower levels of control, such as a minimum security prison, and become eligible for limited periods of release through such means as "temporary absence" and "day parole." Finally, the person might be released to live in the community but under supervision on "full parole." How well a person behaves at the higher levels of security influences whether the level of control will be reduced down the road, but that decision is based primarily on an assessment by penitentiary staff as to the person's risk of reoffending and the seriousness of any offence the person is likely to commit. The decision can be reversed at any time if the assessment changes.

There are a variety of conditional release programs—each with its own purpose, eligibility date, and granting criteria. Here are the major programs:

- unescorted temporary absence (UTA), which usually consists of a few days in the community for a particular purpose;
- work release, consisting of regular daytime release from a prison to work in the community;
- day parole, generally consisting of release to a community residential program from which the person can go out each day for job search, employment, school, and so forth;
- full parole, in which the person lives in his or her own home under community supervision; and
- statutory release, which imposes community supervision during the last third of the sentence on most who are not already on parole, and which might also include a condition to live in a day-parole facility. Not everyone is freed on statutory release. There are provisions that allow for some individuals to be detained until the full expiry of their sentence.

The differences between the various conditional release programs centre on the earliest possible date that a person can be considered for release (the "eligibility date"), and the criteria that must be met before the person can be released. Applications are reviewed and can be approved or rejected outright, or the person may be required to meet specific objectives, such as completing a program, before the case will be reviewed again. The eligibility requirements for statutory release are very different from those of the other programs, and these will be discussed separately later in this chapter.

Figure 11.1 shows the usual eligibility date for the various types of conditional release for those serving fixed sentences.

Although some individuals progress through the various conditional release programs to parole before their warrant expiry date sets them free, most are released only when they reach their statutory release date, which is at two-thirds of their sentence. While legally eligible, others are not released on any of the conditional release programs owing to their assessment as high risk and serve their sentences in full, after which they enter the community free and clear of any obligations to report. In rare cases, the court at the time of sentencing can order a person to be supervised after the term of custody expires for a period of up to 10 years ("long-term supervision orders"); that individual remains under the supervision of a parole officer during that additional time.

FIGURE 11.1   Conditional Release Eligibility Dates*

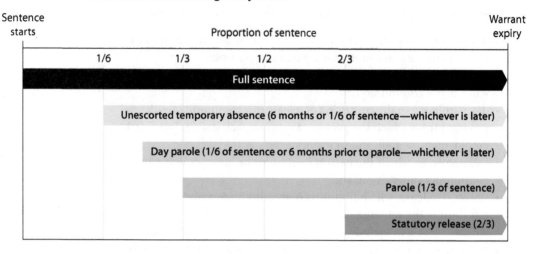

* Notes:
Applies only to those serving fixed terms—not those serving life or indefinite sentences.
Parole eligibility can be set at 50% of sentence by the court at time of sentencing for some offenders.
Does not include court-ordered post-sentence supervision for certain high-risk offenders.

Source: Parole Board of Canada (2010).

The Nature of Community Supervision

Everyone on conditional release is subject to rules and expectations, such as those relating to drugs and alcohol, travel, reporting to the police, and attending specified programs, work, or school. They are also supervised by a federal parole officer to ensure compliance with those rules and expectations, and to provide guidance and referrals to other resources.

Those under supervision might be required or encouraged to see professionals such as a psychiatrist or psychologist, to participate in programs designed to address problems such as anger management or addictions, as well as to attend work or school—all intended to address social, emotional, or psychological difficulties that were factors in the person's past criminal activity or to address barriers to successful reintegration into the community.

An individual can be returned to prison at any time if the parole board concludes that there is an unacceptable risk. The supervision and related restrictions may be intensified or relaxed, depending on the person's perceived risk. An individual can be returned to prison at any time if the parole board concludes that he or she has become an unacceptable risk, based on the belief that the person has violated any conditions of the release, or anything else that, in its opinion, reflects an increased risk. The authority of the parole board is substantial and subject

MINI CASE STUDY

Should Parole Be Revoked?

Tabatha is a single mother of three young children (two of whom have been diagnosed with attention deficit hyperactivity disorder) and is currently on full parole, having served eight months in custody for cheque fraud. She receives no support from the children's father, despite numerous attempts to have his pay garnished for child support. Her own mother wants nothing to do with her or her children, claiming that her troubles are rooted in her lack of remorse and that "God is punishing you for your transgressions."

Tabatha works part-time as an exotic dancer. She has sought out more meaningful work, but with no education and no discernible employment skills, she cannot find a job that will pay her as well as dancing in nightclubs. Given the problems that her children are experiencing, she has become actively involved in their school and assists with extracurricular activities in the community. She works with her children on their homework before going to work and volunteers as a hot lunch coordinator at their school.

Although there have been no reports of alcohol or substance abuse, she has been seen smoking marijuana with her friends. A prohibition on alcohol and drug use is part of her conditions of release, and smoking marijuana is a breach of these conditions.

What Do You Think?

As the parole officer, would you breach her? What would be the ramifications for the children? What are the reasons for your decision?

only to internal review. The most common reason for revoking a conditional release is for a breach of the conditions that were set rather than committing another criminal offence (Public Safety Canada, 2010).

The number of conditional release types and their varying eligibility rules are vast and complicated. This is the result of the many changes to the relevant legislation over the years. Like the *Criminal Code*, the CCRA has become a marvel of detailed rules and exceptions to those rules that only a few experts fully understand.

Premises for Conditional Release

Relatively few prisoners die in jail. The vast majority will be released into the community on or before their warrant expiry date. Not surprisingly, the period during which the person is most at risk of reoffending is during the first few months after release. Based on an analysis of cumulative recidivism, Figure 11.2 shows the high recidivism rate that occurs immediately after release but then flattens quickly after the first 12 months. After seven years of crime-free life, ex-prisoners reoffend at a rate that is no greater than those who have no criminal record (Centre of Criminology, 2007, p. 7).

Many people assume that "tough on crime" measures and, in particular, longer prison sentences will increase public safety. After all, offenders cannot commit more crimes if they are in prison. Also, the fewer ex-convicts there are in the community, the safer everyone feels.

In reality, though, because the risk of reoffending decreases with time, it is not all ex-offenders in the community that present a risk, but rather the number that have been released *recently*. It is true that a longer sentence postpones release, but after a period of adjustment, the number of prisoners actually being released in any given year returns to the same level as before the longer sentences were imposed. The net safety benefit to the community therefore evaporates, while the cost of holding a larger prison population increases—often dramatically (Rajekar & Mathilakath, 2010). In fact, longer periods in prison tend to be related to slightly higher rates of recidivism (French & Gendreau, 2008). Long prison terms also result in the incarceration of many individuals who no longer pose a serious risk of reoffending.

There are potentially huge social and economic benefits to developing initiatives that would reduce the risk of reoffending while also reducing the

FIGURE 11.2 Cumulative Readmissions by Time to New Offence

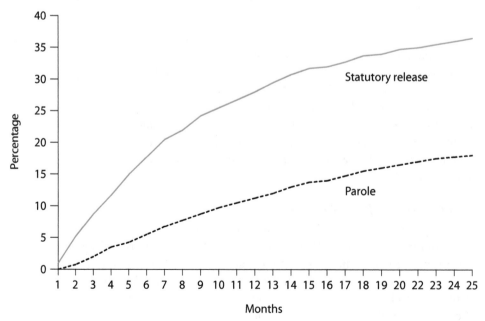

Source: Grant (1996).

size of the prison populations. Indeed, that is the premise on which programs of support, treatment, and supervision immediately following release were developed in Canada over the last century and even earlier.

Does Conditional Release Reduce Crime?

According to the RCMP, about four million Canadians have criminal records (Royal Canadian Mounted Police, 2012). That amounts to more than 10 percent of the adult population, and about 14 to 18 percent of adult males. As of 2008–9, there were 37,201 people in custody in federal and provincial prisons on any given day (Calverley, 2010, Table 3, p. 19). That means that about 0.009 percent of all those with criminal convictions are in jail. The research cited above (Centre of Criminology, 2007) shows that recidivism drops off to an insignificant level over seven years. It is therefore safe to surmise that a large portion of these people have probably given up their criminal activity. Figure 11.3 shows how criminal activity is tied closely to age; relatively few continue committing crimes as they grow older.

The task of conditional release is to help offenders reintegrate successfully into the community. You might think that proving that conditional release is effective would not be difficult to do. In fact, it turns out to not be so easy. As Griffiths found in *The Social Reintegration of Offenders and Crime Prevention*:

FIGURE 11.3   Persons Accused of Crime, by Age, Canada, 2009

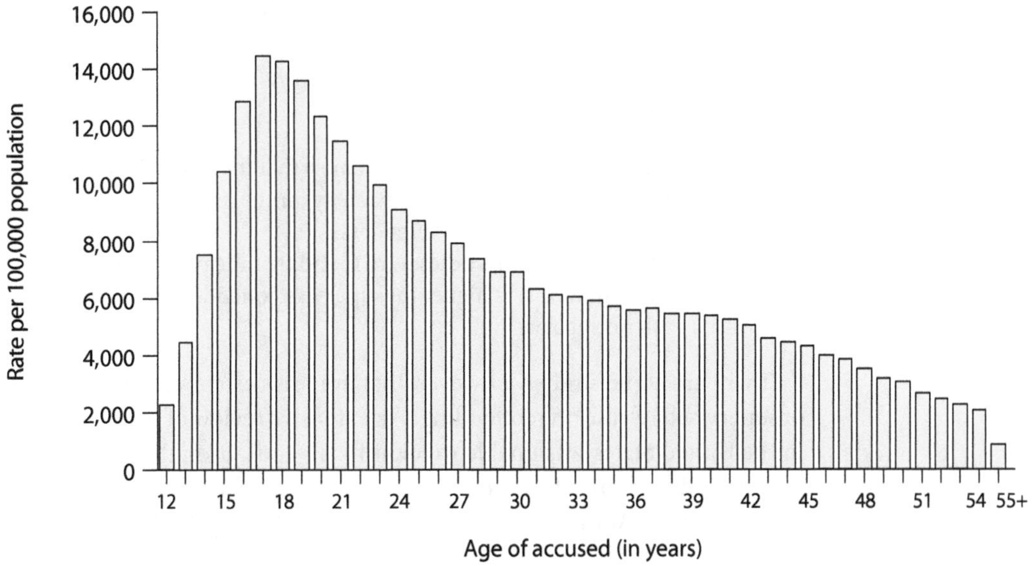

Source: Dauvergne & Turner (2010).

While there is an abundance of ideas as to what, in theory, should work, the findings of program evaluations are often disconcerting. Further, the majority of reintegration programs have not been subjected to controlled evaluations and successful approaches remain to be identified and articulated. (Griffiths, Dandurand, & Murdoch, 2007, p. 2)

To understand how conditional release promotes public safety, you have to look beyond the warrant expiry date. When a person is released before warrant expiry, clearly that person can reoffend before the warrant expiry date—and some do. If the purpose of corrections and conditional release is to reduce the incidence of reoffending over the long term, then the short-term risk of early release needs to be balanced against the long-term benefits of lower criminal recidivism. The important question is not whether some reoffend under conditional release, but whether those released through such programs are less likely to reoffend over the longer term.

There is a compelling logic to conditional release, but research and data are also needed to assess its effectiveness in practice and, therefore, to be able to judge whether the benefits of conditional release outweigh the costs—particularly with respect to recidivism. The best way to evaluate conditional release and to determine whether and for whom it is effective would be to randomly assign prisoners to conditional release and follow up with them for years after. For both legal and ethical reasons, such studies are not possible, and other forms of research and analysis must be relied upon. The Correctional Service of Canada has had for many years an active research program dedicated to determining the most effective ways to reduce recidivism. In 2005, that department summarized its findings in its document *The Safe Return of Offenders to the Community* (Motiuk, Cousineau, & Gileno, 2005, p. 3), which states:

> There is solid evidence to support the premise that the gradual and structured release of offenders is the safest strategy for the protection of society against new offences by released offenders.
>
> For example, recidivism studies have found that the percentage of safe returns to the community is higher for supervised offenders than for those released with no supervision.

There are some studies, however, that are less certain about the impact of supervised release on reoffending. An extensive review of recidivism data in the United States was unable to identify any indication that post-release supervision had any effect on lowering recidivism (Solomon, Kachnowski, & Bhati, 2012). At the same time, the authors acknowledge that the nature of their study made it impossible to sort out whether the lack of data about specific programs might hide good results.

In particular, the research would benefit enormously from system-level data about risk assessment tools, contact standards, caseload averages, case planning, case management strategies, and neighbourhood-based supervision models. Without such information, we are unable to consider how various types of supervision affect rearrest outcomes. For example, perhaps some supervision strategies are very effective, but the aggregate level of the data does not allow observation of these differences. (Solomon et al., 2012, p. 3)

It should not be surprising that community supervision is less effective when caseloads are very high, support services are minimal, supervision is preoccupied with surveillance and apprehension, and the programs are not evidence-based in their design or implementation. Based on his review of the literature, Griffiths identified the following 11 characteristics of programs that were associated with successful reintegration (Griffiths et al., 2007, p. 41). The programs:

1. focus on a specific target group of offenders and their specific challenges;
2. rely on sound methods for assessing the needs and risk factors of offenders;
3. hold the offenders accountable and responsible for their own choices and their actions;
4. begin while the offender is in prison and continue throughout the offender's transition to, and stabilization in, the community (through care);
5. strike a balance between surveillance and control on the one hand, and support and assistance on the other;
6. offer assistance in an integrated and comprehensive manner and address the many interrelated challenges faced by offenders (e.g., wrap-around interventions);
7. are offered as a coordinated effort of all the agencies involved and are supported by strong agency cooperation;
8. are supported by sound case management practices and adequate information management systems;
9. reflect the public safety priorities of the community in which they are developed;
10. engage the community in both the planning and the delivery of the intervention and foster strong community ownership;
11. have a robust evaluation component that allows the program to evolve, self-improve, and remain accountable to the community for crime-reduction results.

Applying the research on effectiveness in the real world is difficult. Even when adequate resources are available (and putting aside politics), ensuring that parole supervisors are adequately trained is a problem. Research by James Bonta of the Corrections Research Department of Public Safety Canada demonstrated that when probation officers were put through just three days of training on effective supervision practices, the recidivism rate of those being supervised dropped 15 percent (Bonta, Wallace-Capretta, & Rooney, 1999).

Blanket statements that conditional release "works" or "does not work" are not helpful or accurate. It is important to know what evidence shows it is effective, for whom, and when. With that information, programs and resources can be developed and targeted to where the best results can be achieved. Otherwise, the promise of conditional release may be defeated because of bad or inadequate practices.

Over the last few decades, a collection of works has emerged that has identified the risk factors in an offender that must be addressed and the best way to do so. Many studies have shown that programs are most effective when based on the three principles of the risk-need-responsivity (RNR) model (discussed in detail in Chapter 9).

> Developed over the last few decades, the risk-need-responsivity model has been used with increasing success to assess and rehabilitate criminals in Canada and around the world. As suggested by its name, it is based on three principles: (1) the *risk principle* asserts that criminal behaviour can be reliably predicted and that treatment should focus on the higher risk offenders; (2) the *need principle* highlights the importance of criminogenic needs [needs that cause or are likely to cause criminal behaviour] in the design and delivery of treatment; and (3) the *responsivity principle* describes how the treatment should be provided. (Bonta & Andrews, 2007, p. i)

Of particular interest is the finding that the greatest benefit in applying the risk-need-responsivity principles was with the more serious offenders (Bonta et al., 2007). After all, low-risk individuals are, by definition, unlikely to reoffend whether engaged in programs or not. This conclusion suggests that restricting conditional release to low-risk offenders makes sense if the intention of the program is only to reduce the immediate costs associated with imprisonment. However, according to the findings, ignoring the mid- and high-risk individuals will likely mean little if any reduction in recidivism rates—especially among those for whom reoffending is most serious.

MINI CASE STUDY

Kirk Clark: Offender Applying for Day Parole

Criteria Considered by the Parole Board

In making a decision whether to grant parole, the members of the parole board must assess

- the offender's criminal, social, and conditional release history
- factors affecting the offender's self-control
- the offender's responsivity to programming and interventions
- the offender's institutional and community behaviour
- the offender's change and progress in addressing his or her correctional plan and crime-cycle indicators
- release plan and community management strategies. (National Parole Board, 2012)

With these criteria in mind, consider the case of Kirk Clark, an offender applying for day parole.

Kirk is 42 years old and has served 13 years of a life sentence for second-degree murder. The victim was a taxicab driver, murdered during a robbery that went wrong. This is Kirk's first federal sentence, but he also has served three provincial sentences of less than 18 months for crimes including driving while intoxicated, two assault convictions, two robbery convictions, possession of stolen property, possession of drugs, and two breaches of a recognizance while on bail. His employment history has been sporadic; he has taken jobs only to quit or be fired within a very short time. His average length of employment is about two months. Drug and alcohol abuse is a common theme, mentioned in pre-sentence reports and in most of his crimes. He began abusing alcohol at age 10 and drugs at age 12. His first conviction was as a youth, at age 14. Kirk currently resides in a minimum-security penitentiary and has applied for day parole.

The particulars of the case for which Kirk is being considered for release are that, while under the influence of drugs, he planned to rob a taxicab. He called for a cab and took a knife with him when he entered the cab. The initial police report indicates that Kirk said he didn't want to be identified, so he killed the driver. He stole $253 from the driver.

Kirk describes his entire life as one filled with chaos, anti-social friends and peers, and chronic substance abuse. Various reports from psychologists, front-line staff, and counsellors note his remorse regarding the offence.

Given the charge and his previous offence history, Kirk was referred for a psychological assessment. He was rated in the moderate range on the **PCL-R**. The reports note his overall good institutional record and his successful completion of various programs (cognitive living, substance abuse, violence prevention). He was also assessed as a moderate–high recidivism risk, based on his **SIR-R** score of −8.

In the first couple of years of incarceration, Kirk had some minor adjustment difficulties, as shown in the institutional charges. One charge was for possession of "brew," and two incidents were noted of disrespectful language to staff. For the past ten years his institutional behaviour has been very good. He has been active in the Lifers Group and has participated in the **LifeLine Program**. He has actively participated in chaplaincy programs, and he reports that he feels he has been reborn. While attending programs inside the institution, he met his current girlfriend, a volunteer with Alcoholics Anonymous and the chaplaincy programs.

Kirk has never been married and has no children. Other than his girlfriend, he has no family or community support.

He has continued attending a substance abuse program and Alcoholics Anonymous while in minimum security. He feels he has his drinking under control, but would be willing to see a psychologist in the community while on day parole.

The community assessment report notes that his girlfriend seems fully aware of his background and that she is a tremendous support for Kirk. He has met the minister of her church, and he plans to join the congregation and volunteer in the church when granted release.

Staff at the halfway house that has accepted Kirk have had frequent contact with him and fully support his release into their care. They have already tentatively found him employment in the local community.

What Do You Think?

If you were a member of the parole board, would you release Kirk on day parole? What would your reasons be? How does your decision reflect the research presented in this chapter related to parole and ultimately the long-term protection of society?

Key Terms

PCL-R (Hare Psychopathy Checklist—Revised): A 20-item tool used for diagnosing an individual's psychopathic or anti-social tendencies. The checklist was developed in the 1990s for use with adult males in prison. Symptoms of psychopathy include the following: lack of conscience or sense of guilt, lack of empathy, egocentricity, pathological lying, repeated violations of social norms, disregard for the law, shallow emotions, and a history of victimizing others.

SIR-R (General Statistical Information on Recidivism Scale): A statistical tool for predicting recidivism; originally developed by Joan Nuffield in the Ministry Secretariat of the Solicitor General of Canada in the 1970s, and introduced as a diagnostic tool for the Parole Board and Correctional Service of Canada in 1988. The scale combines 15 static factors related to criminal activity and social functioning. The factors include current offence, age of admission, age of adult conviction, previous incarceration, previous convictions, employment status, and marital status.

LifeLine Program: A partnership between the Correctional Service of Canada, the National Parole Board, and non-government agencies (e.g., St. Leonard's Society). Under the program, paroled offenders returned to an institution to work with fellow convicts and to assist in their successful release. The program was recently cut by the federal government.

Source: Adapted from a case study from the National Parole Board; courtesy Brian Chase.

The Special Case of Statutory Release

Statutory release needs special attention if for no other reason than that it accounts for 68 percent of all releases from federal prisons in Canada (National Parole Board, 2010, Table 25, p. 69). But it also deserves attention because it demonstrates one of the greatest conflicts relating to the purpose of conditional release. Unlike the other forms of conditional release, where prisoners must convince the parole board that they deserve to be released, with statutory release, the parole board must show why certain prisoners, owing to specific high-risk factors, should remain in custody until their sentence expires. As a result, the majority of prisoners eligible for statutory release are indeed released (National Parole Board, 2010, Tables 92 and 93, p. 105).

The Ouimet Committee's Report on Corrections

Without some understanding of how statutory release developed, it is very easy to be critical of a system that releases into the community those who were refused or did not apply for other forms of conditional release. In 1969, the Ouimet committee, in its *Report of the Canadian Committee on Corrections*, reviewed Canada's experience during the first decade after the *Parole Act* came into force. The committee noted that, while the lowest-risk offenders were being released to community-based supervision through parole, those who had not been granted parole were being released directly into the community without supervision or assistance. In other words, those who would likely have the most difficulty reintegrating were being ignored and left to make it on their own (Ouimet, 1969).

The logic of gradual release was compelling to the Ouimet committee, but, at the same time, it also fully understood that gradual release involved a trade-off between short-term risk and long-term benefits:

> As has been pointed out repeatedly, however, from many sources in many countries and jurisdictions, there are risks in any form of treatment of the offender. The short-term risks of parole are calculated risks and in the opinion of the Committee are less than the risks in the alternative of sudden and dramatic contrast between incarceration and total freedom …
>
> Increasingly, however, it has been pointed out that the practice of paroling only the better risks means that those inmates who are potentially the most dangerous to society are still, as a rule, being released directly into full freedom in the community without the intermediate step represented by parole. (Ouimet, 1969, pp. 331 and 348)

The Ouimet committee chose to recommend a system "under which almost everyone would be released under some form of supervision" (Ouimet,

1969, p. 349). However, members of the committee also were aware of the political implications of releasing the most difficult and potentially dangerous prisoners. To address this problem, they proposed that the period of supervision occur during what had been until then "remission." At that time, remissions allowed for the release, free and clear of any legal restraint or conditions, of all prisoners serving a fixed sentence when they had reached the remission point in their sentence—typically, when two-thirds of their sentence had been served (the maximum remission that could be earned was one-third of the sentence).

Replacing remission with "mandatory supervision," later changed to "statutory release," meant that the effective sentence was increased by 50 percent entirely through laws pertaining to the administration of the sentence, rather than through changes to the sentences itself. Despite statutory release often being referred to as "early release," no one has served less time in prison, many have served more time, and all have been subjected to the loss of freedom through supervision because of it. Indeed, it amounted to a huge increase in the burden of the sentence.

In terms of its justification, statutory release is markedly different from the other forms of release in that it is granted on the basis that the person needs supervision and support after release, as opposed to the person deserving early release because of his or her risk profile. The individual being released to community supervision on statutory release has not earned the trust of correctional officials by demonstrating low risk to reoffend. Quite the contrary, because the person appears much more likely to reoffend, the supervision is imposed as a means to reduce that risk.

What Do You Think?

Is community supervision best used for low-risk "deserving" individuals, or can it be used to reduce the risk of all prisoners regardless of their likelihood to reoffend? Can it do both?

There are many other important questions that arise with statutory release: Is conditional release about reward for good behaviour, or is it about maximizing the potential for successful reintegration? Should prisoners be placed under conditional release because their risk is low, because it is high, or both? If the answer is "both," then the criteria and eligibility dates for conditional release would need to be reconsidered to reconcile the two seemingly contradictory purposes. Perhaps the most important change, however, would be in relation to the role and authority of parole boards.

Data on conditional release outcomes, as reflected in Figure 11.4, show that more persons on parole complete their sentences successfully than do those on statutory release. Most of the difference in the success rates between parole and statutory supervision relates to breaches of the conditions of release, while differences in criminal activity account for much less (Public Safety Canada, 2011, pp. 90 and 92). Although more people committed violence on statutory release than on parole (1.4 percent versus 0.05 percent in 2009–10), the difference in the crime rates committed under both types of release is low and declining.

FIGURE 11.4   Conditional Release Outcomes, 2006-7 to 2010-11

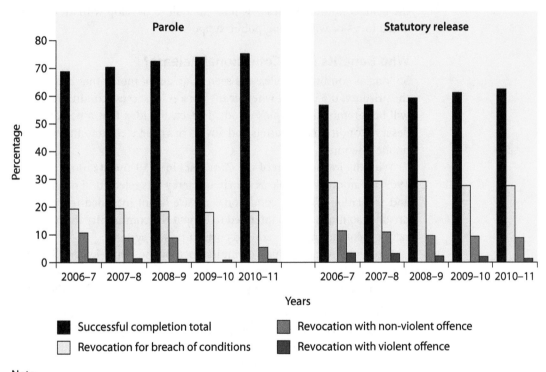

Note:
Excludes offenders serving indeterminate sentences because they do not have a warrant expiry date and can only successfully complete full parole by dying.
Revocation for breach of conditions includes revocation with outstanding charges.
Violent offences include murder and Schedule I offences (listed in the *Corrections and Conditional Release Act*) such as assaults, sexual offences, arson, abduction, robbery and some weapon offences.

Source: Public Safety Canada (2011).

A report published in 2007 by the Correctional Service of Canada Review Panel proposed that statutory release be abolished (Sampson, 2007), having concluded that compared with parole, recidivism under statutory release was excessive. The report was criticized for ignoring the fact that a higher failure rate was an expected outcome from the time of its design and for not addressing the more relevant question of whether the statutory release group's recidivism rate would be lower in the future if released on warrant expiry without supervision (Jackson & Stewart, 2009).

Clearly, the system of conditional release in Canada is intended for both the deserving and the dangerous. It reflects both sides of these seemingly mutually exclusive positions. No wonder the community is conflicted over the purpose and value of conditional release. It appears that until the purposes of conditional release are reconciled and made consistent with practices in the field, conditional release will be difficult to develop with an evidence-based focus or with strong public support.

Who Benefits from Conditional Release?

So long as conditional release is seen as an act of mercy that benefits only the prisoner, the issue of whether the person "deserves" conditional release will be foremost in people's minds. In fact, the idea that a person should deserve conditional release is and always has been a common theme in the public discourse.

With the introduction of the *Parole Act* in 1959 and statutory release in 1969, the notion of parole as a form of mercy was rejected in official policy and regulations. Today, conditional release is not intended to benefit the prisoner so much as it is intended to benefit the community through lower rates of reoffending and reduced costs of prison systems.

A recently released study commissioned by the John Howard Society of Toronto on the costs and benefits of providing housing for ex-prisoners was very careful to frame the analysis in terms of the net benefits to the public.

> If the supports and housing are conceived as interventions on behalf of the public (i.e., a public service), the beneficiary is the community itself. Then the issue of deservedness is really a question of whether the community deserves to be safe, deserves another functioning member, to incur lower costs, and whether the community deserves to have lower incidence of crime. The Cost–benefit analysis concerns itself with the question of whether the intervention achieves these goals. (Stapleton, Pooran, & Doucet, 2012, p. 4)

Without clear public benefit, there is little likelihood of the service ever being supported through government funding and cooperation.

When a person successfully reintegrates into the community, the community benefits by no longer being victimized by that person and no longer having to pay the bills for a very expensive criminal justice system. But the individual also benefits from living a lawful life through restored relationships with family and the community, and from being free and self-sufficient.

Often there is strong public resistance to rehabilitative measures that appear to result in the offender being treated leniently. The problem is that there are no purely painful ways to rehabilitate. It is very difficult to be both harsh and helpful at the same time. Helping a person become a better person is accomplished through learning, and that involves being exposed to positive influences of pro-social people, ideas, and opportunities. Isolating a person in an austere and often anti-social environment like prison, and restricting access to positive learning opportunities such as school, as well as to social events and family visits, can be counterproductive to someone developing the knowledge needed to become a better citizen. Likewise, treatment can only be helpful in an environment where the person is treated respectfully by the therapist.

The only theory that tries to justify pain as rehabilitation is that of deterrence. Deterrence allows us to be punitive—often harshly so—on the ground that harsh treatment prevents further crime. While deterrence might be a convenient theory, it is difficult to confirm through research (Doob & Webster, 2003).

It is perhaps more important to know what factors make crime attractive in spite of any perceived deterrence. For example, a person acting out of fear or the need to be accepted into a social structure—even if it is a gang— or who has a mental illness, or an addiction, might not consider any consequences relating to criminal activity, because any one of these factors, let alone in combination, might overwhelm the deterrent effect.

What Risks Are Being Balanced?

Those responsible for correctional policy and release decisions know that there are potentially great costs to them personally when a person reoffends. The regret that comes from making a decision that led to serious harm, and then being subjected to investigation and appearance at an inquest along with difficult media scrutiny, can result in an intensely painful experience. These same individuals rarely receive recognition or praise when good decisions are made, so it should be no surprise that their decisions by default are as cautious as possible. Their decisions seek to balance personal risk and public risk. The personal risk to the decision-maker is reduced by minimizing the number of people freed on conditional release, even though the public risk is reduced by maximizing the number of people freed on conditional release.

Incidents of failure have far greater impact on public policy than do success rates. It takes a well-informed, principled, and courageous politician or correctional official to stand against this pressure. Consequently, with few exceptions, since the 1970s there has been movement toward increasingly restricting and limiting the use of conditional release, and toughening supervision.

Conclusion

Conditional release could be positive or negative, depending on the design and implementation of the program. Community and political support is generally based on the most recent incidents, rather than success rates. There are strong differences of opinion regarding what the purpose of conditional release should be and how it should operate. Attempts to accommodate these conflicting views have resulted in a system that is at times incoherent and in conflict with the evidence on effective reintegration.

Despite the political and practical difficulties surrounding conditional release, the vast majority of prisoners will be released, and the time when interventions have the best likelihood of reducing recidivism is immediately following release from prison. The challenge then is to make it more effective through principled and evidence-based practices. Public support will be easier to build when the purposes and practices of conditional release are consistent and coherent. There is a long way to go before the promise of conditional release can be fully realized.

▶ IN-CLASS EXERCISE
John Rives: Poet, Parolee, Community Advocate

John Rives was sentenced to life imprisonment at the age of 23. At the time, he was pursuing a bachelor's degree in history at the University of Toronto, having graduated from high school as valedictorian. After a night of drinking, he found himself no longer in the lecture halls, but locked in a cell at the Metro Toronto West Detention Centre awaiting a bail hearing. Rives spent ten years in federal penitentiaries and for the past 21 years has been serving life parole in the Kingston area. He has worked for the LifeLine Program and has trained tutors for Frontier College, who work with inmates in Kingston-area penitentiaries. He is a member of the board of directors of the John Howard Society of Ontario, and is currently chair of the board of directors of the Kingston Community Chaplaincy. He began writing poetry while incarcerated and has since published three volumes: *The Perfection of Guilt*, *Dead Time: Poems from Prison*, and *Shackles and Silence*. The following poem is from *Dead Time*.

Willingness

We peer out from our prisons
at your world.

I see the masses shake their heads
and turn their shriveling minds
back to the single surety of cells.
I see us turn our shriveling lives
back to the single surety of cells.
And we are in agreement.

Television is our window.
And it is yours,
as are our lives,
to free, imprison, labour.
And so become the lives of those we see
dismembered
every noon, at six and at eleven.

Do something now, before the rest of those
you watch
are no longer afraid to die—
something other than change the channel.

But, we prisoners lack even that luxury.
The ugliness dispensed as justice
for our daily bread
could pass for visions of the world
as flashed on colour-pulsing screens.
It's all the same.
Why go beyond the walls?
Why ever leave?
At least in here we're rarely
confused by sincere talk of human kindness, man's responsibility
for fellow man.

Your neighbor thinks that prison keeps him safe.
He's seen it.
Heard the politicians advertise
and swear by its effectiveness.
They say the suffering of certain people
Works
—it does, if holding on to pain and hate
brings life to paradise.

How many times have you heard someone say
he'd die for someone else?
The terrorist, the armchair quarterback,
the crown attorney and the citizens.
How many really would?
It's so much easier to
sacrifice that someone else
for any noble cause,

Or any ad-man's remedy.

Source: Reprinted with permission of John Rives.

Discussion Questions

1. What are the main ideas presented in this poem?
2. Did your decision whether to grant parole to Kirk Clark (earlier in this chapter) change after you read this poem?
3. What does the poem say about the impact of political arguments in the media regarding the success of corrections and parole?
4. Recall the theoretical models of criminal justice presented in Chapter 1. Which model do you think best represents the ideas about crime and punishment expressed in this poem? Where would you put Rives's views along the ideological spectrum of crime control?
5. Chapter 10 discusses some of the reasons that community-based sanctions are preferred over incarceration in certain circumstances. Identify at least two lines from the poem that support the use of community correctional measures. Jot down a few reasons you chose those lines, and discuss them with a classmate.

DISCUSSION QUESTIONS

1. Is the purpose of a sentence undermined or supported by conditional release?
2. Should programs of conditional release be used for those who are most deserving, for those who present the greatest needs and risks, or for both?
3. How might conditional release be changed and/or explained so that its benefits might be better understood by the public?

SUGGESTED FURTHER READINGS

For detailed background information about conditional release: Parole Board of Canada website. http://pbc-clcc.gc.ca/

For an alternative approach to conditional release decision making: John Howard Society of Canada. (2007). *Presumptive gradual release*. Position paper. http://www.johnhoward.ca/document/presumptive/presumptive.pdf

For key policy papers that informed the development of the *Corrections and Conditional Release Act*: Solicitor General Canada. (2002). *Influences on correctional reform: Working papers of the Correctional Law Review, 1986 to 1988*. Ottawa: Author. http://www.naacj.org/en//pdf/res_influences_canadian_correctional_reform.pdf

REFERENCES

Bonta, J., & Andrews, D.A. (2007). *Risk-need-responsivity model for offender assessment and rehabilitation*. User Report 2007-06. Catalogue No. PS3-1/2007-6. Ottawa: Public Safety Canada. Retrieved from http://www.publicsafety.gc.ca/res/cor/rep/_fl/Risk_Need_2007-06_e.pdf

Bonta, J., Wallace-Capretta, S., & Rooney, J. (1999). *Electronic monitoring in Canada*. Ottawa: Solicitor General Canada. Retrieved from http://www.publicsafety.gc.ca/res/cor/rep/_fl/em-eng.pdf

Bonta, J., Wallace-Capretta, S., & Rooney, J. (2007). A quasi-experimental evaluation of an intensive rehabilitation supervision program. *Criminal Justice and Behavior, 27*, 312–329.

Calverley, D. (2010). Adult correctional services in Canada, 2008/2009. *Juristat, 30*(3). Catalogue No. 85-002-X. Ottawa: Statistics Canada. Retrieved from http://www.statcan.gc.ca/pub/85-002-x/2010003/article/11353-eng.pdf

Centre of Criminology. (2007). For how long is a record of offending predictive of future offending? *Criminological Highlights, 8*(4). Toronto: University of Toronto. Retrieved from http://criminology.utoronto.ca/lib/CrimHighlightsV8N4.pdf

Corrections and Conditional Release Act, SC 1992, c. 20.

Dauvergne, M., & Turner, J. (2010). Police-reported crime statistics in Canada, 2009. *Juristat, 30*(2), chart 14. Catalogue No. 85-002-X20100021129. Ottawa: Author. Retrieved from http://www.statcan.gc.ca/pub/85-002-x/2010002/article/11292-eng.htm

Doob, A.N., & Webster, C.M. (2003). Sentence severity and crime: Accepting the null hypothesis. *Crime and Justice, 30*, 143–195.

French, S., & Gendreau, P. (2008). *Safe and humane corrections through effective treatment.* (Research Report). Ottawa: Correctional Service of Canada. Retrieved from http://www.csc-scc.gc.ca/text/rsrch/reports/r139/r139_e.pdf

Grant, B.A. (1996). *Inmates referred for detention (1989–90 to 1993–94): A comparative analysis.* Rep. No. R-45. Ottawa: Correctional Service of Canada. Retrieved from http://publications.gc.ca/site/eng/383650/publication.html

Griffiths, C.T., Dandurand, Y., & Murdoch, D. (2007). *The social reintegration of offenders and crime prevention.* Rep. No. 2007-2. Catalogue No. PS4-49/2007E. Ottawa: Public Safety Canada, National Crime Prevention Centre.

Jackson, M. (2002). *Justice behind the walls: Human rights in Canadian prisons.* Vancouver: Douglas & McIntyre.

Jackson, M., & Stewart, G. (2009). A flawed compass: A human rights analysis of the roadmap to strengthening public safety. Retrieved from http://www.justicebehindthewalls.net/resources/news/flawed_Compass.pdf

Motiuk, L., Cousineau, C., & Gileno, J. (2005). *The safe return of offenders to the community: Statistical overview.* Ottawa: Correctional Service of Canada. Retrieved from http://www.csc-scc.gc.ca/text/rsrch/safe_return2005/safe_return2005_e.pdf

National Parole Board. (2010). Performance Measurement Division. *Performance monitoring report 2009–2010.* Ottawa: Author. Retrieved from http://www.pbc-clcc.gc.ca/rprts/pmr/pmr_2009_2010/2009-2010-eng.pdf

Ouimet, R. (1969). *Report of the Canadian Committee on Corrections: Towards unity–criminal justice and corrections.* Ottawa: Queen's Printer.

Parole Board of Canada. (2010). Fact sheet: Types of release. Retrieved from http://www.pbc-clcc.gc.ca/infocntr/factsh/rls-eng.shtml#2

Parole Board of Canada. (2012). *Policy manual,* Vol. 1, No. 23. Retrieved from http://pbc-clcc.gc.ca/infocntr/policym/polman-eng.shtml#_Toc296953777

Public Safety Canada. (2010). Portfolio Corrections Statistics Committee. *Corrections and conditional release statistical overview: Annual report 2010.* Catalogue No. PS1-3/2010E-PDF. Ottawa: Author. Retrieved from http://www.publicsafety.gc.ca/res/cor/rep/_fl/2010-ccrso-eng.pdf

Public Safety Canada. (2011). Portfolio Corrections Statistics Committee. *Corrections and conditional release statistical overview: Annual report 2011.* Catalogue No. PS1-3/2011E-PDF. Ottawa: Author. Retrieved from http://publications.gc.ca/site/eng/404354/publication.html

Rajekar, A., & Mathilakath, R. (2010). *The funding requirement and impact of the "Truth in Sentencing Act" on the correctional system in Canada.* Catalogue No. YN5-28/2010E-PDF. Ottawa: Office of the Parliamentary Budget Officer.

Rives, J. (1989). *Dead time: Poems from prison*. Hamilton, ON: Mini Mocho Press.

Royal Canadian Mounted Police (RCMP). (2012). Quick facts. In *Canadian Criminal Real Time Identification Services (CCRTIS)*. Retrieved from http://www.rcmp-grc.gc.ca/cr-cj/ccrtis-scictr-eng.pdf

Sampson, R.C. (2007). *Report of the Correctional Service of Canada Review Panel: A roadmap to strengthening public safety*. Catalogue No. PS84-14/2007E-PDF. Ottawa: Public Works and Government Services Canada. Retrieved from http://www.publicsafety.gc.ca/csc-scc/cscrprprt-eng.pdf

Solomon, A.L., Kachnowski, V., & Bhati, A. (2012). *Does parole work? Analyzing the impact of postprison supervision on rearrest outcomes*. Washington, DC: Urban Institute. Retrieved from http://www.urban.org/UploadedPDF/311156_Does_Parole_Work.pdf

Stapleton, J., Pooran, B., & Doucet, R. (2012). *Making Toronto safer: A cost-benefit analysis of transitional housing supports for men leaving incarceration*. Toronto: The John Howard Society of Toronto.

Populations in Focus

<table>
<tr><td colspan="2">

LEARNING OBJECTIVES

After reading this chapter, students will be able to:

- Appreciate the challenges faced by older offenders when they are incarcerated.
- Have a better understanding of the unique problems faced by women inmates.
- Understand the concerns facing transgendered inmates.
- Explain how the use of alcohol and substances in correctional facilities can impact on staff and inmates.
- Know what the term "DO" means and critically evaluate its application in the case of Lisa Neve.
- Understand the unique challenges that sex offenders face in reintegrating into the community.
- Differentiate between suicide and self-injury.
- Explain some of the reasons why Aboriginal offenders are overrepresented in the correctional system.
- Appreciate the challenges faced by correctional staff and management in meeting the needs of a diverse population of inmates

</td><td>

CHAPTER OUTLINE

</td></tr>
</table>

Introduction

In this chapter, we will very briefly outline some specific populations of interest within the Canadian correctional landscape. These include substance abusers, those experiencing mental disorder, sex trade workers, and dangerous offenders. We will also explore issues specific to women, older incarcerated offenders, and sex offenders. It is important to keep in mind that many incarcerated individuals will fall into more than one of these categories, which means the issues they face will often be much more complex than those discussed here.

Within the general population of inmates, there are subpopulations that deserve special consideration in this chapter. These various groups may face unique challenges from the perspective of both the inmates, in terms of how they cope with incarceration, and from staff, in terms of correctional management. Although some of these groups might be few in number (for example, transgendered inmates), they can nonetheless pose significant challenges for corrections with respect to the resources and the staffing necessary to meet their unique needs. The coverage of topics in this chapter is not meant to be exhaustive, and certain other relevant topics, such as racial profiling, are examined elsewhere in this book. The goal of this chapter is to remind you of the diversity of the offender population, and the need to recognize the varied kinds of challenges confronting them and those who work with them in a prison environment.

Older Offenders

Correctional Service of Canada (CSC) considers any offender aged 50 years or more as an "older" offender. (Because Chapters 13 and 14 discuss the unique challenges inherent in dealing with youth in conflict with the law, this chapter will only cover the topic of ages as it relates to the older offender.) Evidence to date suggests that this group of inmates is growing in number. In 2000, about 12 percent of federal inmates were aged 50 and over. This percentage jumped to 18 percent in 2009 (CSC, 2009a). This is not really surprising, given that since the 1970s, the Canadian population has been aging, and is expected to continue to do so into the near future. As crime tends to be a "young man's game," it stands to reason that as the relative proportion of young people in Canada declines and the relative size of the older cohort increases, there should be an overall decline in the crime rate (all other factors being equal).

SIDEBAR

Crime Rates and Age

Peter Carrington has used statistics to forecast the relationship between population age and crime rates. He estimates that there should be a reduction in Canada's overall crime rates from 2000 to 2041 (Carrington, 2001). However, Carrington noted that the crime rates for offences that are more typical of older adults (sexual assault, and drinking and driving, for example) would be less affected by the aging of the country's population.

When considering their incarceration history, the Canadian population of older offenders is not a homogeneous one. There are those who were young when first incarcerated and have grown old in prison while serving a lengthy sentence. These individuals tend to be model inmates and pose a relatively low risk to reoffend. About 10 percent of older inmates fit into this category (Uzoaba, 1998). A second group of older offenders consists of those who have been in and out of prison all of their lives. Estimates suggest that 17 percent of older offenders can be described as "doing life on the instalment plan." These individuals are sometimes referred to by criminologists as "career criminals" who tend to view prison as part of their lifestyle. The final group is made up of those serving their first prison sentence as older adults. While they may have led law-abiding, pro-social lives as younger adults, these individuals later in life, for various reasons, came into conflict with the law. The vast majority (73 percent) of Canadian older offenders fall into this category, and they are likely to have the hardest time coping with institutional life.

The issues associated with incarcerated older offenders are well known in the United States, where they have been researching older offenders, and dealing with the unique needs of this population for a number of years. In the United States, older offenders make up the fastest-growing population among state prisons, increasing 203 percent in a ten-year period (Ortiz, 2000). Further, estimates suggest that the number of older inmates on death row has more than doubled since 1999, with 29.1 percent being aged 50 or older at the end of 2009 (Snell, 2000; Snell, 2010). American researchers have noted that older inmates have more significant health issues than do their younger counterparts, thus increasing the cost of incarcerating them, given that they require additional medical and dietary considerations. Correctional systems face a number of challenges as they prepare to meet the unique needs of this growing population.

One of these challenges is the physical health of older inmates. The aging process is accelerated for many, with estimates suggesting that factors such as lifestyle choices, socio-economic status, and poor access to medical care result in incarcerated individuals appearing ten years older than their non-incarcerated counterparts. This is especially significant given that almost one in five incarcerated offenders in Canada is 50 or older (Office of the Correctional Investigator, 2011). Factors such as poor diet, smoking, drug and alcohol abuse, and limited access to dental or health care have undoubtedly had an overall negative impact on the health of those entering correctional facilities. As such, inmates as a group are more likely to face the effects of aging and to experience chronic health problems earlier in life than is the

SIDEBAR

Managing Older Offenders

The challenges associated with incarcerating older offenders in Canadian prisons, and the lack of a national strategy by Correctional Service of Canada (CSC) to deal with their needs, has recently caught the attention of the Office of the Correctional Investigator (OCI), currently led by Howard Sapers. The correctional investigator is mandated by legislation (*Corrections and Conditional Release Act*) to be an ombudsman for all federal offenders. In addition to investigating complaints by individual offenders, the OCI is responsible for reviewing CSC policies and procedures and for making recommendations specific to areas of concern.

A fairly extensive report on older Canadian offenders was produced by CSC's research branch in 1998 (Uzoaba, 1998). Following this report, CSC created an Older Offender Division in 2000, and a policy group was formed to make recommendations at the national level. However, these initiatives have been apparently abandoned, and none of the recommendations implemented (OCI, 2011).

Sapers (2011) has made four specific recommendations pertaining to the managing of older offenders within CSC:

- that more appropriate programming be developed to better meet the needs of older offenders, including physical fitness programs;
- that more staff with training and experience in gerontology and palliative care be hired;
- that when new buildings are planned, the physical needs of older offenders be taken into consideration (for instance, accessible living arrangements); and
- that the CSC develop a national older offender strategy that will include not only a geriatric release policy, but also improved post-release supports for older offenders.

general population. Cancer, emphysema, diabetes, cardiovascular disease, and various types of dementia are all chronic conditions that require inmates to be treated in-house. This may require the following: continuous monitoring of their condition while incarcerated; frequent appointments with a variety of health-care staff (nurses, doctors, physiotherapists, dentists, psychiatrists); and outside trips to consult with specialists in the community.

Physical health challenges faced by older offenders include not only dealing with chronic illness, but also dealing with mobility issues and sensory impairments. Hearing and seeing difficulties may require that the inmate be given hearing aids and eyeglasses. Mobility issues may require that aids such as canes, walkers, wheelchairs, and prostheses be provided; additional accommodations made to the inmate's physical environment may also be necessary. Because prisons have not traditionally been built with the needs of the older inmate in mind, there are often accessibility challenges when it comes to meeting their daily needs (bathing, toileting, feeding). Many of the prisons that house federal inmates are in desperate need of retrofitting in order to meet these needs. A number of penitentiaries have actually been designated as heritage buildings, and five are more than 100 years old, thus making modernizing these facilities a very expensive endeavour (Sapers, 2011).

Social and Safety Challenges

Older offenders also face considerable challenges when it comes to coping with the stress of incarceration. Issues of safety may be a factor. They may feel threatened by the younger members of the general population, and this can be made worse by their mobility concerns (not being able to fend off a physical attack or flee from one). Similarly, older inmates may be targets of bullying within the prison walls. The fact that they often have very little social status within the institution and that they have limited physical strength can make them an easy target for younger and stronger inmates. In addition to safety concerns, the older offenders may find it challenging to access recreational activities that could assist with lowering their stress levels. If it is difficult for an inmate to partake in yard time because of mobility concerns, then they will not be able to experience fresh air or to participate in yard or even social activities. This may have a harmful effect on their ability to cope (Sapers, 2011). Ultimately, prisons are faced with having to offer palliative care to their terminally ill inmates. While this can be a challenge in a correctional setting with its rigid structure, it is a moral imperative that palliative care be provided in a compassionate and dignified way.

It is important to note that in addition to the above, correctional institutions must also provide appropriate programming options for older offenders, who have different needs from younger ones. Focus on programs that deal with employment or vocational training may be of little relevance to the older offender who is of retirement age. Very few aging inmates typically access the kinds of rehabilitation and reintegration services that are needed to successfully return to the community (Sapers, 2011). They may require special accommodations to be able to fully participate in programs offered in an institution. For example, they may need shorter program sessions, more bathroom breaks, various aids, or material presented in a more accessible format in order to fully benefit from the program.

Female Offenders

Women make up a very small percentage of those who commit crimes. While they constitute about 12 percent of those admitted to provincial or territorial custody and 13 percent of those admitted on remand, women make up far less of the federally incarcerated population—about 6 percent—than men do (Calverley, 2010). In recent decades, however, the percentage of females being admitted to federal programs has been gradually increasing (Statistics Canada, 2007). Prior to the building of five new regional facilities across Canada in the 1990s, most federally sentenced women were incarcerated at the Prison for Women (P4W) in Kingston, Ontario. P4W was officially closed on July 6, 2000.

One study produced a "one-day snapshot" of inmates in Canadian adult correctional institutions (Finn, Trevethan, Carrière, & Kowalski, 1999). Data were collected for all inmates on Saturday, October 5, 1996. Nearly half the women (46 percent) were in maximum-security institutions, compared with 39 percent of men. Overall, most female inmates were between the ages of 25 and 34 and housed in multi-level facilities, whereas only 2 percent of incarcerated men were in such facilities. Relatively speaking, fewer women (3 percent) than men (6 percent) were in segregation, and fewer were serving time for crimes against the person compared with men. In provincial and territorial facilities, 28 percent of women (compared with 34 percent of men) were incarcerated for crimes against the person, whereas in federal facilities, the percentage of women serving time for these types of crimes was higher. At the federal level, 64 percent of women (compared with 74 percent of men) were on register for crimes against the person.

Women were more likely than men to have been unemployed when admitted. The educational levels of both women and men were equally low, with about one-third of all provincial and territorial inmates (and nearly half of federal inmates) having completed no more than grade 9.

Women's offences are varied, but have historically centred around crimes related to prostitution, theft, and drug use. Females were serving time for fewer offences than were men, had much less extensive criminal histories, and shorter **aggregate sentences** (Finn et al., 1999). More recent estimates (for 2004) found that men were more likely to face multiple charges, and women were more likely to be one-time offenders (Kong & AuCoin, 2008). Aboriginal women were overrepresented across provincial, territorial, and federal facilities. Approximately 25 percent of the federally incarcerated women and almost 30 percent of the provincially and territorially sentenced women were Aboriginal (Kong & AuCoin, 2008). In 2008–9, 28 percent of all female remands and 37 percent of women sentenced to custody were Aboriginal

aggregate sentences
The combined total of all sentences being served by an individual.

(Calverley, 2010). There also appears to be a significant increase in federally sentenced women who are deemed to be both high risk and high needs (Kong & AuCoin, 2008).

Incarcerated women face a host of stressors associated with their lives both inside and outside the prison walls. Although many cope adequately, some turn to strategies that have worked for them in the past, but that are ultimately problematic, such as drinking and using drugs, eating disorders, self-injury, and attempts at suicide. Aside from possibly causing serious injury or death, these behaviours may lead to correctional sanctions, such as being placed in segregation for intoxication.

Many women in prison are mothers, and often the primary caregivers for their children. One of their biggest issues is the care of their children. In some cases, the children have been made wards of the court, effectively eliminating any future contact with their mothers. When children themselves start having trouble with the law, mothers in prison may face a double dose of guilt for "not being there" for their children and for "setting a bad example."

The Grand Valley Institution for Women in Kitchener, Ontario opened in 1997 and features "campus-style" housing. Compare this photo with the photo of the Don Jail in Chapter 9 (page 243). How might an inmate's environment affect his or her rehabilitation? Source: Correctional Service of Canada.

The Task Force on Federally Sentenced Women

The mandate of the Task Force on Federally Sentenced Women (TFFSW) was to assess the correctional management of women sentenced to federal prison in Canada—from initial processing to warrant expiry—including the need to develop a strategic plan to guide and direct this process in a way that was respectful of the women's needs (TFFSW, 1990). The CSC faced some clear difficulties when it came to the operation of the new regional facilities for women. The TFFSW's report, *Creating Choices*, and the implementation of its recommendations were met with a number of criticisms (Hannah-Moffat, 2000). As Hannah-Moffat noted in 1995:

> Perhaps one of the most profound difficulties is that feminists have failed to adequately define the meaning and criteria of woman centeredness. The implementation of the task force's recommendations and the definition of *woman centered* have been left to Corrections Canada with little external (feminist) input. (p. 141)

When the new regional facilities were opened, they were not able to accommodate the needs of maximum-security women. This failure to balance the practical aspects of implementing a woman-centred philosophy against the systemic demands inherent in managing violent offenders was glaring. As Shaw (1999, p. 258) pointed out:

> It is unfortunate that the model of the women-centred prison developed in *Creating Choices* failed to take account of the fact that women can be perpetrators of violence as well as victims. The failure to confront the issue of women's use of violence other than as a response to continued partner violence is not restricted to the Task Force alone, but has been characteristic of feminist accounts of women and violence within criminology more generally.

While Shaw's observations raise a valid concern, few would argue that societal issues such as classism, sexism, and racism have not had an impact on who becomes criminalized in Canada. Generally, it is a subset of women—those most negatively affected by these issues in our society—who become criminalized.

Sexual Identity and Sexual Orientation

There are considerable additional challenges to living in a prison environment for anyone who does not identify as a heterosexual. The reality of our sexual culture is that it is diverse, but in prison such diversity is not often acknowledged or accepted. The coalition fighting Lisa Neve's dangerous offender designation (see case study below) made the point that in her case, psychiatric evidence used against her relied on aspects of her sexual orientation as an indicator of pathology. In addition to the heterosexual majority, there are those who identify as homosexual, lesbian, gay, intersex, transsexual, transgendered, queer, questioning, two-spirited, bisexual, pansexual or polysexual or omnisexual, and asexual. Clearly, sexual diversity exists in society and, by extension, in the prison environment as well. A thorough discussion of the marginalization of these groups in society is beyond the scope of this text; however, this section will focus on the realities that some of these individuals face in the correctional system.

In the past, institution-wide homophobic practices such as segregating homosexuals (under the guise that it was for their own safety) were not unusual, and were an early target for gay prison advocates. The evidence to date suggests that coerced or forced sexual activities are more common in male correctional facilities than in female facilities, but coercive sexual activities do occur in female facilities, although they are rare. Further, what may appear at first to be consensual sexual activity between male inmates may, on closer examination, actually have an element of coercion or manipulation fuelled by concerns over safety, security, and financial support (Hensley & Tewksbury, 2002).

To date, there is a real lack of empirical research on transgendered inmates. One study of transgendered inmates in California, published in 2010, showed that they are more likely to have high unemployment rates, be between the ages of 36 and 45, be homeless, be incarcerated for a property crime, be housed in secure facilities, and be classified as sex offenders. While less likely to be gang members, they are more likely to be identified as having a mental disorder, to suffer from alcohol and drug abuse, and to have a history of suicidal thoughts or attempts; more than 40 percent have previously worked in the sex trade. Staggeringly high estimates of HIV infection (60 to 80 percent of transgendered inmates are HIV-positive) have also been reported (Sexton, Jenness, & Sumner, 2010). In sum, the demographic profile of transgendered inmates is quite different from that of the general inmate population.

There are reports of rampant **homophobia**, extensive harassment, and verbal, physical, and sexual assaults at the hands of both staff and other inmates suffered by transgendered inmates. They are also more likely than other inmates to spend time in protective custody—sometimes for their own protection; however, extended periods in isolation are clearly harmful as well. Depending on the jurisdiction, transgendered inmates may have additional health-care concerns associated with their transition (e.g., hormones, surgery) that are not met. As an illustration of just how serious this can be, cases of self-castration and penectomy have been documented where prison officials have denied requests of inmates to access specific transgendered health care (Brown, 2010).

Transgendered inmates face issues with correctional procedure as well. Canada is one of the few countries that actually have a formal policy on **gender identity disorder (GID)**. Transgendered inmates may be recognized as such by CSC if they have been assessed and diagnosed by an expert in GID. They may initiate or continue with hormone therapy while incarcerated and are permitted to cross-dress (under certain conditions); if they are pre-operative, then they will be held in an institution consistent with their birth sex (that is, a man who is in the process of becoming a woman but who has not had an operation yet would be held in a male facility). Sex reassignment surgery may be available to inmates, and paid for by CSC, if they meet a number of conditions.

homophobia
Negative attitudes, including hatred, fear, and/or contempt, directed toward gays and lesbians.

gender identity disorder (GID)
Where there is a conflict between the person's physical gender and his or her self-perceived gender (a person who is born physically male, but believes he is really female, for example). Specific diagnostic criteria for GID are outlined in the Diagnostic and Statistical Manual of Mental Disorders (DSM-IV-TR).

What Do You Think?

Even though there is a formal policy on how transgendered inmates are to be treated, might there still be serious safety concerns for these individuals? What if a pre-operative transgendered inmate is placed in an institution consistent with his or her birth sex? Might this still be counter to his or her sexual identity?

Offenders Who Abuse Drugs and Alcohol

Back in 2004, almost 80 percent of Canadians had used alcohol in the past year, and nearly 45 percent reported having tried cannabis at some point in their lives. Research has shown that offenders, as a group, appear to "mirror the general population's usage patterns of alcohol and other drugs," but problems from their substance use are much more frequent and serious *Almost half of all* (Begin, Weekes, & Thomas, 2006, p. 18). The link between crime and the *crimes committed* use of alcohol and drugs has been well demonstrated in the literature. Be- *in Canada are* tween 40 and 50 percent of the crimes committed in Canada are estimated *attributed to the use* to be attributed to the use of alcohol and/or illicit substances (Pernanen, *of alcohol or drugs.* Cousineau, Brochu, & Sun, 2002).

Substance abuse and crime may have a *direct link* (a person may only become violent and commit assaults when under the influence of alcohol) or an *indirect* one (a mother steals food to bring home for her kids because she spent the last of her money on crack cocaine). In both of these instances, a link between substance abuse and crime can be seen (as was the case with Lisa Neve, who is profiled below). In addition to the various direct and indirect relationships between substance abuse and crime, over a quarter of all offenders under federal jurisdiction were themselves convicted of a drug offence—possession, cultivation, importation, or trafficking. In these cases, their involvement in the drug trade had a direct relationship to their conflict with the law. Substance abuse is considered to be in the top eight predictors of recidivism and is one of the factors that seem to be interconnected with other types of criminogenic needs. So while the substance abuse itself may have a negative impact on a person's ability to finish school or hold down a job, it may also interfere with family and marital relations and negatively affect finances. Further, such abuse may lead to becoming involved with others who are anti-social, thus exposing the user to their anti-social attitudes (Andrews & Bonta, 2010). All of these factors have been found to be related to recidivism.

It is because of the relationships noted above that identification of alcohol and/or drug abuse is a priority for correctional services, and is part of the intake procedure for new inmates (Kunic, 2006). A national substance abuse programming strategy has been employed across the Canadian federal prison landscape, with almost half of all male inmates considered to be appropriate for this intervention (Long, 2006).

Substance Use in Prison

There are numerous issues that arise from substance use and abuse in correctional settings. Initially upon intake, there may be physical health concerns associated with detoxification. While this is more likely something local jails and holding facilities have to deal with, it is also possible that an inmate returning from a pass or one who is new to a federal institution may arrive under the influence. In these situations, ensuring that the inmate has proper medical care is essential. The use of substances within institutions is not unusual, and leads to issues of treatment, security, and safety of both inmates and staff. Results from a study of random urine testing among federal offenders showed that about 11 percent of offenders will have positive tests, suggesting continued use of substances while incarcerated and while on conditional release in the community (MacPherson & Fraser, 2006). From a treatment perspective, having participants who are under the influence can be disruptive to other program participants. Further, the user is unlikely to gain much from the program in such a condition. And while there are always concerns about violence, there could be additional violence from inmates when they are high, as well as violence related to the drug trade in prison. Apart from homemade alcohol (known as "brew") and the misuse of prescribed medications, any substances that are circulating within an institution had to have been brought there by inmates, staff, or visitors. The smuggling of substances into an institution is a major concern for security personnel. Plastic bottles of alcohol being thrown over walls, substances being smuggled in body cavities, and drugs being sent over the walls in tennis balls are just a few of the ways that this contraband comes in. Once these substances are inside, their effects on the people who ingest them can wreak havoc on institutional order fairly quickly (McVie, 2001).

Although it is a priority for correctional officials to prevent and stop inmates from using drugs and alcohol, the reality is that substances do get into prison, and inmates do use them. Because of the myriad health concerns associated with substance use, a harm-reduction approach must be taken when dealing with certain aspects of substance abuse. For example, the rates of HIV and hepatitis C are much higher for inmate populations than for the general population (CSC, 2011a). To address this, a number of programs have been put into place. Various programs (Reception Awareness Program,

Choosing Health in Prisons, National HIV/AIDS Peer Education and Counselling Program, Circles of Knowledge Keepers, and Chee Mamuk) provide education to inmates about infectious diseases and how to reduce their risk of infection (Zakaria, Thompson, & Borgatta, 2010, p. 5). In addition, access to bleach kits (to clean needles), condoms, and dental dams is now standard in Canadian federal institutions, and the availability of **methadone** maintenance programs ensures that opiate addicts have a medical alternative to injecting heroin (CSC, 2011b). All of these practices are aimed at harm reduction. However, needle exchange is not available to inmates, despite recommendations from the Canadian Human Rights Commission, the Correctional Investigator, and the Canadian HIV/AIDS Legal Network (Chu, 2009). While CSC (2005) has stated that it is committed to working with public health agencies to explore whether needle exchanges will fit within prison health-care initiatives, to date there has been no significant progress made, and no needle exchange programs are in operation in any Canadian prisons (Chu, 2009).

methadone
A synthetic narcotic that is orally administered and is used in the treatment of opiate (e.g., heroin) addiction.

Dangerous Offenders

When the term dangerous offender (DO) is brought up, Clifford Olson, Paul Bernardo, or Robert Pickton likely comes immediately to mind, but there is also Lisa Neve, who is featured in the mini case study below. Interestingly, Neve could be included in a number of the specific groups being discussed here: females, Aboriginals, substance abusers, psychiatric survivors, sex trade workers, dangerous offenders, and lesbian, gay, bisexual, transgendered, questioning, and two-spirited (LGBTQ2).

It is important to distinguish between those who are given a DO designation and likely will remain incarcerated for an indefinite period of time and those who will be released but whose past violence necessitates the issuance of a long-term supervision order (LTSO) for when they leave prison.

From a correctional management perspective, there are issues related to both the nature of the offences and the indefinite length of sentence that must be considered. For some dangerous offenders, the heinous nature of their crimes will necessitate that they be housed separately from the general prison population. Convicted killers Paul Bernardo and the late Clifford Olson are examples of dangerous offenders who had to be held in segregation at various points in their sentence for the safety of themselves or of others (Hewitt, 2010). In fact, Olson was held in a super-maximum security Special Handling Unit (SHU), a type of facility reserved for Canada's most violent, difficult-to-manage inmates. Arising from their segregation and their long sentences are issues of programming. Prisoners held in segregation will not be able to attend regularly scheduled programming with other offenders.

MINI CASE STUDY

Lisa Neve

In 1994, at the age of 21, Lisa Neve became the second woman in Canadian history to be declared a dangerous offender (DO). The first female DO was Marlene Moore, who committed suicide in 1988 at the age of 31 while incarcerated at the infamous Prison for Women in Kingston, Ontario. Neve was similar to Moore in a number of ways; however, Neve's DO designation was eventually overturned and she was subsequently released from prison.

Lisa Colleen Neve was born in December of 1972 and her biological mother was Aboriginal. Neve was adopted out at the age of three months to Jim and Colleen Neve. The family lived in Calgary, and included two other adopted children: an older brother and a younger sister. Neve's developmental history was initially unremarkable. She was described as an "outwardly loving, trusting child" (Yeager, 2000, p. 10). However, it was not long before problems started to emerge. Neve experienced learning and behavioural difficulties in school, which the media later speculated was possibly caused by fetal alcohol syndrome (Jimenez, 1999). Over the years her parents hired tutors and referred her to mental health professionals in an attempt to address these issues. By the time she was 13, her acting out had escalated to the point where she was expelled from school for being disruptive and drinking alcohol. It was around this time that she began working in the sex trade and her drug and alcohol abuse increased.

Lisa Neve came to the attention of a variety of child welfare agencies as a youth. She would routinely run away from these facilities, and return to either her parents' home or the street. Under the *Young Offenders Act*, she was found guilty of a total of 15 offences, including carrying a concealed weapon (knife), failing to appear in court, soliciting, escape from custody, failure to comply, uttering death threats, assault with a weapon, and forcible confinement. Neve was sentenced to periods in secure youth custody, and admitted on numerous occasions to the Alberta Hospital, where she first engaged in self-injury.

As an adult, she was convicted of seven criminal offences, including assault with a weapon, uttering threats, robbery, and aggravated assault. The aggravated assault charge was a serious one in which Neve used an exacto knife to slash the neck of her victim. She reported that she had problems recalling the event, as she was drunk and high on cocaine at the time. In another serious offence, she and a co-accused convinced a woman (who they alleged had been involved in an assault on a friend of Neve's) to go out for a ride. They took her to a field in a rural area and stripped her of her clothes and, in so doing, cut the victim. The pair took the victim's belongings and money and left her naked in the field; it was only 5 °C at the time. For her role in this robbery, Neve was declared a DO in November of 1994 and sentenced to an indeterminate term of imprisonment. At that time, about a month shy of her 22nd birthday, she was the youngest offender ever to be designated as a DO.

The DO hearing took three weeks to complete, with the Crown's evidence focusing on police testimony and notes written by Neve both in and out of custody. The police testified that she was a heavy user of cocaine and alcohol, that she was known as an "enforcer" on the street and "someone not to be messed with" (Yeager, 2000, p. 12). The Crown also focused on her hospitalization records, which described numerous instances of "violence, aggressive behaviour, threats of violence to both staff and other patients, and an alarmingly negative attitude toward life in general and the well-being of others" (Yeager, 2000, p. 12). They also identified portions of her own diaries where she described acts that she said she had committed that were sadistic and violent. Neve claimed that she had not committed any such acts, and later explained that she was simply trying to divert attention away from her real issues.

A coalition (made up of the Canadian Association of Elizabeth Fry Societies, the Disabled Women's Network Canada, the Women's Legal Education and Action Fund, and the Native Women's Association of Canada) fought to have the DO designation overturned. They asserted that the designation was made based on myths and stereotypes about women who are involved in the criminal justice system, and who are Aboriginal, lesbian, and working in the sex trade. They noted that the decision to declare Lisa Neve a DO was made without any consideration of the context in which a woman commits crimes, the realities that face sex trade workers, and women's strategies of survival employed in both community and custodial settings. Further, the use of Robert Hare's Psychopathy Checklist (Revised) was heavily criticized for its application in this case, given the lack of published norms for female offender populations. Lastly, the coalition pointed out that a good deal of the Crown's psychiatric evidence relied on Neve's sexual orientation as an indicator of pathology when it described her as "homosexual and sadistic." It was also noted that the problem with the psychiatric evidence was compounded by the fact that it did not seem to adequately consider her extreme alcoholism and dependence on drugs (Yeager, 2000).

The Alberta Court of Appeal reversed Lisa Neve's DO designation on June 28, 1999. This decision was made for a number of statutory reasons, including the recognition that the robbery was not serious enough to warrant the DO application in the first place. Moreover, the court determined that the psychiatric evidence that had been relied upon was tainted, and created new case law such that a sentencing judge must consider the "context in which the criminal conduct occurred" (Yeager, 2000, p. 18).

In July 1999, Lisa Neve was released from prison. In a CBC television interview, she commented:

> Every day I have to deal with part of my dangerous offender sentence and stuff, 'cause it's still a big part of me and it depresses me and it hurts me. It's hard just to forgive and forget. (Stewart, 2000, p. 5)

> ### SIDEBAR
>
> ## Defining a Dangerous Offender
>
> Individuals are designated as dangerous offenders at sentencing if it can be shown that they pose a significant risk of committing a future violent or sexual offence. The dangerous offender provision is found in s. 753 of the *Criminal Code.* In order to be "DO'd," an individual must be convicted of a serious personal injury offence and be deemed a threat to others. This must be evidenced by a pattern of repetitive behaviour that the person is unable to restrain that will likely cause death or serious injury to others, or by a pattern of persistent, aggressive behaviour in which the person is indifferent to the consequences to others. A third criterion is that the behaviour of the person is so brutal that he or she is believed unlikely to be able to be inhibited by normal types of behavioural restraint. The long-term offender provisions address concerns about those who do not meet the criteria for DO designation, but who nonetheless pose a significant risk to society. Under a long-term supervision order (LTSO), an individual may be supervised for up to 10 years following the custodial sentence (Public Safety Canada, 2011a).

Moreover, given the indeterminate nature of their sentences, programming that is offered must be tailored to take into account that they are unlikely to be released in the foreseeable future. According to CSC (2011c, para. 3), programs such as "sexual deviance treatments, intensive violence prevention programs, mental disorder treatments, and educational programs" have all been developed for DOs.

A recent estimate suggests that there are 450 DOs in Canada and most of them remain incarcerated (CSC, 2009b). From 2004 to 2008, there was a 20 percent increase in the number of offenders with a DO designation (CSC, 2009b). The vast majority are male; as of April 2011, there was only one female currently designated as a DO. Renée Acoby was originally sentenced to three and a half years in prison, but received an additional 18 years for crimes committed while incarcerated, culminating in an indefinite sentence as a result of a successful DO application. A similar pattern—that of an ever-increasing sentence as a result of convictions incurred while incarcerated—was also seen in the case of Ashley Smith (see Part Five). In 2005, Acoby and another inmate, while serving time at Grand Valley Institution for Women in Kitchener, Ontario, took two staff members hostage and threatened and tortured them for more than three hours. Interestingly, of the three female DO cases mentioned in this chapter (Marlene Moore, Lisa

Neve, and Renée Acoby), none had been convicted of a sexual offence or of taking anyone's life, and all three had a history of convictions that included forcible confinement or hostage takings. Not to minimize the trauma that these women caused their victims, but it is noteworthy that their crimes are not really comparable to the levels of violence commonly associated with infamous DOs like Bernardo, Olson, or Pickton. In fact, convicted double murderer Russell Williams (who pleaded guilty to a total of 88 charges) was recently handed two life sentences, but the Crown attorney in that case did not pursue a DO designation because he believed Williams would never be paroled given the facts outlined at trial (CBC, 2010). An examination of the most serious offences at time of sentencing for DOs suggests that sexual offences represent by far the highest proportion (more than 70 percent) of these cases, with serious assault, homicide, attempted murder, robbery, and other making up the remainder (CSC, 2009b).

Sexual Offenders

Recent estimates suggest that 4.3 percent of those sentenced to provincial custody and 10.4 percent of those in federal custody have a sexual assault as their most serious offence. This amounts to 3,167 and 2,348 offenders, respectively (Calverley, 2010). Analyzing 95 different studies of more than 31,000 sexual offenders, Hanson & Morton-Bourgon (2004) identified an observed sexual recidivism rate of 13.7 percent, a violent recidivism rate (including both sexual and non-sexual violence) of 25 percent, and a general recidivism rate of almost 37 percent. The average amount of follow-up time for these studies was five to six years.

SIDEBAR

Recidivism Rates

Recidivism rates will vary depending on how the term recidivism is defined (is it rearrest, reconviction, or revocation?) and the follow-up period that is used (longer periods are associated with higher rates). It has been suggested that a reconviction rate range between 41 and 44 percent is a reasonably good estimate for Canadian federal offenders, and can serve as a measure against which to evaluate the success of rehabilitative programs both over time and with one another (Bonta, Rugge, & Dauvergne, 2003).

National Sex Offender Program

At the federal level is the CSC's National Sex Offender Program (NaSOP). This group intervention is appropriate for low- to moderate-risk sex offenders, and is considered a semi-structured therapeutic program to assist offenders with developing self-management skills. NaSOP also targets "cognitive distortions [a sex offender thinking that it is normal to have sex with children, for example], deviant arousal and fantasy, social skills, anger and emotion management, empathy, and victim awareness" (Cortoni & Nunes, 2007, p iii). The program has been evaluated, and the results suggest that it is effective in reducing recidivism. As Cortoni and Nunes pointed out, this is consistent with various research to date that has found sex offender treatment programs to be effective in reducing recidivism.

Female Sex Offenders

While the vast majority of sexual offenders are male, an estimated 4 to 5 percent of sexual offences are committed by women (Cortoni & Hanson, 2005). The approach to assessing and treating female sex offenders in the past tended to mirror what had already been developed for men, but as Cortoni (2009) noted, this has not been without criticism. It has been suggested that treatment for female sexual offenders must be "tailored to their distinct needs and characteristics rather than proceed on the assumption that all individuals should receive exactly the same interventions" (Nathan & Ward, 2002, p. 20).

Comparatively speaking, the recidivism rates for female sexual offenders are much lower. In their review, Cortoni and Hanson (2005) found a sexual recidivism rate of 1 percent for women, a violent recidivism rate (including sexual) of just over 6 percent, and a general recidivism rate (including violent and sexual) of just over 20 percent. Again, follow-up periods averaged five years.

Segregating Sex Offenders

Some sex offenders can request to be placed in administrative segregation for their own safety. As a group, sex offenders are viewed by other inmates as being very low in the inmate hierarchy, and can be subject to abuse. In 1996, a riot at Headingley Correctional Centre in Manitoba saw presumed sex offenders attacked by other inmates, resulting in genital mutilation and three inmates having fingers cut off with exacto knives. In a riot at Mountain Institution in British Columbia, a notorious sex offender, Michael Andrew

Gibbon, died from wounds inflicted upon him by other inmates. While Gibbon was residing among the general population when he was killed, in the case of most of the inmates attacked during the Headingley riot, they were living in protective custody—which rioting inmates had access to once they had taken a set of keys from a guard (Matas, 2008; Roberts, 1996).

In an examination of male segregated offenders in Canada, there were differences found between those placed in segregation for disciplinary reasons and those who requested segregation from the general inmate population for their own safety. Those who were voluntarily segregated were significantly more likely to have a previous conviction for a sex offence (27 percent) compared with inmates who were involuntarily segregated (18 percent) (Motiuk & Blanchette, 1997). This is particularly noteworthy, since it has been found that offenders who request to be voluntarily segregated stay there twice as long (average length of stay is 68 versus 35 days) as those who are segregated involuntarily (Bottos, 2007). In a review of the literature, it was reported that the effects of administrative segregation include a negative impact on the "individual's well-being, their security reclassification status, program participation, discretionary release decisions, and conditional release outcomes" (Bottos, p. 17). This is significant given the disproportionate number of sex offenders who voluntarily seek out protective custody.

Reintegrating Sexual Offenders

There are reintegration issues for sexual offenders that need to be considered as part of release planning. Not only do sex offenders have to deal with the barriers and stigma common to most ex-inmates when looking for employment upon release, but they must also contend with barriers specific to the nature of their offence. For example, a teacher who is being released from prison after serving a sentence for the sexual assault of a child will be unlikely to get his or her teaching licence reinstated. As a result of policies and procedures put into place to protect members of society, some sexual offenders will need to consider the likelihood that they cannot return to their previous employment, and must therefore look into retraining to hopefully find suitable employment upon release. Further, most organizations in Canada that provide service to vulnerable populations (children and the elderly, for example) require a criminal records check to be completed prior to a new worker's being hired or volunteering. In addition to facing employment challenges, sexual offenders will also be subject to community notification as well as to sexual offender registration laws (Harris & Hanson, 2010; Manitoba Department of Justice, 2011; Public Safety Canada, 2011c).

Mental Disorders

Mental disorders are considered health conditions, and can include changes in mood, behaviour and/or thinking that can have an impact on how a person functions and may be associated with distress (Health Canada, 2011). In a review of the literature, McGuire noted that "Globally, there is little evidence to suggest that a diagnosis of mental disorder in itself is clearly linked to increased occurrence of any specific type of crime" (McGuire, 2000, para. 22). Although there may not be a direct link between the two, studies have shown that a significant proportion of inmates meet the criteria for a diagnosis of a mental disorder. Collaborations between correctional and mental health systems are deemed essential because it is a reality that some individuals with a mental disorder will find themselves detained in correctional facilities. At admission, about 13 percent of men and 29 percent of women in federal prisons are identified as having mental health problems (CSC, 2011d). Compared with community samples, both male and female incarcerated offenders appear to have considerably higher lifetime prevalence rates of mental disorder (Folsom, 2009). As you may recall from the case study, Lisa Neve had a history of interactions with the mental health system in addition to correctional systems.

Protocols for mental health assessment in Canadian corrections have been in place for a number of years. All federal institutions are required,

---

SIDEBAR

Computerized Assessment

In an effort to identify an efficient way to screen federally incarcerated offenders for mental disorders, a pilot study of the Computerized Mental Health Intake Screening System (CoMHISS) was undertaken. This assessment tool combines self-report measures such as the Brief Symptom Inventory, the Depression Hopelessness and Suicide Screening Form, and the Paulhus Deception Scales. Results of the study suggested that the CoMHISS could effectively identify those who should be further evaluated for the presence of a mental disorder. The researchers noted that more work is needed to determine corrections-specific norms, and they have speculated that the CoMHISS might evolve to include the merging of tools that already exist to allow for estimates of concurrent disorders (those who are co-diagnosed with both a psychiatric disorder and a substance use and/or a gambling disorder) (Stewart et al., 2010).

under *Commissioner's Directive 840*, to provide psychological services, including assessment, to offenders as needed (CSC, 1994). An initial screening of offenders during the intake process must be done to determine who may require further assessment and possible treatment. Psychological assessments must address mental health needs; those done for the purposes of pre-release must also include reference to the inmate's level of risk. Mental health assessments must be culturally and gender-sensitive. A mental health strategy for female offenders has also been developed, and recommendations have been made that specifically address the needs of incarcerated women with mental disorders (Laishes, 2002).

Safety and Suicide Concerns

Issues of safety are of paramount importance to correctional officials. There are two specific behaviours related to psychological functioning that cause concern: self-injurious behaviour and suicide. Although these two behaviours can appear similar (some instances of self-injury may be misinterpreted as a suicide attempt, for example), the intents behind them are different. It was noted by the Correctional Investigator that a quarter of the female offender population has a history of self-injury (Sapers, 2010). Such behaviour can take many forms, including hanging, cutting, scratching, reopening wounds, head banging, biting, swallowing non-food items (such as glass), and inserting objects into the skin. It has been repeatedly pointed out that self-injurious behaviour must be considered a mental health concern and not treated as a matter of security (Heney, 1990; Sapers, 2010), Historically, this has not been the case, and even today, the Office of the Correctional Investigator has documented cases where CSC has shown an overreliance on the use of seclusion and restraints to manage self-injury (Sapers, 2011). Individuals in federal prison are more at risk to kill themselves than to be murdered (Larivière, 1997). The most likely method of suicide in federal institutions is by hanging, and suicides most often occur in the inmate's cell in general population. Suicide rates for prison populations are much higher than for the general population (Polvi, 1997).

Directives for prison staff specify that all inmates must be screened for suicidal ideation within the first 24 hours of being admitted to an institution, when placed in administrative segregation (whether voluntary or for disciplinary reasons), and when staff have reason to believe an inmate is at risk for suicide. Whenever possible, a mental health professional is expected to assess the inmate, and assign him or her to a suicide watch level.

Psychologists, psychiatrists, and psychiatric nurses are just some of the professionals employed in corrections to address the mental health needs of offenders. While intake assessment and pre-release psychological assessments may be mandated, participation in psychological treatment is usually voluntary. Therapeutic and crisis intervention are two types of psychological services available to federal inmates. In many institutions, however, there are not enough resources available to effectively carry out these interventions. The following quote, from the 2007 report of the CSC Review Panel, summarizes the state of psychological services for federal inmates:

> Most penitentiaries have a limited number of psychologists on staff, and mental health care is usually limited to crisis intervention and suicide prevention. Psychologists spend a significant percentage of their time preparing risk assessments intended to assist the National Parole Board in making decisions regarding conditional release. The primary and intermediate mental health care provided to offenders is insufficient. Offenders with mental health problems usually do not receive appropriate treatment unless their needs reach crisis levels. Many are segregated for protection because of their inability to cope in regular penitentiary settings, and therefore they have limited access to programming or treatment. (Sampson, Gascon, Glen, Louie, & Rosenfeldt, 2007, p. 55)

CSC has not escaped criticism for its handling of individuals with severe forms of mental disorder. While exchange of service agreements exist with some secure psychiatric facilities, inmates can still end up bouncing between correctional facilities and psychiatric facilities, or between their home institution and the regional psychiatric correctional institutions. It has been noted that in some instances, inmates have been transferred to give staff relief. Cases like that of Ashley Smith (outlined in Part Five), who ultimately died in segregation at Grand Valley Institution for Women, bring public attention to the plight of those who are incarcerated and shuffled from institution to institution, all the while trying to cope with serious mental illness.

Race

Some critical issues related to race have been touched on in earlier chapters. In the context of this chapter, race will be discussed in connection with the correctional policies and issues relating to Aboriginal offenders.

Assembly of First Nations National Chief Shawn Atleo has said that "First Nations children are more likely to go to jail than to graduate from high school" (Therien, 2011, para. 1). This statement speaks volumes about the continued marginalization of Aboriginal people in Canada. Aboriginal people are overrepresented in the correctional system, making up 18 percent of federally sentenced offenders but only 2.8 percent of the country's adult population (CSC, 2011e). Similar overrepresentation occurs at the provincial level as well. There is every indication, based on the youthful demographics of the growing Aboriginal population, that this overrepresentation will get worse, not better, over time (Mann, 2009).

Colonialism can be viewed as a major contributor to this overrepresentation. It has been defined as a "systematic oppression of a people through a variety of assimilationist measures that are intended to eradicate the peoples and/or their sense of individual and cultural identity" (Restoule, 2009, p. 272). Colonialist practices continue to exert an influence in Canada, although more subtly than in previous eras.

The Gladue Decision

As an example of the impact of colonialism on the justice system, consider the case of Jamie Lynn Gladue, who was found guilty of murdering her common-law husband while under the influence of alcohol. Gladue successfully appealed her sentence of federal custody by arguing that the court had not taken into account distinct cultural issues affecting Aboriginal peoples. In its 1999 landmark ruling (known as the *Gladue* decision), the Supreme Court of Canada determined that it was imperative that the court system take into account the colonialist actions targeted at Aboriginal people in Canada. Understanding these actions would help explain why Aboriginal people have engaged in criminal acts. As a result, courts must now take into account culture-specific and gender-specific issues to better understand who the offender is as a person, and not just focus on the nature of the criminal act (Restoule, 2009).

Passed in 1992, the *Corrections and Conditional Release Act* (CCRA) was the first piece of legislation to give Aboriginal peoples some involvement in the development of services, policies, and programs in corrections, as well as to ensure that the correctional environment provided opportunity for Aboriginal spirituality and cultural practices. One of the principles in the CCRA is that "correctional policies, programs, and practices respect gender, ethnic, cultural and linguistic differences and be responsive to the special needs of women and Aboriginal peoples, as well as to the needs of other groups of offenders with special requirements." First Introduced in 1995, *Commissioner's Directive 702* outlined CSC policy to accommodate Aboriginal culture and spirituality practices within federal prisons. The use of ceremonial medicines (e.g., sweet grass, sage, cedar, and tobacco), ceremonial and personal spiritual objects (e.g., medicine bags, smudge bowls, and feathers), traditional foods, and the practice of ceremonies (e.g., smudging, sweat lodge, pipe ceremonies, and potlatches) are all covered under this directive (CSC, 2008).

CSC has developed and evaluated programs that target the needs of specific groups of Aboriginal offenders, including programs for Inuit sex offenders, violent females, and substance abusers. In this way, CSC is attempting to offer culturally sensitive programming while still adhering to the principles of effective correctional treatment. The establishment of healing lodges is also an example of this. There are eight healing lodges across Canada being oper-ated in partnership with various Aboriginal communities (CSC, 2011f). The first healing lodge (Okimaw Ohci Healing Lodge for women) was opened in 1995, and the first men's healing lodge in 1997. These facilities are staffed primarily by people of Aboriginal descent and are appropriate for minimum-security inmates. Within federal institutions, an Aboriginal Continuum of Care that includes elders and Aboriginal correctional staff has been estab-lished to address the needs of Aboriginal offenders (CSC, 2006).

Aboriginal corrections has been described as being at a crossroads, with an urgent need for action on the part of CSC and a need to translate "good intentions" into results that will lessen the existing gap between Aboriginal and non-Aboriginal offenders (Mann, 2009, p. 5). Aboriginal inmates are overrepresented in segregation, are more likely to be classified as high needs and high risk, are released at later points in their sentences, and are more likely to serve full sentences, to have their conditional release revoked, and to have had a previous youth or adult sentence (Therien, 2011; Mann, 2009). Factors such as "substance abuse, intergenerational abuse, and residential schools, low levels of education, employment, and income, and substandard housing and health care" have been identified as likely playing a role in this overrepresentation (Mann, 2009, p. 4). Although CSC has developed a stra-tegic plan for Aboriginal corrections that includes almost 200 items, review of the plan by the Office of the Correctional Investigator has found that very few of these "promising and ambitious undertakings" have been accom-plished (Mann, p. 4).

Conclusion

What should be clear after reading this chapter is that Canada's correctional population is a very diverse one. When considering the needs of the offender population, those of the more marginalized groups are of prime importance as well—not just those of the majority.

It was noted in the chapter's introduction that this list of special subpopu-lations was not an exhaustive one, but was meant to highlight some key subgroups within the larger correctional population as a way of emphasizing its diversity. The case study of Lisa Neve was chosen because of the complexities of her case; she herself could be classified as a member of several subpopulations, including female, Aboriginal, and dangerous offender. Her case reminds us that people cannot be neatly classified using one label or another, nor should they be. The reality is that for every individual serving time in a custodial setting, there is a unique story and a unique life. While it may be useful to consider some of the challenges that face these different subpopulations, it is imperative that the individuals themselves are not forgotten. Keep this in mind as you read the next section (Part Five), and about the tragic case of Ashley Smith.

► IN-CLASS EXERCISE

Each student should take five to ten minutes to jot down the impact that being incarcerated would have on aspects of his or her own life, such as family, work, and school, and so on.

- Make note of some of the practical arrangements you would need to make if you faced a prison sentence. What would you do with your apartment, or your pet?
- Make a list of your three key concerns or worries about going to prison.

Regardless of what people are incarcerated for, they are going to face similar kinds of concerns. As a student, trying to imagine just how many aspects of your life would change as a result of being incarcerated, and acknowledging your fears, helps you to realize just how overwhelming a period of incarceration could be.

DISCUSSION QUESTIONS

1. If you were a prison warden, and you were approached by a local AIDS organization to pilot a needle exchange program in your prison, how would you decide whether or not your facility would participate (assuming you were the final decision-maker)? What are the pros of instituting a prison needle exchange program? What are the cons? Be sure to include the issues of security and health care, as well as concerns of staff and inmates in your answer.
2. You are out with a friend for dinner when your friend comments on a recent case in which a 67-year-old male was sent to prison for

life. Your friend jokes that the inmate will probably have a better life at "Club Fed" than he would in the community. How would you respond to the comment? What points would you make to educate your friend on the status of elderly offenders in Canadian prisons?

3. Do you agree with the provisions for transgendered inmates as outlined in *Commissioner's Directive 800* (available at www.csc-scc .gc.ca/text/plcy/cdshtm/800-cde-eng.shtml#Gender)? Do you think that pre-operative transgendered inmates should be housed in an institution consistent with their birth sex? Why?

4. Of the subpopulations that were discussed in this chapter, can you identify any single challenge they all pose with respect to prison management? From an operational perspective, are there similar issues that affect some of these groups? How would you go about addressing these with staff to ensure a smooth operation of your facility?

NOTE

A portion of this chapter was adapted from J. Barker (Ed.), *Women and the Criminal Justice System: A Canadian Perspective* (Toronto: Emond Montgomery, 2008).

SUGGESTED FURTHER READINGS

Andrews, D., & Bonta, J. (2010). *The psychology of criminal conduct* (5th ed.). New Providence, NJ: LexisNexis.

Sapers, H. (2008). *A preventable death*. Retrieved from http://www.oci-bec.gc.ca/ rpt/pdf/oth-aut/oth-aut20080620-eng.pdf

Sapers, H. (2011). *Annual report of the Office of the Correctional Investigator 2010–2011*. Catalogue No. PS100-2011E-PDF. Ottawa: Office of the Correctional Investigator. Retrieved from http://www.oci-bec.gc.ca/rpt/ annrpt/annrpt20102011-eng.aspx#ss1b

Yeager, M.G. (2000). Ideology and dangerousness: The case of Lisa Colleen Neve. *Critical Criminology, 9*(1-2), 9–21. doi:10.1007/BF02461035

REFERENCES

Andrews, D., & Bonta, J. (2010). *The psychology of criminal conduct* (5th ed.). New Providence, NJ: LexisNexis.

Begin, P., Weekes, J., & Thomas, G. (2006). The Canadian addiction survey: Substance use and misuse among the Canadian population. *Forum on Corrections Research, 18*(1), 12–18. Retrieved from http://www.csc-scc.gc.ca/ text/pblct/forum/e181/e181d_e.pdf

Bonta, J., Rugge, T., & Dauvergne, M. (2003). *The reconviction rate of federal offenders*. User Report 2003-02. Ottawa: Solicitor General Canada.

Bottos, S. (2007). Profile of offenders in administrative segregation: A review of the literature. Research Brief B-39. Ottawa: Correctional Service of Canada. Retrieved from http://www.csc-scc.gc.ca/text/rsrch/briefs/b39/b39-eng.pdf

Brown, G. (2010). Autocastration and autopenectomy as surgical self-treatment in incarcerated persons with gender identity disorder. *International Journal of Transgenderism, 12*, 31–39. doi:10.1080/15532731003688970

Calverley, D. (2010). Adult correctional services in Canada, 2008/2009. *Juristat, 30*(3), 1–32.

Carrington, P.J. (2001). Population aging and crime in Canada, 2000–2041. *Canadian Journal of Criminology, 43*(3), 331–356.

CBC. (2010, October 21). Williams gets 2 life terms for "despicable crimes." CBC News. Retrieved from http://www.cbc.ca/news/canada/story/2010/10/21/russell-williams-day-four.html

Chu, S. (2009). Clean switch: The case for prison needle and syringe programs. *HIV/AIDS Policy & Law Review, 14*(2), 5–17. Retrieved from http://www.aidslaw.ca/publications/interfaces/downloadFile.php?ref=1601[0]

Corrections and Conditional Release Act, SC 1992, c. 20.

Cortoni, F. (2009). Violence and women offenders. In J. Barker (Ed.), *Women and the criminal justice system: A Canadian perspective* (pp. 175–200). Toronto: Emond Montgomery.

Cortoni, F., & Hanson, K. (2005). A review of the recidivism rates of adult female sexual offenders. Ottawa: Public Safety and Emergency Preparedness Canada. Retrieved from http://www.csc-scc.gc.ca/text/rsrch/reports/r169/r169_e.pdf

Cortoni, F., & Nunes, K. (2007). *Assessing the effectiveness of the National Sexual Offender Program*. Research Report R-183. Ottawa: Correctional Service of Canada. Retrieved from http://www.csc-scc.gc.ca/text/rsrch/reports/r183/r183-eng.pdf

Finn, A., Trevethan, S., Carrière, G., & Kowalski, M. (1999). Female inmates, aboriginal inmates, and inmates serving life sentences: A one day snapshot. *Juristat, 19*(5). Ottawa: Statistics Canada.

Folsom, J. (2009). Women offenders and mental health. In J. Barker (Ed.), *Women and the criminal justice system: A Canadian perspective* (pp. 175–200). Toronto: Emond Montgomery.

Hannah-Moffat, K. (1995). Feminine fortresses: Woman-centered prisons? *The Prison Journal, 75*(2), 135–164.

Hannah-Moffat, K. (2000). Re-forming the prison: Rethinking our ideals. In K. Hannah-Moffat & M. Shaw (Eds.), *An ideal prison? Critical essays of women's imprisonment in Canada* (pp. 30–40). Halifax: Fernwood.

Hanson, K., & Morton-Bourgon, K. (2004). *Predictors of sexual recidivism: An updated meta-analysis*. Catalogue No. PS3-1/2004-2E-PDF. Ottawa: Public Safety and Emergency Preparedness Canada. Retrieved from http://www.publicsafety.gc.ca/res/cor/rep/_fl/2004-02-pred-se-eng.pdf

Harris, A., & Hanson, K. (2010). Clinical, actuarial and dynamic risk assessment of sexual offenders: Why do things keep changing? *Journal of Sexual Aggression, 16*(3), 296–310.

Health Canada. (2011). Mental health: Mental illness. *It's your health.* Catalogue No. H137/5-2006E-PDF. Ottawa: Author. Retrieved from http://hc-sc.gc.ca/hl-vs/alt_formats/pacrb-dgapcr/pdf/iyh-vsv/diseases-maladies/mental-eng.pdf

Heney, J. (1990). Report on self-injurious behaviour in the Kingston Prison for Women. Ottawa: Correctional Service of Canada. Retrieved from http://www.csc-scc.gc.ca/text/prgrm/fsw/selfinjuries/toce-eng.shtml

Hensley, C., & Tewksbury, R. (2002). Inmate-to-inmate prison sexuality: A review of empirical studies. *Trauma Violence Abuse, 3,* 226–243. doi:10.1177/15248380020033005

Hewitt, P. (2010, October 24). Russell Williams enters a "grim" existence in Kingston Penitentiary. *Toronto Star.* Retrieved from http://www.thestar.com/news/canada/article/880485—russell-williams-enters-a-grim-existence-in-kingston-penitentiary

Jimenez, M. (1999, April 3). The law, violence, and Lisa Neve: Is this the most dangerous woman in Canada? *The National Post.* Retrieved from http://business.highbeam.com/435424/article-1G1-54483432/law-violence-and-lisa-neve

Kong, R., & AuCoin, K. (2008). Female offenders in Canada. *Juristat, 28*(1), 1–23. Ottawa: Statistics Canada.

Kunic, D. (2006). The computerized assessment of substance abuse (CASA). *Forum on Corrections Research, 18*(1). 19–23. Retrieved from http://www.csc-scc.gc.ca/text/pblct/forum/e181/e181e_e.pdf

Laishes, J. (2002). The 2002 mental health strategy for women offenders. Ottawa: Correctional Service of Canada. Retrieved from http://www.csc-scc.gc.ca/text/prgrm/fsw/mhealth/3-eng.shtml

Larivière, M. (1997). *The Correctional Service of Canada 1996–1997 retrospective report on inmate suicides.* Ottawa: Correctional Service of Canada. Retrieved from http://www.csc-scc.gc.ca/text/pblct/health/toce-eng.shtml [Note: Click on "RTF" to download the correct report.]

Long, C. (2006). Developing national substance abuse programs in Canadian federal corrections. *Forum on Corrections Research, 18*(1), 38–41. Retrieved from http://www.csc-scc.gc.ca/text/pblct/forum/e181/e181i_e.pdf

MacPherson, P., & Fraser, C. (2006). Random urinalysis testing in federal corrections. *Forum on Corrections Research, 18*(1), 33–37. Retrieved from http://www.csc-scc.gc.ca/text/pblct/forum/e181/e181h_e.pdf

Manitoba Department of Justice. (2011). Safer communities: Sex offender notifications. Retrieved from http://www.gov.mb.ca/justice/notification/index.html

Mann, M. (2009). *Good intentions, disappointing result: A progress report on federal Aboriginal corrections.* Ottawa: Office of the Correctional Investigator. Retrieved from http://www.oci-bec.gc.ca/rpt/pdf/oth-aut/oth-aut20091113-eng.pdf

Matas, R. (2008, April 3). Ottawa orders full review of prison riot. *The Globe and Mail*, p. A6. http://www.theglobeandmail.com

McGuire, J. (2000). Treatment approaches for offenders with mental disorder. In L. Motiuk and R. Serin (Eds.), *Compendium 2000 on effective correctional programming* (chapter 16). Retrieved from http://www.csc-scc.gc.ca/text/rsrch/compendium/2000/chap_16-eng.shtml

McVie, F. (2001). Drugs in federal corrections: The issues and challenges. *Forum on Corrections Research, 13*(3), 7–9. Retrieved from http://www.csc-scc.gc.ca/text/pblct/forum/e133/133c_e.pdf

Motiuk, L., & Blanchette, K. (1997). *Case characteristics of segregated offenders in federal corrections.* Research Report R-57. Ottawa: Correctional Service of Canada. Retrieved from http://www.csc-scc.gc.ca/text/rsrch/reports/r57/r57_e.pdf

Nathan, P., & Ward, T. (2002). Female sex offenders: Clinical and demographic features. *Journal of Sexual Aggression, 8*(1), 5–21. doi:10.1080/13552600208413329

Office of the Correctional Investigator. (2011). *Backgrounder: Summary of issues and challenges facing older and aging offenders in federal custody.* Ottawa: Author. Retrieved from http://www.oci-bec.gc.ca/comm/presentations/presentationsAR-RA0911-OldOff-eng.aspx

Ortiz, M.M. (2000). Managing special populations. *Corrections Today, 62*(7), 64–68.

Pernanen, K., Cousineau, M., Brochu, S., & Sun, F. (2002). *Proportions of crimes associated with alcohol and other drugs in Canada.* Ottawa: Canadian Centre on Substance Abuse. Retrieved from http://www.ccsa.ca/2003%20and%20earlier%20CCSA%20Documents/ccsa-009105-2002.pdf

Polvi, N.H. (1997). *Prisoner suicide: Literature review.* Ottawa: Correctional Service of Canada. Retrieved from http://www.csc-scc.gc.ca/text/pblct/health/toc-eng.shtml [Note: This is the same link as that in Larivière, above, but the reader needs to scroll down the page to find this particular one.]

Restoule, B. (2009). Aboriginal women and the criminal justice system. In J. Barker (Ed.), *Women and the criminal justice system: A Canadian perspective* (pp. 257–287). Toronto: Emond Montgomery.

Roberts, D. (1996, April 27). Police end riot at Manitoba jail; 8 guards injured, several prisoners attacked by other inmates. *The Globe and Mail*, p. A1. http://www.theglobeandmail.com

Sampson, R., Gascon, S., Glen, I., Louie, C., & Rosenfeldt, S. (2007). *Report of the Correctional Service of Canada Review Panel: A roadmap to strengthening public safety.* Catalogue No. PS84-14/2007E-PDF. Ottawa: Public Works and Government Services Canada. Retrieved from http://www.publicsafety.gc.ca/csc-scc/report-rapport/cur-env-3-eng.aspx

Sapers, H. (2011). *Annual report of the Office of the Correctional Investigator 2010–2011*. Catalogue No. PS100-2011E-PDF. Ottawa: Office of the Correctional Investigator. Retrieved from http://www.oci-bec.gc.ca/rpt/annrpt/annrpt20102011-eng.aspx#ss1b

Sexton, L., Jenness, V., & Sumner, M. (2010). Where the margins meet: A demographic assessment of transgender inmates in men's prisons. *Justice Quarterly, 27*(6), 835–866.

Shaw, M. (1999). "Knowledge without acknowledgement": Violent women, the prison and the cottage. *The Howard Journal, 38*(3), 252–266.

Snell, T.L. (2000). Capital punishment 1999. *Bureary of Justice Statistics Bulletin*, NCJ 184795. Washington, DC: US Department of Justice. Retrieved from http://bjs.ojp.usdoj.gov/content/pub/pdf/cp99.pdf

Snell, T.L. (2010). Capital punishment, 2009: Statistical tables. *Bureau of Justice Statistics Statistical Tables*, NCJ 231676. Washington, DC: US Department of Justice. Retrieved from http://bjs.ojp.usdoj.gov/content/pub/pdf/cp09st.pdf

Statistics Canada. (2007). *Federal, provincial and territorial general government revenue and expenditures for fiscal year ending March 31*. CANSIM table 385-0002. Retrieved from http://www5.statcan.gc.ca/cansim/pick-choisir?lang=eng&p2=33&id=3850002

Stewart, B. (Host). (2000, January 3). *The National Magazine—CBC Television* [Transcript]. Toronto: Canadian Broadcasting Corporation.

Stewart, L., Harris, A., Wilton, G., Archambault, K., Cousineau, C., Varrette, S., & Power, J. (2010). *An initial report on the results of the pilot of the Computerized Mental Health Intake Screening System (CoMHISS)*. Research Report R-218. Ottawa: Correctional Service of Canada. Retrieved from http://www.csc-scc.gc.ca/text/rsrch/reports/r218/r218-eng.pdf

Task Force on Federally Sentenced Women (TFFSW). (1990). *Creating choices: The report of the Task Force on Federally Sentenced Women*. Ottawa: Correctional Service Canada.

Therien, E. (2011, July 20). The national shame of Aboriginal incarceration. *The Globe and Mail*. Retrieved from http://www.theglobeandmail.com/news/opinions/opinion/the-national-shame-of-aboriginal-incarceration/article2102814/

Uzoaba, J.H. (1998). *Managing older offenders: Where do we stand?* Research Report R-70. Ottawa: Correctional Service of Canada. Retrieved from http://www.csc-scc.gc.ca/text/rsrch/reports/r70/r70_e.pdf

Yeager, M.G. (2000). Ideology and dangerousness: The case of Lisa Colleen Neve. *Critical Criminology, 9*(1-2), 9–21. doi:10.1007/BF02461035

Zakaria, D., Thompson, J., & Borgatta, F. (2010). *The relationship between knowledge of HIV and HCV, health education, and risk and harm-reducing behaviours among Canadian federal inmates*. Research Report. Ottawa: Correctional Service of Canada. Retrieved from http://www.csc-scc.gc.ca/text/rsrch/reports/r195/r195-eng.pdf

CSC Policy Directives and Publications

CSC. (1994). Psychological services. *Commissioner's Directive 840*. Retrieved from http://www.csc-scc.gc.ca/text/plcy/doc/840-cd.pdf

CSC. (2005). *CSC action plan in response to the report of the Canadian Human Rights Commission*. Ottawa: Author. Retrieved from http://www.csc-scc.gc.ca/text/prgrm/fsw/gender4/CHRC_response-eng.shtml

CSC. (2006). *Strategic plan for Aboriginal corrections: Innovation, learning and adjustment*. Ottawa: Author. Retrieved from http://www.csc-scc.gc.ca/text/prgrm/abinit/plan06-eng.shtml

CSC. (2008). Aboriginal offenders. *Commissioner's Directive 702*. Retrieved from http://www.csc-scc.gc.ca/text/plcy/doc/702-cd.pdf

CSC. (2009a). *Creating better relations: Aging offenders—Aging community*. Retrieved from http://www.csc-scc.gc.ca/text/benevols/archive/2009/crn/pr-age-eng.shtml

CSC. (2009b). *Dangerous offender designations: A five-year offence profile. Research Snippet*, Number 09-3. Ottawa: Author. Retrieved from http://www.csc-scc.gc.ca/text/rsrch/smmrs/rs/rs09-03/docs/rs09-03-eng.pdf

CSC. (2011a). Health Services Sector. *Infectious disease surveillance in Canadian federal penitentiaries 2005–2006*. Ottawa: Public Works and Government Services. Retrieved from http://www.csc-scc.gc.ca/text/pblct/infdscfp-2005-06/infdscfp-2005-06-eng.pdf

CSC. (2011b). *Specific guidelines for methadone maintenance treatment*. Retrieved from http://www.csc-scc.gc.ca/text/pblct/methadone/b-eng.shtml

CSC. (2011c). A program for every inmate: Meeting specific needs—Specific groups, specific needs—Sexual offenders and dangerous offenders. (Education module). Retrieved from http://www.csc-scc.gc.ca/education/sse1-eng.shtml

CSC. (2011d). The changing federal offender population highlights 2009. Retrieved from http://www.csc-scc.gc.ca/text/rsrch/special_reports/sr2009/Highlights-2009-eng.pdf

CSC. (2011e). Aboriginal offender statistics. Facts and figures. Retrieved from http://www.csc-scc.gc.ca/text/prgrm/abinit/know/4-eng.shtml

CSC. (2011f). Aboriginal healing lodges. Facts and figures. Retrieved from http://www.csc-scc.gc.ca/text/prgrm/abinit/know/6-eng.shtml

PART FIVE
Youth Justice

Ashley Smith: Mental Illness Criminalized

Susan Reid

Ashley Smith

In 2007, Ashley Smith, a 19-year-old woman from Moncton, New Brunswick, committed suicide in an adult penitentiary. She did so after being transferred from the youth system less than one year before. Had Ashley committed a heinous offence to warrant transfer to an adult institution? No. Ashley was disruptive. She did not follow orders and was defiant to staff and to others. Both print and television media have reported extensively on this case. Smith's story was twice featured on CBC's *the fifth estate*. An episode called "Out of Control," which aired in January 2010, introduced viewers to her life and death. A second episode about the Smith case, "Behind the Wall," appeared the following November. This case has rocked the public's sensibilities by giving people a rare glimpse into Canada's correctional facilities. Another reason for the public's shock is that the news coverage repeatedly referred to the incident in Moncton, New Brunswick, in which Ashley, at the age of 15, was charged for throwing a crab apple at a Canada Post worker. The media gave the impression that Ashley's transfer to the adult penitentiary system had come about because of this minor offence.

In fact, the crab apple incident followed a series of convictions for minor offences, for which Ashley received terms of probation and a **deferred custody and supervision order**. There were numerous attempts to provide Ashley with alternatives to the youth justice system, but a lack of resources and no clear treatment plan or diagnosis for her mental illness resulted in her continued defiance and return to closed custody at the New Brunswick Youth Centre (NBYC) in the Miramichi. Ashley's pattern of custody followed by community release

> **deferred custody and supervision order**
> A community-based alternative to a custodial sentence. A judge may order a youth to be placed in custody but then defer custody and release the youth into the community subject to conditions and supervision. The order must not exceed six months. If the youth breaches any of the conditions, he or she may be placed back in custody to complete the remainder of the sentence.

continued until she turned 18 and an application was made to transfer her to the adult system. By the time of the transfer hearing, Ashley had accumulated further criminal charges; the custody time that these charges added to her sentence required that she be placed in an adult penitentiary. She was subsequently moved from penitentiary to penitentiary across Canada until she took her own life in a supervised segregation cell. What went wrong?

Ashley was adopted at five days old and, according to her adoptive parents' reports, had a normal childhood. Early in Ashley's adolescence, however, there was a change in her behaviour, according to her parents. The school system also observed this change. At age 12, Smith received a six-week suspension after she and a friend were caught buying marijuana at school. She started acting out, "playing chicken" in the street with oncoming traffic. By age 13, Ashley was repeatedly being suspended from school for her disruptive behaviour. According to the school forms that tracked her behaviour, Ashley was disciplined for bullying, verbal threats, a disrespectful attitude, and non-compliance. She also stalked one of her teachers. She had very few friends. She was banned from most public areas, including the public transit system, the mall, and her school. Her mother sought the help of a private psychologist, who found no signs of mental illness in Ashley but clear indications of behavioural problems. In a single semester in 2002, Ashley committed 17 infractions of school rules. For these infractions, as well as for being disrespectful and disruptive in class, she received many suspensions. Ashley was removed from the regular school system and sent for half days to an alternative high school. Her parents reported that their relationship with Ashley was strained; she defied their rules, viewing inappropriate content on the internet, speaking with strangers in chat rooms, and racking up long-distance charges of up to $1,600 a month.

Ashley's trouble with the law began in March 2002, when she was 14. Her offences were related to public disturbances, trespass, and violence. For example, she made harassing telephone calls to people she didn't know, assaulted strangers on the streets, insulted a parking attendant, and was banned from public transportation for insulting passengers and drivers. A youth court ordered a one-year probation and, due to the number of Ashley's offences, a referral to the province's Intensive Support Program (ISP), which provides supplementary guidance for youth assessed to be at high risk of re-offending. Despite the extra monitoring and support, Ashley continued to have problems following rules, and she accumulated additional charges.

New Brunswick's Youth Treatment Program team sent Ashley for a 34-day assessment at the Pierre Caissie Centre in Moncton, a six-bed residential program. The psychiatrist ruled out depression, but in an addendum to the report referred to her "narcissistic personality traits." Under the category of "diagnostic impressions," the psychiatric assessment stated that Ashley suffered from "learning disorder, ADHD, [and] borderline personality disorder." The psychological assessment recommended that Ashley's parents receive counselling in how to cope with an "oppositional defiant youth" and that everyone work together in dealing with Ashley's behaviour. While she was at the Pierre Caissie Centre, Ashley's anti-social behaviour escalated; the police were called twice on account of her assaulting staff. It was decided that Ashley's outbursts were negatively affecting the assessments of the other five residents at this very small facility, so her stay was reduced to 27 days and she was remanded to the New Brunswick Youth Centre (NBYC) for one month. Within a few weeks at NBYC, Ashley was responsible for over 30 recorded infractions, which ranged from refusing staff orders and becoming aggressive, to making threats of self-harm. This resulted in Ashley being charged institutionally, removed from the unit, placed in isolation ("therapeutic quiet"), and, in many instances, being placed in restraints.

The incident with the crab apples followed this initial period of incarceration. Rather than putting Ashley back into secure custody, where she had difficulty following the rules, the court placed Ashley in open custody in a foster-home environment. Over the course of two weeks, Ashley was moved through three different foster homes because of her continually defiant behaviour. At the end of the third placement, she had to be removed from a locked bathroom, threatening self-harm with a broken light bulb. She was placed back in the NBYC. From this point on, the pattern continued of Ashley's being incarcerated, then released on community supervision, and then remanded when she incurred additional charges (such as breach of probation, common assault, trespassing, and causing a disturbance).

In less than three months, Ashley was in and out of the NBYC five times. After being released on community supervision, she would either breach her conditions or commit a new offence that would get her sent back to remand at the youth jail. Her lengthiest sentence of incarceration began at the end of December and lasted until February of the following year. Within hours of her February release, she was arrested for pulling a fire alarm and breaching probation, which put her back in the NBYC for an additional 75 days. Further criminal charges were filed and more days were added to the sentence she was already serving. The upshot was a sentence of 14 months, to be served at the NBYC.

Ashley spent approximately three years in custody at the NBYC, where she had over 800 incident reports, with institutional charges resulting from over 500 of these incidents. As reported by New Brunswick ombudsman

Bernard Richard (Ombudsman and Child and Youth Advocate [Ombudsman], 2008, p. 19), "it was nothing out of the ordinary for Ashley to have anywhere from one to five reported and documented incidents per day." Ashley had 158 self-harm incidents while at the NBYC. In addition, she accumulated 50 criminal charges. Many of these came about through the efforts of correctional staff or of other health professionals to prevent or stop her self-harming behaviours.

In January 2006, Ashley turned 18, which meant that if she committed any new offences she would be treated as an adult offender. Richard (Ombudsman, 2008, p. 24) reports that senior staff at the NBYC explained to Ashley what the consequences of her offending behaviour would be, now that she had adult status. The staff recorded that Ashley seemed to understand these consequences and was trying to abide by the rehabilitation plan. However, the familiar pattern asserted itself; Ashley would try to follow the institution's rules and plans but would eventually have one of the outbursts which, she indicated later, she was not able to control.

The superintendent of the NBYC, acting in his role as provincial director, decided to apply, under s. 92 of the *Youth Criminal Justice Act*, to have Ashley transferred to the adult system. Section 92 provides that the judge responsible for deciding on a transfer must consider whether such a move is in the best interests of the young person or of the public. In the two court hearings regarding this transfer, it was suggested that the adult system, compared with the youth system, would provide Ashley with a greater opportunity to attend programs that would assist in her rehabilitation. Ashley, for her part, informed the court, in an affidavit, about her fear of entering the adult system:

> Although I know that my record looks bad, I would never intentionally hurt anyone. I am really scared about the thought of going to an adult facility with dangerous people. It has occupied my mind for a long time. I have wanted to behave to ensure that I would not ever go to adult and was sure that I would succeed. (Ombudsman, 2008, p. 26)

In Ashley's affidavit, she also indicated her belief that she could, with time, "get better and do something productive with my life" (Ombudsman, 2008, p. 25). The judge decided that Ashley should be transferred to the adult system. Within a few hours of her transfer to the Saint John Regional Correctional Centre (SJRCC), Ashley had been sent to segregation and threatened with both pepper spray and a Taser for not complying with institutional rules.

Ashley had 34 incident reports over the 26 days of her incarceration at the SJRCC. As she had at the NBYC, she spent most of this time in segregation.

Her behaviour disqualified her from the programs that had earlier been identified as a possible benefit of her transfer to the adult system. During her short stay, she was threatened with a Taser seven times and with pepper spray twice. According to reports made by the New Brunswick Child and Youth Advocate, the mobile mental health team was not called in to deal with Ashley's outbursts. The reasons given to the advocate were that this team was reserved for situations in which the individual was "really very distraught … really out of control … and we really couldn't get a handle on it" (Ombudsman, 2008, p. 26). In other words, the correctional staff felt that they had the necessary correctional tools to handle Ashley's acting-out behaviour.

On October 24, 2006, Ashley appeared in adult court to answer to the criminal charges laid against her while she was at the NBYC, where she was now remanded for an additional 348 days of custody. An application to have Ashley's youth custodial sentences be treated as if they were adult sentences was approved. When the new custody was added to the already existing 1,455 days, it meant that Ashley's time exceeded the provincial requirement of two years less a day, and she had to be transferred to a federal institution. In 2006, at the age of 18, on what would be her last Halloween, she entered the federal penitentiary (Nova Institution for Women) in Nova Scotia.

In less than 12 months in federal custody, Ashley was moved 17 times between three federal penitentiaries, two treatment facilities, two external hospitals, and one provincial correctional facility, and she moved across four of the five Correctional Service of Canada (CSC) regions (Nova Scotia, Quebec, Ontario, Saskatchewan). Howard Sapers, the federal correctional investigator, told the *Toronto Star* that senior corrections officials were aware that Ashley was in trouble during this period; they had read the many reports concerning her: "In the last 11 months of her life, her name appeared on at least 150 'situation reports' filed by federal penitentiaries detailing Smith's attempts to hurt herself or others" (Zlomislic, 2009). Ashley was continuously housed in administrative segregation (that is, solitary confinement) as she had been at the NBYC. During her short stays in the Regional Psychiatric Centre in Saskatchewan and in a provincial mental health centre in Montreal, she was isolated from the other patients.

Although CSC knew that Ashley had never received a full psychological and psychiatric assessment prior to entering federal corrections, no assessment was ever completed. Sapers (2008, p. 6) explains that because Ashley was constantly transferred from one institution to another, she was never in one place long enough for an assessment to be completed or a treatment plan developed. Despite the fact that Ashley had never been fully assessed,

CSC assigned her administrative segregation status for her entire period of incarceration. According to Sapers (2008, p. 7), administrative segregation status is a highly restrictive and, at times, inhumane regime; owing to its severity, it is subject to review every 60 days. In the case of Ashley Smith, however, corrections officials "lifted" her status whenever she was physically moved from one institution to another, thereby circumventing the requirement for a 60-day review. This meant that Ashley spent all of her time alone, in a security gown, to protect her from self-harm. A psychologist who examined the case interpreted some of Ashley's self-injurious behaviour as a means of drawing the staff into her cell "in order to alleviate the boredom, loneliness and desperation she had been experiencing as a result of her prolonged isolation" (Sapers, 2008, p. 8).

Ashley Smith took her life in the early morning of October 19, 2007, less than one year from the date she was placed in the adult correctional system. Sapers has written the following about her suicide (2008, p. 8):

> In the end, Ms. Smith was identified by an institutional psychologist as being highly suicidal. With misinformed and poorly communicated decisions as a backdrop, Ms. Smith died—wearing nothing but a suicide smock, lying on the floor of her segregation cell, with a ligature tied tightly around her neck—under the direct observation of several correctional staff.

Kim Pate, who is executive director of the Elizabeth Fry Society, reviewed videotapes of Ashley's treatment while under the care of CSC. In a sworn affidavit, Pate (2011) reported a number of instances where Ashley's human rights were violated: "Ashley was physically restrained for hours at a time"; "Ashley's requests to have her tampon changed were ignored for hours"; "Ashley was left in a wet security gown for an extended period of time while strapped to a metal gurney." In 2011, Ashley's family launched an $11 million lawsuit against CSC for wrongful death. This case was settled out of court for an undisclosed amount of money.

It could be argued that, under the UN Convention on the Rights of the Child, Ashley Smith's human rights were violated long before her death. Article 40 of this convention requires that children who have violated the penal law be treated in a manner consistent with their age and with the goal of promoting the child's reintegration and constructive participation in society.

Ashley's case highlights the need to take mental health problems into account when making criminal-justice policy. It is estimated that one in five Canadians will experience a mental health problem. You may remember from the last chapter that this rate is higher for incarcerated offenders; a recent report shows a 60–70 percent increase in the rate of mental illness among federally incarcerated offenders since 1997 (Mental Health Commission of Canada [MHCC], 2012, p. 43). Bingham and Sutton (2012, p. 26) report that one in three federally sentenced women suffer from a mental illness and that nearly half of these have engaged in self-harm. The MHCC (2012, p. 9) document reveals that only one in four children or youth experiencing a mental illness reported having sought and received services and treatment. Further, most of the approximately 4,000 Canadians who commit suicide annually were dealing with a mental health problem (MHCC, 2012, p. 17). According to the MHCC (2012) recommendations, we cannot address the overrepresentation of youth with mental health problems in the criminal justice system without providing these youth with timely access to services, treatments, and supports in the community. According to the MHCC, 85,000 children in Canada are experiencing conduct disorders; it is estimated that preventing these disorders in a single child through early intervention could result in a lifetime savings of $280,000 (MHCC, 2012, p. 126).

The following two chapters will consider the history and evolution of youth justice policy in Canada, outlining the key legal distinctions in the way young people and adults are dealt with. As these chapters will note, the Canadian justice system has always recognized that the inexperience of young offenders reduces their accountability. Juvenile courts at the turn of the century focused on preventing misguided and misdirected children from entering adult lives of crime and on protecting them from the harshness of the adult penitentiary system. Think about the recent case of Ashley Smith as you read these chapters and ask yourself whether her situation would have been better or worse during earlier periods of our youth justice system.

What Do You Think?

CSC issued a new "Commissioner's Directive" in July 2011, in direct response to the incidents surrounding Ashley Smith's suicide. The objective of this policy is to use the least restrictive measures necessary to ensure the safety of prisoners who are self-injurious or suicidal. The CSC goal, in other words, is to preserve life and prevent serious bodily injury while maintaining prisoners' dignity. You will recall from the previous case study that the *Safe Streets and Communities Act* has removed the "least restrictive measures" provision from the *Corrections and Conditional Release Act*. What will this mean for inmates with mental health issues?

REFERENCES

Bingham, E., & Sutton, R. (2012). *Cruel, inhuman and degrading? Canada's treatment of federally-sentenced women with mental health issues.* University of Toronto: International Human Rights Program, Faculty of Law. Retrieved from http://media.thestar.topscms.com/acrobat/ba/55/3c47d5da4a599c0f879c56ebe3e6.pdf

Friedli, L.I., & Parsonage, M. (2009). *Promoting mental health and preventing mental illness: The economic case for investment in Wales.* Cardiff: All Wales Mental Health Promotion Network. Retrieved from http://www.centreformentalhealth.org.uk/pdfs/Promoting_mental_health_Wales.pdf

Mental Health Commission of Canada. (2012). *Changing directions, changing lives: The mental health strategy for Canada.* Calgary. Retrieved from http://strategy.mentalhealthcommission.ca/pdf/strategy-images-en.pdf

Ombudsman and Child and Youth Advocate. (2008). *The Ashley Smith report.* New Brunswick: Office of the Ombudsman & Child and Youth Advocate. Retrieved from http://www.gnb.ca/0073/PDF/AshleySmith-e.pdf

Pate, K. (2011). Affidavit in the matter of an inquest into the death of Ashley Smith. February 28. Retrieved from http://fcbarristers.com/Falconer/documents/AffidavitofKimPate.pdf

Sapers, H. (2008). *A preventable death.* Ottawa: Office of the Correctional Investigator. Retrieved from http://www.oci-bec.gc.ca/rpt/pdf/oth-aut/oth-aut20080620-eng.pdf

Smetanin, P., Stiff, D., Briante, C., Adair, C., Ahmad, S., & Khan, M. (2011). *The life and economic impact of major mental illnesses in Canada: 2011 to 2041.* RiskAnalytica, on behalf of the Mental Health Commission of Canada.

Standing Committee on Public Safety and National Security. (2010). Mental health and drug and alcohol addiction in the federal correctional system. Retrieved from http://www.parl.gc.ca/HousePublications/Publication.aspx?DocId=4864852&Language=E&Mode=1&Parl=40&Ses=3

Zlomislic, Diana. (2009, October 10). From generous girl to "caged animal." *Toronto Star.* Retrieved from http://www.thestar.com/news/canada/article/708429--from-generous-girl-to-caged-animal

Thinking About Youth Justice: Historical Roots and Contemporary Approaches

LEARNING OBJECTIVES

After reading this chapter, students will be able to:

- Understand the ways in which young criminals have been dealt with throughout history and compare current approaches to youth justice practice.
- Explain the impact of the ideological models of criminal justice discussed in Chapter 1 on the development of youth justice policy in Canada.
- Consider how public misperceptions about youth generally and young offenders in particular affect the creation and implementation of youth justice policy.

CHAPTER OUTLINE

Introduction

Historically, we have treated young criminals in a way that recognizes their age and stage of maturity, and have accordingly handled their sentencing with a view to providing them with as much guidance as possible to help them avoid a lifetime of crime. Many young people commit offences as part of a process of growing up and taking risks. As a society, we recognize that fact and look upon minor misbehaviour as a valuable lesson that may prevent young people from engaging in more serious criminal activity in the future. However, when young people do commit serious offences, or "adult crime" as it has been coined, society is hard pressed not to respond with more severe interventions and punishments. As mentioned in the case of Ashley Smith, there were a number of attempts to keep her out of the youth justice system by using alternative sanctions. These approaches will be discussed in more detail in the next chapter. However, keep in mind that when the youth justice system did not have the necessary resources to handle her acting-out behaviour, the default was to send her to the adult penitentiary system. This chapter will explore the conflicting demands to treat youth with care and support as a form of prevention, and the societal demand to punish youthful offenders who violate the criminal law.

The History of Youth and Justice

The Good and Evil Test

As far back as Hebrew law and the writing of Greek philosophers, there is evidence that children were not held to the same degree of responsibility for the commission of crimes as their adult counterparts. According to Aristotle, children were seen as being able to act voluntarily, but like animals and the insane, children were not capable of premeditation and so could not be considered morally responsible for their acts. The legal doctrine of *mens rea* (guilty mind) can be traced to the moral philosophy of these early writers, as was discussed in Chapter 5 (The History and Structure of Criminal Law). The concept of "free will," or the ability to make your own choices, is the cornerstone of the issue surrounding responsibility for crime. You may recall that the crime-control and justice models, discussed in Chapter 1, both rely on the notion that individuals commit crimes based on free will as opposed to deterministic factors outside their control.

The 13th-century medieval Italian philosopher St. Thomas Aquinas wrote of the distinction between children and adults, arguing that there are many things that are allowed in the young for which older people are punished or at least blamed (Davis-Barron, 2009, p. 7). Throughout history, there are many accounts of children not having the ability to form intent in the same manner in which "fools" could not be held responsible because of their inability to choose the "good" from the "evil" (*conisaunt de bien ne de mal*). The

doli incapax doctrine
Belief that a child of tender years is incapable of an unlawful act.

doli incapax doctrine applied to children under the age of seven, who were considered incapable of evil intent. At this time, males were deemed to have reached puberty at age 14; females, at age 12. Children between the seven and 14 were considered accountable for their actions, but only if the proof of their intention to act was clear and certain.

By the time of the reign of Queen Elizabeth I in the late 16th century, children and the insane were excluded from criminal responsibility because they failed to possess the necessary mental capacity to form the intent to commit a crime. They were treated as "non-persons" because of their lack of understanding, intelligence, and moral discretion. During the 17th century, the "good and evil" test continued to be paramount in cases involving children. In cases of children above the age of 14 but under the age of 21, the test was used to determine whether such individuals should be subjected to capital punishment, as would others of "full age." The "good and evil" test continued to be the main test of criminal responsibility through the 18th and early part of the 19 centuries, but increasingly, the term "right from wrong" was used synonymously with "good from evil." This practice in English law became entrenched in common law and became criminal law throughout North America. It was incorporated into Canada's first *Criminal Code* in 1892 (Reid, 2011).

> ### SIDEBAR
> ## "Good and Evil" Test
> A child could be found guilty only if the state could establish that the child was able to distinguish between the concepts of good and evil. If a reasonable doubt were raised concerning the ability to perceive the difference, the child could not be punished.

The defence of *doli incapax* was the only special safeguard for children accused of crimes, but it was not uniformly applied. For example, if young persons were found to not fall within the boundaries of this doctrine, they faced the same penalties as adults did, were housed in the same jails and the same cells as adults, and were subject to the same rules and punitive responses (Carrigan, 1988). If young persons before the court were found to understand and appreciate the nature and consequences of their actions, then they were treated as adults would be under similar circumstances.

In Canada, the doli incapax *doctrine prevailed until its repeal with the* Young Offenders Act *in 1984, when the minimum age of criminal responsibility was set at age 12 and the maximum age jurisdiction of the youth court was set at 18 years.*

John Howard (1777, p. 21) clearly stated that young people should not be housed in the same facilities as adults:

> If it were the wish and aim of Magistrates to effect the destruction present and future of young delinquents, they could not devise a more effectual method, than to confine them so long in our prisons, those seats and seminaries of idleness and every vice.

Some historians have written about the discovery of childhood as a distinct period in Western Europe during the 17th century. Perhaps the best-known work is that of Philippe Ariès from France, who wrote a book called *Centuries of Childhood* in 1962. He wrote that children were not treated differently from adults during the Middle Ages and were absorbed into the adult world between the ages of five and seven, sharing in the work of their adult counterparts (Ariès, 1962). Perhaps most noteworthy is Ariès (p. 42) discussion of the portrayal of children in the art of the Middle Ages, where they appeared as **miniature adults**. Other historians have taken exception to the "discovery of childhood" that was attributed to a set point in time by Ariès, arguing

miniature adults
How children were often depicted in the art of the Middle Ages—i.e., as short adults, with adult facial features.

that his thesis was filled with personal religious and ideological beliefs about the role of parents in childrearing and the need to maintain traditional conservative family values (Smandych, 2001; Gleason, Myers, Paris, & Strong-Boag, 2010). Smandych (2012) suggests that while the historical literature points out that 17th-century European values and sensibilities about the changing role of childhood may have had some influence on the manner in which young people who broke the law were dealt with, there have been additional local, national, and international influences that have also shaped the creation of juvenile justice. We will now turn to the early youth court in Canada.

Early History of Youth Justice in Canada

One of the earliest issues facing colonial Canada in the late 1800s was dealing with the large numbers of orphans who were left to fend for themselves in the new country. While numerous families crossed the Atlantic Ocean from the British Isles, many of the adults died en route. Not only were children orphaned, but many were deserted and abandoned "due to the great concourse of dissolute abandoned women" (i.e., women who were abandoned, poor, and attempting to win favour with the men) who frequented every military garrison. The Irish famine brought additional numbers of orphaned children during the 1840s, with estimates as high as 500 orphans in Montreal alone. Some troublesome children were sent to the colonies, as were other unwanted members of society from slums, jails, poorhouses, and orphanages. Under the sponsorship of child immigration agencies, it is reported that between 1873 and 1903, more than 95,000 "at risk" children came to Canada (Department of Justice [DOJ], 2004, p. 1).

The majority of crime that was documented for young people during these early settlement years was minor in nature, similar to the offences we see today. According to reports, the 300 youth in prison in New Brunswick between 1846 and 1857 were convicted of drunkenness, theft, and vagrancy (i.e., no fixed address) (DOJ, 2004, p. 3). These were the same patterns of criminal behaviour that had sent them to the colonies in the first place!

Adult reformers started to raise the issue of housing youth and adults in the same facilities, suggesting that the prisons and reformatories served as nothing more than professional schools of crime. George Brown was a Scottish-born journalist who became a politician following his arrival in Upper Canada, and went on to found and edit the national newspaper *The Globe and Mail*. Brown voiced concerns about the horrific conditions within the prisons and penitentiaries after touring Kingston Penitentiary, in his seminal royal commission report in 1849. In this two-volume report, Brown discussed the case of a 10-year-old boy who was whipped 57 times over an eight-month period for "staring and laughing." Another case he reported was that of an 11-year-old French Canadian boy who was given 12 lashes on Christmas Eve for speaking French. This report compelled Canadians to reconsider the philosophy of having young people in the same prisons as adults:

> It is distressing to think that no distinction is now made between the child who has strayed for the first time from the path of honesty … and the hardened offender of mature years. All are consigned together to the unutterable contamination of the common gaol; and by the lessons there learnt, soon become inmates of the Penitentiary. (Brown Commission, 1849, p. 73)

What Do You Think?

How does the 2007 case of Ashley Smith relate to these comments from George Brown, made in 1849, or to the earlier comments made by John Howard in 1777? In what ways have society's attitudes toward treatment of young offenders changed? How have they stayed the same?

It was becoming common knowledge that children who were committing offences were more often than not victims of poor living conditions and parental neglect, and should therefore not be seen as offenders. Reports show that during this time, in any large community, youth could be "found loitering around the streets, idle, neglected, and undisciplined." Much of this has been attributed to "parental neglect, a lack of proper diet, malnutrition, unsanitary living conditions, drunken and dissolute parents, and inadequate or no medical care." In addition to youth crime, these young people were not interested in the newly developed public schools and were often charged with truancy (i.e., not being in school) (DOJ, 2004, p. 5). Boudreau (2012, p. 121) suggests that the number of young people who sold newspapers and engaged in other street trades was an influential factor in the insistence that young people be off the streets and attend school. The idea was that if young people were not visible as "street urchins," the general population would feel safer from the perceived concern of rising youth crime. Lobby groups of middle-class reformers became known as the **Child Savers**, raising awareness about the need to do something for these children; this was the beginning of a new era in thinking about youth in conflict with the law. The move away from the harsh treatment of offenders and the subsequent focus on treatment, education, and rehabilitation was also happening in the United States. The

Child Savers
Group of middle-class reformers in 19th-century North America that lobbied for public schools, public health, and the creation of a separate system of youth justice.

focus on the needs of young people who were abandoned and neglected gave the push for reform to ensure that these children and youth had the same benefits of guidance and assistance that might be afforded their peers who had families.

Davis-Barron (2009, p. 38) reported that in introducing the federal bill that became the *Juvenile Delinquents Act* in 1908, the then minister of justice explained the rationale for the legislation as follows:

> WHEREAS it is inexpedient that youthful offenders should be classed or dealt with as ordinary criminals, the welfare of the community demanding that they should on the contrary be guarded against association with crime and criminals, and should be subjected to such wise care, treatment, and control as will tend to check their evil tendencies and to strengthen their better instincts.

The Juvenile Delinquents Act

It was clearly stated in the *Juvenile Delinquents Act* (JDA), s. 26(1), that young people were not to be housed in the same facilities as their adult counterparts:

> No juvenile delinquent shall, under any circumstances, upon or after conviction, be sentenced to or incarcerated in any penitentiary, or county or other gaol, or police station, or any other place in which adults are or may be imprisoned.

However, in those cases where the young person had committed a serious, violent crime, the youth court had a "safety valve" (Doob & Cesaroni, 2004, p. 172), whereby the court could treat the young person as an adult if it was satisfied that "the good of the child and the interests of the community demanded it" (JDA, s. 9(1)).

Unlike legislation which would follow under the *Young Offenders Act* and the *Youth Criminal Justice Act*, direction on the philosophy and principle of the legislation did not appear until s. 38:

> This Act shall be liberally construed in order that its purpose may be carried out; namely, that the care and custody and discipline of a juvenile delinquent shall approximate as nearly as may be that which should be given by his parents, and that as far as practicable every juvenile delinquent shall be treated not as a criminal, but as a misdirected and misguided child, and one needing aid, encouragement, help, and assistance.

parens patriae ("parent of the nation")
The principle that the state acts as a "kindly parent" to dependent delinquents.

The idea of the state providing assistance and guidance to a child in the same manner as a parent would is known as the doctrine of **parens patriae**. The focus of intervention was no longer punishment, but treatment. There was no need for formal court hearings, legal safeguards, or defined sentences because the young person was not before the court to be corrected. Instead, appearing in youth court was seen as an opportunity to save the youth from a life of neglect, poverty, and dysfunction, and for the youth to be given help by those who were in attendance.

In recognition of the importance of preventing the young person from entering a life of crime as an adult, the proceedings were confidential (*in camera*) and the disposition was that the young person was found to be "in a state of delinquency." There were no specified sentences or sentence length (i.e., **indeterminate**). The staff of the court, including the judge, probation officers, and others were looking after the **best interests of the child**, and would provide guidance and assistance. "Delinquents" would receive as much treatment and intervention as was necessary to ensure that they were no longer victimized by neglectful parents. Young persons became wards of the state in the same way that children who are in need of protection in cases of child abuse are removed from the custody of their parents. When the state, under the doctrine of *parens patriae*, took over the responsibility of rearing a delinquent child, it meant that the young person would be in state care until the age of 21 years (or the legal age of majority).

Treating the Needs of the Whole Delinquent

From the time the JDA was enacted in 1908 until its replacement 76 years later with the *Young Offenders Act* in 1984, the youth justice system was philosophically rooted in the welfare model, as discussed in the first chapter. The juvenile court was not concerned about legal rights of due process, nor was it particularly concerned about the crime that had been committed. Those young people who broke the law, any law, were brought before the court to be given aid, encouragement, help, and assistance. It didn't matter if the youth had committed a criminal offence, was truant from school, was habitually late for curfew, or had spit on the sidewalk, jaywalked, or trespassed—the juvenile court was seen as a safe place to receive help for misdeeds. Parents could also receive some reprieve from their **incorrigible** children, who could be "cured" of their delinquent tendencies.

Further, a juvenile could be found to be in a state of delinquency for offences that were only relevant to youth, known as status offences. The juvenile court judges controlled the movements and decision making of young persons until such time as they were no longer "delinquent." Providing treatment and rehabilitation to these "wayward" youth often meant that long periods of custody in a "training school," "industrial school," or "reformatory" were imposed on young persons who may not have committed any criminal offence, but had been deemed incorrigible, truant, or otherwise disruptive to

indeterminate
A disposition for juveniles that was not fixed in length. A young person could be held in custody until the youth was deemed by correctional authorities to no longer be seen as a threat to society or to be rehabilitated.

best interests of the child
The principle that children's interests are different from those of adults, and that all decisions affecting children must be considered in light of article 3 of the UN Convention on the Rights of the Child as being focused on what is best for the children, and not what is best for their parents.

incorrigible
Not able to be corrected or improved; beyond the care and control of parents.

MINI CASE STUDY

Marlene Moore

Canada's first female dangerous offender, Marlene Moore, entered reform school at age 13 as an incorrigible child. When asked to complete a series of questions for a psychologist, she wrote, in one response, that "My friends don't know … *I am afraid of jails.*" Marlene was incarcerated except for brief periods of time from the age of 13 until she committed suicide when she was 31 years old while imprisoned at Ontario's Kingston Prison for Women. Her story is recounted in the book *Rock-a-Bye Baby: A Death Behind Bars* (Kershaw & Lasovich, 1991).

There were many injustices for youth under the *Juvenile Delinquents Act*, where young people were being "treated" for offences that would otherwise not yield significant sanctions had they been adults.

the maintenance of an orderly community. The juvenile court's inability to separate the issue of youth control from that of youth welfare was widely criticized. This led to extensive consultation and discussion regarding the nature and purpose of the juvenile justice system over a 25-year period (Reid-MacNevin, 1991).

By way of summary, the JDA was based on the doctrine of *parens patriae*, its main purpose being to provide for the unfortunate circumstances that young persons found themselves in. The primary concern of the juvenile court was not due process or even the type of crime that had been committed, but rather to remove the youth from the care and control of their parents, and have the state assume the parental role (Reid & Zuker, 2004). In the era under the JDA from 1908 to 1982, the majority of children who appeared in youth court were not represented by legal counsel (Wilson, 2003). The lack of procedural and legal safeguards under the JDA was criticized because somewhere between 95 and 99 percent of the children charged entered guilty pleas (Chapman, 1971, p. 92).

SIDEBAR

Status Offences

Status offences are acts that are considered illegal only because of the age status of the offender. Examples of juvenile status offences include truancy, incorrigibility, and sexual precociousness (i.e., early interest in sexual activities).

Youth Justice in Canada, 1982–2003

Due Process and Accountability Join Best Interests

With the proclamation of the *Canadian Charter of Rights and Freedoms* in 1982 came great criticism for the provisions of the JDA that denied children basic rights of due process. The Act itself stated that no proceedings were to be set aside because of any informality or irregularity where it appeared that the disposition of the case was in the best interests of the child. Further, the JDA had considerable discretion and variability across the country, with different maximum age jurisdictions from province to province; in some jurisdictions the age limit was different for boys and girls (Reid-MacNevin & Kappel, 2003). After almost 25 years of discussion and debate, starting with an intensive review in 1965, the *Young Offenders Act* was proclaimed in 1984.

The Young Offenders Act

As was the case prior to enacting the JDA, much debate centred around the philosophical orientation of the law and such issues as punishment versus treatment, flexible adjudication versus procedural rights, and federal versus provincial jurisdictions (Reid & Reitsma-Street, 2001). Trying to balance the competing interests, the drafters of the 1984 statute set out a series of principles that were to govern the philosophical direction of the new legislation. The *Young Offenders Act* (YOA) was an attempt to balance the social responsibility that young persons must bear for their criminal conduct (ss. 3(1)(b), (c), (d)) against their special needs (ss. 3(1)(a), (c), (f)) and the rights of individual youth (ss. 3(1)(a), (d), (f), (g)). Further, the YOA acknowledged the responsibility of the community to take reasonable measures to prevent and control youthful crime (s. 3(1)(b)). The Act marked

TABLE 13.1 Four Models of Criminal Justice Reflected in the Principles of the YOA

Community change	Society has the responsibility to take reasonable measures to prevent criminal conduct by young persons	YOA s. 3(1)(b)
Welfare	… having regard to the needs of young persons and the best interests of their families	YOA s. 3(1)(f)
Justice	Young persons have the right in every instance where they have rights or freedoms that may be affected by this Act, to be informed as to what those rights and freedoms are	YOA s. 3(1)(g)
Crime control	Society … must be afforded the necessary protection from illegal behaviour	YOA s. 3(1)(b)

Source: Reid & Reitsma-Street (2001).

a shift from the historical child welfare model of the JDA to more of an adult criminal law model (Reid & Zuker, 2004).

The YOA contained principles reflective of four models of criminal justice, and are shown with the relevant section of the **Declaration of Principle** section outlining the ways in which youth are to be dealt with.

Declaration of Principle
The guiding philosophy of the *Young Offenders Act* that is laid out in 13 phrases following a definition of terms. This was a significant change from the *Juvenile Delinquents Act*, which did not explain the philosophy until the end of the legislation.

What Do You Think?

As outlined in Chapter 1, the four models of criminal justice represent various ideological perspectives on such questions as how we as a society view the causes of crime and how we should intervene in the lives of those who come in conflict with the law. Having the principle section of the legislation define how to deal with young persons in four differing ways could be seen as confusing when compared with the JDA, which had only one focus. What issues can you think of that might surface, given that different models are being considered simultaneously?

The implementation of the YOA, with its conflicting goals of rehabilitation and the protection of society, led to an increased use of the youth court and an even greater use of custodial sanctions than had been experienced under the JDA. Many judges, guided by the Act's philosophy of crime control and attention to deterrence, imposed short sentences in custody that came to be referred to as a "short, sharp shock" (Doob & Cesaroni, 2004). The proliferation of these short sentences (averaging about six months) meant that Canada gained the dubious distinction of having the highest youth incarceration rate in the world!

On February 14, 2001, the minister of justice at the time, Anne McLellan, rose in the House of Commons to speak on the first reading of Bill C-7, the proposed *Youth Criminal Justice Act*:

> [T]he existing YOA has resulted in the highest youth incarceration rate in the western world, including our neighbours to the south, the United States. Young persons in Canada often receive harsher custodial sentences than adults receive for the same type of offence. Almost 80% of custodial sentences are for non-violent offences. (Canada, House of Commons, 2001, p. 1530)

The focus on deterrence, within the crime-control model, meant that youth who violated their conditions of probation or who showed a similar lack of respect for the law were likely to find themselves serving a short term of custody. These youth would have formerly been seen as "misguided and misdirected" under the JDA; however, under the YOA, such behaviour was criminalized and youth were charged with administration of justice offences. These offences include failure to comply with a disposition (i.e., sentence), failure to appear in court, breach of probation conditions, and contempt against the youth court. Escaping lawful custody and being unlawfully at large are also administration of justice offences; the latter was quite often used in the case of young offenders walking away from group homes that had been designated as places of open custody. Bell (2012, p. 86) reported that administration of justice offences were more likely to result in a custodial sentence than were most other offence categories, with more than 35 percent of failure-to-comply convictions resulting in such dispositions.

This was addressed by a variety of consultations throughout the country, with concerns being raised that using the provisions within the YOA related to **diversion** and community-based sanctions should be a priority to combat the rising rates of youth custody (DOJ, 1998). Even though there had been numerous amendments to the legislation between 1984 and 1998, the federal government decided to scrap the legislation and begin anew with the introduction of the *Youth Criminal Justice Act* (YCJA) in 2001. The YCJA received royal assent on February 19, 2002 and was proclaimed in force as of April 2003; this Act is the current legislation for dealing with young offenders in Canada.

diversion
Sentencing approach in which offenders are given an opportunity to perform some community service or are referred to a community agency to better address their needs instead of being processed through the youth court system. Under the *Youth Criminal Justice Act*, diversion is called "extrajudicial measures and sanctions."

Youth Justice Today: The Youth Criminal Justice Act

The YCJA addressed one of the main criticisms of the YOA by providing a statement of purpose and principle for sentencing young offenders. A fundamental principle of adult sentencing, as discussed in other chapters, is that of proportionality. There had been no mention of this principle under the YOA, and now there is an entire section focusing on the principles of sentencing. Another similarity to the adult model is the change in the term "dispositions" to "sentences" under the YCJA. These will be further discussed in the next chapter.

The *Young Offenders Act* was criticized for the lack of direction in the philosophy of its principles, because any one of the four ideological models could be used to justify an intervention with youth before the courts. This lack of direction could and did lead to a great deal of inconsistency from one court to the next. The drafters of the YCJA wanted to ensure that there was no confusion about the overriding philosophy of youth justice in Canada. They therefore inserted a **preamble** to the legislation, outlining "moral and legal standards" for the manner in which young people are to be dealt with in the youth justice system (Tustin & Lutes, 2011). The preamble mentions

preamble
The introductory part of a statute that, while not legally enforceable, contains significant statements from Parliament about the values on which the legislation is based. While technically outside the enacted legislation, the preamble is meant to guide the statute's interpretation by the courts, including the Supreme Court of Canada.

SIDEBAR

Themes Within the Youth Criminal Justice Act

Theme 1: The intent is long-term protection of the public through prevention, rehabilitation, and ensuring meaningful consequences for young people who commit offences (s. 3(1)).

    a) the youth criminal justice system is intended to

        i. *prevent* crime by addressing the circumstances underlying a young person's offending behaviour,

        ii. *rehabilitate* young persons who commit offences and reintegrate them into society, and

        iii. ensure that a young person is subject to meaningful *consequences* for his or her offence

in order to promote the long-term *protection* of the public.

Theme 2: Establish a separate system for young persons emphasizing rehabilitation and reintegration, accountability, and timely interventions (s. 3(1)(b)).

    b) the criminal justice system for young persons must be separate from that of adults and emphasize the following:

        i. *rehabilitation* and *reintegration*,

        ii. fair and proportionate *accountability* that is consistent with the greater dependency of young persons and their reduced level of maturity,

        iii. enhanced *procedural protection* to ensure that young persons are treated fairly and that their rights, including their right to privacy, are protected,

        iv. *timely intervention* that reinforces the link between the offending behaviour and its consequences, and

        v. the *promptness* and speed with which persons responsible for enforcing this Act must act, given young persons' perception of time.

Theme 3: The response to young persons who commit offences should reinforce respect, encourage repair of harm done, be meaningful, and respect differences and special needs (s. 3(1)(c)).

    c) within the limits of fair and proportionate accountability, the measures taken against young persons who commit offences should

        i. reinforce *respect* for societal values,

        ii. encourage the *repair of harm done* to victims and the community,

iii. be *meaningful* for the individual young person given his or her needs and level of development and, where appropriate, involve the parents, the extended family, the community, and social or other agencies in the young person's rehabilitation and reintegration, and

iv. *respect* gender, ethnic, cultural, and linguistic *differences* and respond to the needs of *[A]boriginal young persons* and of young *persons with special requirements*.

Theme 4: Special considerations for youth, victims, and parents (s. 3(1)(d)).

d) special considerations apply in respect of proceedings against young persons and, in particular,

i. young persons have rights and freedoms in their own right, such as the right to be heard in the course of and to participate in the processes, other than the decision to prosecute, that lead to decisions that affect them, and young persons have special guarantees of their rights and freedoms,

ii. *victims* should be treated with courtesy, compassion, and respect for their dignity and privacy, and should suffer the minimum degree of inconvenience as a result of their involvement with the youth criminal justice system,

iii. *victims* should be provided with information about the proceedings and given an opportunity to participate and be heard, and

iv. *parents* should be informed of measures or proceedings involving their children and encouraged to support them in addressing their offending behaviour.

Source: Reid-MacNevin & Kappel (2003).

other prevailing legislation, including the Charter, as well as the UN Convention on the Rights of the Child (CRC), to underscore the goal of protecting the rights of young persons. Article 40 of the CRC requires that children who have violated the penal law be treated in a manner consistent with their age and with the desirability of promoting their reintegration and their taking up a constructive role in society. The CRC underscores diversion from criminal proceedings and extrajudicial solutions, and the use of socio-educational interventions; deprivation of liberty should be used only as a last resort. Canada's international obligations to all children who have committed offences support a presumption that juvenile offenders are not to be treated like adults (Reid, 2010).

One of the most significant additions to the new YCJA was that the Declaration of Principle set out four ranked and interlinked statements about the youth court criminal justice system, which:

1. is intended to promote the long-term protection of the public (s. 3(1)(a))
2. is to be separate from the adult criminal justice system (s. 3(1)(b))
3. should reinforce respect, encourage the reparation of harm, and respect differences while being meaningful to the young person (s. 3(1)(c))
4. provides special consideration for youth, victims, and parents (s. 3(1)(d)).

What Do You Think?

Think about the case of Ashley Smith that opened this section and consider the themes outlined above. In what way(s) were these themes upheld? In what way(s) were they ignored? What areas do you think were emphasized in her case?

Now think about the Part One case study. Keeping in mind the details of his youth, what might have been different for J (the offender) if the YCJA had been in place while he was a young person? Identify three factors about J's background that would have influenced your decision about his sentence had he been a young offender at the time of the offence.

Reid and Zuker (2004) suggest that the YCJA reflects at least four ideological models of criminal justice within the Declaration of Principle. Statements drawn from s. 3 of the YCJA that are indicative of the five models discussed in Chapter 1 are provided in Table 13.2.

TABLE 13.2   Five Models of Criminal Justice Reflected in the Principles of the YCJA

Restorative justice	[T]he measures taken against young persons who commit offences should reinforce respect for societal values [and] encourage the repair of harm done to victims and the community	YCJA s. 3(1)(c)(i), (ii)
Community change	[T]he measures taken against young persons who commit offences should ... where appropriate, involve the parents, the extended family, the community and social or other agencies in the young person's rehabilitation and reintegration	YCJA s. 3(1)(c)(iii)
Welfare	[T]he criminal justice system for young persons must be separate from that of adults and emphasize ... rehabilitation and reintegration	YCJA s. 3(1)(b)(i)
Justice	[Y]oung persons have rights and freedoms in their own right, such as a right to be heard in the course of and to participate in the processes, other than the decision to prosecute, that lead to decisions that affect them, and young persons have special guarantees of their rights and freedoms	YCJA s. 3(1)(d)(i)
Crime control	[T]he criminal justice system for young persons must ... emphasize ... timely intervention that reinforces the link between the offending behaviour and its consequences	YCJA s. 3(1)(b)(iv)

What Do You Think?

Look at the other provisions in s. 3 of the YCJA. Where do they fit in terms of the models outlined in Table 13.2 and discussed in more detail in Chapter 1?

Do Young People Know Right from Wrong?

In reviewing the psychosocial literature, there is convincing evidence of changes in moral and cognitive reasoning through the adolescent years. Before the age of ten, children lack the capacity to make moral judgments because there is no awareness of the impact of their actions on others. Children up to the age of 13 lack moral independence from adults, and some research has shown that moral discernment continues to develop up to the age of 17. Both cognitive and moral development continues into the early 20s, with the brain not fully developing until the age of 25.

What Do You Think?

In light of evidence to suggest the brain is not fully developed until the age of 25 years, should the age of criminal responsibility be increased? What age do you think is most appropriate?

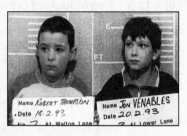

MINI CASE STUDY

The Jamie Bulger Murder

The idea that children and adolescents are not capable of being held responsible for criminal acts seems preposterous to some. There are a number of cases that have been reported in the media that have fuelled this debate. Perhaps the most notorious case was the 1993 murder of 2-year-old Jamie Bulger by a pair of 10-year-old boys in England. Jon Venables and Robert Thompson (the names of the youths were released by the court after the trial, in part due to the public outcry in the media) abducted Jamie from a shopping mall (captured on CCTV), proceeding out of the mall and through the streets. A number of adults saw them and noticed that the young child was crying, but assumed that he was a younger sibling and did not intervene. Venables and Thompson left the toddler on a railroad track, where he was severed in two by a train. Forensic evidence showed that Jamie was dead before being struck by the train. He had suffered a number of skull fractures, so it was difficult to determine which one actually led to his death.

Venables and Thompson are known as the youngest convicted murderers of the 20th century. The sentence was originally set at a minimum of 8 years, but on appeal was increased to 10, and then to 15, which would have meant they would be released at age 25 years. Defence counsel appealed to the European Court of Human Rights, claiming that the boys had not received a fair trial. The court ruled that there had been a violation of article 6 of the European Convention on Human Rights and reduced their sentences to 8 years. They were released in 2001 with a series of conditions for their parole, including curfews and strict reporting requirements. The pair were both given new identities because it was determined that their lives would be in imminent danger upon release. In 2010, Venables was returned to custody for violation of his conditions and additional charges (Franklin & Petley, 1996).

The idea that such a horrendous act could be committed with impunity outraged many and left many to question why we have a separate system of youth justice.

What Do You Think?

In Canada, the minimum age of criminal responsibility is 12 years. Young people under this age who commit offences are dealt with by child welfare authorities as children in need of protection, in much the same way as they were under the former JDA. In some jurisdictions in the United States, the minimum age of criminal responsibility is 5 years. What are the benefits of a child welfare system over a juvenile justice system in dealing with young children who commit crime? What age is the most suitable for the minimum age of criminal responsibility?

The old adage that "The exception does not prove the rule" rings true in the case of youth justice. When a young person has committed a heinous act, the media has a tendency to sensationalize these cases and highlight them as being more common than they are. In fact, they are rare occurrences (Reid, 2004). The public, fed a steady dose of these sensational stories, starts to believe that young offenders are literally "getting away with murder," and various groups begin to put pressure on governments to "do something" about the youth crime problem. It is this balancing of political pressure with the known facts about youth crime that makes the creation of youth justice policy so problematic.

The media tend to sensationalize youth crimes, so they seem more common than they are.

In debunking these myths about youth justice, we are left with a sense that most young persons who come before the court do require guidance and assistance from the adults in their lives. The paradox lies in the minority of cases where a young person commits a very serious offence. Western nations have historically retained the power to either transfer a youth to the adult court system, as was the case under both the JDA and the YOA, or to mete out an adult punishment in youth court, as is the case under the YCJA. More about the sentencing provisions will be provided in the next chapter.

Young Persons Under the Safe Streets and Communities Act

The ongoing debate as to whether young persons who commit criminal offences should be treated as children or as adults continues with the proclamation of the *Safe Streets and Communities Act* (2012). There are a number of sections in this Act that give additional discretion to judges to impose adult punishment on young persons. In light of the case study of Ashley Smith, who was transferred as a youth to an adult penitentiary, we know only too well that the adult penitentiary system did not serve her well and that the idea of retaining a separate system of youth justice will remain steadfast in the future.

The next chapter will look specifically at the issues surrounding the sentencing of young offenders and the provisions within the YCJA for creative sentences that provide a just measure of accountability while also assisting young persons to reduce their **criminogenic needs** and successfully reintegrate into society, thus saving them from embarking on a life of adult criminality.

criminogenic needs
Known risk factors that increase the likelihood that an individual will reoffend.

SIDEBAR

Myths and Facts About Youth Justice

Myth: The increase in the crime rate in Canada is directly related to the increase in youth crime.

Fact: Research has shown that young persons are at higher risk of committing criminal offences. The prevalence of offending peaks during the teenage years (around 17–18) and decreases as youth mature into their 20s and 30s. However, the crime rate in Canada has been steadily declining over the past number of years.

In 2010, police reported the largest drop in violent crime since 1999. When we look specifically at youth crime, we find that the 2010 youth crime rate fell 7 percent from the year before and was 11 percent lower than a decade ago. The severity of youth crime has also declined, with a 6 percent drop in 2010. There was a 29 percent drop in homicide, 12 percent decline in serious assaults, 14 percent decline in motor vehicle thefts, and 10 percent decline in break-ins (Brennan & Dauvergne, 2011).

Myth: Locking up all young offenders is the smartest way to deal with juvenile crime.

Fact: While it is necessary for some young persons to serve some time in custody, ultimately all young persons are going to return to their communities. It is essential that these offenders are provided with appropriate opportunities for their rehabilitation early on so as to reduce the difficulties experienced when reintegrating into their communities. Research has shown that less juvenile justice processing is more likely to be successful in preventing future criminality (see Petrosino, Guckenburg, & Turpin-Petrosino, 2010).

Myth: Just keeping kids in at night would take care of most crime, certainly most violence.

Fact: Contrary to what most people think, the peak times for the commission of crime by young persons is between 2 and 6 p.m., the after-school hours when they are left on their own to pursue "leisure" interests. Most drug sales, assaults, and other offences occur during this period. It should be noted that this is also the time of day where there is no municipally imposed curfew. In those cities that have one, the results have shown that a curfew may inadvertently increase youth crime. Part of the problem is that it may further marginalize young persons, and place additional emotional and financial stress on parents or guardians, leading to more conflicts between parents and children (see Vissing, 2011).

Myth: There's nothing you can do to prevent youth crime.

Fact: Many programs have been proven to be effective in curbing the conditions that lead young persons toward crime, to strengthen the aspects of their lives that tend to keep them from becoming involved with crime, and to work with the community to strengthen capacity to effectively deal with young persons (see Reid, 2010).

Myth: Most teenagers are lazy and don't want to help their communities.

Fact: Six out of ten young persons already volunteer with community agencies. Almost nine out of ten teenagers would volunteer to take part in programs to help prevent crime if they knew how to get involved with their communities (see Centre for Excellence on Youth Engagement, 2009).

Myth: It is cheaper to lock kids in jail than to try to treat them in the community.

Fact: Many programs that prevent youth crime or assist youth in the community are far less expensive than incarceration. The average annual cost of detaining an adult offender in an institution is $50,375, while the estimated annual cost of detaining a young offender is more than $100,000. Youth require additional programming under the YCJA, as well as the provision of education as mandated provincially.

What Do You Think?

What are some of the other "commonsensical" beliefs that you have heard about young persons generally, and young offenders in particular? See if you can list some of these myths and generate ideas on how you would find the "facts" to debunk them.

DISCUSSION QUESTIONS

1. Discuss what might have been the outcome for Ashley Smith had she been living during the time of the JDA. What positive and negative outcomes might there have been during this time period?
2. The YOA and YCJA represent a number of the philosophical models of criminal justice outlined in the first chapter. What are some of the positive and negative features of having more than one model represented in youth justice legislation?
3. Have a look at your local newspaper and see how youth crime is depicted. Do you think that the media present one or more of the models outlined in this chapter? What myths are promoted in the media about young persons and young persons in conflict with the law? In what way(s) can you change how society views young persons who become enmeshed in the youth criminal justice system?

SUGGESTED FURTHER READINGS

Bell, S. (2012). *Young offenders and youth justice: A century after the fact*. Toronto: Nelson.

Davis-Barron, S. (2009). *Canadian youth and the criminal law*. Toronto: LexisNexis.

Kershaw, A., & Lasovich, M. (1991). *Rock-a-bye baby: A death behind bars*. Toronto: McClelland & Stewart.

UN Convention on the Rights of the Child. http://www.unicef.org/crc/

Winterdyk, J., & Smandych, R. (2012) *Youth at risk and youth justice: A Canadian overview*. Toronto: Oxford University Press Canada.

REFERENCES

Ariès, P. (1962). *Centuries of childhood: A social history of family life*. New York: Vintage.

Bell, S. (2012). *Young offenders and youth justice: A century after the fact*. Toronto: Nelson.

Boudreau, M. (2012). *City of order: Crime and society in Halifax, 1918–35*. Vancouver: UBC Press.

Brennan, S., & Dauvergne, M. (2011). Police-reported crime statistics in Canada, 2010. *Juristat*, Catalogue No. 85-002-X. Ottawa: Statistics Canada. Retrieved from http://www.statcan.gc.ca/pub/85-002-x/2011001/article/11523-eng.pdf

Brown Commission. (1849). Appendix to the journals of the Legislative Assembly of the Province of Canada. *Second report of the Royal Commission on the Provincial Penitentiary in Kingston*. Ottawa: King's Printer.

Canada, House of Commons. (2001, February 14). *Debates: Edited Hansard*, No. 013. Retrieved from http://www.parl.gc.ca/HousePublications/Publication.aspx?Language=E&Mode=1&DocId=2332075

Carrigan, D.O. (1988). *Juvenile delinquency in Canada: A history*. Toronto: Irwin.

Centre of Excellence for Youth Engagement. (2009). *What is youth engagement?* Retrieved from http://www.tgmag.ca/aorg/pdf/Whatis_WEB_e.pdf

Chapman, P.B. (1971). The lawyer in juvenile court: A Gulliver among Lilliputians. *Western Ontario Law Review, 10*, 88–92.

Davis-Barron, S. (2009). *Canadian youth and the criminal law*. Toronto: LexisNexis.

Department of Justice Canada. (1998). *A strategy for the renewal of youth justice*. Ottawa: Author.

Department of Justice Canada. (2004). *The evolution of juvenile justice in Canada* Ottawa: Queen's Printer. Retrieved from http://www.justice.gc.ca/eng/pi/icg-gci/jj2-jm2/jj2-jm2.pdf

Doob, A., & Cesaroni, C. (2004). *Responding to youth crime in Canada*. Toronto: University of Toronto Press.

Franklin, B., & Petley, J. (1996). Killing the age of innocence: News reporting of the death of James Bulger. In J. Pitcher & S. Wagg (Eds.), *Thatcher's children? Politics, childhood and society in the 1980s and 1990s*. London: Falmer Press.

Gleason, M., Myers, T., Paris, L., & Strong-Boag, V. (Eds.). (2010). *Lost kids: Vulnerable children and youth in twentieth-century Canada and the United States*. Vancouver: University of British Columbia Press.

Howard, J. (1777). *The state of prisons in England and Wales*. London: Warrington.

Kershaw, A., & Lasovich, M. (1991). *Rock-a-bye baby: A death behind bars*. Toronto: McClelland & Stewart.

Juvenile Delinquents Act, RSC 1970, c. J-3.

Petrosino, A., Guckenburg, S., & Turpin-Petrosino, C. (2010). Formal system processing of juveniles: Effects on delinquency. *The Campbell Collaboration Library of Systematic Reviews*. Retrieved from http://campbellcollaboration .org/lib/project/81/

Reid, S.A. (2004). Youth crime and the media. In K. Campbell (Ed.), *Youth justice in Canada*. Toronto: Pearson.

Reid, S.A. (2010). The untapped potential in our communities to assist youth engaged in risky behavior. *International Journal of Child, Youth and Family Studies*, *1*(2), 179–203.

Reid, S.A. (2011). Age of responsibility. In W.J. Chambliss (Ed.), *Juvenile crime and justice* (pp. 4–13). Thousand Oaks, CA: Sage.

Reid, S.A., & Reitsma-Street, M. (2001). Assumptions and implications of new Canadian legislation for young offenders. In T.A. O'Reilly-Fleming (Ed.), *Youth injustice: Canadian perspectives* (pp. 49–73). Toronto: Canadian Scholars' Press.

Reid, S.A., & Zuker, M.A. (2004). A conceptual framework for understanding youth justice in Canada. In K. Campbell (Ed.), *Youth justice in Canada*. Toronto: Pearson.

Reid-MacNevin, S.A. (1991). A theoretical understanding of current Canadian juvenile justice policy. In A. Leschied, P. Jaffe, & W. Willis (Eds.), *The Young Offenders Act: A revolution in Canadian juvenile justice* (pp. 17–36). Toronto: University of Toronto Press.

Reid-MacNevin, S.A., & Kappel, B.E. (2003). *Youth justice in Canada*. Toronto: Canadian Training Institute.

Safe Streets and Communities Act, SC 2012, c. 1.

Smandych, R.C. (2001). Accounting for changes in Canadian youth justice: From the invention to the disappearance of childhood. In R.C. Smandych (Ed.), *Youth justice: History, legislation and reform* (pp. 10–21). Toronto: Harcourt Canada.

Smandych, R. (2012). From "misguided children" to "criminal youth": Exploring historical and contemporary trends in Canadian youth justice. In J. Winterdyk and R. Smandych (Eds.), *Youth at risk and youth justice: A Canadian overview* (pp. 3–25). Toronto: Oxford University Press Canada.

Tustin, L., & Lutes, R. (2011). *A guide to the Youth Criminal Justice Act*. Markham, ON: LexisNexis.

Vissing, Y. (2011). Curfews. In W.J. Chambliss (Ed.), *Juvenile crime and justice* (pp. 59–72). Thousand Oaks, CA: Sage.

Wilson, L.C. (2003). The role of counsel in the *Youth Criminal Justice Act. Alberta Law Review, 40*(4), 1029–1040.

Young Offenders Act, SC 1981-82-83, c. 110.

Youth Criminal Justice Act, SC 2002, c. 1.

Youth Sentencing

Introduction

The philosophy and principles of the *Youth Criminal Justice Act* (YCJA) are consistent with the academic research that shows that incarcerating young people can do more harm than good, and that our most successful interventions should be doing less criminal-justice processing for the majority of those who present as low-risk, low-need offenders (Petrosino, Turpin-Petrosino, & Guckenburg, 2010). As pointed out in Chapter 13, under the *Young Offenders Act* (YOA; 1984), Canada had the highest youth incarceration rate in the world, with many going into secure custody for a "short sharp shock" (Doob & Cesaroni, 2004).

During that period (1984–2002), youth courts were overused for minor offences that could better be dealt with outside the courts through diversion programs. Sentences were unfair and disproportionate to the seriousness of the offences young persons had committed and were often used instead of appropriate mental health or child welfare programs. The YCJA, proclaimed in 2002, addressed a number of these issues by "shifting the orientation of youth justice to a criminal law and restraint approach" (Barnhorst, 2012, p. 112). The legislation places increased emphasis on both extrajudicial measures to appropriately deal with youth while keeping them out of the formal justice system, and on non-custodial sentences for those who are formally charged and found guilty. Custodial sentences are seen as a measure of last resort for the highest-risk offenders. This chapter will explore the provisions within the YCJA to respond to youth who come into conflict with the criminal law. An overview of alternatives to the court process, the principles of youth sentencing, and a discussion of the implications of these provisions for youth will be provided. The chapter also discusses the continuing tension between the public's demand to get tough on young persons who commit offences and the ways in which the federal government has responded with amendments to the legislation.

See also mini chapter 16.6
*Boot Camps for Young
Offenders*

How Does the Public Learn About Youth Crime?

In Chapter 13, we discussed myths and facts about youth crime. It was pointed out that generally the public believes that youth crime is on the rise while, in actuality, youth crime is decreasing and has been declining over the past number of years. Why is there such a disconnect between the public's perception of youth crime and the reality? What are the implications of these myths about youth crime for the creation of youth justice policy?

When the members of the general public pick up a newspaper on any given day, they are confronted with a variety of images both from the pictures and the printed word that are stored in their "mental data bank for instant playback" (Reynolds, 1996, p. 12). As news reports, whether from the print media or through online sources, continue to provide most individuals with a picture of what is happening in the world around them, it is important to recognize that the storytelling of journalists can have a profound impact on the way in which people interpret their world. In the area of juvenile justice policy, the images from the news media are that youth crime is out of control and increasingly violent; the youth justice system "doesn't work" and is too "lenient" to deal with today's violent youth; and the remedy to the current "youth crime crisis" is to be found in longer and harsher punishments. The public's reliance on the media as their barometer of how safe they feel from victimization by young persons is skewed from the reality of youth crime: the "regular diet of unusual over time seems usual" (Dorfman & Schiraldi, 2001, p. 31).

One of the cornerstones of youth justice is that the identity of a young person should be protected. This is important because publishing the name of the young person is viewed as being harmful to rehabilitation efforts and would negatively affect the youth. In the end, the result of such damaging effects for young persons who are not given an opportunity to mature into young adults is that public safety would be compromised. The *Juvenile Delinquents Act* (JDA) provided that all juvenile court hearings were to be held "without publicity" and without the public in attendance. The JDA also banned the publication of the identity of young persons. This meant that the media could not report on charges against juveniles or on their trials. With the enactment of the *Canadian Charter of Rights and Freedoms* in 1982, the exclusion of the public from attending criminal proceedings involving juveniles was ruled to be unconstitutional for violating the provision of freedom of the press. In *R. v. R.J.* (1982), the Superior Court of Justice in Ontario stated that "[t]he State has not satisfied me that a blanket denial of a public hearing without any cause being shown other than social purposes can be justified" (p. 184). In the period leading up to the proclamation of the YOA, a compromise developed: the ban on the publication of the identity of the young person before the court continued, but with a more open and accountable process that permitted the public and the media in the courtroom. Allowing public accountability and media scrutiny under the provisions of the new legislation meant that, for the first time in Canadian history, the public would learn details about youth crime.

While opening the courtroom to the media and the public had the potential to inform the public of some of the root causes of youth crime and the contexts in which such offences take place, the media did not capitalize on this opportunity. In presenting sensational crimes and relying on "expert" sources such as the police, the voice of youth was not heard in the stories that were being told about them. Bell (2012, p. 26) suggested that "continual and sensationalized" crime reporting produced a **moral panic** about youth crime, which was in turn reinforced through the "selective reporting" of public outrage toward not only "out-of-control youth" but also the legislation that was supposed to control crime.

A study conducted from May to August in 1996 of the content of four newspapers (*Toronto Star*, *Toronto Sun*, *Guelph Mercury*, and *Kitchener-Waterloo Record*) revealed that almost two-thirds (56.7 percent) of the articles about youth were crime-related and 52 percent were about violent crime. At that time, violent crime accounted for only 18 percent and property crime accounted for about half (Reid, 2005). As news started to be increasingly reported on the Internet, the study was again conducted in 2002, looking at news stories about youth that were available online for the months of June, July, and August. While there were fewer stories about youth crime

moral panic
A concept that refers to those times when people, groups, or events are defined and perceived to be a threat to security and public order (Cohen, 1972). Moral panic may be exacerbated when negative images of the target are presented in the media, which may lead to harsh and oppressive treatment of the target.

than found in newspapers (30 percent), the emphasis on youth violence was staggering, with 64 percent of the Internet articles focused on violent crime (p. 147).

Seskus and Mofina (2000, p. 140) suggested, "It is not the newspaper's job to tell people what to think, but rather to tell people what to think about." Moreover, they suggested that "[i]t is a reader's responsibility to use the information as a stepping stone to further participate in the democratic process" (p. 141). However, how many readers actually critically evaluate the information being presented in the newspapers they read? Considering that very few people have had any direct experience with the youth justice system or with young persons who commit criminal offences, there is no basis for comparison beyond what is reported in the news.

How many readers actually critically evaluate the information in newspapers they read?

What Do You Think?

What is your impression of youth crime based on reading the news? What are the impressions of your parents' or grandparents' generation? Take a look at your local newspaper or do a quick Internet news search to see how many articles depict youth in any way (positively or negatively), and then count the number of articles that are youth-crime related. How does your analysis compare with the studies conducted in 1996 and 2002?

What Do We Do with Young Criminals?

rehabilitation
The treatment of offenders in order to prevent future criminal activity; the process whereby a person recognizes that his or her behaviour was wrong, fully understands why it was wrong, and decides not to behave that way in the future.

reintegration
The process whereby a person lives in the community in a law-abiding manner and maintains his or her decision not to continue with past destructive behaviour.

As discussed in Chapter 13, the changes that came about in the YCJA were the result of several years of consultation and review of the YOA. After a lengthy parliamentary committee review, the federal minister of justice released *Strategy for the Renewal of Youth Justice* (Department of Justice, 1998), a policy paper that outlined the federal government's response to the review and set the tone for the legislation. The paper responded to public pressure to "get tough" on young offenders by drawing a clear distinction between the small number of violent offenders and the vast majority who are non-violent. The strategy, which would form the philosophical intent of the YCJA, was based on three guiding principles:

- crime prevention
- meaningful consequences
- **rehabilitation** and **reintegration**.

The government's approach acknowledged the research literature that clearly showed that preventing crime is the most effective way to protect communities (see Chapter 15 for more on this approach). The strategy paper promoted alternatives to the youth court system as a means of crime prevention. These extrajudicial measures and sanctions will be discussed later in this chapter.

Meaningful Consequences

Strategy for the Renewal of Youth Justice pointed out the importance of ensuring that young persons who commit crimes are made aware of the connection between their crime and the effect that the crime has had on the victim and the community.

You will recall from Chapter 1 the discussion about the restorative justice model, which outlined this approach. In many cases, youth crime, like adult crime, takes an emotional toll on victims, witnesses, friends, and communities. From a restorative justice perspective, the most significant aspect of crime is that it victimizes citizens and communities. The youth justice system should focus on repairing this harm by ensuring that the young persons are held accountable for making amends for the damage and suffering they have caused. Large segments of the Canadian public consider imprisonment to be the only true measure of justice and the only yardstick by which to measure whether society's response is "tough" enough. Yet the reality is that much crime involves conflict, and it is not possible to create opportunities to resolve conflict or encourage healing for either party with a focus on incarceration for young offenders. The world over, we question the value of raw punishment in socializing our children in an attempt to ensure compliance. We need to apply this same questioning to our public policy: Why hurt people who hurt people? To show that hurting is wrong?

See also mini chapter 16.5 Restorative Justice in Focus: Sentencing Circles

---

SIDEBAR

Questions Asked by the Restorative Justice Model

The most important questions for restorative justice do not focus on whether to punish or treat offenders. Rather, the primary questions to be answered are:

- What harm has been done?
- What needs to be done to make it right?
- Who is responsible?

Source: Based on Centre for Research on Youth at Risk (1998).

SIDEBAR

A Point of Illustration

Prior to the enactment of the YCJA, the author was involved in some research with young people at the New Brunswick Youth Centre. The interview started with what might be referred to as straightforward demographic questions (e.g., How long have you been incarcerated? Was this your first experience with custody?). When asked what the charge was that they were currently serving in custody, a number of them said "breach," meaning a breach of conditions of their probation. When further asked what was the original offence for which they received the probation, they responded, "This time?" When she answered yes, a number of them responded again with "breach."

It became clear to the author not only that the courts were issuing a large number of custodial sentences for "administration of justice offences" (e.g., failing to comply with a sentence), but also that the youth who were receiving these sentences did not really even remember what the original offence was that led to their youth sentence. The concept of meaningful consequences in the YCJA was a response to this issue.

What Do You Think?

Take a look at some of the sentences that are given to young persons today (as might be found in an Internet news search). Do you think that these sentences provide meaningful consequences? What else might have been done that would have responded to the questions posed by the restorative justice model?

preamble
The introductory part of a statute that, while not legally enforceable, contains significant statements from Parliament about the values on which the legislation is based.

Declaration of Principle
The policy framework expressed in s. 3 of the *Youth Criminal Justice Act* that is meant to guide interpretation of the Act and to inform every process contained in the Act.

The concept of meaningful consequences was introduced in the YCJA in response to the high rate of youth incarceration under the YOA, when a large number of youth were being placed in custody for minor offences (see "A Point of Illustration" sidebar). The term "meaningful consequence" is found in three places in the YCJA: in the **preamble**, in the **Declaration of Principle** (s. 3), and in the sentencing principles in s. 38.

Preamble

The preamble to the YCJA states in part:

> AND WHEREAS Canadian society should have a youth criminal justice system that commands respect, takes into account the interests of victims, fosters responsibility, and ensures accountability through meaningful consequences and effective rehabilitation and reintegration, and that reserves its most serious intervention for the most serious crimes and reduces the over-reliance on incarceration for non-violent young persons ...

Declaration of Principle

Section 3 is a statement of overriding principles, meant to inform every process in the YCJA:

> 3(1) The following principles apply in this Act:
> (a) the youth criminal justice system is intended to ...
> (iii) ensure that a young person is subject to meaningful consequences for his or her offence in order to promote the long-term protection of the public.

Purpose and Principles of Sentencing

Part 4 of the YCJA concerns sentencing and begins with the following statement of purpose:

> 38(1) The purpose of sentencing under section 42 (youth sentences) is to hold a young person accountable for an offence through the imposition of just sanctions that have meaningful consequences for the young person and that promote his or her rehabilitation and reintegration into society, thereby contributing to the long-term protection of the public.

The Supreme Court of Canada in *R. v. B.W.P; R. v. B.V.N.* (2006) held that in the interpretation of "meaningful consequence," the intent is not deterrence. Justice Charron discussed the meaning as an "individualized sentencing process by focusing on underlying causes, rehabilitation, [and] reintegration," and that the concepts in s. 3(1)(a) were to be "viewed from the perspective of the young person rather than from society at large" (p. 27).

The YCJA has provided a sequential approach to youth justice: even the layout of the legislation is designed in sequence, emphasized in various layers, from the preamble to the Declaration of Principle to the nature of the treatment of offenders, drawing attention to the principles that shall guide extrajudicial measures in s. 4. The final layer in s. 38 sets out the purpose and principles of sentencing, underscoring the "long-term protection of society" through the imposition of "just sanctions" that hold a "young person accountable" through "meaningful consequences" that will "promote his or her rehabilitation and reintegration into society."

Early prevention and intervention through school networks, through communities, and through the assistance of families help to avoid stigma and labelling, and may be the most suitable alternative for the majority of young persons who offend. There will always be, however, a small number of youth who are persistent offenders requiring a range of multidisciplinary assistance set within a clear path over a fairly substantial period of time.

Evidence has shown that a great deal of damage is done when society provides intensive treatments to low-risk offenders, which sets them off on a trajectory of net-widening and further entrenchment within the system.

Alternatives to the Youth Court

As discussed in Chapter 13, the original proponents of a juvenile justice system in North America, the "Child Savers," as they came to be known, advocated the diversion of young persons from the harshness of the adult system. Diversion programs were developed in response to the research evidence that suggested that keeping youth in their families and communities, supported by a package of services aimed at their individual needs—including family treatment and restorative justice practices—has a positive effect and is successful in reducing recidivism (Moyer, 1980; Whitaker, Severy, & Morton, 1984; Latimer, 2001; Ungar, 2004; Schwalbe, Gearing, Mackenzie, Brewer, & Ibrahim, 2012). Keeping youth in their community allows for a "holistic intervention approach" focused on identifying individual, family, and community risks and strengths, and treating them comprehensively (Sullivan, Veysey, Hamilton, & Grillo, 2007). Such an approach exemplifies the tenets of the community change, welfare, and restorative justice models described in Chapter 1.

Perhaps the most successful sections of the YCJA are those that promote diversion of minor offenders out of the formal youth justice system through a series of **extrajudicial measures** by the police in the form of warnings and cautions, and more intensive options such as referrals to community agencies in the form of extrajudicial sanctions.

extrajudicial measures
Informal ways in which police may keep a young person out of the youth justice system by using such means as warnings, cautions, or referrals to a community agency for help.

Principles and Objectives for Extrajudicial Measures

In addition to the Declaration of Principle in s. 3 of the YCJA, the following principles found in s. 4 apply to extrajudicial measures:

(a) Extrajudicial measures are often the most appropriate and effective way to address youth crime.
(b) Extrajudicial measures allow for effective and timely interventions focused on correcting offending behaviour.
(c) In the case of a non-violent offender, with no previous convictions, extrajudicial measures are to be presumed to be adequate to hold the young person accountable for his or her actions.
(d) Extrajudicial measures should be used whenever they are adequate to hold the young person accountable for offending behaviour, including cases where the young person has previously committed offences.

The YCJA then sets out objectives for extrajudicial measures in s. 5. Such measures should be designed to

(a) provide an effective and timely non-judicial response to offending behaviour;
(b) encourage young persons to acknowledge and repair the harm caused to the victim and the community;
(c) encourage families of young persons to be involved in the design and implementation of the measures;
(d) provide an opportunity for victim participation in the decision on the measures selected and to receive reparation; and
(e) respect the rights and freedoms of young persons and be proportionate to the seriousness of the offence. (adapted from Reid-MacNevin & Kappel, 2003, pp. 28–29)

What Do You Think?

Which models (crime control, justice, welfare, community change, restorative justice) are represented in the principles and objectives of extrajudicial measures? Is there one model that takes precedence over another?

Police and Extrajudicial Measures

Before starting any judicial proceeding against a young person, a police officer is *required* by the YCJA (s. 6(1)) to consider whether it would be sufficient to:

1. *Take no further action.* Generally, the police officer decides that it is not necessary to do anything further because the parents, school officials, and in some cases the victim have taken measures to hold the young person accountable.
2. *Warn the young person.* Usually this is a one-to-one lecture by the officer explaining the possible outcomes if the behaviour is repeated and comes to the attention of the police again.
3. *Administer a caution.* This is a more formal warning by the police, generally put in writing in a letter that may be issued in person in the presence of the parents so that they are aware of the caution. The letter advises the youth that the police believe that he or she has committed a crime but that he or she is not going to be charged at this time; however, if the youth is found committing similar conduct in the future, he or she could be charged.

4. *Make a referral to a community program.* Police may refer the young person, with his or her consent, to a program (e.g., drug addiction program, homework program) that may help the youth not to commit further offences.

What Would You Do?

Jordan, 14, has been warned once before, for a prank that he and another young person played when they threw eggs at a house one early summer morning. He has come to the attention of the police again for spray-painting a rude message under a bridge. What would you do as the police officer attending this case?

A 2009 report prepared for the New Brunswick Department of Public Safety reviewing extrajudicial measures and sanctions was entitled *125 Warnings* (Reid, 2009). This title reflected the comment given by a former probation officer who suggested that police cautions should be used whenever possible for minor offenders, and that it should not matter if the officer has given one warning or 125 warnings if that is the right solution to the situation presented.

Extrajudicial Sanctions

If the police believe that a warning, caution, or referral is not sufficient to hold the young person accountable through meaningful consequences, the case will be referred to the Crown, who will then have the option of using **extrajudicial sanctions** that have been developed as part of a program authorized by the province, outside the formal court system. The YCJA requires that parents be notified if such a sanction is used, and victims have the right to be informed of the sanction that was given. The Act also describes when an extrajudicial sanction may be used (s. 10):

- It must be seen as an appropriate response with regard to the needs of the young person and the interests of society. This is in keeping with the concept of meaningful consequences.
- There must be, in the opinion of the Crown, sufficient evidence to justify proceeding with the prosecution.
- The young person must first accept responsibility for the act or omission that forms the basis of the offence. Before consenting, a young person must be advised of his or her right to legal representation and

extrajudicial sanctions
More formal ways of handling a youth case outside of court, administered by the Crown. As with the alternative measures programs under the *Young Offenders Act*, youth may be required to complete community service.

be given the opportunity to consult with counsel. The young person must not express the wish to have the charge dealt with by the court.

- No admission of guilt by a young person as a condition of being dealt with by an extrajudicial sanction is admissible as evidence against a young person in any criminal proceeding. However, if the youth does not complete the extrajudicial sanction and is later tried and convicted of the offence, the fact that the young person did not complete the extrajudicial sanction may be raised during sentencing.

It is important to underscore that an extrajudicial sanction is not a sentence. While some youth may participate in very similar programs and activities as part of a term of probation or as a form of community service imposed as part of a sentence upon conviction, the youth who receive extrajudicial sanctions have not been convicted, and therefore do not have a youth criminal record.

This approach is in keeping with a recent **meta-analysis** of 29 studies that indicated that more juvenile justice system processing led to higher rates of recidivism. The researchers looked at the impact of juvenile justice system processing over a 35-year period in studies that included 7,300 juveniles. They concluded that not only does formal processing of juveniles appear not to control crime, it actually seems to increase it on all measures studied (Petrosina, Turpin-Petrosino, & Guckenberg, 2010).

meta-analysis
A statistical technique that compares a group of studies; a study of other studies that have been conducted on a particular topic or in a specific area of research.

Youth Justice Courts

Young persons appear in a separate court from adults, with a judge alone. Part 3 of the YCJA deals with judicial matters and includes procedures on dealing with the young person's right to a lawyer independent of the youth's parent(s), appearance in court, detention or bail provisions, as well as the notices to parents. Also included are other procedures related to medical and psychological reports, referrals to child welfare agencies, trials, and appeals. For the purposes of this chapter, a few highlights will be identified to provide a contrast with the adult criminal court proceedings that were discussed in Chapter 6.

The Declaration of Principle states that young persons must have enhanced procedural protections to ensure that they are treated fairly and that their rights, including their right to privacy, are protected (s. 3(1)(b)(iii)). Such enhanced protections include making sure not only that young persons have their rights read to them by a person in authority, but that they understand those rights. This can require the appointment of more people to assist a young person, in addition to family members and independent legal counsel.

Parental notification is required as soon as possible after a young person is arrested or detained pending a court appearance. A parent can be ordered to attend court at any stage of the proceedings if the judge is of the opinion that it is necessary or in the young person's best interest.

What Do You Think?

Are there any situations where it would not be appropriate to have a parent attend a court hearing for a young person? What if a young person who has been living on the streets for a number of years has not had any contact with the parent? What if the parent is a co-accused? What if a youth has been abused by the parent and is currently under the care of child welfare authorities? Can you think of any other situations?

Unlike previous youth justice legislation, the YCJA states that pretrial detention cannot be used as a substitute for appropriate child protection, mental health, or other social measures, as shown in the mini case study "Theft of Pepperoni: No Longer a Youth Court Matter."

Principles of Sentencing

The YCJA states that the purpose of sentencing is to hold a young offender *accountable* for his or her crime through the imposition of just sanctions that have meaningful consequences for the young person and that promote rehabilitation and reintegration into society, which thereby contributes to the long-term protection of the public. In addition to the principles outlined in s. 3 of the YCJA, the following sentencing principles also apply:

- *No greater than adult punishment.* In handing out a sentence, a young person shall not receive a punishment that would be greater than the punishment for an adult who has been convicted for the same offence committed in similar circumstances.
- *Regional consistency.* The sentence must be similar to the sentences imposed in the region on similar young persons found guilty of the same offence committed in similar circumstances.
- *Proportionate to offence and responsibility.* The sentence must be proportionate to the seriousness of the offence and the degree of responsibility of the young person for the offence.
- *Priority to non-custodial.* All available sanctions other than custody are to be considered for all young persons. Particular attention should be paid to using non-custodial sentences for Aboriginal youth.

MINI CASE STUDY

Theft of Pepperoni: No Longer a Youth Court Matter

In *R. v. M.J.S.* (2004), the Nova Scotia Supreme Court ruled in a case where a 14-year-old girl had been charged in 2002 with theft of pepperoni, and was subsequently charged with breaching a number of conditions of her release related to missing curfew, failing to live where directed, and failing to go to school. The young person had been remanded in pretrial detention for approximately one month prior to her sentencing hearing on both the theft charge and the breach of her conditions. Despite both the Crown prosecutor and defence counsel recommending a non-custodial sentence, the judge imposed a period of custody for 90 days. The defence then sought intervention from the Nova Scotia Supreme Court to release the young person pending appeal, but before the case could be heard, the young person spent another week in custody.

The Nova Scotia Supreme Court **quashed** the original custodial sentence and in-sisted that there be no additional sentence given because it would "simply be repeating the errors of the Youth Court Judge by imposing a sentence that is disproportionate to the offences" (para. 27). In reviewing the sentencing judge's decision, it was clear that there were a number of errors in law, and the appeal court went so far as to say that the sentencing judge "misinterpreted or misapplied each of the sections she re-ferred to" (para. 12). The issue before the sentencing court was that the young person was a troubled 14-year-old who was not able to return home to live with her parents, and it was believed that she was living on the streets. Based on the submissions and the sentencing judge's remarks, the issues presented by the young person were more child welfare matters, and the use of custody as a substitute for child protection, mental health, or other social measures violated s. 39(5) of the *Youth Criminal Justice Act* (YCJA).

This Supreme Court decision clearly underscored and corrected many of the prob-lems under the *Young Offenders Act*, whereby young persons who would have been better served through social services were being incarcerated due to the lack of ap-propriate child welfare services. According to the Supreme Court reasons, the sentencing judge also erred in ordering a custodial sentence based on the proportionality principle under the YCJA. The justice remarked, "The entire series of events started with the primary offence where this troubled young person took a piece of pepperoni" (para. 24).

Further, said the justice, "A young person who has committed a relatively minor offence but has serious psychological needs that seem to have contributed to the behaviour should receive a sentence that reflects the seriousness of the offence, not the seriousness of the psychological needs" (para. 15). This highlights the move away from the welfare model reminiscent of the *Juvenile Delinquents Act*.

quash
To reject or void the original sentence, thereby making it invalid.

What Do You Think?

Because the YCJA does not provide for those young persons who find themselves homeless or without child welfare services, what needs to be done for youth who come in conflict with the law *because* of their need for child welfare services?

- *Rehabilitation/reintegration.* The sentence is to be one that is likely to rehabilitate the young person and reintegrate him or her into society and promote a sense of responsibility in him or her, and an acknowledgement of the harm done to victims and the community.

What Do You Think?

Which models (crime control, justice, welfare, community change, restorative justice) are represented in these principles?

Factors to Consider in Sentencing Youth

The YCJA requires the court to also take into account the following when determining a youth sentence:

- the degree of participation by the young person in the offence
- the harm done to victims and whether it was intentional or reasonably foreseeable
- any reparations made by the young person to the victim or the community
- time already spent in custody for pretrial detention
- previous findings of guilt
- any other aggravating and mitigating circumstances related to the young person or the offense that are relevant to the purpose and principles.

What Do You Think?

How do these factors compare with the sentencing factors for adults that you learned about in Chapter 8?

Aboriginal Youth and Sentencing

The Declaration of Principle as outlined in s. 3 of the YCJA includes the requirement to respect and respond to the needs of Aboriginal young persons, which means that the sentence must also respond to their needs. The circumstances of young Aboriginal offenders must be taken into account at the time of sentencing according to this principle. This is similar to the provision for adults in the *Criminal Code* that was a result of the Supreme Court of Canada decision in *R. v. Gladue* (1999) (discussed in detail in Chapter 12). According to the case, Aboriginal people in 1997 made up about 3 percent of the population but amounted to 12 percent of federal adult inmates. In the provinces of Manitoba and Saskatchewan, reports indicated that Aboriginal adult offenders accounted for between 55 and 72 percent of all admissions to provincial corrections.

The Department of Justice reported on a one-day snapshot of Aboriginal youth in custody and found that in 2001, they represented about 7 percent of the juvenile population in select provinces and territories, but made up 25 percent of admissions to custodial facilities (Bittle, Hattem, Quann, & Muise, 2002). Latimer and Foss (2004) reported on a follow-up snapshot of Aboriginal youth in custody, and despite the YCJA being in effect, Aboriginal youth continued to experience significantly higher incarceration rates— nearly eight times more likely to be in custody than their non-Aboriginal counterparts. In 2004, Aboriginal youth accounted for 5 percent of the population but 33 percent of youth in custody.

Green (2012, p. 68) reported that since the implementation of the YCJA, the number of Aboriginal youth in custody has increased from 28 percent in 2002–3 to 36 percent in 2008–9, despite Aboriginal youth representing only 6 percent of the youth population.

What Do You Think?

Recall the case study of J at the beginning of this book (Part One) and think about the provisions in *R. v. Gladue* and the statistical profile presented. What could be done differently for both youth and adults to reduce the number of offenders going into our prison system?

Community Sanctions for Convicted Youth

In keeping with the desire to reduce the number of youth who are sentenced to custody, the YCJA focuses on continuing to look at other ways of handling young persons who commit the majority of offences, while reserving custody for the small number of youth who commit serious offences.

Section 42 of the YCJA provides the following non-custodial options for a youth court to impose on a convicted young person, listed in order from the least onerous to the most onerous:

1. A *judicial reprimand* (i.e., a stern warning from the judge) means that a finding of guilt is entered, but it is as if the sentence has already been served, in the belief that the processing of the young person before the court is a sanction in itself.

2. An *absolute discharge* is like a reprimand in that the processing of the young person through the formal court system is the sentence.

3. A *conditional discharge* adds a series of conditions that the court considers appropriate, and may include reporting to a probation officer. Once the conditions have been satisfied, the young person will be discharged. However, if a young person does not fulfill the conditions, the youth can be charged with another criminal offence (failure to comply with the sentence, s. 137 YCJA).

4. Although a *fine* of up to $1,000 is an option, some courts are hesitant to give fines as a sentence because they are punitive with very little rehabilitative value, and this is seen as contrary to the principle of the legislation. Further, fines may be viewed as unfair for those young persons who have parents with the ability to pay, even though the judge must ask about the young person's present and future ability to pay the fine on his or her own.

5. A young person may be ordered to make *compensation* (payment) or *restitution* (services) for personal injury, for loss of or damage to property, or for loss of income or support. The judge cannot order personal service without the consent of the victim to be compensated, because not all victims may want to have contact or involvement with the young person. An order to perform personal service cannot exceed 240 hours and must be completed within one year of the date of the order.

6. A *community service order* may be issued, which includes personal or community service if the judge deems the young person a suitable candidate and the service does not interfere with the young person's normal work or educational hours. Again, the community service hours may not exceed 240 hours and must be completed within one year of the date of the order.

7. Order of *prohibition, seizure,* or *forfeiture* for at least two years; this may relate to such items as firearms or other dangerous weapons.

8. *Probation* has been one of the most preferred sanctions since the inception of the JDA. Under the YOA, there were many young persons who breached their conditions of probation, leading to another criminal charge that often put them into custody. The YCJA provides for the conditions to be reviewed and altered if breached, rather than always laying a new charge. Probation includes the requirement to report periodically to a probation officer, to avoid contact with known offenders, and to meet other conditions that are meant to address the offence committed and respond in a meaningful manner. Community service may also be part of a probation order.

R. v. K.D.

In *R. v. K.D.* (2003), one of the first reported cases under the YCJA from the Nova Scotia Supreme Court, Justice Lynch gave a judicial reprimand to a 15-year-old girl who had been charged with assault and uttering threats while she was being restrained at her group home residence. The young girl had eight prior findings of guilt related to uttering threats and assault committed under similar circumstances whereby she received as a sentence community service work caring for animals. The pre-sentence report indicated that she had a "horrendous" background; she had been the victim of physical abuse and neglect, including having been locked in cupboards (para. 2).

Since the age of nine, the youth had been living in the Children's Response Program, which is part of the IWK Health Centre in Halifax. Her psychiatric and psychological assessment reports prepared for the court indicated a number of behavioural problems and mental health conditions (e.g., ADHD, oppositional defiant disorder, conduct disorder, post-traumatic stress disorder, and attachment disorder). K.D. acted out in an aggressive manner when physical restraints were put on her for disciplinary measures, and this had been the case in her previous charges. The doctor who had been treating the young girl for the past six years wrote in the pre-sentence report: "K.D. is a young adolescent who requires specialized care within a nurturing environment in an attempt to undo the effects of institutionalized behaviour patterns" (para. 7). Further, the team leader of the Children's Response Program wrote, "The child has been failed by the system. A lot of her behaviours in the past two years have been out of despair and institutionalization" (para. 10).

In her reasons, the justice discussed meaningful consequences in the context of the young person's multiple psychological and psychiatric diagnoses and her limited cognitive abilities. The judge made it clear that the agencies responsible for assisting this young girl were not to offload their responsibility onto the justice system:

> The requests that have been made or the suggestions that have been made in the pre-sentence report with regard to why I should sentence her to probation or why I should sentence her to community service work are, as I said, not the job of sentencing. They are the job of the Department of Community Services and the Department of Health. They are to provide those opportunities to her. (para. 17)

The pre-sentence report indicated that there had been some success with a change in medication and the completion of anger management programs; she had fewer incidents of being removed to a secure unit at the IWK hospital. The following provides the text of the judicial reprimand to the youth:

> I understand that the situation is not a good one at this point, but I want you to understand that those people do not deserve to be physically assaulted by you. Do you understand that? You have to use your best efforts, as it appears you have been trying to, to keep your anger under control. (para. 20)

You have a history of this type of behaviour and I have to take that into account. I have to take into account the fact that the description of your last six years at the Children's Response Program, the fact that it has not been an appropriate placement for you, but I think that you have to bear in mind that the people that work with you do not deserve the behaviour that you have shown to them. I want you to keep that in mind. (para. 21)

What Do You Think?

Consider the case study of Ashley Smith (at the beginning of Part Five) and the fact that she also experienced institutionalization and acted out toward staff in a similar manner as K.D. Do you think a judicial reprimand would have been a just sanction for Ashley?

9. *Intensive Support and Supervision Program* (ISSP) is a new provision under the YCJA that calls for a more intensive probation order in those provinces where it is available. Rather than the young person having to serve a term in custody, this keeps the youth in the community and adds support in the form of intensive monitoring, and additional resources and referrals to community-based agencies as a condition of the order; this cannot exceed two years.

10. *Attendance at non-residential centres* is also a new provision to keep young persons out of custody. In addition to reporting to a probation officer, the young person is required to attend a centre that offers programs and services for up to 240 hours for a maximum of six months. This allows the judge an opportunity to address some of the risk factors that the young person presents, by ordering, for example, attendance at a drug and alcohol treatment centre after school. These attendance centre programs are not available in all provinces.

More Intensive Interventions: Custodial Sanctions

As discussed in Chapter 13, under the *Juvenile Delinquents Act*, juvenile offenders were found to be in a state of "delinquency," and it was the responsibility of the state through its government programs to treat delinquency as if it were a disease. The sentences were indeterminate because it could not be ascertained how much of a dose of "treatment" was required to cure young persons of their delinquent ways. Juvenile delinquents were placed in reformatories, industrial schools, and youth facilities for treatment; between 1908 and 1984, such facilities were often thought of as private educational and training institutions, with the added benefit of offering counselling, therapy, and psychological intervention. These institutions, however, did not live up to this "gold standard" of treatment and rehabilitation, and were often merely a secure place to warehouse **throwaway children.**

The *Young Offenders Act* was designed to specifically address the problems of indeterminate sentencing and to move away from the welfare-only focus of the JDA. As you may recall from Chapter 13, the philosophy of the YOA reflected a combination of four models of procedure (i.e., welfare, crime control, justice, and community change) (Reid & Reitsma-Street, 1984). Without a priority assigned to any one approach, judges were left with a delicate balancing act of looking after the needs of young persons while also satisfying the need to protect society from their criminal acts. Further, you may recall that because Canada was sending so many young offenders to custody for short sentences, there were more youth in custody in this country than anywhere in the world. The purpose of youth custody and supervision is set out in s. 83 of the YCJA, which states that this sentence is designed to contribute to the protection of society through safe, fair, and humane measures while at the same time assisting the young person to be rehabilitated and reintegrated back into society. The focus of this section is to follow the principle of the **least restrictive measure** that would hold a young person accountable for his or her crime while also recognizing the age and stage of development of the young person.

The YCJA sets out clear principles of sentencing and adds a number of limitations on the use of custody. As was outlined in the list of principles of sentencing, a non-custodial option is preferred and the court is prohibited from imposing custody on any young person if an appropriate alternative is available.

In order for a judge to consider custody, the case must meet at least one of the following four criteria:

- The youth has committed a violent offence.
- The youth has failed to comply with two or more previous non-custodial sentences.
- The youth has a "pattern of findings of guilt" (i.e., two or more previous occasions) *and* the offence is one in which an adult would receive a sentence of more than two years.
- It is an "exceptional" case where the aggravating circumstances make it impossible to provide a non-custodial sanction. The judge must explain why this is an exceptional case.

Even if only one of the conditions is met, the court is obligated to consider all alternatives to custody that are reasonable. In those "exceptional"

throwaway children
Children who have become state wards and fallen through the cracks of the various systems (child welfare, health, education, youth justice) and do not have guardians or parents to advocate on their behalf for services and treatment.

least restrictive measure
The principle that when there is a less onerous method of holding a young person accountable, it should be used rather than a more restrictive sanction, such as custody.

SIDEBAR

Youth Court Records

When a young person is found guilty of a criminal offence, the individual will receive a youth record (YCJA, s. 119(2)). The period of time that a youth record may be accessed after a finding of guilt varies, depending on the type of sentence. Generally, the more severe the offence, and therefore the more severe the sentence, the longer the period of access to the record by police, victims, judges, courts of review, and persons carrying out a criminal record check.

- A judicial reprimand can only be accessed for two months (see the mini case study on *R. v. K.D.*).
- An absolute discharge can be accessed for a year.
- A conditional discharge can be accessed for three years.
- All other summary conviction offences can be accessed for three years from the time the young person completes the sentence.
- Indictable offences can be accessed for five years from the time the young person completes the sentence.

If a young person is convicted of a subsequent offence, the access period is recalculated. Youth records are not protected from adult proceedings while the access period is still open, which means that a youth record can be brought forward at time of sentencing as an adult; the fact that a young adult before the court has a youth record can also be published.

What Do You Think?

If a young person receives an absolute discharge at age 17.5 years, will a criminal record check for a job at age 18 show that the youth has a criminal record? What would a criminal record check show for the same individual if an extrajudicial sanction had been imposed instead?

cases, a judge might consider custody based on issues of child protection, mental health, or concern about other social measures, but is not able to use custody for those reasons (see the "Theft of Pepperoni" mini case study on page 367). In other words, a judge cannot impose custody for a young person's "own good" or to teach the young person a lesson.

However, a judge does have the opportunity to use a deferred custody and supervision order. This new sentencing provision imposes strict conditions on a young person who will serve his or her sentence in the community, but has the option to bring the young person into custody to serve the remainder of the sentence.

One of the shortcomings of the YOA was that it imposed terms of custody without allowing an opportunity for reintegration unless the judge specified. For example, if a young person was sentenced to three years in secure custody, the youth would serve all three years in a locked facility unless the judge ordered a sentence to be two years secure, followed by six months open custody and six months on probation. The YCJA remedied this by including a provision whereby the final third of all custodial sentences is to be served in the community under a reintegration order. Reflecting this change, all custodial sentences are now referred to as custody and supervision orders. Under the YCJA, for a youth who is given custody, the time in custody must be followed by a period of community supervision that is half as long as the custody order (s. 42(2)(n)).

If all four criteria are met with respect to a custody order, the length of the custody imposed is determined by the offence and the degree of responsibility of the young person, and is not to be determined by such factors as the time needed to treat the youth in a custodial program. Some evaluation research has suggested, for example, that drug rehabilitation could take more than six months in a residential facility, which could be longer than an appropriate sentence for the type of offence committed. (Remember, under the JDA, juveniles could be kept in custody until their 21st birthday, regardless of the offence.) All offences except the most serious ones (known as "presumptive offences") are considered to receive one-third custody and two-thirds community/reintegrative supervision orders. The maximum total length of custody and supervision is two years, or three years if the offence is one for which an adult could receive a life sentence under the *Criminal Code*.

Serious Offenders

According to s. 2(1) of the YCJA, a serious violent offence is one in which, in the commission of the offence, the young person causes or attempts to cause **serious bodily harm** as defined in s. 2 of the *Criminal Code* and further expressed in case law (*R. v. C.D.K.* (2005)). This designation is made in a separate court process after a young person has been convicted of the offence. Such a designation has repercussions for a youth: three such determinations mean that a young person may be eligible for an "intensive rehabilitative custody and supervision (IRCS) order."

Although an IRCS order is a rehabilitative treatment, there are not many young persons who are given this order, due to the stringent nature of the requirements. As indicated, a young person must agree to the treatment plan, and no young person can be subject to physical or mental health treatment without his or her consent (s. 42(8) YCJA).

serious bodily harm
Harm that includes any physical or psychological hurt or injury, as well as any interference with a person's comfort level, and that is not temporary (transient) or insignificant (trifling) in nature.

> ## SIDEBAR
>
> ### Intensive Rehabilitative Custody and Supervision Orders
>
> Intensive rehabilitative custody and supervision (IRCS) orders are a treatment sentence for youth who have been found guilty of murder, manslaughter, or aggravated sexual assault *or* who have committed three serious violent offences *and* are suffering from a mental, psychological, or emotional disorder. The IRCS order includes a treatment plan that the young person must agree to participate in while in custody and while being supervised during the reintegrative community portion of his or her sentence. It is estimated to cost more than $100,000 per year due to the intensive therapy; the federal government has recently reaffirmed its support to continue this funding.

If a young person is at least 14 years old and has been convicted of an offence for which an adult would receive more than two years in prison, the Crown can make an application to the youth court for an order deeming the young person to be liable for an adult sentence. In making such a decision, the youth court judge must consider the seriousness and the circumstances of the offence, as well as the age, maturity, character, background, and previous record of the young person, and any other relevant factors; the judge must also have determined that a youth sentence would not be of sufficient length to hold the young offender accountable. While there is no mention of the balance between the need to protect society and the rehabilitation of the young person—as there had been in previous legislation, which used a transfer hearing to lead to the imposition of an adult sentence—the concept of **accountability** in the YCJA presumes a greater degree of care due to the age and stage of development of young persons.

accountability
Being held responsible for the actions that lead to a crime. Youth are seen as less accountable than adults; their accountability is measured on the basis of the greater dependency of young persons and their lower level of maturity.

Where Should Youth Serve Their Custodial Sentences?

The youth justice court is expected to be guided by the basic presumption that a young person who is under 18 at the time of sentencing will be placed in a youth facility and, if over the age of 18, in an adult facility unless the court is satisfied that it would not be in the best interests of the young person or would jeopardize the safety of others. In the *Annual Report of the Correctional Investigator*, prior to the death of Ashley Smith in custody, it was recommended that legislative amendments be made to ensure that

MINI CASE STUDY

When Youth Commit Murder

For the offences of attempt to commit murder, manslaughter, and aggravated sexual assault, the maximum length of a custody and supervision order for a youth sentence is three years.

For first-degree murder, a young person can receive a maximum youth custodial sentence of ten years, with six years served in custody. Second-degree murder carries a maximum sentence of seven years, with at most four years served in custody.

If the Crown is successful in its application to have a young person liable to an adult sentence, the young person could receive a sentence of life imprisonment. One of the most significant changes under the YCJA was that youth were no longer transferred to adult court to be tried in the case of serious violent offences. This change has meant that a young person must be found guilty in youth court; after a finding of guilt, the Crown may make an application for an adult sentence.

In deciding whether a young person should receive an adult sentence, the test is focused on the principle of accountability and whether a youth sentence would be of sufficient length to hold the young person accountable. The judge must be mindful of the youth justice principle of proportionate accountability, which is in keeping with the greater dependency and lower level of maturity of young persons generally.

One of the most notorious cases in recent years is that of the highly publicized "bathtub girls" murder in Brampton, Ontario. In 2003, two sisters, Sandra and Beth Anderson, aged 16 and 15 at the time, were angry about living with an alcoholic mother. They drugged their mother's drink with lethal levels of codeine from Tylenol No. 3 and invited her to take a warm bath, where they then held her head under water until she drowned. The girls were convicted of first-degree murder and sentenced to ten years as youth. The Crown had sought an adult sentence, but the trial judge stated that the circumstances of the case were not sufficient to render the case exceptional as required by s. 72 of the YCJA. In his remarks, he reiterated that it was important to remember that with youth, we are talking about fair and proportionate accountability that is consistent with the greater dependency of young persons and their reduced level of maturity (Mitchell, 2008). They were the first to serve youth sentences in an adult penitentiary since the YCJA was passed.

In 2006, both of the girls were sent to the Grand Valley Institution for Women in Kitchener, Ontario. By 2009, the eldest sister had served four years of the maximum ten-year sentence and was residing in a halfway house when she was accepted into a first-year science and engineering program at the University of Waterloo, where she is taking courses. The younger sister was released from custody after serving four years and is taking courses at a different university. In a 2009 article, Justice Bruce Duncan, referring to his decision to release the eldest sister to a halfway house, was quoted as saying that to "keep the gifted and intelligent woman with superior intelligence in prison would be little more than warehousing her" (as cited in Mitchell, 2009). They will both be required to return to court each year for the remainder of their ten-year sentence for a mandatory review (Mitchell, 2010).

What Do You Think?

Considering the range of sentences available for young persons in youth court, what arguments are there to suggest that the youth court sentence was not sufficient to hold the two girls accountable? What do you think about the girls attending university?

young persons under the age of 20 are not placed in penitentiaries and that youth courts are given information about the dangers of being placed in adult institutions (Office of the Correctional Investigator, 2003). Research has shown that young persons who are placed in adult facilities are more likely to reoffend, and to reoffend more quickly and more often than those who remain in the juvenile system (Steiner, Hemmens, & Bell, 2006).

In those cases where a young person has been sentenced to custody in a youth facility and then turns 18 while in custody, an application to transfer the young person to an adult facility can be made under s. 92 of the YCJA. In the application, it must be shown to the court that the transfer is in the best interests of the young person or in the public interest.

What Do You Think?

In the case of Ashley Smith, an application to transfer her to an adult facility was successful. Under which condition do you feel this application was most successful—her best interests or the public interest?

Growing Up in Jail

Confinement of youth in correctional facilities has a high economic cost as well as other social costs. What evidence there is suggests that custody has a weak deterrent effect on youth, and in many cases, the impact of incarceration actually increases the likelihood of reoffending. In calculating the costs and benefits of a custodial policy for young persons, it must also be kept in mind that almost all young offenders will be released into the community, and there runs the risk of a huge social cost to youth when they "grow up" in jail (think back to the case of J that began Part One).

In order to make a successful transition to young adulthood, youth must have opportunities and environmental conditions that support this transition.

SIDEBAR

John Howard: Gaols as Seminaries of Crime for the Young

In England during the 1700s, there were a number of reformers who fought for social justice reform; among the most ardent was John Howard. Writing in the *State of Prisons in England and Wales*, Howard (1777) spoke of the need to create separate facilities for youth, calling attention to the "seminaries" of crime that currently existed:

> I have now to complain of what is pernicious to their morals; and that is, the confining all sorts of prisoners together: debtors and felons, men and women, the young beginner and the old offender; and with all these ... some are guilty of misdemeanours only.
>
> In some Gaols you see (and who can see it without pain?) boys of 12 or 14 eagerly listening to the stories told by practised and experienced criminals of their adventures, successes, stratagems, and escapes.
>
> In some few Gaols are confined idiots and lunatics. The insane, where they are not kept separate, disturb and terrify other prisoners. No care is taken of them, although it is probable that by medicines, and proper regimen, some of them might be restored to their senses, and to usefulness in life. (pp. 15–16)

What Do You Think?

In the case of Ashley Smith, you will recall that she did not want to be placed in the adult system and that she was also suffering from a mental illness. If John Howard were to write *The State of Prisons in Canada, 2012*, would he find problems that were similar to or different from those he wrote about in 1777?

For example, the developmental psychology literature suggests that healthy transitions to adulthood include the presence or absence of an authoritative adult parent figure, association with pro-social peers, and participation in educational, extracurricular, or employment activities that foster the development of independent decision making and critical thinking (Bender & Losel, 1997; Farrington, 2002; Hawkins et al., 2008; Lipsey, 2009). In the correctional system, correctional officers, whose main job is to maintain security, often have impersonal, authoritarian, and hostile relationships with the young offenders (Schubert, Mulvey, Loughran, & Losoya, 2012). The lack of pro-social peers further complicates the situation for young persons who don't have a caring adult to help them develop social skills, improve relationships, or deal with problems. While there are some opportunities for education and extracurricular activities within our youth custodial facilities, much time is spent in cells or in the prison yard under the watchful surveillance of guards. This social context is not conducive to the healthy development of youth and to the successful transition to young adulthood. Upon release, the stigma of having been in custody can thwart efforts to seek out legal and meaningful employment or education. The lack of opportunity to develop social skills can make it very difficult to establish stable pro-social relationships. The two most important factors related to no longer engaging in crime are marriage or a stable intimate relationship and meaningful employment (Reid, 2010). Hindering the natural development of meaningful relationships and the skills necessary for meaningful employment through the use of more custody for young persons will jeopardize their successful transition to adulthood (Franke, 2010; Corrado & Freedman, 2011).

SIDEBAR

Youth and Social Justice

The following is an excerpt from the author's expert testimony to the House of Commons Standing Committee on Justice and Human Rights (Reid, 2011) regarding proposed changes to the YCJA that would include adding the principles of deterrence and denunciation to proceedings with young persons:

> The *Youth Criminal Justice Act* has had the effect of reducing the number of young people who have been sentenced to custody right across Canada, thereby removing our international embarrassment under the former legislation as being the nation which had the highest youth incarceration rate in the world. I am afraid that with the introduction of "specific deterrence and denunciation" to the principles of sentencing in the proposed amendments, we are headed back to that most embarrassing time. I am saddened by the thought of more young people being held in custody when our research evidence shows that incarceration does little to reduce offending patterns of young people and, in most cases, increases the likelihood that a young person will reoffend upon release. I believe that this will be most pronounced for the most vulnerable youth in our communities: the poor, the disenfranchised, and our First Nations youth. I am worried that the message that we will be sending to young people is contrary to the philosophy and principle of the YCJA; young people will feel like "throwaways," discarded because we couldn't take the time to apply evidence-based research and practice.

Safe Streets and Communities Act: Implications for Youth Justice

The *Safe Streets and Communities Act*, discussed in the case study in Part Four, also has implications for young people in the youth justice system. Requiring police officers to keep records of those situations where a young person has received a caution, warning, or referral under extrajudicial measures seems contrary to the intent of an alternative to the youth system and will likely increase the number of youth coming into the system. Lifting the ban on publication of names of youth when the court decides that the case is a serious one also seemingly defeats the intent of the provisions related to confidentiality in youth court proceedings. Finally, adding the principles of deterrence and denunciation to youth sentencing will move us again closer to the adult system and reduce the emphasis on the other principles directly relevant to youth based on their age and stage of maturity. The success of decreasing the number of youth in custody owing to the clear procedures and alternatives to the formal court process under the YCJA is likely to be jeopardized with the inclusion of these principles. Further, as shown in some of the research literature, the likelihood of imposing custody in more cases also increases the likelihood of failure. Significantly, it also runs contrary to the UN Convention on the Rights of the Child (1989) and, in particular, the Beijing Rules (1985), which state that "[t]he placement of a juvenile in an institution shall always be a disposition of last resort and for the minimum necessary period" (rule 19.1).

As discussed in previous chapters, governments often bow to public pressure to "do something" about the few sensational cases that draw utter disgust from the public. However, moral panics, as history has shown, are transitory and will subside over time. This is not at all to diminish the pain and anguish that is suffered by the victims and their families when such horrific crimes occur. On the contrary: when such panic is perpetuated through the institutionalization of fear through legislation and policy innovations directed at the perceived threat, more harm is often done than good.

The *Youth Criminal Justice Act* has been built on sound research evidence that reserves the most serious interventions for those young persons most at risk. Since its implementation, the number of young people in custody has been reduced, and innovative alternatives that assist them in their journey into adulthood have been created. Moving away from a model that acknowledges the lower level of maturity of young persons, toward a system more akin to the adult system, is most likely a step back in history.

SIDEBAR

Scared Straight Does Not Prevent Youth Crime

In 1978, the documentary *Scared Straight!* followed a group of delinquent youth into Rahway State Prison in New Jersey, where they were taunted by a group of "lifers" who had volunteered to provide a glimpse of what prison life might be like if these youth continued in their path of delinquency. A further documentary, *Scared Straight! Ten Years Later*, aired in 1987. A systematic evaluation of the experimental evidence found that, contrary to the images presented in the follow-up documentary, *Scared Straight!* did not prevent future delinquency. Rather, the deterrence-based program had the opposite effect and actually encouraged more involvement in crime (Petrosino, Turpin-Petrosino, & Buehler, 2003). Research since this meta-analysis has confirmed that such shock incarceration programs do not work (MacKenzie, 2006; Drake, Aos, & Miller, 2009; Henggeler & Schoenwald, 2011; Guerra & Williams, 2012).

In the fall of 2011, the original producer of *Scared Straight!* developed a new program called *Beyond Scared Straight*. This newer version is still based on the confrontation with inmates, but includes additional information and communication with the youth to assist them in making the right choice. The evidence was overwhelming from the research on *Scared Straight!* that such programs do not work; the creation of this second series, and its receiving much air time, appears to be catering to public pressure to "do something" about youth crime.

What Do You Think?

Have a look at some of the episodes of *Beyond Scared Straight* at www.aetv.com/beyond-scared-straight and consider why this deterrence-based program would be popular with the general public.

DISCUSSION QUESTIONS

1. Review the principles and objectives of extrajudicial measures and consider the ways in which Ashley Smith was dealt with at the beginning of the process. As was pointed out in the case study, Ashley was involved in extrajudicial measures before being incarcerated. What could have been done to assist her?

2. Earlier in this book, you learned that deterrence does not work to reduce recidivism among offenders. What is the value of adding denunciation and deterrence as a principle of sentencing for young persons as outlined in the *Safe Streets and Communities Act*?

3. The YCJA has made it more difficult to send a young person into custody than was the case under previous juvenile justice legislation. When, in your opinion, should youth be sentenced to custody?

SUGGESTED FURTHER READINGS

Davis-Barron, S. (2009). *Canadian youth and the criminal law*. Markham, ON: LexisNexis Canada.

Perelman, A.M. (2009). Beliefs about what works in juvenile rehabilitation: The influence of attitudes on support for "get tough" and evidence-based interventions. *Criminal Justice and Behavior, 36*(2), 184–197.

Scott, E.S., & Steinberg, L. (2008). *Rethinking juvenile justice*. Cambridge, MA: Harvard University Press.

REFERENCES

Barnhorst, R. (2012). Youth justice policy reform: The Youth Criminal Justice Act. In K. Ismaili, J. Sprott, & K. Varma (Eds.), *Canadian criminal justice policy: Contemporary perspectives*. Don Mills, ON: Oxford University Press.

Bell, S. (2012). *Young offenders and youth justice: A century after the fact*. Toronto: Nelson.

Bender, D., & Losel, F. (1997). Protective and risk effects of peer relations and social support on antisocial behavior in adolescents from multi-problem milieus. *Journal of Adolescence, 20*(6), 661–678.

Bittle, S., Hattem, T., Quann, N., & Muise, D. (2002). *A one-day snapshot of Aboriginal youth in custody across Canada*. Ottawa: Department of Justice.

Canadian Charter of Rights and Freedoms, part I of the *Constitution Act, 1982*, RSC 1985, app. II, no. 44.

Centre for Research on Youth at Risk. (1998). *Restorative justice* (Fact Sheet), St. Thomas University. Retrieved from http://www.stthomasu.ca/research/youth/restorative.htm

Cohen, S. (1972). *Folk devils and moral panic*. Oxford: MacGibbon and Kee.

Corrado, R., & Freedman, L. (2011). Risk profiles, trajectories and intervention points for serious and chronic young offenders. *International Journal of Child, Youth and Family Studies, 2*(1), 197–232.

Department of Justice. (1998). *A strategy for the renewal of youth justice*. Ottawa: Department of Justice Canada.

Doob, A., & Cesaroni, C. (2004). *Responding to youth crime in Canada*. Toronto: University of Toronto Press.

Dorfman, L., & Schiraldi, V. (2001). *Off balance: Youth, race and crime in the news*. Washington, DC: Office of Juvenile Justice and Delinquency Prevention, US Department of Justice.

Drake, E.K., Aos, S., & Miller, M.G. (2009). Evidence-based public policy options to reduce crime and criminal justice costs: Implications in Washington state. *Victims and Offenders, 4*: 170–196.

Farrington, D. (2002). Developmental criminology and risk-focused prevention. In M. Maguire, R. Morgan, & R. Reiner (Eds.), *Oxford handbook of criminology* (3rd ed., pp. 602–640). Oxford, UK: Oxford University Press.

Franke, S. (2010). *Current realities and emerging issues facing youth in Canada: An analytical framework for public policy research*. Ottawa: Government of Canada, Policy Research Institute.

Green, R. (2012). Explaining the Youth Criminal Justice Act. In J. Winterdyk & R. Smandych (Eds.), *Youth at risk and youth justice: A Canadian overview*. Toronto: Nelson.

Guerra, N.G., & Williams, K.R. (2012). Implementing evidence-based practices for juvenile justice in communities. In E.L. Grigorenko (Ed.), *Handbook of juvenile forensic psychology and psychiatry* (pp. 297–307). New Haven, CT: Springer.

Hawkins, J.D., Brown, E.C., Oesterle, S., Arthur, M.W., Abbott, R.D., & Catalano, R.F. (2008). Early effects of communities that care on targeted risks and initiation of delinquent behavior and substance use. *Journal of Adolescent Health, 43*(1), 15–22.

Henggeler, S.W., & Schoenwald, S.K. (2011) Evidence-based interventions for juvenile offenders and juvenile justice policies that support them. *Social Policy Report, 25*(1), 3–20. Retrieved from http://www.jmcgvlkpd.mtfc.com/2011_EB_Interventions_for_Juv_Offenders.pdf

Howard, J. (1777). *The state of prisons in England and Wales*. London: Warrington. Retrieved from http://books.google.ca/books?id=4EhNAAAAYAAJ

Juvenile Delinquents Act, RSC 1970, c. J-3.

Latimer, J. (2001). A meta-analytical examination of youth delinquency, family treatment, and recidivism. *Canadian Journal of Criminology, 43*(2), 237–253.

Latimer, J., & Foss, L.C. (2004). *A one-day snapshot of aboriginal youth in custody across Canada: Phase II*. Ottawa: Youth Justice Policy, Department of Justice Canada.

Lipsey, M.W. (2009). The primary factors that characterize effective interventions with juvenile offenders. *Victims & Offenders, 4*(2), 124–147.

MacKenzie, D.L. (2006). *What works in corrections? Reducing the criminal activities of offenders and delinquents*. New York: Cambridge University Press.

Mitchell, B. (2008). *The class project: How to kill a mother—The true story of Canada's infamous bathtub girls*. Toronto: Key Porter.

Mitchell, B. (2009, June 22). Bathtub girl granted release to attend school. *The Toronto Star*. Retrieved from http://www.thestar.com/news/crime/article/654696--bathtub-girl-granted-release-to-attend-school

Mitchell, B. (2010, July 27). Bathtub girl to attend Waterloo University. *The Toronto Star*. Retrieved from http://www.thestar.com/news/gta/crime/article/840680--bathtub-girl-to-attend-waterloo-u-in-the-fall

Moyer, S. (1980). *Diversion from the juvenile justice system and its impact on children: A review of the literature*. Ottawa: Queen's Printer.

Office of the Correctional Investigator. (2002). *Annual report of the Office of the Correctional Investigator 2002–2003*. Ottawa: Public Works and Government Services Canada. Retrieved from http://www.oci-bec.gc.ca/rpt/annrpt/annrpt20022003-eng.aspx#IVP

Petrosino, A., Turpin-Petrosino, C., & Buehler, J. (2003). Scared Straight and other juvenile awareness programs for preventing delinquency: A systematic review of randomized experimental evidence. *The Annals of the American Academy of Political and Social Science, 589*(1), 41–62.

Petrosino, A., Turpin-Petrosino, C., & Guckenburg, S. (2010). Formal system processing of juveniles: Effects on delinquency. *Campbell Systematic Reviews.* doi:10.4073/csr.2010.1. Retrieved from http://www.campbellcollaboration.org/lib/download/761/

R. v. B.W.P; R. v. B.V.N., 2006 SCC 27.

R. v. C.D.K., [2005] SCJ No. 79.

R. v. Gladue, [1999] 1 SCR 688.

R.v. K.D., [2003] NSJ No. 165 (SC Fam. Div.).

R. v. M.J.S., [2004] NSJ No. 64 (SC).

R. v. R.J. (1982), 37 OR (2d) 173 (HC).

Reid, S.A. (2005). Youth crime and the media. In K. Campbell (Ed.), *Youth justice in Canada*. Toronto: Pearson.

Reid, S.A. (2009). *125 Warnings: A review of extrajudicial measures and extrajudicial sanctions related to youth with highly complex needs within the criminal justice system in New Brunswick*. Fredericton, NB: Department of Public Safety.

Reid, S.A. (2010). The untapped potential in our communities to assist youth engaged in risky behavior. *International Journal of Child, Youth and Family Studies, 1*(2), 179–203.

Reid, S.A. (2011, March 23). Evidence to Standing Committee on Justice and Human Rights, 40th Parliament, 3rd Sess. Retrieved from http://www.parl.gc.ca/HousePublications/Publication.aspx?DocId=5069873&Language=E&Mode=1

Reid, S.A., & Reitsma-Street, M. (1984). Assumptions and implications of new Canadian legislation for young offenders. *Canadian Criminology Forum, 7*(1), 1–19.

Reid-MacNevin, S.A., & Kappel, B.E. (2003). *Youth justice in Canada*. Toronto: Canadian Training Institute.

Safe Streets and Communities Act, SC 2012, c. 1.

Schubert, C.A., Mulvey, E.P., Loughran, T.A., & Losoya, S.H. (2011). Perceptions of institutional experience and community outcomes for serious adolescent offenders. *Criminal Justice and Behavior, 39*(71), 71–93.

Schwalbe, C.S., Gearing, R.E., MacKenzie, M.J., Brewer, K.B., & Ibrahim, R. (2012). A meta-analysis of experimental studies of diversion programs for juvenile offenders, *Clinical Psychology Review, 32*(1): 26–33.

Seskus, T., & Mofina, R. (2000). Young offenders and the press. In J. Winterdyk (Ed.), *Issues and perspectives on young offenders in Canada* (2nd ed.). Toronto: Harcourt.

Steiner, B., Hemmens, C., & Bell, V. (2006). Legislative waiver re-considered: General deterrent effects of statutory exclusion laws enacted post-1979. *Justice Quarterly, 23*(1), 32–48.

Sullivan, C.J., Veysey, B.M., Hamilton, Z.K., & Grillo, M. (2007). Reducing out-of-community placement and recidivism: Diversion of delinquent youth with mental health and substance use problems from the justice system. *International Journal of Offender Therapy and Comparative Criminology, 51,* 555–577.

UN General Assembly. (1989). Convention on the rights of the child. UNTS Vol. 1577. Retrieved from http://www2.ohchr.org/english/law/crc.htm

UN General Assembly. (1985). Standard minimum rules for the administration of juvenile justice (the Beijing rules). Retrieved from http://www2.ohchr.org/english/law/pdf/beijingrules.pdf

Ungar, M. (2004). Resilience among children in child welfare, corrections, mental health and educational settings: Recommendations for service. *Child and Youth Care Forum, 34*(6), 445–464.

Whitaker, J., Severy, L., & Morton, D. (1984). A comprehensive community based youth diversion program. *Child Welfare, 63*(2), 175–181.

Young Offenders Act, SC 1981-82-83, c. 110.

Youth Criminal Justice Act, SC 2002, c. 1.

PART SIX
System Challenges: Problems, Prevention, and Potential

You Be the Judge (Revisited)

Karla O'Regan

Have a quick look back at the case that opened this book. Do you remember what sentence you thought J should receive? Can you recall your reasons for choosing that sentence? Now that you've had a chance to consider the many agencies, approaches, and guiding principles involved in Canada's criminal justice system, has your view of that case changed in any way? Which of the sentencing principles discussed in Chapter 8 does your initial judgment reflect? Did you give priority to a particular sentencing principle? Which ones were less important to you? Are there sentencing objectives that, as you now see, your chosen penalty didn't address well?

J's actual name is Marcel Jacob. His case was heard by Barry Stuart, a former judge and a prominent proponent of restorative justice in Canada who has worked extensively with a number of Canada's First Nations communities in the Yukon. He has worked over his career to explore and develop alternative processes that build on Aboriginal traditions. He is currently an associate at the Centre for Restorative Justice at Simon Fraser University, where he continues to work on alternative dispute processes that engage parties in a consensus-based approach to resolving conflict. Some of Stuart's thinking about the Jacob case is reflected in the following paragraphs, taken from his judgment in that case:

> We see in our court both the beginning and the end of tragic stories, over and over again. The story begins with taking a child into the permanent care of the state because the child's family has failed to provide the basic level of care. The story ends when the child, years later as a young man, is sentenced for a terribly violent crime, or as a young woman, has her child taken into care. This is a common story. There are exceptions. However, some exceptions differ only in the degree of sad or tragic events that characterize their lives.
>
> The parade of children from broken homes, to permanent care, to substance abuse, to dysfunctional lives, to crime, and ultimately to jail,

and/or to parent children, who in turn feed the system with another round of permanent wardships, seems endless; seems diabolically planned to employ an ever-increasing number of professionals. From the perspective of the bench, the frustration, anger and despair in this tragic and senseless parade generates an overwhelming desire to blame the department that cares for these neglected children as they evolve into dysfunctional and, at times, very dangerous young adults, or to blame correction agencies that send offenders back to the community to offend again. It would be easy to blame these agencies, but it would be wrong to do so. In over 20 years, I have never found a single social worker or correction officer who did not stretch beyond their resources to make a difference. Many were burned out by the overwhelming challenges they confronted and accepted.

If blame is being passed out, no one can elude taking their share. The parents whose neglect caused their child to be taken into care, the extended family and community who failed to become involved, all of the professionals—public health workers, social workers, teachers, police officers, probation officers and, yes, judges—who have done our job in the same old way, all of us must share the blame for the endless parade of children through our hands and into dysfunctional lives. By now, we should know better. We must do much better.

To do better, we need to stop looking for someone to blame. Scapegoating will dig us deeper into our abysmal incapacity to make a difference. To do better, we need to share a systemic understanding of the larger process. We need to understand that what each does, connects to what others do and creates a pattern. The pattern influences each of us in ways that are often not apparent. To do better, we need to take more than an isolated snapshot, frozen around one case or one event, as the basis for understanding what to change. We will not understand what to do unless we understand the larger ramifications of our actions that play out over years, if not generations.

The tragedy in this case, as in the case of so many young people like Marcel Jacob, is not that any one person failed to do their job—everyone may have done their specific job, but collectively we failed to do the job required to make a difference. Until we slow down, step aside from the crush of daily challenges, to acquire a systemic understanding, we will each continue to do our job well, but continue to fail to do the job needed to change the endless parade of devastated lives.

The enemy is us. The villain in this piece, as in so many other cases, is no one person, no one agency or department, but rather the system. The fragmented, truncated system that has no integrated vision or holistic approach is the villain. The system we accept so readily and tinker with wee changes to address its massive failings is the paramount contributing cause of Marcel's circumstances. (*R. v. Jacob*, 2002, paras. 120–127)

Sentence: Eight years in prison, DNA sample, lifetime firearms prohibition

What Do You Think?

You now have an opportunity to rethink your own decision about the appropriate sentence for Jacob (a decision you made after reading Chapter 1 of this book) in light of the decision reached by Judge Stuart:

- What do you think of Judge Stuart's decision in this case? Do you agree with it? How different is his decision from the one you reached?
- What sentencing principles do you think Judge Stuart's judgment reflects? Are there others that you think it misses or underemphasizes?
- In his judgment, Judge Stuart mentions a number of issues within Canada's criminal justice system that were discussed in the previous chapters. These include the social context of crime, the strain on institutional resources to adequately address it, and how easy it can be to look outside ourselves when assigning blame for society's crime. Are there others you can identify?
- Think back on the theoretical models discussed in Chapter 1. Where on the ideological continuum would you place Judge Stuart's approach to crime and its punishment? Does his judgment represent a collectivist or an individualist view of society?
- Although Judge Stuart is widely recognized as a proponent of restorative justice, does his decision in the Jacob case reflect other theoretical models of crime control?

See also mini chapter 16.5 Restorative Justice in Focus: Sentencing Circles

The next chapter will address many of these issues within the context of crime prevention. You will learn about the differences between crime prevention approaches and the strategies more commonly found among criminal justice agencies. As noted by Judge Stuart, successful crime prevention and community restoration require many hands—strong family supports, educational programs, successful labour markets, and healthy communities. The challenges facing each of you, as students of criminal justice, are numerous and daunting. A full exploration of the trials and opportunities awaiting you is beyond the scope of this introductory text, but Chapter 16 briefly discusses these topics. What role do you foresee for yourself in Canada's criminal justice system? How will you meet the challenge of vanquishing its "villains"?

REFERENCE

R. v. Jacob, 2002 YKTC 15. Retrieved from http://www.sfu.ca/crj/fulltext/rvjacob.pdf

Crime Prevention

MINI CASE STUDY

Community-Based Crime Prevention in an Inner-City Toronto Neighbourhood

Standing near a bright new playground watching smiling children taking tennis lessons and neighbours chatting as they tend a community garden, Stephanie Payne marvels at how quickly the scene has changed at Toronto's most notorious intersection.

"Two years ago, everyone was scared and cautious. There were a lot of kids hanging out and smoking and swearing. You don't see that any more," said the Barbados-born Ms. Payne, who helped organize a community effort that cut the rate of major crimes by half in a troubled trio of apartment buildings on the northeast corner of Jane and Finch.

A survey done in 2000 showed the crime rate in the area of high-rises and malls near York University was well over twice the national average, and much of it was youth-related. Assaults, shootings, stabbings, and standoffs with police occurred with alarming frequency.

Breaking the cycle required creative thinking and a lot of detailed work, but the success can serve as a model for other communities, said Kevin Green, principal of Greenwin Property Management, which owns the buildings and manages 50,000 apartment units across Canada.

"We had a vision that we could get the community involved and bring down crime, but landlords are not the ones most renters turn to unless the heat is off," Mr. Green said.

He approached Ms. Payne and other prominent tenants to start the San Romanoway Revitalization Association, which includes residents, businesses, and the police.

Ms. Payne, who has lived in Canada since 1967 and works as a nurse, said she knew that giving the residents a sense of community and empowerment was important, but she was skeptical.

"Over the years there's been a lot of negativity attached to the area," she said. "I hemmed and hawed but I finally said I'll give it a try."

Complicating matters were the 76 different languages spoken by tenants of the three buildings on San Romanoway. They are mostly recent immigrants from the Caribbean, Guyana, south and east Asia, and Africa, all of whom are still adapting to life in a new country. Of the 4,400 residents, nearly 3,000 are under the age of 18.

Because many of the residents come from places where speaking out can invite trouble, the association's early meetings drew as few as half a dozen residents, Ms. Payne said. But as people talked, momentum and membership grew. They found everyone wanted more security but had been waiting for someone else to do something about it. They also wanted more recreational and social activities for children, who played noisily and destructively in the hallways.

The crime figures became the basis of Ms. Payne's proposal to the National Crime Prevention Centre, a federal Justice Department initiative that provides up to $100,000 a year in project support for up to three years if a group can get local corporate and private partners.

Meanwhile, Greenwin worked with the Toronto-based private firm Intelligarde International to rethink the security system to keep out people who do not belong. Brighter lighting and security cameras were installed around the complex to eliminate places where people could congregate without being seen, Mr. Green said.

But there were challenges within as well. A few tenants who were perennial problems, such as drug dealers who had set up shop in apartments, were evicted.

Then the association began to get corporate help to find activities and jobs for the youthful residents.

Rogers Cable donated computers and Internet access for a computer centre that is continually busy. Tennis Canada refinished a long-neglected tennis court and the Ontario Tennis Association agreed to provide free tennis lessons. In the past year, 120 children enrolled for the course.

Human Resources Development Canada is paying the salaries of counsellors for a nine-week children's day-camp program this summer. As part of a $300,000 HRDC grant, a youth internship program was also set up with the Jewish Vocational Services of Greater Toronto.

The latest addition is the playground, completed last weekend with the help of 200 volunteers and material provided by Home Depot Canada. The inspiration for that was a tenant who found a Web site for Kaboom!, a U.S.-based foundation linking corporations to community groups seeking to build safe play spaces.

Andrea Allen, a single parent of two boys who came to Toronto from Jamaica three years ago, says she wonders why people used to be wary of living at Jane and Finch.

"Honestly, I would not want to leave here."

Source: Immen (2003). Reprinted by permission of the *Globe and Mail*.

What Do You Think?

1. On the basis of this case study, what factors do you believe contribute to the crime and disorder problems in this community?

2. What criminal justice (law enforcement) approaches do you think would traditionally be implemented to address the problems in this community? What are the shortcomings of these traditional approaches?

3. Identify the preventive approaches that have been implemented in this community. How do they differ from the traditional criminal justice approaches?

Introduction

Although there is no universally accepted definition of the term "crime prevention," it can be broadly defined as any pre-emptive intervention intended to block or reduce the risk of a criminal act occurring or the onset of criminal behaviour within an individual. This expansive definition is purposeful, for it reflects the expansiveness of the crime prevention field, in both theoretical and applied terms. There are a number of philosophies, strategies, programs, and practices that could be classified as "crime prevention." This definition acknowledges the unfinished debate among scholars over the conceptual parameters that should be applied to crime prevention to distinguish it from traditional criminal justice approaches to crime.

Indeed, crime prevention is distinguished from the criminal justice system in several ways: through its proactive nature in dealing with crime (usually before it occurs); the central role played by private citizens and communities; and the reliance on institutions and strategies that often fall outside the criminal justice system. Notwithstanding its distinction as an "alternative approach to the more traditional responses to crime," Welsh and Farrington (2012, p. 3) contend that crime prevention should nonetheless be "considered the fourth pillar of crime reduction, alongside the institutions of police, courts, and corrections."

The aim of this chapter is to provide an overview of crime prevention, with particular emphasis on contrasting its unique conceptual underpinnings and approaches with those of the criminal justice system.

Crime Prevention Versus the Criminal Justice System

The contemporary field of crime prevention arose as a critique of and an alternative to the criminal justice system. In particular, the traditional "cops, courts, and corrections" approach was seen as being insufficient to control or deter acts that threaten public safety. More specifically, according to the proponents of crime prevention, the criminal justice system is unable to cope with the actual quantity of crime, and it fails to identify many criminal offenders and bring them to justice, to rehabilitate those offenders who are identified, and to address the root causes of crime and criminality (Canada, 1993, p. 1).

In theory, crime prevention is contrary to the criminal justice system in many respects, including the following:

- It is inherently proactive, not reactive.
- It stresses flexibility in applying strategies that are individualized for specific circumstances and that generally fall outside the criminal justice system, rather than taking the cookie-cutter approach of the criminal justice system, which relies on the same set of strategies in controlling crime (arrest, prosecute, punish).
- It puts responsibility primarily in the hands of citizens, not of the state, although great emphasis is placed on partnerships between state and non-state actors.
- Greater emphasis is placed on "informal" social control (which is carried out by private actors) as opposed to "formal" social control (which is exercised by the state).
- It focuses on potential offenders (at-risk individuals) and potential victims, rather than on the offenders.
- It targets not only crime, but also fear, disorder, and public incivilities.

Each of these distinguishing characteristics is detailed below. Table 15.1 summarizes the differences between crime prevention and the criminal justice system.

TABLE 15.1   A Comparison of Crime Prevention and the Criminal Justice System

	Crime prevention	Criminal justice system
Timing	Proactive	Reactive
Approach	Predict, assess, and intervene	Intervene (no real prediction)
Response	Problem-oriented (wide range of appropriate solutions)	Narrow range of solutions
Lead responsibility	Citizenry	State
Partnerships and collaboration	Partnerships and collaboration fundamental and extensive	Limited partnerships between criminal justice agencies and non-state actors
Organizations providing services	Community groups, NGOs, schools, public health, social welfare agencies	Police, public prosecutors, correctional facilities, parole boards, legislative branches
Control	Informal social control	Formal social control
Scope	Criminal act, criminality (causes), disorder, incivilities, fear	Criminal act
Targets	Victim (and offender)	Offender
Setting	Natural: Home, school, or community	Artificial: State institution
Primary goal	Improved functioning	Control of individuals

Source: Author, with contributions from Greenwood (2006, p. 15).

What Do You Think?

1. What are some similarities between the criminal justice system and crime prevention?

2. For high-crime neighbourhoods, what criminal justice strategies discussed in previous chapters do you believe best complement crime prevention strategies?

3. What do you think a comprehensive approach to crime control should entail in a high-crime neighbourhood?

Proactive Crime Prevention Efforts

One critique of the criminal justice system is that it is overwhelmingly reactive when it comes to combating crime and does not have the capacity to proactively address the root causes of crime. The most fundamental characteristic of crime prevention, by contrast, is that it is proactive; it strives to anticipate and prevent crime either by reducing the opportunity for a criminal act to occur in a particular time or place, or by addressing the root causes of criminal behaviour. Proactive crime prevention strategies are epitomized by social problem-solving interventions that primarily cater to children and youth who are at risk of future delinquent and criminal behaviour.

A "Problem-Oriented" Approach

According to Cherney (2006, p. 1), "A core component of crime prevention good practice" is a "problem-solving methodology." This approach to crime control encompasses three components: (1) an *analytical process*, whereby the scope and nature of a (potential) crime problem or criminal behaviour are predicted and assessed by collecting and analyzing relevant information (which includes identifying and separating out the causes of the problem from the symptoms and aggravating factors); (2) an intervention that is *crafted specifically for the problem being addressed* (which includes determining the most appropriate institutions through which interventions can be delivered); and (3) consideration of *a wide range of alternative and flexible solutions* in anticipation of or reaction to a crime risk or onset of criminal behaviour (recognizing the highly individualized nature of each risk).

The Central Role of Private Actors and Partnerships

The criminal justice system is symptomatic of a state-imposed, top-down approach to social problem solving: the government defines the problem (through laws and legislation), then takes responsibility for addressing the problem (through the enforcement of criminal laws by police, prosecutors, the judiciary, correctional facilities, parole agencies, etc.).

Crime prevention is based on a bottom-up approach, with citizens playing a major role.

In contrast, crime prevention is based on a bottom-up approach, which in turn assumes that private citizens play a major role in maintaining order in a free society and should therefore accept some responsibility for the prevention of crime, criminality, and incivilities. This is a fundamental change that results in the responsibility for crime prevention being partially transferred from the state to the citizenry.

That said, the state still plays a major role in crime prevention, beyond its traditional criminal justice responsibilities. Crime prevention is thus ultimately a shared responsibility between private and public actors. A hallmark of crime prevention initiatives is that they should be planned and implemented as partnerships between government (public) agencies and other key (private) stakeholders (community groups, schools, private sector businesses, etc.). In addition to police, other government agencies, professionals, and services that are important players in crime prevention include schools, social workers, publicly funded health-care facilities and professionals, municipal engineering and urban planning departments, as well as municipal recreational facilities and community centres, to name just a few.

FIGURE 15.1   The Players in Crime Prevention

CRIME PREVENTION PARTNERS

Public Stakeholders
- police
- schools
- social workers
- health-care facilities and professionals
- municipal engineering and urban planning departments
- municipal recreational facilities and community centres

Private Stakeholders
- private citizens
- community groups
- local businesses
- property owners and managers
- private security professionals
- urban design professionals (e.g., architects)

▶ IN-CLASS EXERCISE

Identify various institutions, organizations, and/or programs in your town or city that play a role in addressing the root causes of criminal behaviour. As part of a class discussion, describe the role they play (and specific programs they implement) in addressing factors that put children and youth at risk of future criminal or delinquent behaviour.

Informal Social Control

The shift in crime prevention responsibilities from the state to local communities means greater emphasis is placed on informal forms of social control, exerted by private actors working together, as opposed to formal methods of social control, which are state-imposed sanctions codified in written laws and regulations, and enforced by the police and the courts.

informal social control

The development, observance, and enforcement of local norms for appropriate public behaviour (Greenberg & Rohe, 1986, p. 80).

Informal social control is central to community crime prevention, and is concerned with reinforcing or modifying the individual and collective behaviours of residents to produce or strengthen a local social environment that can informally regulate itself, including the regulation and prevention of criminal, delinquent, disorderly, and uncivil behaviour. Informal social control is based on customs, common agreement, or social norms. Within the context of neighbourhoods, it refers to "the observance of standards of right conducted in the public places in which one lives and moves, those standards to be consistent with, and supportive of, the values and lifestyle of the particular neighbourhood" (Wilson, 1975, p. 24). Informal social control is said to restrict crime and disorder through a vigorous enforcement of local norms and standards by the legitimate users of a space. The activities involved in such community-based enforcement include creating conditions whereby offenders are at greater risk of being detected, reporting offenders to police, confronting offenders, and undertaking structured activities by neighbourhood groups, such as Neighbourhood Watch or citizen patrols (Greenberg, Rohe, & Williams, 1983; Greenberg, Rohe, & Williams, 1985, p. 1; Rosenbaum, 1988, p. 327).

Focusing on Potential Victims and Offenders

The criminal justice system is overwhelmingly focused on offenders—catching them, charging them, prosecuting them, sentencing them, punishing them, and, to a lesser extent, rehabilitating them. The field of crime prevention is also directly concerned with offenders through strategies that attempt to reduce opportunities for them to commit crimes in a particular time and place. However, it tends to pay more attention to the potential victim or target; not only are situational crime prevention strategies geared toward protecting people and places from victimization, but the planning and implementation of these interventions are often carried out by the very people who are at risk of becoming victims. Attention is also shifted from the offender to the potential offender; this is the hallmark of social developmental approaches to crime prevention that seek to address the factors that place children and youth at risk of (future) delinquency and criminality.

Targeting Criminality, Fear, and Disorder

As discussed above, crime prevention through social development is very much focused on addressing the root causes of criminal and delinquent behaviour. This contrasts with the criminal justice system, which was never created to address the root causes of criminality (although corrections-based treatment and rehabilitation does attempt to prevent recidivism).

Moreoever, crime prevention interventions do not simply address crime; in some cases, they are meant to provide individuals and communities with the education, tools, power, and collective security to alleviate fear of crime (see Chapter 1 for further discussion of fear of crime).

Certain crime prevention theories and strategies also advocate a focus on disorder and incivilities, which are not criminal or illegal acts as defined by the law, but can contribute to local instability that may invite more serious crime problems. For Lab (2004, p. 15), there are two categories of disorder and incivilities: physical ("the physical deterioration of buildings, litter, graffiti, vandalism, and abandoned buildings and cars, among others") and social ("public drunkenness, vagrancy, groups of loitering youths, harassment [such as begging and panhandling], and visible drug sales and use"). Such behaviours may be addressed by mobilizing and organizing neighbourhood residents, which include promoting a level of informal social control. Some situational crime prevention and law enforcement strategies emphasize **zero tolerance** toward incivilities and disorder problems in the belief that such enforcement may help alleviate factors that encourage more serious crime problems (Wilson & Kelling, 1982).

zero tolerance
A disciplinary approach that advocates automatic punitive responses to all types of disorder and crime problems, no matter how minor, with the intention of eliminating undesirable conduct through punishment and deterrence. For example, fighting in school means an automatic suspension.

The Goals of Crime Prevention

Greenwood (2006, pp. 12 and 13) distinguishes between the ultimate goals of criminality (crime) prevention and the criminal justice system. He implies that the main role of the criminal justice system in helping to produce a civil and orderly society is the "control of individuals" (in particular offenders, although it can be argued that the state's social control function also targets the broader public through the general deterrence effect of criminal laws, enforcement, and punishment). In contrast, crime prevention through social development—through its targeting of at-risk children and youth and emphasis on social problem solving, community cohesion, and strong local institutions (e.g., schools, families, communities)—is ultimately geared toward the improved functioning of the individual.

Dominant Crime Prevention Approaches

Crime prevention strategies can be separated into four broad categories:

1. crime prevention through social development
2. situational crime prevention
3. community crime prevention
4. community and problem-oriented policing.

Crime Prevention Through Social Development

Crime prevention through social development (CPSD) encompasses interventions that target the root causes of criminal behaviour. Research shows that many chronic offenders come from some type of negative social environment during their childhood, which can include poverty, parental neglect and abuse, exposure to violence, poor schooling, or poor role models. Children and youth who are at risk of future criminal offending may also suffer from personal **risk factors** such as hyperactivity, anger management problems, learning disabilities, or psychological disorders. The underlying premise of CPSD is that risk-focused interventions, implemented during childhood and the teen years, can alleviate factors that may lead to future delinquent, criminal, and antisocial behaviours. According to Welsh and Farrington (2010), the basic idea of risk-focused criminality prevention is simple: "Identify the key risk factors for offending and implement prevention methods designed to counteract them. There is often a related attempt to identify key **protective factors** against offending and to implement prevention methods designed to enhance them" (p. 9).

A central institution through which social problem-solving approaches to crime prevention are delivered is the family. The family is society's most crucial institution in promoting or hindering the future criminal behaviour of a child. Child development is highly influenced by various family characteristics and practices; for instance, parent–child relationships, discipline, family mental health, neglect or abuse, and family history of substance abuse or criminal behaviour. A significant focus of social problem-solving approaches to prevent criminality is to strengthen high-risk family environments by helping to develop and support good parenting skills, while addressing problems and negative behaviours experienced by parents that can affect their children (e.g., poverty, substance abuse, aggression). These approaches also entail interventions that cater directly to at-risk children by increasing their personal resilience through mentoring, remedial education, psychological counselling, social and life skills development, and recreational activities. (See Chapter 13 on youth justice for more on risk and protective factors.)

Schools are second only to families in significance as a crime prevention institution. First and foremost, education is a critical protective factor in offsetting **criminogenic** conditions. The most important role that schools can play is to teach kids to read, write, compute, and think. Like families, schools also provide young people with an environment that is critical to their positive socialization and the development of basic social competencies. Many innovative approaches to school culture and education have been introduced in recent years that can also help deter criminality insofar as such

risk factors
Factors that increase the risk of criminal or delinquent behaviour.

protective factors
Positive conditions, influences, or interventions that can increase the health and well-being of children and families by counteracting risk factors.

criminogenic
Producing or tending to produce crime or criminal behaviour.

innovations promote learning, attendance, completion of high school, and pro-social behaviour among high-risk students. These innovations include:

- customizing academic programs to the needs of each student
- developing more interactive and experiential teaching practices
- providing alternative curricula for struggling students
- allowing students more say in a school's policies
- providing rewards for academic achievement and consistent attendance
- providing programs that foster important social competencies and life skills that can prevent future criminality.

In recent years, schools have also become the central vehicle through which programs are delivered to reduce specific criminogenic risk factors such as aggression, bullying, violence, negative peer pressure, substance abuse, and gang involvement.

After analyzing the evaluations of various crime prevention projects, Sherman (1997) concluded that the following CPSD interventions targeting children and youth were effective or promising in reducing criminogenic risk factors:

Within the home:

- Frequent home visits to infants (ages 0–2) by trained nurses and other professionals, which reduces child abuse and other injuries to infants.
- Preschool and weekly home visits by teachers to children under age 5, which substantially reduces arrests when the children are older.
- Family therapy and parent training, which reduce aggression and hyperactivity.

Within the school:

- Clarifying and communicating norms about behaviour through rules, reinforcement of positive behaviour, and school-wide initiatives (such as anti-bullying campaigns), which reduce crime, delinquency, and substance abuse among students.
- Life, social competency, and coping skills training (emphasizing capacities such as stress management, critical thinking, problem solving, self-control, and emotional intelligence), which reduces delinquency and substance abuse.
- Training or coaching at-risk youth in thinking skills (using rewards-based behaviour modification techniques), which reduces substance abuse.

- Innovative classroom management and instructional initiatives (such as grouping students into smaller units for cooperative learning or using flexible and intensive instruction methods for underachieving or disruptive students), which reduce drug abuse and delinquency.

Within the community:

- Community-based mentoring by Big Brothers Big Sisters, which substantially reduced drug abuse in one experiment (although evaluations of other mentoring programs did not reveal the same impressive results).
- Community-based, supervised after-school recreation programs, which can reduce juvenile crime in the immediate area.

Situational Crime Prevention

situational crime prevention (SCP)

The management, design, or manipulation of the immediate physical and human environment so as to remove or reduce the opportunities for specific types of crimes.

Situational crime prevention (SCP) involves the management, design, or manipulation of the immediate physical and human environment so as to remove or reduce the opportunities for specific types of crimes. In particular, SCP operates on three hypotheses concerning crime (Cohen & Felson, 1979; Clarke & Cornish, 1985; Clarke, 1997):

1. Most criminal acts require the coming together of motivated offenders and potential victims at a particular time and place (for this reason, situational measures focus on securing places).
2. Many types of crime—property crime in particular—are opportunistic; that is, offenders take advantage of certain opportunities they perceive can be exploited within a particular physical (and human) environment (for this reason, situational measures attempt to reduce opportunities for criminal acts to take place).
3. Criminal behaviour involves a rational decision-making process whereby the offender weighs the advantages and disadvantages of a specific criminal act (this being the case, offenders can be deterred from committing crimes).

What Do You Think?
Situational Crime Prevention

1. What are the fundamental differences between situational crime prevention and a social problem-solving approach?
2. What are the similarities between situational crime prevention and traditional policing approaches discussed in Chapter 3?

Each of these hypotheses draws attention to one of the most important assumptions underlying situational crime prevention: human behaviour is affected by the immediate physical environment. Within the context of crime and its prevention, this means that specific settings can create opportunities for an illegal act to occur by transforming thoughts or inclinations into a criminal act. "The theory of crime settings rests on a single principle: that easy or tempting opportunities entice people into criminal action" (Felson & Clarke, 1998, pp. 1 and 2).

Based on this **etiological** theory of crime, the essential characteristic of situational crime prevention is that it concentrates on reducing the *opportunity* for a criminal act to occur at a particular time and place. Because SCP strategies intervene directly in the opportunistic portion of the criminal process, its solutions are restricted to variables that can be manipulated in the context of the relationship between people and their physical environment. Approaches to reducing opportunity have been grouped into five categories (Clarke, 1997; Cornish & Clarke, 2003):

etiology
The study of causation or origination.

1. Increasing the effort needed by the offender to commit a crime, by making the targets of crime harder to get at or otherwise hindering the commission of crime.
2. Increasing the risks to the offender, whether real or perceived, of detection and apprehension.
3. Reducing the rewards to the offender, which in some cases may involve removing the targets of crime altogether.
4. Removing people's excuses to commit crimes.
5. Reducing provocations—for example, reducing frustration and stress, avoiding disputes, reducing emotional arousal, and neutralizing peer pressure.

What Do You Think?

What strategies has your community or city put in place to reduce opportunities for criminal acts?

The Built Environment

Environmental design is an important factor in crime prevention. Crime prevention through environmental design (CPTED) is a situational approach that advocates the proper design and use of a physical space as well as the built environment (houses, buildings, landscapes, streets, parks, and entire neighbourhoods) to reduce the opportunity for crime. CPTED uses

environmental design
Fashioning and developing the physical and built landscape, most often in an urban or suburban setting.

Crime Prevention Through Environmental Design (CPTED)

Some CPTED guidelines that are commonly used to reduce the opportunity for crime at a particular time and place include the following:

- target hardening, including locking doors and windows and using fences and security gates
- entry control mechanisms, such as computerized pass cards or apartment building entrance intercoms
- limiting the number of entry and exit points in a neighbourhood
- "intentional" surveillance techniques and technology, such as convex mirrors, security cameras, and raised cashier kiosks
- maximizing "natural surveillance" by legitimate users through certain building designs (such as locating windows so they overlook sidewalks and parking lots) and interior and exterior lighting (stressing bright white lights)
- designing buildings and/or pruning ground-level planting to minimize potential hiding or entrapment areas
- promoting legitimate use of public spaces (encouraging "eyes on the street") by building attractors such as parks, playgrounds, wide sidewalks, and community gardens
- designing spaces to promote social interaction and cohesion among residents
- keeping surrounding areas clean, well maintained, graffiti-free, and attractive to prevent a perception of neglect by potential offenders.

| BEFORE | AFTER |

Source: Peel Police.

opportunity reduction strategies that are both direct (modifying the built environment to prevent crime) and indirect (influencing residents to assume greater responsibility over their neighbourhood).

▶ IN-CLASS EXERCISE

Walk around your neighbourhood with a camera and take photos of physical and built characteristics you believe increase the opportunity for a crime to occur. At the same time, take photos of physical and built characteristics you believe decrease the opportunity for a crime to occur. Present these images in class and describe how some designs adhere to SCP and CPTED principles, while others do not.

Community Crime Prevention

Community crime prevention (CCP) incorporates the community defence model and the community development model. Both share one defining element essential to CCP: the existence of a socially cohesive collective of residents who join together to prevent and control crime. It is believed that the loss of the socially cohesive community has contributed to crime and disorder within advanced Western societies (Wirth, 1938; Forrest & Kearns, 2001). Accordingly, the effectiveness of community-based crime prevention efforts often depends on the extent to which local social cohesion, or a sense of community, exists within a particular locale. While some may view the neighbourhood as simply the area in which situational or social developmental crime prevention programs are implemented, the sociological concept of community in and of itself forms the heart of a distinct crime prevention philosophy and institution.

Particularly important to CCP, according to Sampson, Raudenbush, and Earls (1997), is **collective efficacy**, a concept that combines social cohesion with informal social control and is defined as "the linkage of mutual trust and the willingness to intervene for the common good" (p. 919), as well as the realization of "common values and the ability of groups to regulate their members according to desired principles" (Crawford, 1999, p. 518).

collective efficacy
The willingness of individuals in a neighbourhood to work together toward a common goal, such as crime control.

The community defence model is geared toward preventing criminal opportunities by organizing local residents to keep a watchful eye out for suspicious activities or individuals. The theory behind this approach is that the implementation of crime prevention programs will mobilize residents around a shared control over private and public spaces. The crime prevention program that has become universally associated with the community defence model is Neighbourhood Watch.

Neighbourhood Watch

Also called Block Watch or Crime Watch, this structured program involves a group of neighbours organized to prevent crime and disorder problems within a residential neighbourhood or apartment building. Residents are trained to keep an eye out for suspicious individuals or activities and to call police when such circumstances are spotted.

The community development model promotes the physical, social, and socio-economic development of a neighbourhood, which can include organized residents, economic development, beautification projects, **gentrification**, and other types of physical development.

A community development approach is said to help prevent crime in a number of ways:

- by addressing physical dilapidation and disorder problems that can contribute to a downward spiral of communities, which invites more serious crime problems
- through the nurturing of local social cohesion and informal social control
- through social and economic developments that address local criminogenic risk factors.

gentrification
The changes that result when middle-class or upper-middle-class individuals acquire and upgrade property in low-income and working-class neighbourhoods.

What Do You Think?

Consider the campus that you attend and discuss ways in which the community development approach has been applied. How might the campus go further with this approach?

Community and Problem-Oriented Policing

For police agencies, the philosophy and strategies of crime prevention are realized through community policing and problem-oriented policing (see

Chapter 3 on policing strategies). The theory of community policing has a number of profound implications for the delivery of policing services. Its goal is much more than to simply enforce laws; community policing is about contributing to the broader safety, security, and health of a community. It advocates that police agencies and their individual members forge a strong partnership with local communities, empowering citizens and neighbourhoods to help prevent crime. The community policing mandate, as it reflects the broader goals of community crime prevention, is to support citizen-based initiatives and reinforce the informal social control mechanisms of the local community (Wilson & Kelling, 1982). By extension, community policing requires the police agency and its members to be accountable to the communities they serve. For Friedmann (1992), a police service must be seen as a part of, not separate and isolated from, the general public. Community policing recognizes that the police cannot impose a lasting order on a community from the outside; they are instead one of many resources to which a community can turn to help empower them to solve local problems.

In theory, community policing bestows greater responsibility, autonomy, and discretion on front-line constables (Skolnick & Bayley, 1988). It also often involves establishing community policing stations in different neighbourhoods. The composition of a police agency committed to community policing should also better reflect the demographic and social makeup of the communities it serves (Leighton, 1991, p. 10).

Central to community policing is a problem-oriented approach that strives to address the causes and facilitators of local crime problems in order to prevent such problems from emerging, continuing, or worsening. A problem-solving approach means that police seek out solutions that are most appropriate to the problem and that often entail alternatives to the criminal justice system (Goldstein, 1987, p. 15). As Sherman and Eck (2006, p. 299) put it, "Where the core concept of community policing was community involvement for its own sake, the core concept for problem-oriented policing was *results*: the effect of police activity on public safety, including (but not limited to) crime prevention."

Conclusion

Crime prevention interventions encompass and are often delivered through a society's most basic institutions by a wide range of governmental agencies and private actors, including those whose mandate is tangential to crime. These include daycare facilities, schools, social welfare agencies, community centres, substance abuse clinics, neighbourhood associations, youth drop-in centres, employment training agencies, and health-care facilities, to name just a few. As Sherman (1997, p. 1) writes, "Most crime prevention results from the web of institutional settings of human development and daily life."

While the crime prevention institutions and strategies described in this chapter have been listed separately, the impact and success of each are maximized when they work in a coordinated and complementary fashion. In other words, "Schools cannot succeed without supportive families, labour markets cannot succeed without well-policed safe streets, and police cannot succeed without community participation in the labor market" (Sherman, 1997, p. 5).

This observation underscores the importance of a comprehensive approach to crime prevention, especially in disadvantaged neighbourhoods, where residents are often confronted with myriad problems that can give rise to and facilitate criminal behaviour. A comprehensive approach to crime prevention, according to the National Crime Council in Ireland (2003, p. 20), must aim to reduce crime by

- reducing the opportunities to commit crime;
- promoting social inclusion and reducing the socio-economic, educational, societal, and environmental factors that can leave children and young people "at risk" of engaging in criminal activities;
- reducing recidivism through the reintegration of young and adult offenders into the community in a planned and supportive way, involving training and education, skills development, and personal support; and
- providing appropriate interventions through an interagency/partnership approach where knowledge, expertise, and best practice are shared to the maximum.

Most crime problems or criminogenic preconditions cannot be solved through spur-of-the-moment, arbitrary actions based on gut feelings or common sense. What is most required is a problem-oriented approach that relies on rigorous information collection and analysis and the application of crime prevention strategies that have been proven to work (while ensuring these strategies are appropriate to each individual setting).

This systematic approach includes:

- putting together a plan that entails researching and understanding targeted crime problems (and their causes and aggravating factors) within a particular setting,
- understanding the environment in which the problems are taking place,
- identifying and mobilizing community members and other key partners,

- developing a strategy to address the identified problems (and their causes),
- implementing the strategy,
- sustaining the strategy,
- monitoring and evaluating the plan, and
- making any necessary modifications.

DISCUSSION QUESTIONS

1. How would you define crime prevention? Do you believe it should be defined broadly or narrowly? Should it be defined by its methods or its consequences? What parameters would you apply to a definition of crime prevention? Do you believe that the design of the physical environment can actually affect people's behaviour in those spaces?

2. Do you believe that certain architectural and urban designs can motivate people to assume more interest in the safety of their neighbourhood?

3. What are some of the most successful approaches to improving the root causes of criminal and violent behaviour?

4. Some have argued that police services should not simply focus on law enforcement, but should also help address a wide range of problems, including those that give rise to crime and criminality. Yet the multi-agency approach that is advocated by community policing means that police officers can rely on other professionals who may be better suited to address such causal problems. Within the context of this multi-agency approach to community policing, do you believe that police should stay focused on what they do best (enforcing the laws, responding to calls for service, arresting of-fenders) and allow their partners to focus on the social problems that give rise to crime? Or do you think officers should engage in problem-oriented policing involving tasks that fall outside their law enforcement mandate? Explain your answer.

SUGGESTED FURTHER READINGS

International Centre for the Prevention of Crime. (2008). *Compendium of crime prevention practices to inspire action across the world*. Montreal: Author.

Lab, S.P. (2010). *Crime prevention approaches, practices, and evaluations* (7th ed.). New York: Anderson.

Schneider, S. (2009). *Crime prevention: Theory and practice*. Boca Raton, FL: CRC Press.

Sherman, L.W., Farrington, D.P., Welsh, B.C., & MacKenzie, D.L. (Eds.). (2006). *Evidence-based crime prevention* (Rev. ed.). London: Routledge.

Welsh, B.C., & Farrington, D.P. (Eds.). (2012). *Oxford handbook of crime prevention*. Oxford: Oxford University Press.

REFERENCES

Canada. (1993). *Crime prevention in Canada: Toward a national strategy—Twelfth Report of the Standing Committee on Justice and the Solicitor General.* Ottawa: House of Commons Canada.

Clarke, R.V. (1997). Introduction. In R.V. Clarke (Ed.), *Situational crime prevention: Successful case studies* (2nd ed., pp. 2–43). Albany, NY: Harrow and Heston.

Clarke, R.V., & Cornish, D.B. (1985). Modeling offenders' decisions: A framework for policy and research. In M. Tonry & N. Morris (Eds.), *Crime and justice: An annual review of research* (Vol. 6, pp. 147–185). Chicago: University of Chicago Press.

Cherney, A. (2006). Problem-solving for crime prevention. *Trends and Issues in Crime Prevention, 314.* [Canberra: Australian Institute of Criminology.]

Cohen, L.E., & Felson, M. (1979). Social change and crime rate trends: A routine activity approach. *American Sociological Review, 44,* 588–608.

Cornish, D.B., & Clarke, R.V. (2003). Opportunities, precipitators, and criminal decisions: A reply to Wortley's critique of situational crime prevention. In M.J. Smith & D.B. Cornish (Eds.), *Theory for practice in situational crime prevention* (pp. 41–96). Monsey, NY: Criminal Justice Press.

Crawford, A. (1999). Questioning appeals to community within crime prevention and control. *European Journal on Criminal Policy and Research, 7,* 509–530.

Department of Health and Human Services. (2011). Administration for Children and Families. *Strengthening families and communities: 2011 resource guide.* Washington, DC: Author.

Eckblom, P. (1994). Proximal circumstances: A mechanism-based classification of crime prevention. In R.V. Clarke (Ed.), *Crime prevention studies* (Vol. 2, pp. 185–232). Monsey, NY: Criminal Justice Press.

Felson, M., & Clarke, R.V. (1998). *Opportunity makes the thief: Practical theory for crime prevention.* Police Research Series Paper 98. London: Home Office.

Forrest, R., & Kearns, A. (2001). Social cohesion, social capital and the neighbourhood. *Urban Studies, 38*(12), 2125–2143.

Friedmann, R.R. (1992). *Community policing: Comparative perspectives and prospects.* New York: St. Martin's Press.

Goldstein, H. (1987). Toward community oriented policing: Potential, basic requirements, and threshold questions. *Crime and Delinquency, 33*(1), 6–30.

Greenberg, S.W., & Rohe, W.M. (1986). Informal social control and crime prevention in modern urban neighborhoods. In R.B. Taylor (Ed.), *Urban neighborhoods: Research and policy* (pp. 79–118). New York: Praeger.

Greenberg, S.W., Rohe, M., & Williams, J. (1983). Neighborhood conditions and community crime control. *Journal of Community Action*, *19*(5), 39–42.

Greenberg, S.W., Rohe, M., & Williams, J. (1985). *Informal citizen action and crime prevention at the neighborhood level: Synthesis and assessment of the research.* Washington, DC: US Department of Justice, National Institute of Justice.

Greenwood, P.W. (2006). *Changing lives: Delinquency prevention as crime-control policy.* Chicago: University of Chicago Press.

Immen, W. (2003, June 9). Team effort to cut crime transforms Jane-Finch. *Globe and Mail*, p. A10.

Lab, S.P. (2004). *Crime prevention approaches, practices, and evaluations* (5th ed.). New York: Anderson.

Leighton, B. (1991). Visions of community policing: Rhetoric and reality in Canada. *Canadian Journal of Criminology*, *33*(3/4), 485–522.

National Crime Council of Ireland. (2003). *A crime prevention strategy for Ireland: Tackling the concerns of local communities.* Dublin: The Stationery Office. Retrieved from http://www.irlgov.ie/crimecouncil/downloads/ CrimePrevention.pdf

Rosenbaum, D.P. (1988). Community crime prevention: A review and synthesis of the literature. *Justice Quarterly*, *5*, 323–395.

Sampson, R.J., Raudenbush, S.W., & Earls, F. (1997). Neighborhoods and violent crime: A multilevel study of collective efficacy. *Science*, *277*, 918–923.

Sherman, L.W. (1997). Thinking about crime prevention. In L.W. Sherman, D. Gottfredson, D. MacKenzie, J. Eck, P. Reuter, & S. Bushway (Eds.), *Preventing crime: What works, what doesn't, what's promising* (pp. 1–31). Report to the United States Congress. Washington, DC: National Institute of Justice.

Sherman, L.W., & Eck, J. (2006). Policing for crime prevention. In L.W. Sherman, D.P. Farrington, B.C. Welsh, & D.L. MacKenzie (Eds.), *Evidence-based crime prevention* (Rev. ed., pp. 295–329). London: Routledge.

Skolnick, J.H., & Bayley, D.H. (1988). *Community policing: Issues and practices around the world.* Washington, DC: US Government Printing Office.

Skolnick, J.H., & Bayley, D.H. (1988). *Community policing: Issues and practices around the world.* Washington, DC: US Government Printing Office.

Welsh, B.C., & Farrington, D.P. (2010). *The future of crime prevention: Developmental and situational strategies.* Document No. 237329. Washington, DC: National Institute of Justice. Available at https://www.ncjrs.gov/ pdffiles1/nij/grants/237329.pdf

Welsh, B.C., & Farrington, D.P. (2012). Crime prevention and public policy. In B.C. Welsh & D.P. Farrington (Eds.), *Oxford handbook of crime prevention* (pp. 3–20). Oxford: Oxford University Press.

Wilson, J. (1975). *Thinking about crime.* New York: Academic Press.

Wilson, J., & Kelling, G. (1982, March 31). Broken windows. *Atlantic Monthly*, 29–38.

Wirth, L. (1938). Urbanism, migration and tolerance: A reassessment. *American Sociological Review*, *56*, 117–123.

Selected Issues in Criminal Justice

Introduction: Recurrent Issues and Applications

How the law defines crime and the way society chooses to respond to it are processes that are in a constant state of flux. In recent years, Canada has seen significant changes to its criminal law, its correctional system, and its accountability measures for police action. For example, in March 2012 the Ontario Court of Appeal decision in *Bedford v. Canada* made it legal for the first time in Canadian history to sell sex on the street. This has challenged many people's views about the criminal law, its history, and its future. Similarly, in June 2012 a BC court granted Gloria Taylor, a woman dying from a debilitating disorder, the right to die with the assistance of a physician. This judgment also marked a historic first for Canadian law. In 1993, Sue Rodriguez, a woman dying of the same disease, went all the way to the Supreme Court seeking a right to assisted suicide, and lost. Gloria Taylor's case has been appealed by the federal government and will likely go all the way to the Supreme Court before a conclusion is reached. Many people are wondering whether Canada's views on crime and punishment have changed enough in 20 years to warrant a new position on euthanasia.

The future of criminal justice will continue to be riddled with a host of concerns over the best way to intervene in the lives of people who violate the laws designed to promote public safety. This chapter is designed to set out a series of potential issues that may have prominence in the years to come, or that have had a resounding historical tone as debates about the most effective or desirable forms of criminal justice intervention have taken place. Each issue is set out as a mini chapter, with critical thinking questions designed to help push you forward in your study of criminal justice. It is our hope that these issues will spark further discussion and analysis as you conclude the book. Just as an introductory course aims to familiarize you with the topics and key players within a field, allowing you to pursue more advanced topics in upper-level courses, this chapter aims to provide you with a survey of some of the more specialized issues in criminal justice studies. It will be up to you to pursue these issues and questions in more detail, perhaps in a research paper, a class presentation, or in your next criminal justice course!

Although the topics explored in this chapter are by no means an exhaustive list, they cover several issues relevant to the "three C's" of criminal justice study that have been examined in this book so far: cops, courts, and corrections. There are also a few topics from the neighbouring field of criminology. You may remember from Chapter 1 that although criminology and criminal justice are distinct fields of study, there are many areas of overlap where the theoretical interests of criminology aid the investigative and treatment goals of criminal justice. This is particularly true with regard to the more advanced and complex problems facing criminal justice professionals. For example, a discussion of the use of sentencing circles (one of the topics included in this chapter) will require input from criminology to help us determine which theories of crime control and punishment are available and how they might be applied. Such a discussion will also require that we consult with the criminal law and courtroom procedures to determine how sentencing circles might operate within the existing criminal justice system. Further, familiarity with Canada's correctional system is necessary when contemplating alternatives to existing penalties. Finally, sentencing circles directly affect the role of the police in protecting and serving communities.

"The world is a dangerous place, not because of those who do evil, but because of those who look on and do nothing."

—Albert Einstein

This chapter cannot, of course, cover all of the topics that are of interest to criminal justice professionals. Nor should it be viewed as highlighting only the "important ones." Rather, you might think of this chapter as an opportunity to listen in on conversations between criminologists, police, courts, and corrections professionals about police tactics, Charter rights, crime prevention, youth crime, and capital punishment. Although voicing an opinion in a conversation about such complicated topics can be a daunting prospect, it is our hope that this book will not only have prepared you to "speak up" about criminal justice, but also helped you to do so.

16.1 "Nothing Works" Revisited

In 1974, researchers Douglas Lipton, Robert Martinson, and J. Wilks used meta-analysis to assess all the evaluations of criminal rehabilitation programs between 1945 and 1967. They concluded: "With few and isolated exceptions, the rehabilitative efforts that have been reported so far have had no appreciable effect on recidivism" (1974, p. 25). Martinson subsequently publicized this conclusion much more widely through a short essay in the American public policy journal *The Public Interest*, asserting that "nothing works." The phrase has been associated with his name ever since.

In a 1975 book (Lipton, Martinson, & Wilks, 1975), Martinson admitted that he and his co-authors had left out of their study some research that may have shown rehabilitation to be more effective than they had publicly stated, but he maintained that there was consistent enough evidence to suggest that rehabilitation should not be the guiding philosophy of corrections. Martinson later commented that he did not care for the slogan that the media used to sum up what he had said, stating, "the press has no time for scientific quibbling and got to the heart of the matter better than I did" (Martinson, 1979, p. 254). The phrase "nothing works" became the mantra of those opposed to rehabilitation, and had some influence in shifting public opinion away from liberal programs of rehabilitation and toward retribution or deterrence as justifications for punishment.

> *"Does nothing work? Do all of these studies lead us irrevocably to the conclusion that nothing works, that we haven't the faintest clue about how to rehabilitate offenders and reduce recidivism?"*
>
> —*Robert Martinson (1974, p. 48)*

Cullen, Smith, Lowenkamp, and Latessa (2009) suggest that, by the time Martinson's article appeared, there was already a broad movement to reject rehabilitation and that Martinson was treated as a "criminological celebrity" for confirming what everyone knew (2009, p. 104). At the time, prisons were already being portrayed as inhumane, as shown in Zimbardo's Stanford Prison experiment, which first appeared in a *New York Times* article (Zimbardo, Banks, Haney, & Jaffe, 1973). Cullen and Gendreau (2001) argue that "nothing works" was deeply ingrained in the professional ideology of criminologists.

Some commentators have suggested that Martinson committed suicide as a result of the publicity around his controversial statement. David Farabee (2005, p. xvi) suggests that Martinson "grew angrier and more alienated and a few years after taking his unpopular stand—although he had begun to waver—he took his own life." Further, detractors who were arguing based on ideology had, according to Farabee, a "passionate reaction against his findings and against him personally," which "revealed a powerful bias in academic circles that encourage those who 'prove' that these programs work and dismiss those who suggest otherwise as being opposed to rehabilitation" (2005, p. xvi).

Cullen et al. (2009, p. 106) suggest that Martinson was not a lonely voice but part of a "growing chorus" of researchers who had found similar results. Raynor (2008) suggests that "nothing works" was a "powerful, resilient and simplistic doctrine" that attracted support not only from "monetarist welfare cutters" but also from a whole host of others. Radical criminologists such as Taylor, Walton, and Young (1973) were supportive of the doctrine because they were opposed to the pathologizing of offenders as objects of treatment. The number of diverse individuals who found the "nothing works" doctrine appealing led to a consensus that facilitated what Andrews and Bonta (1998) have called "knowledge destruction."

More recently, Farabee published *Rethinking Rehabilitation: Why Can't We Reform Our Criminals?* (2005) in collaboration with the American Enterprise Institute, a neo-conservative Washington, DC think tank. Reminiscent of Martinson himself, Farabee published an op-ed article in the *Washington Post* in 2006 opposing legislation that would provide treatment for offenders.

The Debate Continues

"Tackling prisoner recidivism is serious business requiring serious solutions, and it is unlikely to involve workbooks, videos or talk therapy."

—David Farabee (2006)

Farabee (2005, p. 76) argues that people who are "ideologically inclined" to deal with crime through social programs will draw upon the "treatment works" literature, while "those of us who advocate returning responsibility to the offender draw upon the classical criminological literature that suggests that offenders make rational decisions to commit crimes and can therefore make a rational decision to abstain." Farabee makes six recommendations for the future of criminal justice:

1. Deemphasize prison as a sanction for nonviolent re-offences and increase the use of intermediate sanctions.
2. Use prison programs to serve as institutional management tools, not as instruments for rehabilitation.
3. Mandate experimental designs for all program evaluations.
4. Establish evaluation contracts with independent agencies.
5. Increase the use of indeterminate community supervision, requiring three consecutive years without a new offense or violation.
6. Reduce parole caseloads to fifteen to one [twenty-five or more], and increase the use of new tracking technologies (i.e., electronic monitoring). (Farabee, 2005, p. 78)

Farabee suggests that the first two recommendations will save costs by reducing reliance on incarceration and "replacing therapeutic programs with less costly activities that will serve the same prison-management function." For Farabee, the third and fourth recommendations are seen as a way to establish and maintain rigorous standards to evaluate the effectiveness of the practices in the fifth and sixth recommendations (Farabee, 2005, p. 79).

In commenting on these recommendations, Cullen et al. (2009, p. 116) suggest that, "in Farabee's future, prisons would be reduced to custodial institutions, community corrections reduced to a police function, and offenders would be stripped of their criminogenic personal histories and reduced to rational decision makers. Farabee sees this as a sober, realistic view; we see it as needlessly hopeless and dangerous." Although Cullen et al. agree that corrections must be an instrument of punishment and justice, they believe that the correctional system "should also serve a social welfare function." They argue that social welfare may "infuse corrections with a dose of humanity ... but its presence should not be confused with some sort of misguided leniency." Throughout their paper, they cite numerous studies that show a contrary view (Gendreau & Ross, 1979; Gendreau, Little, & Goggin, 1996), and they conclude by citing Mark Lipsey (2003), arguing that "rehabilitation is not only about improving offenders but also about protecting public safety" (Cullen et al., 2009, p. 116).

In a rather passionate critique of the methodology of the "what works" research, Farrall (2003) argues for more detailed, qualitative study of how front-line correctional workers impact offenders and their circumstances, and further analysis of what practices and approaches have been helpful and why. Farrall made the same argument in later publications, suggesting that our understanding of how rehabilitation "works" needs to be informed by research on the process of desistance from crime, something that is currently missing in the quantitative meta-analyses.

The question of whether one's choice of research methodology—quantitative or qualitative—depends on one's ideological viewpoint is worthy of further consideration.

How does the promotion of "nothing works" as a criminal justice policy get interpreted within the theoretical models of criminal justice?

Restorative justice	In a "nothing works" world, restorative justice practices would focus on reintegrative shaming and looking after the needs of the victim and the wider community.
Community change	Community change advocates would recognize the benefit of providing and advocating for the prevention of crime, so that all members of the community would benefit.
Welfare	Welfare advocates would find the lack of rehabilitation and treatment for individual offenders completely unacceptable.

| Justice | For justice advocates, the rights of individuals who are coerced into treatment programs would be upheld under a "nothing works" system. |
| Crime control | Crime-control advocates would applaud a focus on denunciation, punishment, and deterrence. |

What Do You Think?

1. Throughout this book you have looked at a variety of issues using the models of criminal justice outlined in Chapter 1. The argument about the effectiveness of correctional treatment is one that lends itself well to a consideration of the ideas presented in each of these models. The ideas presented in this section suggest a clear dichotomy between punishment and treatment. Having read this book and considered a number of the issues related to this debate, what do you think now?

2. Consider the provisions of the *Safe Streets and Communities Act* (explored in the Part Four case study). On which side of the debate does this legislation stand? What are some of the provisions in the Act regarding correctional treatment that help you to understand the dichotomy in this debate?

3. The youth-led organization Lead Now (leadnow.ca) took a very strong activist stance against the changes enacted in the *Safe Streets and Communities Act*. What are the similarities and differences between an activist group, such as Lead Now, and recognized experts, such as Martinson and Farabee, commenting in the media?

REFERENCES

Andrews, D.A., & Bonta, J. (1998). *The psychology of criminal conduct*. Cincinnati, OH: Anderson.

Cullen, F.T., & Gendreau, P. (2001). From nothing works to what works: Changing professional ideology in the 21st century. *Prison Journal, 81*, 313–338.

Cullen, F.T., Smith, P., Lowenkamp, C.T., & Latessa, E. (2009). Nothing works revisited: Deconstructing Farabee's "Rethinking Rehabilitation." *Victims and Offenders*, 101–123.

Farabee, D. (2005). *Rethinking rehabilitation: Why can't we reform our criminals?* Washington, DC: AEI Press. Retrieved from http://www.heart-intl.net/HEART/100507/RethinkingRehabilitation.pdf

Farabee, D. (2006, February 11). Reinventing criminal justice. *Washington Post*, p. A9.

Farrall, S. (2003). J'accuse: Probation evaluation-research epistemologies. Part one: The critique. *Criminal Justice, 3*(2), 161–179.

Gendreau, P., & Ross, R.R. (1979). Effective correctional treatment: Bibliotherapy for cynics. *Crime and Delinquency, 25*, 463–489.

Gendreau, P., Little, T., & Goggin, C. (1996). A meta-analysis of the predictors of adult offender recidivism: What works! *Criminology, 34*, 575–607.

Lipsey, M.W. (2003). *Effective correctional treatment enhances public safety*. ICCA Monograph Series, Publication No. 3. La Crosse, WI: International Community Corrections Association.

Lipton, D., Martinson, R., & Wilks, J. (1974). *The effectiveness of correctional treatment: A survey of treatment evaluation studies*. New York: Praeger Press.

Martinson, R. (1974). What works? Questions and answers about prison reform. *The Public Interest* (Spring), 22–54.

Martinson, R. (1979). New findings, new views: A note of caution regarding sentencing reform. *Hofstra Law Review, 7*, 242–258.

Raynor, P. (2008). Community penalties and home office research: On the way back to "nothing works"? *Criminology, 8*, 73–87.

Safe Streets and Communities Act, SC 2012, c. 1. Retrieved from http://laws-lois .justice.gc.ca/eng/AnnualStatutes/2012_1/FullText.html

Taylor, I., Walton, P., & Young, J. (1973). *The new criminology*. London: Routledge & Kegan Paul.

Zimbardo, P.G., Banks, W.C., Haney, C., & Jaffe, D. (1973, April 8). A Pirandellian prison: The mind is a formidable jailer. *New York Times Magazine*, pp. 38–40.

16.2 Section 1 of the Charter: The Oakes Test

Although lawyers are often criticized for making simple things seem more complicated than they need to be, one of the areas where this habit is particularly relevant is the interpretation of Charter rights. We can be assured that each word found in the Charter was carefully chosen (after, no doubt, painstakingly detailed debate), so understanding what each word means is integral to knowing what protections are guaranteed by Canada's supreme law. Section 9, for example, protects every person who comes into contact with Canadian police from "arbitrary detention." But what does "arbitrary" mean? And what counts as "detention"? You may remember from the discussion of these terms in Chapter 4 that the criminal justice system uses very particular legal definitions that can sometimes differ from everyday meanings.

One place where the exact legal meaning of the words used in the Charter is particularly important is in its first section. Section 1 of the Charter reads:

> The *Canadian Charter of Rights and Freedoms* guarantees the rights and freedoms set out in it subject only to such reasonable limits prescribed by law as can be demonstrably justified in a free and democratic society.

This section informs us that the rights protected by the Charter cannot be violated unless the government can offer a sufficiently good reason for doing so, and even then, that the rights must be overridden in the least intrusive way possible. This is what is meant by a "reasonable limit." In other words, if the government wants to enact a law that would limit any of the freedoms guaranteed by the Charter (such as freedom of expression), it must do so *reasonably*. Further, the reason the government offers for limiting the right must be justified "in a free and democratic society." But what do these words mean in the context of protecting and guaranteeing Charter rights?

Shortly after the Charter came into force, the Supreme Court of Canada was asked to define the meaning of the words in s. 1 when David Oakes was arrested while in possession of eight vials of hashish oil. Although Oakes argued the oil was for his own personal use, the *Narcotic Control Act* at the time contained a provision that allowed police to assume that anyone carrying a narcotic was doing so with the intention of trafficking (that is, selling it to others). Oakes argued that this provision violated his right to be presumed innocent until proven guilty (under s. 11(d) of the Charter). The court agreed but then had to consider whether this violation of his right could be "justified in a free and democratic society." The steps the court took in answering this question have become known as the *Oakes* test.

This test is applied each time a Charter right has been violated. Each step of the test must be passed in order for the violation to be allowable—that is, to be "justified in a free and democratic society." There are two steps to the test, with the second step having three parts. Let's look at the various stages of the test in detail.

Step 1: Determining a "Pressing and Substantial Objective"

The first step of the *Oakes* test asks the following questions:

- What is the reason offered for the right violation?
- What is the objective of the law or action that has infringed the Charter?
- Is it important enough to override the most important rights and freedoms Canada offers?

Assuming that the law or action in question passes this first step of the test, the court moves on to the second step, examining three specific aspects of the Charter violation.

Step 2: Proportionality (Three Parts)

Assuming that the reason for violating the Charter right is important enough, are the measures taken to reach that objective "proportional"? In other words:

- *Rational connection:* Does the law or action that has violated the right make sense? Given the "pressing and substantial" objective offered in step 1, does the law or action seem like a rational way to achieve it?
- *Minimal impairment:* Does the infringing law or action violate the Charter right as little as is possible? Is there another way to achieve the same objective without violating the Charter at all? Or perhaps not as much?
- *Deleterious effects:* What might be the negative consequences of violating the right? Even though the law or action has an objective that is very important, and the means by which the government is trying to achieve it are rational and infringe on the Charter as little as possible, are the consequences of allowing a right violation too damaging to permit? In other words, do the means ultimately justify the ends?

This test is applied each time a law or a police action is found to violate a Charter right. If the violation passes the *Oakes* test, it is allowed. If it fails the test, the law must be changed or the police action reprimanded. The

Oakes test therefore plays a major role in defining the scope and limits of the legal powers of Canada's police and legislators.

How might the justification of random police searches under the *Oakes* test be interpreted by the theoretical models of criminal justice?

Restorative justice	For restorative justice advocates, individual rights often take a backseat to concerns about the community as a whole. For example, restorative justice places great emphasis on the offender's acknowledgement of responsibility; yet, from a Charter perspective, accused persons have a right to be protected against self-incrimination.
Community change	Community change advocates would not be so concerned about whether an individual's rights were violated if the random searches were beneficial to the broader community interests.
Welfare	Welfare advocates would not be as concerned about an individual's right not to be searched if the police were trying to find offenders who needed drug treatment or counselling. The important point about police searching an individual for drugs would be to convict the offender so that he or she could receive appropriate treatment for addiction.
Justice	Justice proponents would be the strongest advocates of the rights of the individual to be searched according to carefully regulated procedure.
Crime control	Crime-control advocates might not appreciate the number of cases that may be rendered ineligible for prosecution because of a violation of an individual's rights. This would lead to lengthier court hearings and fewer cases moving through the system in an expedient manner.

What Do You Think?

1. A 1998 Supreme Court of Canada case, *R. v. Hufsky*, held that the police practice of conducting random roadside stops of drivers violates s. 9 of the Charter. Random spot checks are conducted under provincial motor vehicle laws for the purpose of reducing the number of impaired drivers. Police ask drivers a series of questions during the stop in order to determine the sobriety of the driver, to check the mechanical fitness of the vehicle, and to confirm that the driver is licensed and insured. You may be asking yourself, why, if these roadside stops are a violation of the Charter, have they been allowed to continue? The answer lies in the *Oakes* test. Imagine you are a member of the Supreme Court hearing the *Hufsky* case. You have found a violation of s. 9 and must now proceed with the *Oakes* test to determine whether the violation is justifiable in a "free and democratic society." How will you answer the questions posed in the *Oakes* test? Will you allow roadside stops to continue? Be sure to provide your reasons.

2. Review the material found in Chapters 4 and 6 of this book. Select and analyze one or two of the Charter violations mentioned in the chapters using the *Oakes* test. Do your findings differ from those of the court(s)?

3. In the *Oakes* case itself, the court did not actually complete all of the stages of the s. 1 analysis. Although the trafficking provision was found to have a pressing and substantial objective, the court found that it could not satisfy the rational connection test. Because the law failed one of the steps of the *Oakes* test, the court did not need to consider the remaining branches. For the moment, assume that the rational connection test was passed in *Oakes* and continue to the remaining two steps (minimal impairment and deleterious effects) to conduct your own analysis. Would a presumption of trafficking pass the *Oakes* test in your court?

4. Some legal scholars have critiqued the use of the *Oakes* test, suggesting that it is not really a relevant test, given how many other balancing and analytical tests the courts use when assessing Charter rights violations. Others argue that the *Oakes* test should not be universally applied to all rights violations, but rather that different types of Charter rights require different kinds of analyses. Explore this debate on your own and determine whether you agree with these critiques, and why.

REFERENCES AND FURTHER READING

Bredt, C.D., & Dodek, A.M. (2001). The increasing irrelevance of section 1 of the Charter. *Supreme Court Law Review* (2d), *14*, 175–187.

Canadian Charter of Rights and Freedoms, part I of the *Constitution Act, 1982*, being Schedule B to the *Canada Act 1982* (UK), 1982, c. 11.

Choudry, S. (2006). So what is the real legacy of Oakes? Two decades of proportionality analysis under the Canadian Charter's section 1. *Supreme Court Law Review* (2d), *34*, 501–525.

Ikpa, T.S. (2007). Balancing restorative justice principles and due process rights in order to reform the criminal justice system. *Journal of Law & Policy, 24*, 301–325.

R. v. Hufsky, [1988] 1 SCR 621.

R. v. Oakes, [1986] 1 SCR 103.

Rothstein, M. (2000). Section 1: Justifying breaches of Charter rights and freedoms. *Manitoba Law Journal, 27*(2), 171–184.

Sharpe, R.J., & Roach, K. (2005). *Essentials of Canadian law: The Charter of Rights and Freedoms*. Toronto: Irwin Law.

Siebrasse, N. (1991). The Oakes test: An old ghost impeding bold new initiatives. *Ottawa Law Review, 23*(1), 99–138.

16.3 Victims' Rights

In 1979, the World Society of Victimology was formed to provide a forum for researchers, policy-makers, and service providers to pursue their common interests and exchange knowledge. The Society began to use its combined knowledge to influence the United Nations, and in 1985 the UN General Assembly adopted a resolution on the Declaration of Basic Principles of Justice for Victims of Crime and Abuse of Power. The resolution committed every government in the world to a transformational shift in the manner in which the criminal justice system operated, requiring that there be a recognition that crime has an impact on **victims** and families, and not just on the state. Further, it required a recognition that victims may be subject to abuses of power when they come in contact with the agencies of criminal justice.

victims
Persons who, individually or collectively, have suffered harm, including physical or mental injury, emotional suffering, economic loss or substantial impairment of their fundamental rights, through acts or omissions that are a violation of criminal law (UN Resolution 40/34, Part A[1]).

In 1988 the federal and provincial justice ministers agreed to a Canadian statement of principles of justice for victims of crime to respond to the UN resolution. However, the principles fell short of those expressed in the UN resolution. In a meeting on October 1, 2003, justice ministers endorsed a renewed version. This statement of principles is a guide to how victims *should* be treated during the criminal justice process, and guides the development of policies and programs. However, because the statement is not law, it does not provide victims with additional rights beyond those provided in the *Criminal Code* or the *Corrections and Conditional Release Act* (CCRA).

victim impact statement
A written document made by the victim that describes the harm done to the victim and the effect the crime has had on his or her life.

In 1988, Parliament passed Bill C-89, which gave victims various rights, including the right to file a **victim impact statement** or speak to the court during a sentencing hearing. The federal government expanded its legislation on victims in 1996 with the passage of Bill C-41. Amendments to the *Criminal Code* (see s. 722) codified the rights of victims of crime, making it possible for impact statements to be admitted during sentencing, for restitution to be provided to the victims, and for victims to attend some parole hearings (Bacchus, 1999).

These amendments marked the emergence of a victims' rights movement in Canadian criminal justice. Sparked by an interest among criminologists in the social and emotional experiences of the victims of crime, the field of **victimology** was developed to better understand the processes and effects

Victimology is a subfield of criminology interested in the study of victims. This includes understanding the experiences of victims during and after crime, as well as examining the factors that may influence who becomes a victim, or how offenders choose victims. This field of study is also associated with strong activism for victims' rights, support, and advocacy for greater involvement during the various stages of the criminal justice system.

SIDEBAR

Canadian Statement of Basic Principles of Justice for Victims of Crime (2003)

In honour of the United Nations' Declaration of Basic Principles of Justice for Victims of Crime, and with concern for the harmful impact of criminal victimization on individuals and on society, and in recognition that all persons have the full protection of rights guaranteed by the *Canadian Charter of Rights and Freedoms* and other provincial Charters governing rights and freedoms; that the rights of victims and offenders need to be balanced; and of the shared jurisdiction of federal, provincial, and territorial governments, the federal, provincial, and territorial Ministers Responsible for Criminal Justice agree that the following principles should guide the treatment of victims, particularly during the criminal justice process.

The following principles are intended to promote fair treatment of victims and should be reflected in federal/provincial/territorial laws, policies and procedures:

- Victims of crime should be treated with courtesy, compassion, and respect.
- The privacy of victims should be considered and respected to the greatest extent possible.
- All reasonable measures should be taken to minimize inconvenience to victims.
- The safety and security of victims should be considered at all stages of the criminal justice process and appropriate measures should be taken when necessary to protect victims from intimidation and retaliation.
- Information should be provided to victims about the criminal justice system and the victim's role and opportunities to participate in criminal justice processes.
- Victims should be given information, in accordance with prevailing law, policies, and procedures, about the status of the investigation; the scheduling, progress and final outcome of the proceedings; and the status of the offender in the correctional system.
- Information should be provided to victims about available victim assistance services, other programs and assistance available to them, and means of obtaining financial reparation.
- The views, concerns and representations of victims are an important consideration in criminal justice processes and should be considered in accordance with prevailing law, policies and procedures.
- The needs, concerns and diversity of victims should be considered in the development and delivery of programs and services, and in related education and training.
- Information should be provided to victims about available options to raise their concerns when they believe that these principles have not been followed.

Source: Department of Justice Canada (2003). Retrieved from http://www.victimsfirst.gc.ca/serv/wvr-qdv.html

of victimization. Advancements in this field of study have led to an increased awareness among criminal justice agents and scholars of the importance of supporting victims through the various stages of a criminal prosecution, and of advocating for the place of victims within these processes. Although it is common for victims of a crime to think of the trial as "their case," this is not how Canada's criminal justice system is structured. Strictly speaking, when a person commits a criminal offence, he or she is considered to have injured the state, rather than individual victims. This is why criminal cases are cited as *R. v. Offender*, where *R.* stands for *regina* (the Latin word for queen). In other words, a criminal case is a matter between the Queen, or state, and the individual offender. This structure leaves little room for the voice of a victim. The victims' rights movement has changed this in a number of ways, moving the victim of a crime closer to being recognized as a participant in the criminal process. However, the extent of this participation remains a matter of debate within criminal justice research.

Once an offender has been convicted of a crime, there are additional opportunities for victims to have their voice heard. The CCRA, proclaimed in 1992, formally recognized victims—a first in correctional legislation. The Act requires the Correctional Service of Canada (CSC) and the Parole Board of Canada (PBC) to disclose the following information to a victim:

- the offender's name, the offence and the court that convicted him or her, and the start date and length of the offender's sentence (s. 26(1)(a))
- eligibility dates and review dates for unescorted, escorted temporary absences, or parole for the offender (s. 142(1)(a)).

The CCRA also permits the CSC and the PBC to disclose additional information to the victim if they deem that the interests of the victim outweigh any invasion of the offender's privacy that could result from the disclosure. This information may include:

- the offender's age
- the location of the penitentiary in which the offender is serving his or her sentence
- the date when the offender is to be released on temporary absence, work release, parole, or statutory release, as well as the location of release and any conditions attached to the release
- the date of any hearing for the purposes of a detention review
- whether or not the offender has appealed a decision of the PBC, and the outcome of that appeal.

The *Safe Streets and Communities Act* (2012) introduced further amendments to the CCRA, including the following:

- victim participation in conditional release hearings and the disclosure of more information to victims about their offender
- more offender accountability, including the requirement of a correctional plan that sets out behavioural objectives for program participation, as well as the meeting of court-ordered obligations such as victim restitution or child support.

Although the federal government has provided some support through such avenues as the Policy Centre for Victim Issues (Department of Justice), the National Office for Victims (Public Safety Canada), and the Office of the Federal Ombudsman for Victims of Crime, Irvin Waller (2011) argues that in order to reduce crime and harm to victims of crime in Canada, the *Safe Streets and Communities Act* should create a permanent Crime Reduction Board for Canada. Through the promotion and comprehensive implementation of effective "pre-crime prevention programs" and fair services and rights for victims of crime, such a board would:

- provide leadership to federal action
- collaborate with the provinces and other relevant entities to agree on and implement a national strategic plan and long-term framework
- gather and analyze practical information in order to foster widespread application of effective and cost-efficient programs
- develop national standards and ways to foster practices and guidelines that meet those standards
- monitor achievements in reducing crime and harm to victims, and make recommendations for additional actions.

How might a policy of enhanced rights for victims of crime be interpreted within the framework of the theoretical models of criminal justice?

Restorative justice	Restorative justice advocates would be pleased with the greater involvement of victims in the criminal justice process, provided that the broader community could also be an active participant.
Community change	For the broader community to be able to prevent and control crime, community change advocates would argue that all members must have access to the machinery of the criminal justice system. Victim participation is enhanced with additional rights and services, thereby benefiting the whole community.

Welfare	Ensuring that all individuals and families have access to appropriate services and counselling to heal from the damage caused by a criminal event would be seen as a positive step by welfare advocates.
Justice	Ensuring that individual rights are protected, whether for a victim or an offender, would be applauded by justice proponents.
Crime control	Provided that victims are still available to assist in the prosecution and conviction of offenders, additional rights would not be seen by crime-control advocates as a problem after the initial conviction.

What Do You Think?

1. What is the general history of the victims' rights movement in Canada? What were its key catalysts, and how has the role of the victim in the criminal justice process changed? The ancient Code of Hammurabi gave victims of crime a central role in determining the appropriate punishment for offenders, and mandated a strict scheme for compensation. What changed from having a strict scheme of compensation to victims and a clear role in terms of the punishment of offenders in the evolution of the criminal justice system?

2. Almost half of all victims' services that are currently offered in Canada are police-based (Sauvé, 2009). This means that these services are located in police departments and often staffed by members of the police department. Other victims' services are staffed by volunteers and civilians. What is the effect of a police-based victims' service? Are certain services better offered by police or by other criminal justice agents? What might be the pros and cons of each approach?

3. a. The victim impact statement (an excerpt of which you read in the Part One case study) is one of the most common ways by which victims participate in the criminal justice system. How did these statements come to be part of the sentencing process? Victims can choose whether to submit their statement in writing or to deliver it orally to the court. Why might a victim choose one or the other form of submission?

   b. Although victims can submit a victim impact statement at an offender's sentencing, they must make a special application to do so at a parole hearing. Why does the system create this distinction? Is it compatible with the UN resolution?

   c. You have a definition of a "victim" of a crime from the UN resolution. Is this definition comprehensive, or is something missing?

Who should be included in the definition? Should any parties be excluded? Landau (2009, pp. 26–27) suggests that in defining who the victim is, we cannot rely on the criminal process as our only frame of reference, because it marginalizes the victim to the role of witness for the prosecution. Once the case has been solved, the victim ceases to exist in a technical sense. What is your opinion of this interpretation?

4. Kent Roach (1999) presents two models of victims' rights: punitive and non-punitive. What does he mean by these? Which model do you think is more prevalent in Canada's criminal justice system?

5. What are the services offered by the Policy Centre for Victim Issues (Department of Justice), the National Office for Victims (Public Safety Canada), and the Office of the Federal Ombudsman for Victims of Crime? Do they overlap, or are they distinct?

6. What purpose would be served by the provision of a permanent Crime Reduction Board for Canada? How would such a board be similar to or different from the present National Crime Prevention Centre, discussed in Chapter 15 on crime prevention?

7. Should the role of victims in Canada's criminal justice system be changed? Why or why not? What changes to the current situation would you recommend?

REFERENCES AND FURTHER READING

Canadian Resource Centre for Victims of Crime (CRCVC). http://crcvc.ca

Canadian Resource Centre for Victims of Crime (CRCVC). (2006). *Victims' rights in Canada*. Ottawa: Author. Retrieved from http://www.crcvc.ca/docs/vicrights.pdf

Corrections and Conditional Release Act, SC 1992, c. 20.

Criminal Code, RSC 1985, c. C-46.

Landau, T. (2006). *Challenging notions: Critical victimology in Canada*. Toronto: Canadian Scholars' Press.

Roach, K. (1999). *Due process and victims' rights: The new law and politics of criminal justice*. Toronto: University of Toronto Press.

Safe Streets and Communities Act, SC 2012, c. 1.

Sauvé, J. (2009). Victim services in Canada, 2007/2008. *Juristat*, 29(4). Catalogue No. 85-002-X. Ottawa: Statistics Canada.

Scott, H. (2010). *Victimology: A Canadian perspective*. Oxford: Oxford University Press.

UN General Assembly. (1985, November 29). *Declaration of basic principles of justice for victims of crime and abuse of power*. Resolution 40/34. New York: Author. Retrieved from http://www2.ohchr.org/english/law/victims.htm

Waller, I. (2011). Rights for victims of crime: Rebalancing justice. Retrieved from http://irvinwaller.org/speaker/

Wemmers, J.-A. (2004). Victims' perspectives on restorative justice: How much involvement are victims looking for? *International Review of Victimology, 11*(2/3), 259–274.

Young, A.N. (2001). The role of the victim in the criminal law process: A literature review—1989 to 1999. Victims of Crime Research Series. Ottawa: Department of Justice. Retrieved from http://www.justice.gc.ca/eng/pi/rs/rep-rap/2000/rr00_vic20/rr00_vic20.pdf

16.4 Intimate Partner Violence and Specialized Courts

Domestic violence is recognized as a crime by the criminal justice system. However, the justice system's treatment of it varies from place to place, because it falls under provincial/territorial jurisdiction. Even the definition varies, as explained by Gill (2005), who suggests that the term selected by those doing research in the area will reflect a particular understanding of the issue. For the Alliance of Canadian Research Centres on Violence, the term *intimate partner violence* has been adopted to reflect the diversity of situations (Gill, 2006).

What Do You Think?

Researchers, in their definition of terms, might select one or more of the following terms: "conjugal violence," "domestic violence," "family violence," "violence between intimate partners," "woman abuse," "violence against women," or "intimate partner violence." What distinctions might a researcher make in selecting one of these terms? How would the choice of term influence the kind of "knowledge" generated and passed on to policy-makers who make decisions about how to intervene in these situations?

The way in which the police, Crown attorneys, and courts handle cases of intimate partner violence varies significantly from one province to the next. Research conducted on specialization in provincial/territorial court jurisdictions (Hornick, Boyes, Tutty, & White, 2005; Dawson & Dinovitzer, 2001; Ursel, 2003) points to the diverse models in place and how differently domestic violence cases are treated in the justice system.

Children who experience intimate partner violence are indirect victims of violence. According to research, children who are exposed to their parents' violence are at increased risk of experiencing emotional, physical, and sexual abuse, of developing emotional and behavioural problems, and of increased exposure to other adversities in their lives (Holt, Buckley, & Whalen, 2006). Amato's (2000) review of a 12-year longitudinal study found that young adults who had been exposed to parental violence as children were 189 percent more likely to experience violence in their own adult relationships than were those who had not been exposed to parental violence. In response to this research, some provinces implemented a system of mandatory reporting to child welfare agencies, in cases of where children witness domestic violence. This may mean that the child is removed from the home and placed in foster care.

What Do You Think?

Should children who are exposed to intimate partner violence be considered victims of child abuse, and therefore be referred to a child welfare authority? What are the implications for the parents in terms of seeking help for their situation if there is a mandatory reporting requirement?

A number of jurisdictions in Canada have implemented problem-oriented courts to deal with cases of intimate partner violence. The Winnipeg Family Violence Court was established in 1990, followed by the early-intervention Domestic Violence Court in Toronto (1997), the Domestic Violence Treatment Option of the Yukon Territorial Court (2000), and the Calgary Domestic Violence Courtroom, now known as HomeFront (2000). Similar courts were established in Saskatchewan (2003), New Brunswick (2007), and Newfoundland and Labrador (2008). Each of these courts operates under different models of specialized courts. For example, the Winnipeg court has five full-time Crown attorneys who are specialized prosecutors, a women's advocacy and child victim/witness program, specially designed courtrooms, and one full-time judge. The focus is on expediting cases and on post-adjudication treatment (that is, after a finding of guilt).

In Ontario, the focus is on early intervention through the use of extended bail provisions. Offenders can plead guilty and be referred to counselling (the Partner Assault Response [PAR] program) as a condition of bail. This court-mandated counselling consists of 16 weeks of specialized counselling and education during which participants learn non-violent ways to manage anger. Successful completion of the PAR program is a mitigating factor at sentencing. The Domestic Violence Court in Toronto features a specialized prosecution with a thorough police investigation, a victim/witness assistance program, and specialized Crown attorneys.

In the Yukon, the Domestic Violence Treatment Option (DVTO) offers treatment to offenders in a specialized court as a condition of bail, or offenders may be offered similar treatment as a condition of probation. Offenders are monitored regularly by the court and the judge throughout bail and probation.

Hannah-Moffat and Maurutto (2012) report that in some domestic violence courts, clients are also told that participation in the program can enable continued contact with partners and children, but this claim was not borne out in interviews with clients who went through the PAR program in Ontario.

It has been found that, historically, very few victims of intimate partner assault contact the police for assistance (Hotton, 2001, p. 5). In the past, victims often felt pressure to lay a charge, and this additional stress often dissuaded them from going through with it. The mandatory charging policy relieves this pressure on victims.

In Ontario, Hannah-Moffat and Maurutto (2012, p. 213) report that many of the women who appeared in a domestic violence court were there as a result of Ontario's **dual charge policy**, under which police may avoid arbitrating disputes and instead criminally charge both parties. Once the police lay a charge, only the Crown can withdraw the charge, and then only in limited circumstances. Jaffe, Hastings, Ketizel, and Austin (1991) found that patrol officers chose the existence of corroborating evidence as the primary factor in laying a charge, with the willingness of the victim to cooperate and the seriousness of the injuries as secondary factors. For a specialized court,

dual charge policy
In cases of domestic violence, where the police are not able to discern which of the two parties is the perpetrator, both partners will be charged.

MINI CASE STUDY

Mandatory Charging

Late one night, Kyle receives a disturbing telephone call from his sister, Jenny. During an argument between Jenny and her partner, violence erupted and the couple's oldest daughter called 911. Because a mandatory charging policy has been implemented in Ontario, the police must lay charges if there are reasonable grounds to do so. In light of the circumstances, the police officer made a dual arrest, because he had reasonable grounds to charge both the offender and the victim. Both parties must now appear in court.

What Do You Think?

1. Who are the direct and indirect victims in this case?

2. What do you think about the mandatory charging policy and the dual charging policy? Are there circumstances in which this policy might make the situation better? Might it make the situation worse?

3. What outcome would you want to see in this case if you were Kyle? What outcome would the daughter who made the call want to see? What outcome would Jenny like? How do these outcomes differ, or are they all the same?

the patrol officer turns the case over to a detective sergeant who acts as a liaison to the court and leads the investigative team. Eley (2006, p. 117) reports that investigations include detailed crime scene descriptions, documentation of details seen as aggravators (such as broken furniture), seizures for the purpose of evidence, and photographs at the crime scene and of the victim's and perpetrator's injuries. The complainant's statement is videotaped as soon as possible after the incident. In evaluating the effectiveness of this change in procedures, Eley (2006) reports that, in Ontario, police have gathered more evidence, the quality of police investigations has improved, and case-processing times have decreased significantly.

Prior to the establishment of specialized courts, Crown attorneys saw domestic violence cases as "low profile, messy cases with poor prospects for conviction" and, as such, not very rewarding for Crowns to pursue (Brown, 2000, p. 10). This view was also reported by Landau (2000), who found that domestic violence victims perceived the Crown to be quite insensitive to their needs. In order to address these concerns, prosecutors now receive specialized training prior to volunteering to work in domestic violence courts.

Eley (2005, p. 121), in her analysis of one domestic violence court in Toronto, concludes that while the court does focus on case processing, judicial leadership, and management of court time, its primary process is managing people from justice and non-justice agencies, offenders, victims, and service providers, and therefore it "requires an ordinary courtroom with extraordinary practices for the key actors." Hannah-Moffat and Maurutto (2012, p. 212) suggest that the involvement of community agents in crime control means that these agencies play a direct role in the production of new forms of expert knowledge that shape how offenders and their behaviours are perceived, assessed, and managed.

Generally, each specialized court partners with agencies in its own community, which can lead to a great deal of variation across the country. In Ontario, the Coalition Against Violence (CAV) is actively involved in the delivery of services as well as the creation of the PAR program. Informed by a feminist perspective, CAV was instrumental in altering the "no contact" condition (whereby bail conditions are set to prohibit contact between the offender and the victim) to "contact with written revocable consent," which is more in keeping with the reality that many women may want to attempt reconciliation with their partners. This approach, according to Hannah-Moffat and Maurutto (2012), is not consistent with the approach taken by other community agencies across the country. In Alberta, the authors suggest, the domestic violence court relies on actuarial risk assessment as a main criterion, and this focus is in striking contrast to the Ontario PAR program's focus on danger to the victim.

How do specialized courts (such as domestic violence courts), as a criminal justice policy, get interpreted within the theoretical models of criminal justice?

Restorative justice	Provided that these specialized courts include opportunities for victim participation and mediation, restorative justice advocates would appreciate the approach of individualized justice.
Community change	Community change agencies would consider such an approach to be an opportunity to share their knowledge and programs for the benefit of the larger community.
Welfare	A focus on the individualized needs of offenders who come before the court would be applauded by welfare advocates.
Justice	Justice advocates would raise concerns that individual rights are violated when offenders are compelled to accept a diversionary approach (e.g., extended bail provisions).
Crime control	Police and Crown attorneys will accept such specialized courts, provided that the processing of offenders is efficient and cases are handled expeditiously.

What Do You Think?

1. The issues that are brought to the criminal court in cases of intimate partner violence may cross many government agencies and departments. Which departments would be directly and indirectly involved, and what kinds of services and support would be offered or needed for these cases?

2. Is it realistic to create specialized courts for other kinds of problems that appear before the criminal court? What issues and concerns might warrant a specialized court?

REFERENCES

Amato, P.R. (2000). The consequences of divorce for adults and children. *Journal of Marriage and the Family, 62*, 1269–1287.

Brown, T. (2000). *Charging and prosecution policies in cases of spousal assault: A synthesis of research, academic, and judicial responses—rr2001-5e.* Final report to the Department of Justice, Canada. Ottawa: Department of Justice Canada.

Dawson, M., & Dinovitzer, R. (2001). Victim cooperation and the prosecution of domestic violence in a specialized court. *Justice Quarterly, 18*, 593–622.

Eley, S. (2005). Changing practices: The specialised domestic violence court process. *The Howard Journal, 44*(2), 113–124.

Gill, C. (2005). The justice system's response to intimate partner abuse across Canada: Moving towards a Canadian observatory. Cluster Concept Paper. Fredericton: University of New Brunswick. Retrieved from http://www.unb.ca/observ/documents/cluster-concept-paper.pdf

Gill, C. (2006). Violence between intimate partners: Understanding theories and their links to intervention strategies. In M.R. Hampton & N. Gerrard (Eds.), *Intimate partner violence: Reflections on experience, theory and policy*. Toronto: Cormorant Books.

Hannah-Moffat, K., & Maurutto, P. (2012). Shifting and targeted forms of penal governance: Bail, punishment and specialized courts. *Theoretical Criminology, 16*(2), 201–219.

Holt, S., Buckley, H., & Whelan, S. (2006). The impact of exposure to domestic violence on children and young people: A review of the literature. *Child Abuse and Neglect, 32,* 797–810.

Hornick, J., Boyes, M., Tutty, L., & White, L. (2005). *The domestic violence treatment option (DVTO): Final evaluation report*. Whitehorse, YT and Ottawa: National Crime Prevention.

Jaffe, P.G., Hastings, G., Ketizel, D., & Austin, G.W. (1991). The impact of police laying charges. In N.Z. Hilton (Ed.), *Legal responses to wife assault*. Newbury Park, CA: Sage.

Landau, T.C. (2000). Women's experiences with mandatory charging for wife assault in Ontario, Canada: A case against the prosecution. *International Review of Victimology, 7,* 141–157.

Ursel, J. (2003). Using the justice system in Winnipeg. In H. Johnson & K. AuCoin (Eds.), *Family violence in Canada: A statistical profile 2003*. Catalogue No. 85-224-XIE. Ottawa: Canadian Centre for Justice Statistics. Retrieved from http://www.statcan.gc.ca/pub/85-224-x/85-224-x2003000-eng.pdf

16.5 Restorative Justice in Focus: Sentencing Circles

One of the dominant policy perspectives seen in the sentencing judge's decision in the *R. v. Jacob* case study is restorative justice. You may remember from Chapter 1 that restorative justice represents an approach to crime that falls under the theoretical model of community change. This is due in part to an understanding, endorsed within restorative justice, of crime as a *social* event that affects not only the offender and the victim, but also the wider community in which the crime takes place. The aim of restorative justice, as the name implies, is to address the harm that crime has done to a community and its members in such a way that peace and harmony are *restored*. In other words, restorative justice seeks (ideally) to bring communities back to where they were before the crime occurred.

One of the central rationales for the community-based approaches used in restorative justice is the strengthening of communities through the empowerment of its individual members to address problems, recognize harms, and devise solutions that promote healing, thus reducing the need for more formal punishments. This results in a shift in focus from **legal justice** (what the law says) to an emphasis on **social justice** (what is socially and morally just) when the appropriate punishment or legal response to crime is being considered. This brings restorative justice measures in line with a number of other social justice approaches to crime control, including the recent discipline of **peacemaking criminology**. Although there are variations in the way crime is addressed under these different approaches, each can be seen as subscribing to the following four principles:

- a shared sense of responsibility among community members for addressing crime
- the use of informal community mechanisms rather than formal criminal justice measures

> **Legal justice** refers to a system of principles by which individuals within a society should be treated and should treat one another, based on what the law dictates. The result, provided that the law is followed, is thought to be fair. Legal justice requires that the law be applied equally and fairly to everyone.

Social justice is concerned less with what the formal law says and more with defining justice in terms of human rights. In other words, the different social circumstances of individuals' lives, levels of inequality, and degrees of disadvantage are key considerations in determining how the law should be applied and what principles should govern individuals' relations with one another and the state.

Peacemaking criminology, a relatively new subfield of study within criminology and criminal justice studies, is largely associated with the work of American sociologist Richard Quinney. With roots in both Christian and Eastern philosophies and a strong connection to restorative justice practices, peacemaking approaches to crime control emphasize the social component of crime, including the strong influence of inequality and oppression on offending. Its focus is on alleviating suffering, fostering peace, and advancing practices such as reconciliation, mediation, and conflict resolution as effective responses to crime.

- the inclusion of victims as legal parties to the dispute in their own right
- the understanding of crime as an injury and not just an instance of law breaking. (LaPrairie, 1995, p. 80)

Restorative justice rose to prominence in criminology and criminal justice circles in the mid-1970s as a variety of movements began to change how crime and crime control were regarded. Greater attention to victims' rights, the development of community-based approaches to policing, and the advancement of social justice issues in both social and political circles each served to influence what some criminal justice scholars have identified as a **paradigm shift** in the definition and treatment of crime (Jones & Nestor, 2011). Although these developments help to explain how restorative justice approaches to crime and punishment gained prominence within the formal criminal justice system, many of the techniques and methods of addressing

Paradigm shift, a term first used by Thomas Kuhn, an American historian and philosopher of science, in *The Structure of Scientific Revolutions* (1962), describes a change from one way of thinking to another, usually on a wide scale. It involves a revolution in basic assumptions about how a particular phenomenon or system works, resulting in a completely different worldview. A good example is Galileo Galilei's discovery that the world was not flat but round. His discovery eventually changed the thinking about almost everything in the social and scientific world—a true paradigm shift.

crime that are used in restorative justice initiatives have existed for centuries, with roots in many ancient civilizations, including Arab, Roman, and Greek societies (Braithwaite, 1999). Some of the most influential traditions informing restorative justice practices have been found among the Aboriginal communities of Canada, Australia, and the United States that have a long-standing tradition of community-based approaches to crime and the harm it causes. One of the central challenges for the restorative justice movement has been finding ways of integrating these more traditional forms of punishment and crime response into the formal criminal justice system.

Restorative Justice in Practice: Sentencing Circles

Sentencing circles have proven to be one of the most successful applications of Aboriginal and restorative justice practices within current legal systems. Circles have a profound significance for many First Nations communities in Canada. Thought to symbolize the interconnectedness of all living things with the planet and with one another, the circle is meant to remind members of a community that each decision made and each action taken affects everyone else (Dickson-Gillmore & LaPrairie, 2005). In Canada, the first sentencing circle was held in 1992, in the case *R. v. Moses.* Presided over by Judge Barry Stuart (the same judge who delivered the sentence in *R. v. Jacob*), the *Moses* case prompted many other judges in Canada to attempt sentencing circles in their own jurisdictions. Sentencing circles occur in a number of ways. They can be established on a judge's recommendation or on a request by the offender, defence counsel, the Crown attorney, or a community justice committee, where available (LaPrairie, 1995).

A sentencing circle performs the same task as a sentencing hearing (explored in Chapter 8). It determines the appropriate punishment for a person who has committed a crime. This decision is reached in a very different way during a sentencing circle. Perhaps most distinctively, a sentencing circle does not take place in a courtroom with a judge observing from high above and the accused sitting in a prisoner's box. Rather, everyone who attends sits in a circle; no one is excluded or privileged in how or where they sit in the room. Anyone from the community may attend and participate in the process. Usually, the circle is held in a venue that is much less formal than a courtroom, such as a community centre or dance hall. Many sentencing circles are composed of two circles: an inner circle (where those most affected by the crime are seated) and an outer circle (where members of the community may attend to observe, and speak when asked, or if they volunteer to do so) (LaPrairie, 1995). Although many different people can attend the sentencing circle, each circle usually includes the following participants:

- the offender
- the victim
- the judge
- the Crown attorney
- defence counsel
- the court recorder
- some members from the community (e.g., family members of the victim or the offender).

In addition to these participants, many other criminal justice professionals might attend, including victims' services workers, police officers, substance abuse counsellors, and probation officers. Similarly, many other members of the community may participate in order to speak about the harm the crime has caused to them and their social groups.

The procedure of a sentencing circle is far more informal than that of a sentencing hearing in the criminal justice system. There are no witnesses, for example, and no direct or cross-examinations. Aside from the inner and outer circles (which are not always employed), there are no rules about who sits where or what must be said. This allows for a great degree of variation from circle to circle. Generally, though, the judge welcomes everyone, introduces the relevant parties and the facts of the case, and then invites discussion. Each member of the circle takes turns in speaking, passing an object (sometimes referred to as a "talking feather" or "talking stone") to anyone who wishes to speak. There are no interruptions. If a person is holding the talking stone and speaking, those wishing to speak must wait for the stone to be passed to them before they can begin. This allows everyone to be heard without the fear of being immediately rejected or shut out through interruptions or discrediting remarks.

"The principal value of Community Sentencing Circles cannot be measured by what happens to offenders, but rather by what happens to communities. In reinforcing and building a sense of community, Circle Sentencing improves the capacity of communities to heal individuals and families and ultimately to prevent crime."

—Judge Barry Stuart (1994, pp. 18–19)

The goal of the circle is to reach a consensus about what sentence will best restore harmony and promote healing for the community and its individual members. The judge will usually indicate what the available sentencing options are (as provided for in the *Criminal Code*); but which of these options the circle agrees on, or the reasons for that agreement, are left open to the participants of the circle. As might be expected, the discussions that take place during a sentencing circle are often highly emotionally charged. Unlike a criminal trial and sentencing process, the offender and the victim are provided with an opportunity to speak directly, often for the first time since the offence occurred. While sometimes painful, these conversations frequently enable all parties involved to gain some sense of closure and greater opportunity for healing.

How are sentencing circles, as a criminal justice policy, interpreted within the theoretical models of criminal justice?

Restorative justice	Restorative justice proponents are strong advocates for sentencing circles because they allow the offender to speak with the victim and his or her family, and address concerns of the wider community.
Community change	Provided that the wider community is included in the deliberations about a specific sentence, community change advocates are strong supporters of this approach.
Welfare	The individualized approach to a sentencing circle, which allows for the offender's needs to be addressed through a recommendation at sentencing for treatment, is seen as a positive feature for welfare proponents.
Justice	Justice advocates might be concerned about the individual offender and whether his or her rights have been violated by the informal processes used in circle sentencing. They would also not favour the way sentencing circles treat each case on an individual basis rather than imposing the same sentence for the same offence irrespective of the unique needs or circumstances of the victim, offender, and community.
Crime control	Crime-control advocates are not impressed with the time taken to complete an intensive sentencing circle, which can create a backlog of cases before the courts.

What Do You Think?

1. Restorative justice approaches to crime have a long history in the indigenous communities of North America and Australia. Although sentencing circles represent one of the better-known applications of these approaches to crime control, there are a number of other techniques endorsed by Aboriginal communities both to punish offenders and to assist them in healing and reintegrating into society, such as shaming, banishment, and restitution. Select two or three of these other practices to examine and contrast them with the sentencing options available in Canada's *Criminal Code* and current criminal justice system. What differences and similarities can you identify? What theoretical models do these practices speak to? How is crime defined in each of these approaches?

2. In theory, sentencing circles can be used for any offence. There are some debates within law and criminal justice studies about whether they are better suited for some offences and offenders than for others. For example, some victims' rights advocates argue that circle sentencing is not well suited to sexual offences, because they can cause more trauma than healing. Others debate whether they should be used for young offenders. Do you think criteria should be established for the

cases in which sentencing circles can be used? Are there problems with judges being the figures who decide whether a circle will take place?

3. Although many First Nations communities endorse the use of sentencing and healing circles within Canada's criminal justice system, some are opposed to this integration. They argue that these practices are sacred to Aboriginal people and their use within non-Aboriginal contexts may be inappropriate. The use of sentencing circles is sometimes characterized as a further instance of colonization or oppression of Aboriginal culture. Explore this debate on your own, identifying arguments for each side before determining where you stand on the issue.

4. Using the *R. v. Jacob* case study, imagine that a sentencing circle has been set up to address this offence and its harm to the community. Who would be present in the circle, and why? What do you think each participant might say? Do you think this case is an appropriate one for a sentencing circle? Why or why not? What effect, if any, do you think a circle would have had on the outcome of this case?

5. Investigate the distinction between social justice and legal justice. How dissimilar are they? Review the theoretical models discussed in Chapter 1 and decide whether each model focuses more on social justice or on legal justice. Provide one example of a punishment for each model that supports your argument.

REFERENCES AND FURTHER READING

Belknap, J., & MacDonald, C. (2010). Judges' attitudes about and experiences with sentencing circles in intimate-partner abuse cases. *Canadian Journal of Criminology and Criminal Justice, 52*(4), 369–395.

Braithwaite, J. (1989). *Crime, shame, and reintegration.* Cambridge: Cambridge University Press.

Braithwaite, J. (2002). *Restorative justice and responsive regulation.* Oxford: Oxford University Press.

Cunliffe, E., & Cameron, A. (2007). Writing the circle: Judicially convened sentencing circles and the textual organization of criminal justice. *Canadian Journal of Women and the Law, 19*(1), 1–35.

Dickson-Gilmore, J., & LaPrairie, C. (2005). *Will the circle be unbroken? Aboriginal communities, restorative justice, and the challenges of conflict and change.* Toronto: University of Toronto Press.

Jones, N.A., & Nestor, R. (2011). Sentencing circles in Canada and the Gacaca in Rwanda: A comparative analysis. *International Criminal Justice Review, 21*(1), 39–66.

LaPrairie, C. (2005). Altering course: New directions in criminal justice— Sentencing circles and family group conferences. *Australian and New Zealand Journal of Criminology, 28*(1), 78–99.

Pepinsky, H.E., & Quinney, R. (Eds.). (1991). *Criminology as peacekeeping.* Bloomington, IN: Indiana University Press.

R. v. Moses (1992), 11 CR (4th) 357 (Yuk. Terr. Ct.).

Stuart, B. (1994). Sentencing circles: Purpose and impact. National Canadian Bar Association.

Whonnock, K. (2008, April). Aboriginal courts in Canada. Report prepared for the Scow Institute of Canada, Granville Island, BC. Retrieved from http://www.scowinstitute.ca/library/documents/Aboriginal_Courts.pdf

16.6 Boot Camps for Young Offenders

Boot camps are sometimes referred to as "shock incarceration programs" owing to their high-intensity, physically demanding nature. Boot camps are most commonly known as military-style training for new recruits, with a heavy dose of physical activity. For this reason, it is not surprising that personal fitness trainers and gyms across the country have taken this name for their high-intensity "shock" fitness programs. In the case of penal boot camps, they have been very popular with those people who believe that young people need to be taught a lesson and that the strict discipline and physical activity characteristic of a military-style boot camp will help achieve this. Such programs promise greater self-discipline, respect, and potentially reduced reoffending rates. However, as Cullen, Blevins, Trager, and Gendreau (2005, p. 68) note, "the consensus in the criminological community is that the evidence is persuasive that boot camps are largely a failed enterprise." A more recent analysis found that while boot camps may improve individuals' attitudes during the program, there is no effect on participant's reoffence rates (Meade & Steiner, 2010). In fact, some studies have found that participation in boot camp may increase the likelihood of recidivism (Wilson, MacKenzie, & Mitchell, 2003). As Latessa, Cullen, and Gendreau (2002) have argued, boot camps are known in the profession as *correctional quackery* because they satisfy the desire to punish but fail to produce a result. (See the sidebar on page 447.)

Supporters of boot camp programs argue that recidivism rates are poor indicators of program success because recidivism studies may not reveal the truly important figure, which is the *eventual probability* of recidivism. The fact that 50 percent of the participants fail within the first three months may mean that either all of the graduates will likely recidivate at some point, or that all of those individuals who are going to recidivate have done so within the first three months following completion of the program (Osler, 1991; Reid-MacNevin, 1997).

Some supporters of boot camps argue that they are effective means of dealing with offenders because the structure and discipline enforced at the camps build a foundation of discipline, responsibility, and self-esteem (Reid-MacNevin, 1997). Clark, Moscicki, and Perry (2009) suggest that the skills that young people can gain from a military-style boot camp experience are transferable to the workplace. Discipline, such as "being at the appointed place at the appointed time in the proper uniform, doing what you're told, when you're told and how you're told," will assist young people when they

SIDEBAR

What Is the Appeal of Boot Camps?

Cullen, Blevins, Trager, and Gendreau (2005, p. 60) suggest that there is a certain uplifting and heart-warming quality to the image of boot camps that has been promoted in television and films, such as *An Officer and a Gentleman*, which appeals to the general public:

> We see the slightly delinquent, confused, perhaps self-centred youthful rebel saved from personal and social failure by the demanding but ultimately caring drill sergeant who pulls the recruit back from the brink of going AWOL. The ending of these films is particularly revealing. They invariably show the group that had survived boot camp proudly marching out in their pristine dress uniforms just as a new group of recruits sporting long hair and ill-fitting clothes staggers off the bus to the inhospitable greetings of the drill sergeant. We all know what awaits them!

Waller (2009, p. 297) asks us to consider a variation on boot camps:

> Suppose that instead of *boot camps* we tried *beach camps*: youthful offenders are sent for an eight-week crash program of rehabilitation at a beautiful sandy beach resort, where they would sip cool beverages, frolic in the surf, go sailing and scuba diving, live in luxury hotels, and do pleasant lessons on finding alternatives to criminal behaviour. And we discover that not only are these beach camps less expensive than harsh boot camps, but they are also incredibly effective in turning youthful offenders away from lives of crime (while the more expensive boot camps report marginal effectiveness at best).

What Do You Think?

1. What is the appeal to the general public of the military-style boot camp? What makes it so powerful compared with Waller's (2009) alternative of a beach camp? Are both kinds of camps correctional quackery?

2. Perhaps you have answered that a beach camp is not good common sense! However, Cullen, Trager, and Gendreau (2005, 65) suggest that "[a]ll of us should continue to be wary of common sense. It is dangerous precisely because it seems so correct, leaves our biases unchallenged and requires virtually no effort to activate." Think about the protective factors that might be supported in a beach camp for those youth who have never had such opportunities, and make a list of the pros and cons of such an approach.

go to work for someone else: "Unless you're Bill Gates, you're going to work for someone else. You aren't going to last long at McDonald's if you don't understand that basic fact" (Clark, Moscicki, & Perry, 2009, p. 304).

What Do You Think?

Should correctional and rehabilitation programs for young offenders aspire to train people for something more than a McJob? (A "McJob" is a low-paying, often part-time or temporary position in the retail or service sector, offering minimal or no benefits. The name is derived from McDonald's restaurants.)

Others have pointed out that there are several components of boot camps that are not appropriate for working with youth. Peters, Thomas, and Zamberlan (1997) suggests that youth respond to encouragement better than they do to criticism and punishment, because the very nature of adolescence is to reject rule structure imposed by adults and authority figures.

The popularity of boot camps for youth has declined since the 1990s, partly as a result of research showing no difference in recidivism rates, but also as a result of a number of lawsuits related to human rights violations, such as cruel and unusual punishment. Campie (2011) reports on three examples highlighted in a US Government Accountability Office investigation in 2007 regarding abuse allegations against youth boot camps.

- A 15-year-old died from a severed neck artery after being held face down in dirt for 45 minutes.
- A 14-year-old died of dehydration after being forced to sit in 113 °F desert heat as punishment for asking to go home. (The director was sentenced to six years in prison for manslaughter.)
- A number of boys were required to stand with bags over their heads and a hangman's noose around their necks as a reminder of their punishment.
- A 14-year-old boy died from having ammonia tablets pushed up his nose by boot camp staff for minor misbehaviour.

Coupled with these allegations of abuse and the lack of scientific evidence to support the use of boot camps as an effective correctional intervention, the number of boot camps has steadily declined throughout the United States (Russell, 2006). However, as Campie (2011, p. 50) argues, the boot camp cottage industry remains a "robust supplier of disciplinary services for parents dealing with troubled teens." Private programs range in cost from $10,000 for a 30-day program to about $18,000 when the program combines wilderness therapy with the boot camp regimen (Campie, 2011).

The popularity of the boot camp has also been reflected in the reality TV series *Brat Camp*. (The original UK version of the series ran for five years, the German version for three, the US version for one.) The youth on these shows appeared to be from wealthier families, and the shows featured an emphasis on parent–teen conflict (such as not following house rules, partying, getting into fights). When the series aired in Canada, an article in the *Toronto Star* described the program as abusive (Menon, 2005). When the show was launched in Britain, Barnardo's, a children's charity, expressed concern that the show was sending the wrong message to parents—namely, that a short period of "tough love" can resolve mental health and behavioural issues (Lee, 2004).

Despite conflicting evidence about the usefulness of boot camps, they are so appealing to the public's desire to "get tough on crime" that evidence refuting their effectiveness may fall on deaf ears. A case in point is New Zealand's youth justice legislation, which was amended in 2010 under the *Children, Young Persons and Their Families (Youth Court Jurisdiction Orders) Amendment Act* (Lynch, 2010). New Zealand had gained international acclaim for a youth justice system that was built on the tenets of restorative justice (Braithwaite, 1989; Zehr, 1990). The former legislation was noted for its non-punitive response to youth, with diversion being used in approximately 80 percent of apprehensions, even with serious offenders (Lynch, 2011). However, the new legislation, which includes youth boot camps, is a sign that the country is becoming more punitive with juvenile offenders.

According to New Zealand's minister of social development, the new reforms, known as Fresh Start Reforms, incorporate army-style discipline with a full range of rehabilitation programs, including alcohol and drug counselling, mentoring, and cognitive behavioural treatment (Lynch, 2011). Reports within the first few months of the operation of the Fresh Start Reforms indicated that, of the 17 youth who had completed the program, four had been sentenced to prison and the majority had reoffended. The "success" of the program included a commentary suggesting that while the program participants had recidivated, 60 percent committed a less serious crime and 53 percent offended less frequently (Lynch, 2011, p. 10).

With Canada's enactment of the *Safe Streets and Communities Act* (2012) and its principles of denunciation and deterrence as a guiding philosophy for youth justice, we may also see the return of boot camps. When a strict-discipline program was started in Ontario in the 1990s, there was considerable support from the public that was echoed throughout provincial public safety policies. Reid-MacNevin (1997) reports that even though the research evidence did not support a deterrence-based criminal justice policy, the Ministry of Correctional Services moved forward with the government's election promises: "there will be boot camps for violent young offenders, hollow-point bullets for police, a law allowing police to warn the public when violent sex offenders are released, and removal of bleeding hearts from the provincial parole board" (Brennan, 1995, p. 63, cited in Reid-MacNevin, 1997, p. 156).

How might a policy of boot camps for young offenders be interpreted within the framework of the theoretical models of criminal justice?

Restorative justice	Restorative justice advocates would not be pleased with the punitive nature of boot camps and the lack of involvement of victims. The fact that boot camps are generally closed to community involvement would also be a problem for restorative justice advocates, who seek restoration for the broader community.
Community change	Because boot camps remove the offender from the community and isolate them in small wilderness camps or military-style barracks, community change advocates would not see the benefit to the broader community of such isolation.
Welfare	Boot camps have shown the most promise when they are focused on individual cognitive therapy and treatment for individual offenders. If boot camp programs focused on these outcomes, welfare advocates would see them as more helpful than standard military-style boot camps.
Justice	Provided that offenders were given the possibility of a reduced sentence if they selected a boot camp, justice proponents would support the individual's freedom to choose an outcome.
Crime control	With boot camps' focus on deterrence and denunciation, as well as the speedy disposition of cases, crime-control advocates would be pleased with such a policy.

What Do You Think?

1. What do you think will be the outcomes of New Zealand's move away from a youth justice system founded on restorative justice principles toward a more punitive system?

2. What do you think will be the implications of the *Safe Streets and Communities Act* (2012) with respect to the creation of programs and policies to ensure that the principles of denunciation and deterrence are implemented for young persons who commit crime?

3. Do you think there will be a resurgence of research interest in evaluating the effectiveness of boot camps? Do you think new research will find new evidence to support such programs?

REFERENCES

Braithwaite, J. (1989). *Crime, shame, and reintegration*. Cambridge: Cambridge University Press.

Campie, P.E. (2011). Boot camps. In W.J. Chambliss (Ed.), *Juvenile crime and justice*. Washington, DC: Sage.

Clark, C.L., Moscicki, R., & Perry, J. (2009). To march or not to march: Is that the question? In B.N. Waller (Ed.), *You decide! Current debates in criminal justice*. Boston: Allyn & Bacon.

Cullen, F.T., Blevins, K.R., Trager, J.S., & Gendreau, P. (2005). The rise and fall of boot camps: A case study in common sense corrections. *Journal of Offender Rehabilitation, 4*(3–4), 53–70.

Latessa, E.J., Cullen, F.T., & Gendreau, P. (2002). Beyond correctional quackery: Professionalism and the possibility of effective treatment. *Federal Probation, 66*(2), 43–49.

Lee, D. (2004, March 25). Teenage fix. *The Guardian*. Retrieved from http://www.guardian.co.uk/education/2004/mar/25/schools.uk

Lynch, N. (2010). A change in the law for child offenders: The Children, Young Persons, and Their Families (Youth Courts Jurisdiction and Orders) Amendment Act 2010. *New Zealand Family Law Journal, 6*(10), 289–293.

Lynch, N. (2011). Playing catch-up? Recent reform of New Zealand's youth justice system. *Criminology and Criminal Justice* (forthcoming).

MacKenzie, D., Wilson, D., & Kider, S. (2001). Effects of correctional boot camps on offending. *Annals of the American Academy of Political and Social Science, 126*, 578. doi:10.1177/000271620157800108

Meade, B., & Steiner, B. (2010). The total effects of boot camps that house juveniles: A systematic review of the evidence. *Journal of Criminal Justice, 38*(5), 841–853.

Menon, V. (2005, July 14). Boot camp for teens is abusive. *The Toronto Star*, p. A22.

Osler, M. (1991). Shock incarceration: Hard realities and real possibilities. *Federal Probation* (March), 34–41.

Peters, M., Thomas, D., & Zamberlan, C. (1997). *Boot camps for juvenile offenders*. Washington, DC: Office of Juvenile Justice and Delinquency Prevention, US Department of Justice.

Reid-MacNevin, S. (1997). Boot camps for young offenders: A politically acceptable punishment. *Journal of Contemporary Criminal Justice, 13*(2), 155–171.

Russell, K.C. (2006). Brat camp, boot camp or … ? Exploring wilderness therapy program theory. *Journal of Adventure Education and Outdoor Learning, 6*(1), 51–68.

Waller, B.N. (2009). *You decide! Current debates in criminal justice*. Boston: Allyn & Bacon.

Wilson, D.B., MacKenzie, D.L., & Mitchell, F.N. (2003). Effects of correctional boot camps on offending. *Campbell Systematic Reviews*. doi:10.4073/csr.2003.1. Retrieved from http://www.campbellcollaboration.org/lib/download/3/

Zehr, H. (1990). *Changing lenses: A new focus for crime and justice*. Scottsdale, PA: Herald Press.

16.7 Wrongful Convictions and Jailhouse Informants

Of all the mistakes that are possible in a criminal justice system as large and complex as Canada's, there is no error as grievous as sending an innocent person to jail. Although wrongful convictions are often thought to be a rare occurrence, the development of forensic science (and DNA analysis in particular) has brought far more wrongful convictions to the forefront of criminal justice studies. Recent scholarship in Canada, the United States, and the United Kingdom has begun to explore these miscarriages of justice, prompting the establishment of a number of governmental inquiries and commissions aimed at identifying the causes and effects of wrongful convictions.

One of the leading factors thought to contribute to incidents of wrongful conviction is the use of jailhouse informants. An informant is a person who provides the police and prosecution with information about a crime. A number of different types of informants are typically used in criminal investigations. "Citizen informants" are law-abiding individuals who provide the police with information about a crime they may have witnessed or learned about (for example, they may have overheard a conversation, or seen a missing person or stolen vehicle). Information relayed to the police by these individuals is usually kept confidential so as to protect the informant; sometimes, however, citizen informants may be asked to testify at trial. "Criminal informants" are individuals who have provided information to the police based on their own involvement in criminal activity and associations. They are also sometimes referred to as "street informants" (Bloom, 2003). A "jailhouse informant" is a subtype of criminal informant who is being held in custody, usually awaiting trial or sentencing (Sherrin, 1997a).

The information provided by a jailhouse informant is based on what the informant has seen or overheard while in custody. Most often, it is a claim that another prisoner has made an admission of guilt about a pending case. This information is exchanged or "traded" with police in return for some favour or benefit for the informant, such as leniency in sentencing or a transfer to a lower-security facility. Sometimes, a police officer will pose as a fellow inmate or a member of a criminal association in order to gain the trust of the accused and gather evidence about the case. Such officers are referred to as "undercover informants." The use of information gathered by undercover informants can raise questions about Charter rights violations, especially where the accused has already asked to speak to a lawyer, and may be subject to exclusion at trial. Courts have viewed the use of undercover informants as an attempt by the police to bypass the Charter through "the back door," and have dealt with such practices very harshly.

The fact that jailhouse informants usually "trade" the information they have about a case in return for a benefit is one of the main reasons the credibility of their testimony is doubted. Often, a case is reported in enough detail in the media to enable an inmate seeking a reduced sentence or prosecutorial leniency to offer a convincing account of an admission or confession without even speaking to the accused. This problem has become even more widespread with the availability of the Internet in prisons, leading to the recent nickname of **e-snitches** (Alter, 2005). The stigma of having a criminal record is another reason that jailhouse informant evidence is not easily trusted. This was acknowledged explicitly by the Supreme Court of Canada in *R. v. Bevan* (1993), when the court commented on two of the Crown's jailhouse witnesses:

> Both of them had lengthy criminal records, had strong motivations to lie, and approached the police only when each perceived that some benefit— such as release from prison, a discontinuation of charges against them, or cash payments—could be obtained in exchange for their testimony. Both of them explicitly told the police at the time they came forward that they were seeking a "deal" in exchange for their evidence against the appellants. (p. 327)

This distrust of jailhouse informants has a long history, traceable back to the 13th century, when English common law used the "approver system," which allowed anyone who was charged with a capital offence (such as treason or murder) to obtain a pardon if he or she reported the crimes of another (Sherrin, 1997a). A pardon would be issued only if the person named by the approver was found guilty. If the person named was not found guilty, the approver was put to death! While the consequences for jailhouse informants who give false evidence about what they may have seen or heard while in custody are not as severe as death, the number of wrongful convictions that have resulted from criminal informants committing **perjury** suggests that lives are still at stake.

One of the more famous cases of a wrongful conviction in Canada was that of Guy Paul Morin, who was convicted in 1992 of the sexual assault and murder of his eight-year-old neighbour. He was sentenced to life imprisonment. Three years later, DNA analysis cleared Morin of any guilt and his conviction was overturned (Katz, 2011). A key component of the Crown's

e-snitch
A term for jailhouse informants who gather information about a case using the Internet. News reports, blogs, and personal websites often provide enough detail about a crime to enable informants to falsify entire confessions rather convincingly.

perjury
The act of wilfully lying under oath usually before a judge (and/or jury) during a trial. It is a criminal offence in many countries, including Canada, as defined in s. 131 of the *Criminal Code*.

case against Morin was the testimony of two jailhouse informants who claimed they heard Morin confess to the crime while sharing a cell with him (Skurka, 2002). A public inquiry launched after Morin's release revealed a number of questionable circumstances related to the reliability of the evidence offered by the jailhouse informants. One of these informants was paroled on his first day of eligibility, within a week of testifying against Morin (Kaufman, 1998). This led Justice Kaufman, the commissioner of the Morin inquiry, to comment on the danger of relying on jailhouse informants, suggesting that their testimony was often "tainted by self-interest" (Katz, 2011). He further stated:

> The systemic evidence emanating from Canada, Great Britain, Australia and the United States demonstrated that the dangers associated with jailhouse informants were not unique to the Morin case. Indeed, a number of miscarriages of justice throughout the world are likely explained, at least in part, by the false, self-serving evidence given by such informants. (Katz, 2011, p. 122)

The actual number of wrongful convictions is difficult to determine, although data offered by the Innocence Project, an American organization established to help free the wrongfully convicted, suggest that 292 wrongful convictions have been overturned in the United States since 1989 through DNA testing. This figure is also supported in the academic literature (Raeder, 2007). In jurisdictions like the United States, where capital punishment is still in use, the dangers of using unreliable or false informant testimony are amplified. The Innocence Project reports that of the 292 cases they were successful in having overturned, 17 of the convicted had been serving time on death row. In more than two-thirds (70 percent) of these cases, the accused was a racial minority, with 62 percent being African-American. When considered in the context of the overrepresentation of racial minorities in prison and research demonstrating the systemic forms of bias and discrimination that operate in the criminal justice system, these issues become all the more serious.

These many difficulties with the use of jailhouse informants have led some to argue that this kind of testimony should be eliminated from the criminal justice system altogether. Although inmates cannot be prevented from talking with police about what they see or hear while in their cells, if this information were not usable in court, it might reduce the number of informants who would choose to lie to the police in the hopes of gaining something (Sherrin, 1997b). However, police are quick to note how helpful informants can be in solving a case, and that not all cases involving jailhouse informants lead to wrongful convictions. Some people argue that changes should be made to the way in which informant statements are used as evidence. For example, some maintain that **corroboration** should be required before a jailhouse informant can testify. Others suggest that juries be warned about the problems with relying on jailhouse informant testimony in cases where it is being used. Other arguments include limiting or eliminating the benefits that informants can gain from police so as to remove the incentive for informants to lie (Sherrin, 1997b). Each of these reform proposals has its difficulties, and none of the states and countries that use jailhouse informants use them in the same way. Although this is a complicated issue, the links that have been drawn between jailhouse informants and wrongful convictions make this an important problem to think through.

> **Corroboration** is a legal term that refers to evidence that supports or "backs up" information the police already have. It serves to confirm information that has been reported to police. For example, if a witness to a bank robbery told police she saw three people running from the bank wearing Homer Simpson masks, and video footage from the bank's security system showed the robbers wearing such masks, then the video would corroborate the witness's testimony.

The use of jailhouse informants to enhance the likelihood of conviction might be interpreted with the theoretical models of criminal justice as follows:

Restorative justice	Similar to welfare advocates, restorative justice advocates would not approve of the use of jailhouse informants unless such use would benefit the offender, the victim, and the wider community. Like community change advocates, restorative justice advocates would not see the value to the community of such "snitching."
Community change	The way the use of jailhouse informants pits offenders against one another and fosters mistrust between offenders and criminal justice professionals would not be seen by community change advocates as being beneficial to the community of the prison, or the wider community (society). A win–lose scenario is not in keeping with a community change approach where all members of society are to receive some benefit.
Welfare	Welfare advocates would not approve of the use of informants in the criminal justice process because such use would jeopardize gains made in treatment programs that may be working on issues of dishonesty. If the sharing of information was seen to be of therapeutic value to the individual giving testimony, it might be seen as a more palatable option.
Justice	The testimony of informants is seen as problematic for both the informant and the individual being defended. Justice advocates would want to ensure that the informant received appropriate compensation (i.e., sentence reduction) for such testimony. At the same time, justice advocates would question the reliability of the testimony of an individual who had something to gain at the expense of a defendant.
Crime control	If the use of testimony from informants can expedite convictions, crime-control advocates would see it as a positive contribution to the criminal justice process.

What Do You Think?

1. One of the problems raised by the use of undercover officers posing as jailhouse informants is the potential for Charter rights violations. Thinking back on the Charter rights that were discussed in Chapters 4 and 6, which rights are most likely to be at issue in these cases? Do you think the use of undercover informants should be allowed in criminal investigations? What are some of the arguments in favour of their use? If you were a defence lawyer, what arguments might you make against the admission of undercover informant evidence?

2. Although there are many problems associated with the use of jailhouse informants, many police organizations argue that they continue to serve as a valuable investigative tool in difficult cases. This is a good example of the kind of tension within the criminal justice system when balancing competing interests—on the one hand, the protection of society (largely through police investigative powers), and on the other, the protection of individual rights. How do you think this balance should be struck with jailhouse informants? Should their use be permitted? Why or why not?

3. Explore the link between wrongful convictions and jailhouse informants. How many cases of wrongful conviction can you discover where testimony from a criminal informant was used? Is there enough evidence to establish a strong connection? Do you think jailhouse informants get a bad name?

4. Given the many problems associated with the use of jailhouse informants, a number of suggestions have been made for improving their use. Some argue that jailhouse informants should not be used at all. Do you agree? Why or why not? Investigate this reform debate and determine your own position on the issue. What changes (if any) would you recommend to the way in which the criminal justice system uses jailhouse informants?

REFERENCES AND FURTHER READING

Alter, V. (2005). Jailhouse informants: A lesson in e-snitching. *Journal of Technology Law and Policy, 10*(2), 223–242.

Anderson, B. (2003). *Manufacturing guilt: Wrongful convictions in Canada.* Halifax: Fernwood.

Bloom, R. (2003). Jailhouse informants. *Criminal Justice, 18*(1), 20–27.

Innocence Project. (2012). Cardozo School of Law, New York. http://www.innocenceproject.org

Katz, H. (2011). *Justice miscarried: Inside wrongful convictions in Canada.* Toronto: Dundurn Press.

Kaufman Commission. (1998). *The Commission on Proceedings Involving Guy Paul Morin*. Toronto: Ontario Ministry of the Attorney General. Retrieved from http://www.attorneygeneral.jus.gov.on.ca/english/about/pubs/morin/

Maidment, M. (2010). *When justice is a game: Unravelling wrongful conviction in Canada*. Halifax: Fernwood.

Manitoba Justice. (2001). *The inquiry regarding Thomas Sophonow: Jailhouse informants, their unreliability and the importance of complete Crown disclosure pertaining to them*. Winnipeg: Manitoba Office of the Attorney General. Retrieved from http://www.gov.mb.ca/justice/publications/sophonow/jailhouse/recommend.html

Martin, D.L. (2002). Lessons about justice from the "laboratory" of wrongful convictions: Tunnel vision, the construction of guilt, and informer evidence. *UMKC Law Review, 70*(4), 847–864.

Natapoff, A. (2009). *Snitching: Criminal informants and the erosion of American justice*. New York: New York University Press.

R. v. Bevan (1993), 82 CCC (3d) 310 (SCC).

Raeder, M.S. (2007). See no evil: Wrongful convictions and the prosecutorial ethics of offering testimony by jailhouse informants and dishonest experts. *Fordham Law Review, 76*(3), 1413–1452.

Sherrin, C. (1997a). Jailhouse informants, part I: Problems with their use. *Criminal Law Quarterly, 40*, 106–122.

Sherrin, C. (1997b). Jailhouse informants, part II: Options for reform. *Criminal Law Quarterly, 40*, 157–187.

Skurka, S. (2002). A Canadian perspective on the role of cooperators and informants. *Cardozo Law Review, 23*(2), 759–770.

Zimmerman, C. (2001). From the jailhouse to the courthouse: The role of informants in wrongful convictions. In S.D. Westervelt & J.A. Humphrey (Eds.), *Wrongly convicted: Perspectives on failed justice* (pp. 55–76). Piscataway, NJ: Rutgers University Press.

16.8 Capital Punishment

It might seem strange to find a discussion of the death penalty in a 21st-century Canadian textbook. The last execution in Canada was in 1962, 14 years before an impassioned Prime Minister Pierre Trudeau spoke on the floor of the House of Commons in favour of a bill to abolish capital punishment. He argued:

> It is not open to anyone among us to take refuge in the comforting illusion that we are debating nothing more than an abstract theory of criminal justice. … I want to make it very clear that, if a majority of honourable members vote against abolition, some people are going to be hanged. … I say that, Mister Speaker, not from any desire to be morbid or melodramatic. … I say it in order to impress upon the House as strongly as I can that what we will actually be deciding, when we vote on this bill, is not merely how the law of the land will be written, but also whether some human beings will live or die. (Canada, 1976, p. 14500)

Although it has been more than 35 years since the death penalty could be found "on the books" in Canada, it remains a controversial issue, frequently making appearances in political platforms and election agendas. In a 2011 television interview with the CBC's Peter Mansbridge, Prime Minister Stephen Harper supported the use of capital punishment for some offences, arguing that sometimes the death penalty "fits the crime" (Taber, 2011). Despite this position, Harper was clear that his government would not reopen the debate on capital punishment in Canada.

One reason a government might shy away from reintroducing the death penalty into Canadian criminal law is the *Charter of Rights and Freedoms*. Section 12 of the Charter provides protection against the use of "cruel and unusual punishment." Although Canada abolished the death penalty six years before the Charter was written, a number of other countries have followed suit, on the basis that it constitutes an unusually severe penalty. South Africa, for example, outlawed capital punishment in 1995 on the basis that it violated the country's prohibition of "torture of any kind, whether physical, mental, or emotional" and "cruel, inhuman or degrading treatment or punishment" (Schabas, 1996).

Another reason capital punishment remains a relevant issue in criminal justice studies is its persistence elsewhere in the world. Amnesty International reports that 58 countries still use the death penalty and that 21 executions took place in 2011 (Amnesty International, 2012). The United

"Everyone has the right not to be subjected to any cruel and unusual treatment or punishment."

—*Section 12 of the Charter of Rights and Freedoms*

States continues to execute its prisoners by lethal injection, electrocution, firing squad, hanging, and the gas chamber (Radelet, 1989). Until 2002, the United States allowed the execution of offenders who were mentally disabled (*Atkins v. Virginia*, 2002). Since Canada's abolition of the death penalty, the United States has executed 1,290 offenders (Death Penalty Information Center [DPIC], 2012). Twenty-two were under the age of 18, making the United States one of nine countries that allow the use of the death penalty in young offender cases (despite its prohibition under international law). With the decision in the *Roper v. Simmons* case in 2005, however, America banned capital punishment for juveniles. Prior to this, the United States and Iran executed more child offenders than the combined total executed in the other seven countries that permit it. Iran is now the leading executioner of young offenders, with 145 juveniles currently sentenced to death (Amnesty International, 2012).

Capital punishment continues to be a hotly debated topic in many regions of the world. Supporters of the death penalty are sometimes referred to as "retentionists," while those who oppose it are called "abolitionists." Although there are a number of arguments on both sides of the debate on capital punishment, recent research examining systemic forms of racism in the criminal justice system and high levels of overrepresentation of visible minorities in prisons suggests an even greater need to consider the implications

---

SIDEBAR

Two Views on Capital Punishment

The abolitionist view holds that:

- life is sacred
- capital punishment does not deter crime
- capital punishment is implemented with a class bias
- the innocent may die
- retribution is uncivilized
- capital punishment precludes rehabilitation
- capital punishment injures the criminal justice system.

The retentionist view holds that:

- capital punishment is the only prevention against certain crimes
- capital punishment balances the scales of justice
- capital punishment deters crime
- capital punishment is an economical way to manage offenders.

of state-sanctioned killing. Data from the United States reveal that although only 50 percent of all murder victims (nationally) are white, 75 percent of the cases resulting in an execution involved a white victim (DPIC, 2012). In instances of interracial murder, the numbers are even more disturbing: cases involving a white offender and a black victim accounted for only 18 executions, compared with 254 executions in cases involving a black offender and a white victim (DPIC, 2012). State-specific studies reveal a similar pattern. In California, offenders who killed white victims were three times more likely to receive a death sentence than offenders who killed black victims, and four times more likely than offenders who killed Latino victims (Pierce & Radelet, 2005).

How might reinstating capital punishment as a criminal justice policy be interpreted within the theoretical models of criminal justice?

Restorative justice	Restorative justice advocates would be opposed to the reinstatement of capital punishment because it would not repair the damage that the crime has caused to the victim and the wider community, nor would it allow individual offenders to make restitution.
Community change	Community change advocates would be opposed to the reinstatement of capital punishment on the basis that the community would not be served through general deterrence.
Welfare	Welfare proponents would be opposed to the reinstatement of capital punishment because it would suggest that individualized treatment was not effective.
Justice	Justice proponents would be opposed to the reinstatement of capital punishment, arguing that individuals have the right to life and liberty.
Crime control	With a focus on the classical tenets of "an eye for an eye," crime-control advocates would welcome the reinstatement of capital punishment, provided that it did not get caught up in the appeal process, which would lengthen the time of incarceration and increase costs.

What Do You Think?

1. In *Roper v. Simmons*, the US Supreme Court ruled that executing offenders for crimes that were committed while the offender was under 18 violated the Eighth Amendment of the US Constitution. The Eighth Amendment is very similar to s. 12 of Canada's Charter and prohibits the use of cruel and unusual punishment. Examine the *Roper* case in greater depth to determine how the arguments made with respect to young offenders might affect the debate on the use of the death penalty for adults.

2. Explore the debate on capital punishment, choosing one country to focus on. Outline the arguments made by abolitionists and those made by retentionists. Assess what your own position is, and why. Try to include at least one theoretical model discussed in Chapter 1 in your analysis.

3. Imagine that Canada's Conservative government changes its position and decides to reinstate the death penalty. Would s. 12 of the Charter prevent reinstatement? If so, would the violation be justified under the *Oakes* test?

4. Some debate occurs around the question of whether all murderers should be subject to capital punishment, or whether some murderers might be considered less deserving of death than others. Amnesty International provides information on each of the 58 countries that currently use the death penalty. While some of these employ it only for instances of murder, many other countries allow its use for many other less serious offences, including embezzlement, vehicle theft, arson, and, in the Democratic Republic of the Congo, cowardice (Schabas, 2002, pp. 106–107). At least nine countries still use capital punishment as a penalty for homosexuality. How should these differences in application be addressed? Do the crimes that are eligible for the death penalty affect your views on whether it should be allowed or not?

REFERENCES AND FURTHER READING

Amnesty International. (2012). Death penalty. Amnesty.Org. Retrieved from http://www.amnesty.org/en/death-penalty/

Atkins v. Virginia, 536 US 304 (2002).

Canada. (1976, June 15). Parliament. House of Commons Debates, 30th Parl., 1st sess.

Cliff, C. (Ed.). (2003). *Capital punishment: A bibliography with indexes*. New York: Nova Science.

Death Penalty Information Center (DPIC). (2012, June 18). Facts about the death penalty. DeathPenaltyInfo.Org. Retrieved from http://www.deathpenaltyinfo.org/documents/FactSheet.pdf

Hodgkinson, P., & Rutherford, A. (1996). *Capital punishment: Global issues and prospects*. Winchester, UK: Waterside Press.

Hoshowsky, R.J. (2007). *The last to die: Ronald Turpin, Arthur Lucas, and the end of capital punishment in Canada*. Toronto: Dundurn Press.

Kronenwetter, M. (2001). *Capital punishment: A reference handbook*. Santa Barbara, CA: ABC-Clio Press.

Pierce, G., & Radelet, M. (2005). The impact of legally inappropriate factors on death sentencing for California homicides, 1990–1999. *Santa Clara Law Review, 46*(1), 1–48.

Radelet, M.L. (1989). *Facing the death penalty: Essays on a cruel and unusual punishment.* Philadelphia: Temple University Press.

Roper v. Simmons, 543 US 551 (2005).

Schabas, W.A. (1996). *The death penalty as cruel treatment and torture: Capital punishment challenged in the world's courts.* Richmond, VA: Northeastern University Press.

Schabas, W.A. (2002). *The abolition of the death penalty in international law* (3rd ed.). Cambridge: Cambridge University Press.

Steiker, C.S., & Steiker, J.M. (2010). Capital punishment: A century of discontinuous debate. *Journal of Criminal Law and Criminology, 101*(3), 643–689.

Strange, C. (1992). The lottery of death: Capital punishment, 1867–1976. *Manitoba Law Journal, 23*(3), 594–619.

Taber, J. (2011, January 19). Opposition heaps scorn on Harper's death-penalty "agenda." *The Globe and Mail.* Retrieved from http://www.theglobeandmail.com/news/politics/ottawa-notebook/opposition-heaps-scorn-on-harpers-death-penalty-agenda/article610989/

Index